FROM ANCIENT ISRAEL TO MODERN JUDAISM
INTELLECT IN QUEST OF UNDERSTANDING

Number 159
FROM ANCIENT ISRAEL TO MODERN JUDAISM
INTELLECT IN QUEST OF UNDERSTANDING

Edited by
Jacob Neusner
Ernest S. Frerichs
Nahum M. Sarna

FROM ANCIENT ISRAEL TO MODERN JUDAISM

INTELLECT IN QUEST OF UNDERSTANDING

Essays in Honor of Marvin Fox

Volume One

What Is at Stake in the Judaic Quest for Understanding
Judaic Learning and the Locus of Education
Ancient Israel
Formative Christianity
Judaism in the Formative Age: Religion

Edited by
Jacob Neusner
Ernest S. Frerichs
Nahum M. Sarna

Managing Editor
Joshua Bell

Scholars Press
Atlanta, Georgia

FROM ANCIENT ISRAEL TO MODERN JUDAISM
Intellect in Quest of Understanding

The editors acknowledge with thanks the support of the
Tisch Family Foundation in the publication of this volume.

Library of Congress Cataloging in Publication Data

From ancient Israel to modern Judaism : intellect in quest of
understanding : essays in honor of Marvin Fox / edited by Jacob
Neusner, Ernest S. Frerichs, Nahum M. Sarna.
    p. cm. -- (Brown Judaic studies ; no. 159, 173-175)
    Contents: v. 1. What is at stake in the Judaic quest for
understanding. Judaic learning and the locus of education. Ancient
Israel. Formative Christianity. Judaism in the formative age:
religion -- v. 2. Judaism in the formative age: theology and
literature. Judaism in the Middle Ages: the encounter with
Christianity, the encounter with Scripture, philosophy, and theology
-- v. 3. Judaism in the Middle Ages: philosophers. Hasidism,
Messianism in modern times. The modern age: philosophy -- v. 4. The
modern age: theology, literature, history.
    ISBN 1-55540-335-2 (v. 1 : alk. paper)
    1. Judaism--History. 2. Philosophy, Jewish. 3. Fox, Marvin.
I. Fox, Marvin. II. Neusner, Jacob, 1932- . III. Frerichs,
Ernest S. IV. Sarna, Nahum M. V. Series: Brown Judaic studies ;
no. 159, etc.
BM157.F76 1989
296'.09--dc20   89-61111

Printed in the United States of America
on acid-free paper

TABLE OF CONTENTS

Preface xiii

Bibliography of the Works of Marvin Fox xvii

Part One
WHAT IS AT STAKE IN THE JUDAIC QUEST FOR UNDERSTANDING

1.   History as a Jewish Problem 3
     Ben Halpern, Brandeis University

Part Two
JUDAIC LEARNING AND THE LOCUS OF EDUCATION

2.   Judaic Studies and the College Curriculum 25
     William Scott Green, University of Rochester

3.   The University as a Locus for the Judaic Life of Intellect:
     Why the New Is Not Necessarily Better than the Old, but
     Only Different 41
     Jacob Neusner, Brown University

Part Three
ANCIENT ISRAEL AND THE ANCIENT NEAR EAST

4.   The Role of Inspiration Relative to Other Explanations of
     the Formation of the Hebrew Bible 59
     Ernest S. Frerichs, Brown University

5.   Genesis 21:33: A Study in the Development of a Biblical
     Text and its Rabbinic Transformation 69
     Nahum M. Sarna, Brandeis University

6.   "He Should Continue to Bear the Penalty of That Case:"
     An Interpretation of Codex Hammurabi Paragraphs 3-4
     and 13 77
     Tsvi Abush, Brandeis University

7.   Dealing with Fundamental Regime Change: The Biblical
     Paradigm of the Transition from Tribal Federation to
     Federal Monarchy under David 97
     Daniel J. Elazar, Bar Ilan and Temple Universities

Part Four
FORMATIVE CHRISTIANITY

8. The Transformation of a Religious Document: From Early Christian Writings to Canon 133
Mauro Pesce, University of Bologna

9. Anti-Semitism in John's Gospel 149
William A. Johnson, Brandeis University

10. The New Testament, the Early Church, and Anti-Semitism...171
John T. Townsend, Episcopal Divinity School

11. Four Christian Writers on Jews and Judaism in the Second Century 187
Robert MacLennon, Hitchcock Presbyterian Church, Scarsdale

Part Five
FORMATIVE JUDAISM:
RELIGION

12. "Teach Us to Count Our Days:" A Note on Sefirat HaOmer...205
Harold Fisch, Bar Ilan University

13. Are Women Property in the System of the Mishnah? 219
Paul V. M. Flesher, Northwestern University

14. Three Stages in the Development of Early Rabbinic Prayer..233
Tzvee Zahavy, University of Minnesota

15. Architecture and Laws: The Temple and its Courtyards in the Temple Scroll 267
Lawrence H. Schiffman, New York University

Index 285

VOLUME TWO

Preface...xiii
Bibliography of the Works of Marvin Fox..xvii

PART SIX:
FORMATIVE JUDAISM: THEOLOGY

16. Judaism in Crisis? Institutions and Systematic Theology in Rabbinism....................3
     Roger Brooks, University of Notre Dame
17. The Problem of Originality in Talmudic Thought...19
     Robert Goldenberg, State University of New York at Stony Brook
18. On Man's Role in Revelation...29
     David Weiss Halivni, Columbia University

PART SEVEN:
FORMATIVE JUDAISM: LITERATURE

19. Did the Talmud's Authorship Utilize Prior "Sources"? A Response to Halivni's
     Sources and Traditions...53
     Jacob Neusner, Brown University
20. The Rabbis of the Babylonian Talmud: A Statistical Analysis...................................81
     Harold Goldblatt, University of Maryland
21. Matching Patterns at the Seams: A Literary Study...95
     Herbert Basser, Queens University
22. Recent and Prospective Discussion of Memra...119
     Bruce Chilton, Bard College
23. The Am Ha'Arets as Literary Character...139
     Peter Haas, Vanderbilt University

PART EIGHT:
JUDAISM IN THE MIDDLE AGES:
THE ENCOUNTER WITH CHRISTIANITY

24. The Christian Position in Jacob Ben Reuben's Milhamot Ha-Shem...........................157
     Robert Chazan, New York University

PART NINE:
JUDAISM IN THE MIDDLE AGES:
THE ENCOUNTER WITH SCRIPTURE

25. Tradition or Context: Two Exegetes Struggle with Peshat...173
     Martin I. Lockshin, York University
26. "Introduction to the Commentary on Song of Songs Composed by the Sage Levi Ben
     Gershom" – An Annotated Translation..187
     Menachem Kellner, University of Haifa
27. Late-Fourteenth Century Perception of Classical Jewish Lore: Shem Tob ben Isaac
     Shaprut's Aggadic Exegesis...207
     Lester A. Segal, University of Massachusetts-Boston

PART TEN:
JUDAISM IN THE MIDDLE AGES:
PHILOSOPHY AND THEOLOGY

28. Creation in Medieval Philosophical, Rabbinic Commentaries...................................231
     Norbert M. Samuelson, Temple University
29. Some Forms of Divine Appearance in Ancient Jewish Thought................................261
     Michael Fishbane, Brandeis University
30. Female Imaging of the Torah: From Literary Metaphor to Religious Symbol..........271
     Elliot Wolfson, New York University

Index 309

VOLUME THREE

Preface..xiii
Bibliography of the Works of Marvin Fox...xvii

PART ELEVEN:
JUDAISM IN THE MIDDLE AGES:
PHILOSOPHERS: MAIMONIDES AND HIS HEIRS

31. Aspects of Maimonidean Epistemology: Halakah and Science..3
Isadore Twersky, Harvard University
32. Intellectual Perfection and the Role of the Law in the Philosophy of Maimonides...............25
Howard Kreisel, Ben-Gurion University of the Negev
33. Maimonides and the Alternatives Concerning the World's Being Everlasting.......................47
Keith E. Yandell, University of Wisconsin
34. Maimonides' Fundamental Principles Redivivus...77
Charles M. Raffel, American Jewish Committee
35. Another More Nevukhim: The Italian Background and the Educational Program of
Leon Modena's More Nevukhim Bikhtivah Bilshonenu Hakodosh..89
Howard Adelman, Smith College

PART TWELVE:
JUDAISM IN THE MIDDLE AGES:
PHILOSOPHERS: JUDAH HALEVI

36. Judah Halevi and Karaism..111
Daniel J. Lasker, Ben Gurion University of the Negev
37. The Superiority of Oral over Written Communication: Judah Ha-Levi's Kuzari and
Modern Jewish Thought...127
Raphael Jospe, The Open University of Israel

PART THIRTEEN:
HASIDISM. MESSIANISM IN MODERN TIMES

38. Hasidism as the Image of Demonism: The Satiric Writings of Judah Leib Mises................159
Yehudah Friedlander, Bar Ilan University
39. When a Rabbi Is Accused of Heresy: R. Ezekiel Landau's Attitude toward R. Jonathan
Eibeschuetz in the Emden-Eibeschuetz Controversy...179
Sid Z. Leiman, Brooklyn College

PART FOURTEEN:
THE MODERN AGE: PHILOSOPHY

40. The Character and Status of the Concept of History in Three Twentieth Century
Systems of Judaic Thought: Cohen, Rosenzweig, Lévinas..197
Wendell S. Dietrich, Brown University
41. Heschel's Critique of Kant..213
Lawrence Perlman, Vassar College
42. Ararat and its Fortress: Excerpts from the Rawidowicz-Margulies Correspondence...........227
Benjamin Ravid, Brandeis University

Index...249

VOLUME FOUR

Preface..xiii
Bibliography of the Works of Marvin Fox..xvii

PART FIFTEEN:
THE MODERN AGE: THEOLOGY AND IDEOLOGY

43. Samson Raphael Hirsch's Doctrine of Inner Revelation...3
    Walter S. Wurzburger, Yeshiva University
44. Non-Jews in a Jewish Polity: Subject or Sovereign?..13
    David Novak, University of Virginia
45. Tikkun: A Lurianic Motif in Contemporary Jewish Thought....................................35
    Lawrence Fine, Mount Holyoke College
46. From Tanakh to Modern Times: Aspects of Jewish Religion....................................55
    Moshe Goshen-Gottstein, Hebrew University of Jerusalem
47. Universal Mission and Jewish Survivalism in American Zionist Ideology...............61
    Allon Gal, Ben Gurion University of the Negev

PART SIXTEEN:
THE MODERN AGE: LITERATURE

48. Paradise Lost as a Midrash on the Biblical Bride of God...87
    Sylvia Barack Fishman, Brandeis University
49. "Sacred Sriptures or Bibles of Mankind" in Walden by Henry David Thoreau....................105
    Pier Cesare Bori, University of Bologna
50. L. A. Arieli and the Literature of the Second Aliyah..115
    Gila Ramras-Rauch, Hebrew College
51. In Search of "Authentic" Anglo-Jewish Poetry: The Debate over A. M. Klein's Poems
    (1944)..125
    Jonathan D. Sarna, Hebrew Union College-Jewish Institute of Religion, Cincinnati
52. Tadeusz Rozewicz Faces the Holocaust Past...137
    David H. Hirsch, Brown University

PART SEVENTEEN:
THE MODERN AGE: HISTORY

53. The Politics of Yiddish in Tsarist Russia...155
    David E. Fishman, Jewish Theological Seminary of America and YIVO Institute for
    Jewish Research
54. From Yishuv to Sovereign State: Changes in the Social Structure of the Jewish State
    in the 1940s..173
    Jehuda Reinharz, Brandeis University
55. The Ideology of Antisemitism: The American Jewish View.....................................189
    Gary A. Tobin, Brandeis University
56. French Jewry and the Centrality of The State of Israel: The Public Debate, 1968-1988.........203
    Phyllis Cohen Albert, Harvard University

Index...229

Preface

In these essays, collected in four volumes, we honor as principal and leader of Judaic Studies in our generation Professor Marvin Fox, Philip W. Lown Professor of Jewish Philosophy and Director of the Lown School of Near Eastern and Judaic Studies at Brandeis University, because in our generation, Professor Fox has occupied the position of *doyen* of Judaic Studies in the academy. This position has come to him through force of character and conscience and is one that expresses the man's moral authority, as much as his acknowledged excellence as scholar and teacher. His scholarship is attested by the bibliography that follows, his teaching by the excellent contributions to this volume of many of his doctoral students. But while in learning and teaching he competes on equal terms with many, in stature and universal respect there is none anywhere in the world of Judaic Studies, at home or in the State of Israel, who compares. It is a simple fact that the scholars who contributed to these volumes, have nothing whatsoever in common save that they concur in expressing esteem for this remarkable colleague. This is a scholars' tribute to a great man; in paying this honor to Marvin Fox, we identify the kind of person we want as our representative and academic avatar. In our generation, this is the sort of scholar we have cherished.

The facts of his career do not account for the honor in which he is held, even though he has pursued, and now pursues, a splendid career in higher education. But the facts do explain something about the man. Professor Marvin Fox received his B.A. in philosophy in 1942 from Northwestern University, the M.A. in the same field in 1946, and the Ph.D. from the University of Chicago in 1950 in that field as well. His education in Judaic texts was certified by rabbinical ordination as Rabbi by the Hebrew Theological College of Chicago in 1942. He taught at Ohio State University from 1948 through 1974, rising from Instructor to Professor of Philosophy. During those years he served also as Visiting Professor of Philosophy at the Hebrew Theological College of Chicago (1955) and also at the Hebrew University of Jerusalem and Bar Ilan

University (1970-1971). In 1974 he came to Brandeis University as Appleman Professor of Jewish Thought, and from 1976 onward he has held the Lown Professorship. From 1975 through 1982 and from 1984 through 1987 he was Chairman of the Department of Near Eastern and Judaic Studies at Brandeis. From 1976 he has also served as Director of the Lown School of Near Eastern and Judaic Studies. In 1980-1981 he was Visiting Scholar in Jewish Philosophy at the Center for Jewish Studies of nearby Harvard University.

He has received numerous academic awards, a selected list of which includes the following: 1956-1957: Elizabeth Clay Howald Post-Doctoral Scholarship; 1962-1963, Fellow of the American Council of Learned Societies; 1975-1978, Director of the Association for Jewish Studies regional conferences, funded by the National Endowment for the Humanities; 1977-1980, Director of the project, "For the Strengthening of Judaic Studies at Brandeis and their Links to the General Humanities," also funded by the National Endowment for the Humanities. From 1979 he has been Fellow of the Academy of Jewish Philosophy; 1980-1981, Senior Faculty Fellow, National Endowment for the Humanities. He has served on the editorial boards of the *AJS Review, Daat, Judaism, Tradition, Journal for the History of Philosophy,* and other journals. He has lectured widely at universities and at national and international academic conferences and served as Member of the National Endowment for the Humanities National Board of Consultants for new programs at colleges and universities. Over the years he has counseled various universities and academic publishers as well.

His ties to institutions of Jewish learning under Jewish sponsorship are strong. He has served on the Advisory Committee of the Jewish Studies Adaptation Program of the International Center for University Teaching of Jewish Civilization (Israel), since 1982; International Planning Committee of the Institute for Contemporary Jewry of the Hebrew University since that same year; member of the governing council of the World Union of Jewish Studies since 1975; secretary, 1971-1972, vice president, from 1973-1975, and then president, from 1975-1978, of the Association for Jewish Studies; and he has been on the board of directors of that organization since 1970. From 1964 through 1968 he served on the Executive Committee of the Conference on Jewish Philosophy; from 1970 to the present on the Executive Committee of the Institute of Judaism and Contemporary Thought of Bar Ilan University; from 1972 as member of the Academic Board of the Melton Research Center of the Jewish Theological Seminary of America; member of the board of directors of the Institute for Jewish Life from 1972 through 1975; member of the board of directors of the Library of Living

Philosophers, from 1948; Associate of the Columbia University Seminar on Israel and Jewish Studies from 1968 through 1974; and many other organizations.

His committee service at Brandeis University has covered these committees: Graduate School Council; Philosophy Department Advisory Committee and Reappointment and Promotions Committee; University Tenure Panels; Academic Planning Committee (Chairman, 1982-1984); Faculty Committee for the Hiatt Institute; Tauber Institute Faculty Advisory Committee and its academic policy subcommittee; Committee on University Studies in the Humanities; Faculty representative on the Brandeis University Board of Trustees (1978-1980). His professional memberships include the American Philosophical Association, the Metaphysical Society of America, the Medieval Academy of America, as well as the Association for Jewish Studies, Conference on Jewish Philosophy, and American Academy for Jewish Research.

The editors of this volume bear special ties of collegiality and friendship with Professor Fox. In this project Professor Sarna represents Brandeis University and also has been a close and intimate colleague and friend for many years. Professors Frerichs and Neusner have called upon Professor Fox for counsel in the fifteen years since Professor Fox came to Brandeis University. And Professor Fox has responded, always giving his best judgment and his wisest counsel. Professor Fox has been a good neighbor, a constant counsellor, and valued friend. In the sequence of eight academic conferences, run annually at Brown University in the 1970s, Professor Fox played a leading role in the planning of the programs and in scholarly interchange. Through him and the editors of this volume Brown and Brandeis Universities held a conference at which graduate students in the respective graduate programs met and engaged in shared discussion of common interests. Professor Fox moreover has taken a position on numerous dissertation committees in Brown's graduate program in the History of Judaism. His conscientious and careful reading of these dissertations give to the students the benefit not only of his learning but also of his distinct and rich perspective on the problem of the dissertation. Consequently, among the many other universities besides Ohio State and Brandeis at which Professor Fox has made his contribution, Brown University stands out as particularly indebted to him for wisdom and learning.

The editors express their thanks to President Evelyn Handler of Brandeis University for sponsoring the public event at which the contributors to these volumes presented the books to Professor Fox and enjoyed the opportunity of expressing in person their esteem and affection for him; and to the Max Richter Foundation of Rhode Island

and the Program in Judaic Studies at Brown University for financial and other support in organizing and carrying out this project. Mr. Joshua Bell, Verbatim, of Providence, Rhode Island, produced the camera ready copy with the usual attention to aesthetic excellence and also accuracy of detail that have characterized all of his work for Brown Judaic Studies, Brown Studies in Jews and their Societies, Brown Studies in Religion (Scholars Press), and also Studies in Judaism (University Press of America). The staff of Scholars Press, particularly Dr. Dennis Ford, gave to this project their conscientious attention. Professors Frerichs and Neusner therefore express thanks to Verbatim, Scholars Press, and University Press of America, which in the past ten years have made Brown University's Judaic Studies Program the world's largest publisher of scholarly books and monographs in the field of Judaic Studies. All three editors thank the contributors to these volumes for their willingness to collaborate in what we believe is an important tribute to greatness in our field and in our time.

Jacob Neusner   Nahum M. Sarna
Ernest S. Frerichs   Department of Near Eastern
Program in Judaic Studies   and Judaic Studies
Brown University   Brandeis University
Providence, Rhode Island   Waltham, Massachusetts

Bibliography of Marvin Fox
1946-1989

1. "Three Approaches to the Jewish Problem," *Antioch Review,* 6(1), Spring 1946, pp. 54-68.

2. "Towards a Life of Joy: A Theological Critique," *Menorah Journal,* 36(2), Spring 1948, pp. 248-251.

3. "On Calling Women to the Reading of the Torah," *The Reconstructionist,* 13(19), January 1948. An exchange of letters with Robert Gordis. For Gordis' reply see *idem.,* 14(7), May 1948.

4. *Kant's Fundamental Principles of the Metaphysic of Morals,* edited with an introduction (Liberal Arts Press, 1949). Reprinted in numerous editions by the original publisher, then acquired by Bobbs-Merrill, and most recently by Macmillan.

5. Review of Chaim Weizmann, *Trial and Error,* in *Heritage,* Spring 1949, pp. 16-18.

6. Review of Morris R. Cohen, *Reason and Law,* in *Illinois Law Review,* 45(2), May 1950, pp. 305 -307.

7. *Moral Fact and Moral Theory: A Study of Some Methodological Problems in Contemporary Ethics.* Unpublished doctoral dissertation, University of Chicago, 1950.

8. Review of John A. Nicholson, *Philosophy of Religion,* in *Philosophy and Phenomenological Research,* 11(3), March 1951.

9. Review of Maxwell Silver, *The Way to God,* in *Philosophy and Phenomenological Research,* 11(4), June 1951.

10. "On the Diversity of Methods in Dewey's Ethical Theory," *Philosophy and Phenomenological Research,* 12(1), September 1951.

11. Review of Abraham Joshua Heschel, *Man is Not Alone,* in *Commentary,* 12(2), August 1951, pp. 193-195.

12. "Kierkegaard and Rabbinic Judaism," *Judaism,* 2(2), April 1953, pp. 160-169.

13. "Day Schools and the American Educational Pattern," *The Jewish Parent*, September 1953.

14. Review of J. Guttmann, *Maimonides' Guide of the Perplexed*, in *Judaism*, 2(4), October 1953, pp. 363-367.

15. "Moral Facts and Moral Theory," in *Perspectives* (Ohio State University Press, 1953), pp. 111-127.

16. Review of Martin Buber, *At the Turning, New Mexico Quarterly*, 24(2), Summer 1954, pp. 217-220.

17. "What Can the Modern Jew Believe?" Alfred Jospe, ed., *Judaism for the Modern Age* (B'nai B'rith Hillel Foundations, 1955).

18. "Our Missing Intellectuals: Another View," *National Jewish Monthly*, December 1954, pp. 10-13.

19. Review of Abraham Cronbach, *Judaism for Today*, in *Judaism*, 4(1), Winter 1955, pp. 82-84.

20. "Amicus Jacobus, sed Magis Amica Veritas," *Conservative Judaism*, 10(3), Spring 1956, pp. 9-17.

21. "The Trials of Socrates: An Analysis of the First Tetralogy," *Archiv fuer Philosophie*, 6(3/4), 1956, pp. 226-261.

22. "What's Wrong – and Right – with Deweyism," *The Jewish Parent*, December 1956.

23. Review of Abraham Joshua Heschel, *God in Search of Man: A Philosophy of Judaism*, in *Judaism*, 6(1), Winter 1957, pp. 77-81.

24. "Can Modern Man Believe in God," in Alfred Jospe, ed., *The Jewish Heritage and the Jewish Student* (New York, 1959), pp. 40-50.

25. "Who is Competent to Teach Religion," *Religious Education*, 54(2), March-April 1959, pp. 112-114.

26. "Torah Jews in the Making," *The Jewish Parent*, April 1960, pp. 4-5, 22.

27. "Heschel, Intuition, and the Halakhah," *Tradition*, 3(1), Fall 1960, pp. 5-15.

28. "Tillich's Ontology and God," *Anglican Theological Review*, 43(3), July 1961, pp. 260-267.

29. "Ve-al ha-Medinot Bo Ye'amer," *Panim el Panim*, No. 124-125, September 10, 1961, pp. 18-19. A symposium with Professor Salo Baron.

30. Review of Samuel Dresner, *The Zaddik*, in *Conservative Judaism*, 15(4), Summer 1961, pp. 39-42.

31. Review of Robert Gordis, *A Faith for Moderns*, in *Commentary*, 32(4), October 1961.

32. "Modern Faith," *Commentary*, 33(2), February 1962. An exchange of letters with Robert Gordis.

33. Review of Jakob Petuchowski, *Ever Since Sinai, Judaism*, 10(4), Fall 1961.

34. Review of Harry A. Wolfson, *Religious Philosophy: A Group of Essays*, in *The Classical Journal*, 58(2), November 1962.

35. "Einige Probleme in Buber's Moralphilosophie," in Paul A. Schilpp and Maurice Friedman, eds., *Philosophen des 20. Jahrhunderts: Martin Buber* (Kohlhammer, 1963), pp. 135-152. German translation of # 47.

36. "Theistic Bases of Ethics," in Robert Bartels, ed., *Ethics in Business* (Ohio State University Press, 1963).

37. Reviews of Joseph Blau, *The Story of Jewish Philosophy*, and Gerald Abrahams, *The Jewish Mind*, in *Commentary* , 35(1), January 1963.

38. Review of Arthur A. Cohen, *The Natural and the Super-Natural Jew*, in *Commentary*, 35(4), April 1963.

39. Review of Ephraim Shmueli, *Bein Emunah Likfirah*, in *Commentary*, 36(2), August 1963.

40. "Religion and Human Nature in the Philosophy of David Hume," in William L. Reese and Eugene Freeman, eds., *Process and Divinity: Philosophical Essays Presented to Charles Hartshorne* (Open Court, 1964), pp. 561-577.

41. "Character Training and Environmental Pressures," in *The Jewish Parent*, October 1964.

42. Review of W. Gunther Plaut, *The Rise of Reform Judaism*, in *Commentary*, 37(6), June 1964.

43. Review of Max Kadushin, *Worship and Ethics*, in *Commentary*, 38(6), December 1964.

44. Review of Israel Efros, *Ancient Jewish Philosophy*, in *Commentary*, 40(1), July 1965.

45. "Religion and the Public Schools – A Philosopher's Analysis," in *Theory into Practice*, 4(1), February 1965, pp. 40-44.

46. Review Essay on *Maimonides" Guide to the Perplexed*, Shlomo Pines, tr., with introductory essays by Leo Strauss and Shlomo Pines, in *Journal of the History of Philosophy*, 3(2), October 1965, pp. 265-274.

47. "Some Problems in Buber's Moral Philosophy," in Paul A. Schilpp and Maurice Friedman, eds., *The Philosophy of Martin Buber* (Open Court, 1966), pp. 151-170.

48. "The Case for the Jewish Day School," in Judah Pilch and Meir Ben-Horin, eds., *Judaism and the Jewish School* (New York, 1966), pp. 207-213.

49. "The State of Jewish Belief: A Symposium," *Commentary*, 42(2), August 1966, pp. 89-92.

50. "Heschel's Theology of Man," *Tradition*, 8(3), Fall 1966, pp. 79-84.

51. "Jewish Education in a Pluralistic Community," *Proceedings of the Rabbinical Assembly of America*, 30, 1966, pp. 31-40, 47-51.

52. Review of Arnold Jacob Wolf, ed., *Rediscovering Judaism: Reflections on a New Theology, Commentary*, 41(2), February 1966.

53. "Sakkanah Lishelemutah shel ha-Yahadut," *Hadoar*, 47(38), October 1967.

54. Chapter in *The State of Jewish Belief* (Macmillan, 1967), pp. 59-69. Reprint of #49.

55. "Heschel, Intuition, and the Halakhah," in Norman Lamm and Walter S. Wurzburger, eds., *A Treasury of Tradition* (New York, 1967), pp. 426-435. Reprint of #27.

56. Review of *Harry Austryn Wolfson Jubilee Volumes*, in *Judaism*, 16(4), Fall 1967.

57. "Prolegomenon" to A. Cohen, *The Teachings of Maimonides* (New York, 1968), pp. xv-xliv.

58. "The Meaning of Theology Today," *Bulletin of the Central Ohio Academy of Theology*, January 1968.

59. Review Article on Sidney Hook, in *Religion in a Free Society, The Journal of Value Inquiry*, 2(4), Winter 1968, pp. 308-314.

60. "The Function of Religion," *Congress Bi-Weekly*, 36(3), February 1969, pp. 56-63.

61. "La Teologia Dell'uomo Nel Pensiero di Abraham J. Heschel," *La Rassegna Mensile di Israel*, 25(4), April 1969. Italian translation of #50.

62. Review of Zvi Adar, *Humanistic Values in the Bible*, in *Commentary* 47(1), January 1969.

63. Review of Richard L. Rubenstein, *After Auschwitz* and *The Religious Imagination*, in *Commentary*, 47(6), June 1969.

64. "Religion and the Public Schools," Kaoru Jamamotie, ed., *Teaching* (Houghton Mifflin, 1969), pp. 239-248. Reprint of #45.

65. "The 'Commentary' Problem," *Judaism*, 18(1), Winter 1969, pp. 108-110.

66. Review of Nathan Rotenstreich, *Jewish Philosophy in Modern Times*, in *Commentary*, 49(5), May 1970.

67. "Naturalism, Rationalism and Jewish Faith," *Tradition,* 11(3), Fall 1970, pp. 90-96.

68. "Day Schools and the American Educational Pattern," in Joseph Kaminetsky, ed., *Hebrew Day School Education: An Overview* (New York, 1970). Reprint of #13.

69. "Day Schools and the American Educational Pattern," in Lloyd P. Gartner, ed., *Jewish Education in the United States* (Teachers College, Columbia University Press, 1970), Classics in Education Series, No. 41. Reprint of #13.

70. "Continuity and Change in Jewish Theology," *Niv Hamidrashia,* Spring-Summer 1971, pp. 15-23.

71. Review of Mendell Lewittes, *The Light of Redemption,* in *The Jerusalem Post Magazine,* April 9, 1971.

72. "Moral Facts and Moral Theory," in Julius Weinberg and Keith Yandell, eds., *Problems in Philosophical Inquiry* (Holt Rinehart Winston, 1971), pp. 368-381. Reprint of #15.

73. "Freedom and Freedom of Thought," *Encyclopaedia Judaica,* Vol. 7, 119-121.

74. "God, Conceptions of," *Encyclopaedia Judaica,* Vol. 7, 670-673.

75. "God in Medieval Jewish Philosophy," *Encyclopaedia Judaica,* Vol. 7, 658-661.

76. "God in Modern Jewish Philosophy, " *Encyclopaedia Judaica,* Vol. 7, 662-664.

77. "God, Names of in Medieval Jewish Philosophy," *Encyclopaedia Judaica,* Vol. 7, 684-685.

78. "God, Names of in Modern Jewish Philosophy, *Encyclopaedia Judaica,* Vol. 7. 685.

79. "Maimonides and Aquinas on Natural Law," *Dine Israel: An Annual of Jewish Law, Tel-Aviv University,* Vol. 3, 1972, pp. 5-36.

80. "Kierkegaard and Rabbinic Judaism," in Robert Gordis and Ruth B. Waxman, eds., *Faith and Reason* (New York, 1972), pp. 115-124. Reprint of #12.

81. "Tillich's Ontology and God," in Keith Yandell, *God, Man and Religion* (McGraw-Hill, 1972). Reprint of #28.

82. Review of Nathan Rotenstreich, *Tradition and Reality,* in *Commentary,* 55(2), February 1973.

83. "Philosophy and Contemporary Jewish Studies," *American Jewish Historical Quarterly,* 53(4), June 1974, pp. 350-355.

84. "Berkovits on the Problem of Evil," *Tradition,* 14(3), Spring 1974, pp. 116-124.

85. "God in Modern Jewish Philosophy," *Jewish Values* (Keter, Jerusalem, 1974). Reprinted from #76.

86. "Conceptions of God," *Jewish Values* (Keter, Jerusalem, 1974). Reprinted from #74.

87. "The Future of Hillel from the Perspective of the University," in Alfred Jospe, ed., *The Test of Time* (Washington, 1974).

88. "Philosophy and Contemporary Jewish Studies," in Moshe Davis, ed., *Contemporary Jewish Civilization on the American Campus* (Jerusalem, 1974). Reprinted from # 83.

89. *Modern Jewish Ethics: Theory and Practice* (Ohio State University Press, 1975). Edited with introduction.

90. "Judaism, Secularism and Textual Interpretation," in M. Fox, ed., *Modern Jewish Ethics: Theory and Practice,* pp. 3-26.

91. "On the Rational Commandments in Saadia: A Re-examination," in M. Fox, ed., *Modern Jewish Ethics: Theory and Practice,* pp. 174-187.

92. "Philosophy and Religious Values in Modern Jewish Thought," in Jacob Katz, ed., *The Role of Religion in Modern Jewish History* (AJS, 1975), pp. 69-86.

93. Review of *The Code of Maimonides: Book IV, The Book of Women,* in *Journal of the American Academy of Religion,* March 1975.

94. "Maimonides and Aquinas on Natural Law," in Jacob I. Dienstag, ed., *Studies in Maimonides and St. Thomas Aquinas* (New York, 1975), pp. 75-106. Reprint of #79.

95. "Law and Ethics in Modern Jewish Philosophy: The Case of Moses Mendelssohn," *Proceedings of the American Academy for Jewish Research,* Vol. 43, 1976, pp. 1-13.

96. "Translating Jewish Thought into Curriculum," in Seymour Fox and Geraldine Rosenfeld, eds., *From the Scholar to the Classroom* (Jewish Theological Seminary, 1977), pp. 59-85.

97. Discussion on the "Centrality of Israel in the World Jewish Community," in Moshe Davis, ed., *World Jewry and the State of Israel* (New York, 1977).

98. "On the Rational Commandments in Saadia's Philosophy," *Proceedings of the Sixth World Congress of Jewish Studies,* Vol. 3 (Jerusalem, 1977), pp. 34-43. Slight revision of #91.

99. "Ha-Tefillah be-Mishnato shel ha-Rambam," in Gabriel Cohn, ed., *Ha-Tefillah Ha-Yehudit* (Jerusalem, 1978). pp. 142-167.

100. Review of Louis Jacobs, *Theology in the Responsa, AJS Newsletter*, No. 22, March 1978.

101. Review of Frank Talmage, *David Kimhi: The Man and his Commentaries, Speculum*, 53(3), July 1978.

102. "The Doctrine of the Mean in Aristotle and Maimonides: A Comparative Study," in S. Stern and R. Loewe, eds., *Studies in Jewish Intellectual and Religious History. Presented to Alexander Altmann* (Alabama, 1979), pp. 43-70.

103. Foreword to Abraham Chill, *The Minhagim* (New York, 1979).

104. *The Philosophical Foundations of Jewish Ethics: Some Initial Reflections.* The Second Annual Rabbi Louis Feinberg Memorial Lecture in Judaic Studies at the University of Cincinnati, 1979, pp. 1-24.

105. "Reflections on the Foundations of Jewish Ethics and their Relation to Public Policy," in Joseph L. Allen, ed., *The Society of Christian Ethics, 1980 Selected Papers* (Dallas, 1980), pp. 23-62. An expansion of #104.

106. Introduction to the *Collected Papers of Rabbi Harry Kaplan* (Columbus, 1980).

107. Review of Jacob Neusner, *A History of the Mishnaic Law of Women*, 5 Vols., in AJS Newsletter, No. 29, 1981.

108. "Human Suffering and Religious Faith: A Jewish Response to the Holocaust," *Questions of Jewish Survival* (University of Denver, 1980), pp. 8-22.

109. "The Role of Philosophy in Jewish Studies," in Raphael Jospe and Samuel Z. Fishman, eds., *Go and Study: Essays and Studies in Honor of Alfred Jospe* (Washington, D.C., 1980). pp. 125-142.

110. "Conservative Tendencies in the Halakhah," *Judaism*, 29(1), Winter 1980, pp. 12-18.

111. Review of Isadore Twersky, *Introduction to the Code of Maimonides, AJS Newsletter*, No. 31, 1982.

112. "The Moral Philosophy of MaHaRaL," in Bernard Cooperman, ed., *Jewish Thought in the Sixteenth Century* (Cambridge, 1983), pp. 167-185.

113. Review of Michael Wyschogrod, *The Body of Faith: Judaism as Corporeal Election*, in *The Journal of Religion*, 67(1), January 1987.

114. "Change is Not Modern in Jewish Law," *Sh'ma*, 13/257, September 16, 1983.

115. "Graduate Education in Jewish Philosophy," in Jacob Neusner, ed., *New Humanities and Academic Disciplines: The Case of Jewish Studies* (University of Wisconsin Press, 1984), pp. 121-134.

116. "Some Reflections on Jewish Studies in American Universities," *Judaism,* 35(2), Spring 1986, pp. 140-146.

117. "The Holiness of the Holy Land," Jonathan Sacks, ed., *Tradition and Transition: Essays Presented to Chief Rabbi Sir Immanuel Jakobovits* (London, 1986), pp. 155-170.

118. "The Jewish Educator: The Ideology of the Profession in Jewish Tradition and its Contemporary Meaning," in Joseph Reimer, ed., *To Build a Profession: Careers in Jewish Education* (Waltham, 1987).

119. "A New View of Maimonides' Method of Contradictions," in Moshe Hallamish, ed., *Bar-Ilan: Annual of Bar-Ilan University Studies in Judaica and the Humanities: Moshe Schwarcz Memorial Volume,* 22-23 (Ramat-Gan, 1987), pp. 19-43.

120. "Law and Morality in the Thought of Maimonides," in Nahum Rakover, ed., *Maimonides as Codifier of Jewish Law* (Jerusalem, 1987), pp. 105-120.

121. "Maimonides on the Foundations of Morality," *Proceedings of the Institute for Distinguished Community Leaders* (Brandeis University, 1987), pp. 15-19.

122. Foreword to Morris Weitz, *Theories of Concepts* (London & New York, 1988) pp. vii-xi.

123. "The Doctrine of the Mean in Aristotle and Maimonides: A Comparative Study," in Joseph A. Buijs, ed., *Maimonides: A Collection of Critical Essays* (University of Notre Dame Press, 1988), pp. 234-263. Reprint of #102.

124. "Nahmanides on the Status of Aggadot: Perspectives on the Disputation at Barcelona, 1263," *Journal of Jewish Studies,* 40(1), Spring 1989.

125. "The Holiness of the Holy Land," in Shubert Spero, ed., *Studies in Religious Zionism* (Jerusalem, 1989). Reprint of #117.

126. *Interpreting Maimonides: Studies in Methodology, Metaphysics and Moral Philosophy* (Jewish Publication Society, 1989).

127. "The Unity and Structure of Rav Joseph B. Soloveitchik's Thought," *Tradition,* 24(3), Fall 1989.

128. "Rav Kook: Neither Philosopher nor Kabbalist," in David Shatz and Lawrence Kaplan, eds., *Studies in the Thought of Rav Kook* (New York, 1989).

Part One
WHAT IS AT STAKE IN THE JUDAIC QUEST FOR UNDERSTANDING

1

History as a Jewish Problem

Ben Halpern
Brandeis University

History, as everyone knows, is to a people as memory is to an individual: the source and assurance of its identity. An identity is a principle that peoples, as well as persons, construct in order to give direction to their existence. It is a bridge they seek to build between the past that no longer exists and the inevitable future, between what has happened and is unalterable and what will happen and is uncertain. History, like memory, pins an identity to the certainty of its past; it is a sheet-anchor to windward that holds a people to its own course in the face of the uncertain future.

But, as everyone also knows, both memory and history are far from reliable, either as to what really happened in the unalterable past or as to the proper direction for the risky exploration of the future. For one thing, the certainty of the past is often a matter of belief and desire more than of well-warranted knowledge – and when there are aspects of the past one may not wish, but cannot help knowing, they present severe problems for the project of rooting one's identity in a secure and desirable base. For this reason, memory and history, as constructions of the past, are often more clearly adjusted to what serves present intentions than to what may "really" have happened and cannot in fact be altered.

History, consequently, is as troublesome for peoples as memory is for persons. This is a fairly universal and widely-observed problem. The form in which it appears in the case of the Jews, as in any other particular case, is a reflection of the special relation between the people and its peculiar history.

3

A people's identity, and the self-image in which it is grounded, is an exercise in self-definition as against the world that it constructs as its imagined environment. What is important in the imagined world varies according to the circumstances of each people. There is a major difference between the world as it appears to peoples whose lives are largely determined by their physical environment, or who are sparsely settled and relatively isolated from menacing strangers, and the world as it appears to peoples who manage rather than adjust to their physical environment, or find themselves in long-lasting relations of mutual tension with other peoples. In the first case, the collective identity may be defined primarily in terms of creation myths and similar cosmological genealogies; in the latter case, ideologically colored political history may serve as the symbolic framework of identification. In the first case, totem poles or the shrines of household gods and patron saints; in the second case, statues commemorating national heroes and monuments symbolizing famous victories assert the people's identity.

Such a distinction is, of course, artificial: many cases overlap the dichotomy. The Jews obviously are such a case – and this is, indeed, one of the reasons why, particularly in our time, history has become problematic for the Jews.

As an ancient people that has preserved the scriptures of its antiquity as a national tradition, the Jews retain in their traditional self-image a version of antique Mediterranean, Middle Eastern cosmological myth: Genesis is the first book of the Hebrew Bible, and it recounts in its lengthy begats the unbroken line of descent of the children of Israel from the beginning of cosmic creation. Yet Yehezkel Kaufmann is not alone in noting the sharp departure of the Hebrew scriptures from the Nature-bound mythology of their immediate environment as well as of the entire world of antiquity. It is common ground for many who have noted the differences between the Hebrew scriptures and their classic contemporaries to remark that the Bible has a distinctive historical quality quite different from parallel antique and classic writings.[1]

One clear source of the difference is the Biblical conception of the covenantal relation between God and the Chosen People. The cosmological tie of the Jewish lineage to the universe of its imagination is not, as in other primal and contemporaneous cultures, one of filiation to the gods or tribal totems, either by descending from or ascending to

---

[1] Eric Voegelin, *Israel and Revolution* (Baton Rouge, 1956); Arnoldo Momigliano, "Time in Ancient Historiography," *History and Theory*, Beiheft 6 (1966) 1-23.

their company in ritual and in social legitimation. God remains apart and Jews do not become incarnated gods, but God and the Jews are distinct entities who stand opposed in a compact of reciprocal obligations and entitlements. The consequence for Jewish culture, and for Jewish communal organization, is that both the culture and the community acquire a strongly ideological, legal character: they affirm in principle a national code, not merely a national myth, as their core structure. *Halakhah*, and not simply *aggadah*, is in one form or another a constitutive element of Jewish peoplehood.

God's covenant with the Jews is from one point of view a strongly historical one: they were promised a land to which they had to migrate; after occupying it, their tenure was to be conditional on their faithful performance of the commandments – both devotional and (even more significantly) ethical and social. God's instruments for the enforcement of their compliance were the other peoples among whom Jews lived. Thus, the covenantal history of the Jew is recorded in their traditions of bondage in Egypt, of the exodus under divinely inspired leadership and the return into the national heritage of the Promised Land, and of their long Exile and the millennial hope for the messianic Redemption: in these historical transformations, there appear the Egyptian Pharaoh, the Babylonian Nebuchadnezzar, the Greco-Syrian Antiochus and the Roman Titus, and a host of others who worked through the process of history to enact God's will.

From another point of view the historical tradition of Judaism seems strangely unhistorical: it is a common remark that Jewishness was experienced not in time but in eternity.[2] The significant relationship, that by which Jewish identity was defined, was the covenanted relation with God and the Torah. This relation with the transcendent was the (active) political core of Jewishness so long as the normative tradition prevailed. Political reality in the form of the relation with other peoples, as traditionally imagined, was overcast with the pale camouflage of *aggadah*: the successor generations of noteworthy oppressors, the Torquemadas and Khmelnitzkis, were all seen as avatars of Haman or Amalek. There was little interest in imagining their individual qualities or in defining oneself in relation to them. The ideological core of traditional Jewish culture was anchored

---

[2]Franz Rosenzweig, *Der Stern der Erlosung* (Frankfurt a. Main, 1921), pp. 374 ff; *Time and Eternity* is, of course, the title of the collection of readings from Jewish sources published by Rosenzweig's associate, Nahum Glatzer.

in eternity, in the transcendental source of the Torah; its concrete historical experience was transmuted into the fluid substance of myth.[3]

This was true, at least, insofar as the history experienced as Jewish was concerned; for the struggles of the *goyim* among themselves were well-understood as subject to natural causes, and they were too full of dangerous consequences to be met simply with pious quietism, in the transcendental dimension of eternity. The gentile nations, to use the traditional imagery, had each its guiding star that ruled its horoscope; the Jews alone lived under the direct providence of God and had no part in the great game of temporal, political history. One had to keep close watch, of course, in order to avoid immediate dangers, but the deeper meaning of history, that which was ultimately relevant for Jews and gentiles alike, was the drama of Exile and Redemption, enacted primarily in the intimate experience of the Jewish people.[4]

This traditional Jewish attitude to history, with its inherent paradoxicality, is problematic enough, objectively speaking, but it long served as a reasonable basis for Jewish life in the dimension of time. The perception of the Jews as a people in exile, dispersed and subject to the rule of diverse gentile nations, was common ground for both the Jews and those who ruled them. The political cultures of the Christian and Muslim societies that tolerated Jews were based on a theological tradition, continuous with the Jewish Bible, that on the one hand granted the Jews a certain legitimacy and on the other hand justified their perpetual subjugation – not only as a practical necessity for gentiles but (especially in the Christian domain) as a God-ordained penalty. Jews themselves saw their Exile as a penance rather than a penalty – that is, as the preparation for their future national Redemption rather than the termination of their election as God's Chosen People. But, as a rule this did not prevent them from deriving from the common theologico-historical base the same conclusion that Christians and Muslims did: that chronic subjugation (and occasional acute oppression) in the Diaspora was a legitimate and justified condition for Jews under God's plan. There were, to be sure, sporadic pseudo-Messianic revolts against the Jewish fate, but in their failure they only reinforced the general Jewish response of quietist acquiescence in their subjugated condition and penitential Exile.

The hallmark of modern Jewish history is the disruption of the Jews' traditional, paradoxical perception of the historical base of their

---

[3]The terms "ideology" and "myth," as used here, need no special definition, but for explication of certain implied meanings, see Ben Halpern, "The Dynamic Elements of Culture," *Ethics* (July 1955), pp. 39-52.

[4]Yitzhak F. Baer, *Galut* (New York, 1947).

national identity. The material base of an exiled Jewry in premodern Europe was the corporate order of society, in which the subjugated, but autonomous, Jewish community had a more or less natural place. The French Revolution abruptly abolished corporate privileges, already eroded by the reforms of eighteenth century absolutism, and it projected a new regime of the secular nation-state, to which all citizens owed unmediated allegiance, and in which all shared a common, undifferentiated franchise. It was an unavoidable, logical conclusion that the legal subjugation and communal autonomy of the Jews had no place in a nation-state. Instead, Jews considered themselves invited to a new national self-identification, based on citizenship in the nation-state, with only their religious belief remaining as the base of their Jewish identity.

The consequences in the institutional history of modern Jewry are familiar. The logic of citizenship in a secular nation-state, so it seemed to emancipated Jews, required them not only to dismantle the structure of their communal autonomy but to revise the forms of their religious practice and belief. In particular, the core conceptions of the Jewish historical self-image, the mythos of Exile and the messianic Redemption, had to undergo another in the series of revisions that mark their long tradition. Past cycles of messianic enthusiasm and pietistic quietism had never questioned the ultimate – even if eschatological rather than historical – restoration of the Jews to national freedom in Zion. Now the covenant with God upon which Jewishness was based was interpreted in Reformed Judaism as a perpetual Mission to the gentiles, a commitment to Dispersion, with no national restoration to Zion at its close. Instead, the French Revolution and the general spread of enlightenment were invested with messianic significance and the enfranchisement of Jews and other subjugated people – and, as many Jews hoped, new conquests of social justice by future revolutions – were interpreted as the true meaning of the long-awaited Redemption.

This radical revision of the traditional mythos served well enough as a rationalization for the inner circle of Jews who subscribed to it. It justified for themselves their continuing religious separation from their gentile fellow-citizens, with many of whom they shared in an overwhelming measure most other features of a common culture, including basic elements of a common, contemporary religious or areligious sensibility. But if it were meant to justify Jewish separatism in the eyes of interested gentiles, it was a clear failure: at the very time when liberal Jews were developing the doctrine of the everlasting Jewish Mission as their response to the spirit of the age, they were under attack by liberal Christian ideologues for their continuing adherence to an outlived religion. And on the gentile side, not only was the expected acceptance of Jews into society painfully limited, but the gentile version of the Exile-Redemption theme lived on in new transformations, both religious and areligious, that stood in sharp contrast to the liberal Jews' conception of their historic role. In contemporary gentile historiography, Jews were treated as largely irrelevant, and their tribulations, whether old or new, were seen in good part as the natural consequence of their questionable historical character or conduct. History presented in this light became a Jewish problem, one that Jewish ideologues and historians in particular had to deal with.[5]

Modern, self-styled "scientific" historiography was part of the expropriation of Western culture from the hegemonic, universal-ecclesiastic to the local, secular-national domain. The concentrated power-centers which in the nineteenth century emerged as nation-states claimed as their own the realms of vernacular literature, music, art styles, and above all history. Land and landscape; the national tongue, folklore, and folkways; and especially the annals of local warfare and power struggles – these supplied the base and substance for the historicist revision of the Western perception of man's past and present condition.

Every group that saw itself as distinctive in its language, culture, or consciousness of kind, or as rooted in its land and thus entitled to national status and sovereignty was impelled to articulate and justify its claim by documenting its legitimacy with a history constructed in the new style. But this was a fertile field for controversy and adversarial contention; and the smaller, weaker claimants labored under the handicap of certain principles introduced into history, as written in the grand style by the major players in the historiographical competition. A distinction between "world-historical nations" and those minor "nationalities" or "ethnic" elements whose history had only parochial interest – and thus, for example, warranted no title to national sovereignty – was an obstacle that such contenders had to struggle over in their race for recognition.

The basis for the distinction between histories of universal and those of merely local or parochial interest was a certain peculiarity of the rise of Western European nationalism. The nation-state, as noted earlier, won its dominant role in historiography by a process that expropriated from the universal hegemony of the Church many other aspects of culture and social control as well. But the autonomy that the

---

[5]Nathan Rotenstreich, *The Recurring Pattern: Studies in Anti-Judaism in Modern Thought* (New York, 1963).

secular nation-state won for itself was not simply an application of a rule that whatever was individual and distinctive deserved freedom. From the beginning, national historiography also applied a principle of universality as its criterion for awarding the right of autonomous expression to certain particularistic values and denying it to others. The centralized national state arose precisely by suppressing the autonomy of lesser, local or parochial systems of social norms – including among others the tradition of Jewish communal autonomy.

Western European nationalism also recognized, explicitly or implicitly, certain limits on its own hegemonic claims and respected the more universal sway of a common culture that transcended national boundaries. The classic nineteenth century nation-state appropriated as its own the domains of politics, literature, the arts – and history; but only the totalitarian regimes of the twentieth century laid claim to science and the realm of ultimate, absolute values and beliefs as subject to their authority.

Nineteenth century European nationalism recognized two traditions – the humanism that gave rise to modern science and the Christianity that formed the deep structure of its ethical values – as beyond its limited dominion. To qualify as a "world-historical" people in the judgment of nineteenth century historiography, a national group had consequently to be able to document a claim to have had a significant role in the development of humanist science or of the common tradition of ethical and metaphysical values that prevailed in Western civilization. Thus, for example, Italy's role in the Renaissance, the role of Germany in the Protestant Reformation, or the roots of democratic liberalism in English or French history gave the protagonists of each national tradition the grounds for writing their national history as a world-historical epic.

Such a criterion, of course, could serve to depreciate the historical significance of others, particularly the smaller, weaker national groups. The records of their past, which they might preserve out of a sentiment of clannish piety, belonged in the same class as the ethnologies of primitive tribes or the chronicles and hagiographies of medieval annalists – a class of antiquarian, irrelevant fables – in the eyes of historians who considered the rise of Western civilization to be the essential core of the history of mankind.

There are two ways in which discredited groups could defend their history against such denigration. One way would be to contest the basic assumptions of the regnant historiography: to deny that the history of man could be truly summed up from the sole perspective of Western civilization or as consummated in the rise of the European nation-state system, or its imperialistic outgrowths. The new histories of our own time – not only the feminist, black nationalist, or third-world revisions but also the currently fashionable concentration on social history and popular culture – have taken up this line with energy and enthusiasm. There have been similar tendencies in Jewish historiography as well, as we shall see, subject to the special conditions of the Jewish experience. But the initial response of Jewish scholars and ideologues took a different tack.

Both Jews and Jewish history continued to be distinctly depreciated by leading modern thinkers and historians from the early Deists and eighteenth century *philosophes* to recent writers like Arnold Toynbee. Derogatory attitudes to Jewish history (unlike the case of other small or weak peoples, ethnic groups, slaves, serfs, plebeians and women) were only in part a matter of neglecting or ignoring the experience of Jews themselves. In greater part, they arose from the significant attention gentile historians paid to their own experience with Jews or Judaism.[6]

For one thing, the Bible was too important a part of the self-image of those among whom Jews lived for the people of the Bible to be overlooked in standard world-historical accounts. In addition, the marginal situation of Jews in premodern Europe made them seek their livelihood in high-risk, insecurely-established economic pursuits. As a result, they figured in the development of major historical innovations, such as the rise of capitalism, in a way that forced itself on the attention of general historians.

On both counts, the historic role of the Jews was often regarded in a negative light. The anticlerical ideologues who viewed revealed religion as superseded by science often accepted the traditional Christian classification of Judaism as a phase in the advance of humanity rendered obsolete by the Church, which was now in turn outdated by the rise of science. Ideologues concerned in a major way with the problem of capitalism often ascribed its unpleasant features to the characteristic traits of the Jewish spirit that allegedly inspired its origins.[7]

---

[6]Shmuel Ettinger, "Yehudim veYahadut b'Einei haDeistim ha-Anglim baMeah ha-18" *Zion*, Vol. XXIV (1964), 182-207; Arthur Hertzberg, *The French Enlightenment and the Jews* (New York and London, 1968), pp. 268-313.

[7]Of the extensive literature on this subject, the writings of Karl Marx and Werner Sombart had the widest audience; see Steven E. Aschheim, "'The Jew Within': The Myth of 'Judaization' in Germany," in Jehuda Reinharz and Walter Schatzberg, ed., *The Jewish Response to German Culture from the Enlightenment to the Second World War* (Hanover and London, 1985), pp. 212-241.

The challenge of a derogatory or contemptuous account of their place in history was one that Jewish historians and ideologues, like those of other slightly-regarded peoples and social groups, felt themselves compelled to meet. One method, similar to that of others whose experience was felt to be inadequately reflected in the standard histories, was to collect and publish records that purported to document a significant Jewish contribution to the general histories, particularly those of major nation-states. Such publications were pointedly directed against negative stereotypes of Jews as wartime slackers or uncultured aliens that were common in gentile cultures. Thus the historical societies founded by Jews in France, England, or the United States would publish accounts of Jewish participation in their country's wars; lists and biographical sketches of eminent Jews in literature, industry, and science; and records of early Jewish settlement in their respective domiciles.

But Jewish apologetics had to justify a claim for historical significance far beyond the bounds of particular nation-states or regions. The discreditation of Jews and Judaism was applied over a broad world-historical canvas: it depicted them in a negative light but as an acknowledged, significant factor in the general history of civilization; and accordingly it viewed them against a landscape-background abstracted not from one national history but from the experience with Jews shared by many nations. Consequently, Jewish ideologues and historians had to contend not simply with the neglect of parts of their historical experience by general, nation-state histories; they also had to frame a defense against explicitly derogatory views of the Jewish role in world-history.

Only the Bible, the most ancient layer of Jewish culture, was universally conceded a major role in the history of Western civilization. A debate over how that role should be evaluated was conducted among gentiles amid the religious controversies of the seventeenth and eighteenth centuries. Christian theologians defended the biblical tradition against the attacks of anticlerical iconoclasts. But both sides agreed in considering the Old Testament, and the whole system of Judaism, as a long-superseded phase of human development. The argument between them was based on the Christian metamorphosis of biblical religion, in which the Jewish source had been so thoroughly transformed that its antique, original version had no substantive relevance, however vigorously the contending ideologues argued its merits. The anticlericals attacked the Jewish Bible as an expedient way to strike at the Christian Church, and the pietists defended ancient Judaism and the Hebrew Scriptures in the form accepted by Christian-theological tradition.

 Jewish writers in the era of Enlightenment and the Emancipation could not develop a position of their own in this debate by taking sides on issues framed in such terms. Only by dissenting from the assumptions on which the gentile antagonists were agreed could an independent, specifically-Jewish approach be formulated. The early writers who articulated such a view, men like the French Joseph Salvador or the German Moses Hess, were marginal both as Jews and as critics of the current state of the gentile society in which they lived, and not merely of its religious (or antireligious) assumptions about Judaism. They claimed for Mosaism a social vision that was superior to that of contemporary bourgeois society, and they looked forward to a new, revolutionary era in which a rejuvenated Jewish tradition would emerge in a leading, world-historical role. (In later years, the defense of Judaism as a socially-oriented, innerwordly religious culture became one of the standard apologetic postulates of more moderate writers, like the protagonists of Reform or Conservative Judaism and Zionist thinkers like Ahad Ha'am.)

 However, the early Jewish historians who wrote during the protracted, halting process of Jewish emancipation in Europe were more concerned to justify Judaism as a relevant part of the accepted, contemporary view of world history than to envision a leading role in a new, brave world of the future. It was not the evaluation of the Bible that was their immediate historiographical problem, but above all the evaluation of post-biblical Judaism: of Pharisaism and the Talmud, and of the whole cultural production and social-institutional tradition of the Jewish past. Their aim was to reinterpret the experience of the past in "modern" terms: that is, in conformity with the standards of evaluation accepted by the enlightened general public, and which they too had made their own.

 Thus, they intended to show that, far from being the rigid, legalistic literalists of stereotypical "pharisaism," the real Pharisees of history were those who made the Law flexible and responsive to changing conditions. This approach (exemplified by Zunz's work on the homiletical and liturgical tradition) was meant, of course, to justify religious reform in the face of hard-line, conservative opposition in the Jewish community itself; but it was also a defense against the common gentile denigration of the Talmud and of rabbinic culture as a whole. Another line of defense, given the highest degree of prominence, was the attention paid to the history of Sephardic Judeo-Arabic culture. The role that Spanish Jewish scholars and philosophers played in transmitting Greek philosophy and science to the reawakening West was a favorite theme in the argument for the world-historical relevance of postbiblical Judaism.

But the very past they sought to rehabilitate was a source of embarrassment for that generation of scholars, owing to their dislike for many of its established contemporary representatives. They stressed the flexibility of the rabbinic tradition of the Talmud partly, at least, in order to contest the authority of contemporary rabbis who relied on a legal code fixed centuries earlier. Another part of the past, the mystical kabbalistic tradition, was viewed with unrelieved aversion by the enlightened, rationalistic scholars of the early nineteenth century, and they gave it as little attention as possible. Their favorite theme, the golden era of Spanish Jewry, which was the main prop of their claim to a place of honor for postbiblical Judaism in world-historical *Ideengeschichte*, was subject to limitations of its own. Many centuries had passed since Jewish culture had achieved that historical peak. Thereafter (especially in the Ashkenazic community of Germany and Eastern Europe) Jewish culture had retreated behind the walls of its self-enclosed rabbinic tradition and detached itself from the flow of world-historical development. Nor could a historian like Zunz place much credence in the apologetic claim of more pragmatic idealogues for the world-historical significance of modernized and reformed versions of Judaism. If he believed that Jewish culture-history indeed deserved scholarly attention, it was the kind of attention merited by a distinguished, but terminated past. What promise the present and future might hold could not be confidently asserted by sound and critical Jewish scholarship.[8]

Recounting the past as *Ideengeschichte* seems particularly appropriate in the case of the Jewish people, whose identity is so strongly anchored in a unique religious culture. Other aspects of the Jewish past, the social, economic, legal-political, and inner-institutional history of a widely-scattered community, obviously had to be taken into account in a full report. Given the hard facts of a millennial Diaspora experience, the perspective that most readily brought into focus the panorama of Jewish history coincided closely with the traditional mythos of Exile. Nineteenth century Jewish historiography was thus made up in roughly equal parts of *Ideen* – and of *Leidensgeschichte*, the mournful chronicle of continuous subjugation and cyclical oppression of the Wandering Jew.

The fact that *Leidensgeschichte* – what Salo Baron later decried as the "lachrymose conception of Jewish history" – seemed so natural a reflection of their people's past forced Jewish historians of the liberal, rationalist school into difficult and embarrassing positions. It was bad

---

[8]Nahum N. Glatzer, ed., *Leopold and Adelheid Zunz: An Account in Letters, 1815-1885* (London, 1958).

enough that secular, profane aspects of the Jewish experience should continue to fall into a pattern all-too-reminiscent of the traditional sacred myth. Yet, when Jewish history was cast as *Ideengeschichte*, the Covenant mythos offered a certain advantage (even in secular transpositions of the theme), since it could build on the established recognition of a Jewish role in "world-history." The obvious task for Jewish historians who followed this line was to magnify the proportions of the Jewish role by revising the evaluation of postbiblical Judaism. If they could present a cogent case for the continuing universal relevance of Jewish history, they might produce a Jewish self-image that their gentile peers would accept as deserving a significant place in the history of modern civilization. The Jewish past would feed more smoothly into the living present and a new Jewish-gentile historiographic agreement might emerge, not equivocal like the traditional Exile conception but more nearly uniform in its positive appreciation of the continuous world-historical role of Judaism and the Jews.

The case was different for Jewish history written as *Leidensgeschichte*. When Jewish suffering was no longer perceived as a divinely-imposed penance, there was no way in which it could be presented by Jewish historians without branding many heroes of gentile history as brutal oppressors. Heinrich Graetz's *History of the Jews* severely indicted Martin Luther and other icons of German historiography for the treatment of Jews (and, on the other hand, hailed Heine and Boerne as founding fathers of modern German culture) in a way that enraged the historian, Heinrich von Treitschke. Treitschke's response viewed Graetz's *History* as a kind of arrogant, anti-gentile, Jewish clannishness that explained, it if did not excuse, the current (1879), newly-spawned "anti-Semitic" movement. Even Theodor Mommsen, in a reply defending Jews against Treitschke, argued that an implicitly countercultural history like Graetz's, which opposed the profound identification of modern, humane, Western civilization with "Christianity" (in its modern, liberal form) could only disturb the harmonious integration of Jews in the German nation – a conclusion to which most Jewish contemporaries who commented on the controversy tacitly submitted. Indeed, Graetz himself, while intent on justifying the Jews in his *History*, hardly meant to mount a general attack on German, or Western culture. He, too, wished to write Jewish *Ideengeschichte* as an integral part of the world-historical development of humane culture. But Jewish *Leidensgeschichte* reflected an experience that he could not easily present within the usual categories (of nation-state relations) and dimensions (of periodization); nor could he accept its evaluation by general historians. When treated as a subject worthy of being studied in its own terms, Jewish history inherently challenged the perspectives conventionally accepted in the general, Western history of which it claimed to be a relevant part.[9]

Dismissive judgments about the significance of postbiblical Judaism were a recurrent theme in major modern overviews of world-history from Hegel to Toynbee. Not only theologians had to justify modern Judaism as a valid alternative to, or subculture of, the Christian-humanism which was the common ground on which the nation-state system rested; Jewish historians were under the same compulsion. The careful special studies they carried out within the wide expanse of their field generally failed to convince other historians that Jewish subjects had more than a parochial interest. Jewish scholars had to present evidence that made the case, by implication or explicitly, for a more universal significance of the Jewish experience.

This could lead to a boldly revisionist reconstruction of general history, when the apologetic impulse was supported by meticulous and comprehensive research and cogent interpretive insight. A signal example was the monumental undertaking of Harry A. Wolfson to reinterpret the entire philosophical corpus of the Scripture-oriented, Jewish-Christian-Muslim world as a coherent chapter in the history of thought. In his construction, the Jewish contribution was not confined to that of transmitting Muslim to Christian culture at a particular period. He claimed a larger Jewish role as the initiators of the entire development, in the person of the Alexandrian Jew, Philo, and in bringing it to a conclusion, in the person of Baruch-Benedict Spinoza, in Amsterdam.

Yet Wolfson's challenging achievement remained totally within the frame of a traditional Western comprehension of the history of culture – one especially congenial to Catholic thinkers. Wolfson (in a manner strikingly reminiscent of his predecessor, Zunz) took the traditional Jewish culture that he elevated to the rank of paradigm for all of traditional Western culture to be a closed chapter, terminated by Spinoza. He found no intellectual warrant – whether in Jewish or in universal terms, – for any innovations that had happened since. Yet in personal practice, if not in personal belief, he lived as a modern, rootless man. His often stated definition of his personal stance was altogether revealing: he called himself, only partially in jest, a "non-observant Orthodox Jew" – in theory, Orthodox, in practice, free. He was, moreover, a Zionist who rejected invitations to visit Israel and a

---

[9]Treitschke's and Mommsen's comments are available in translated excerpts in Paul Mendes Flohr and Jehuda Reinharz, ed., *The Jew in the Modern World: A Documentary History* (New York and Oxford, 1980), pp. 280-286.

Hebraist who said, only partially in jest, that his real vocation –
abandoned after his early years – was to have been a Hebrew poet.

When Gershom Scholem had occasion to review a biography of
Wolfson, it was such paradoxes, and particularly the murky question of
Wolfson's ultimate commitment to the theology underlying the
philosophical tradition to which he devoted a lifetime of unremitting
study, that appeared to the reviewer the most interesting, because the
most questionable, aspect of an enigmatic life.

Scholems's own life and *oeuvre* arouse precisely the same kind of
interest and dubiety. His decisive rejection of the German-Jewish
symbiosis, implicit in his early *aliya* to Palestine, was written out in
explicit, drastic terms in the years after the Holocaust.[10] A vague
rumor long circulated that he nursed a private faith in the capacity of
Judaism, revived in its natural homeland, to offer modern men a valid
alternative to other theologies and to Marxism, among other civil
religions, as well. Yet the matter of his theological commitment, the
question whether his lifelong scholarly concern with Jewish mysticism
implied any corresponding personal belief, remained a puzzle; one
which he did not hesitate to complicate even further by playful, if not
mischievous, evasions of the issue.

As for the other question, of immediate concern to this discussion,
whether his scholarship represents a Jewish rebellion against the
stereotypes of general historiography, the case seems surprisingly
clear. His work was not at all such a rebellion but precisely the reverse:
it was a monumental attempt to revise the stereotyped Jewish
Ideengeschichte, as written by his predecessors, in conformity with
certain established models in the general history of ideas.

Scholem's pioneering exploration of Jewish mysticism was a
rebellion against the liberal, rationalist school that had treated such
phenomena as merely beclouding what was essential in Jewish history.
But this rebellion simply brought Jewish history into harmony with
the ruling trend of German historicism. If one considers the broader
apologetic function of such scholarship, Scholem's rediscovery of
Jewish mysticism served the same purpose as Buber's literary
reconstructions: it defended Judaism against the prevailing view that it
lacked the spontaneity and emotive power of Christianity.

The reorientation to emotive Judaism (shared by many
contemporaries, writing in Hebrew and Yiddish as well as German) was
applied by Scholem with vast industry and keen penetration in

---

[10]"Against the Myth of the German-Jewish Dialogue," in Werner J.
Dannhauser, ed., Gershom Scholem, *On Jews and Judaism in Crisis* (New York,
1976), pp. 61-64.

questions of *Ideengeschichte*. He also extended this approach to more mundane topics of political and social history; here, too, he applied models that were well-established in general history. Christian mystics had been commonly held to have acted as a revolutionary ferment that dissolved the grip of ecclesiastical dogmatism and set free currents of change that brought into being liberal nationalism and bourgeois democracy in Europe. Scholem, in a number of special studies on the participation of an antinomian mystic in the French Revolution, the role of Kabbalist influence on the Masonic lodge of the Asian Brethren, and of the Frankist legacy in the rise of Reform Judaism, tried to demonstrate a similar pattern in Jewish history.[11]

This was a version of Jewish history much valued by Scholem and his appreciative readers as written "against the grain"; but its extension into areas beyond *Ideengeschichte* was only marginally useful.[12] It illuminated eddies rather than the mainstream of modern Jewish historical development. In this respect, Scholem encountered a problem that burdened other historians as well: the materials of Jewish social and political history proved to be stubbornly resistant to the patterns of periodization and categorization current in general historiography.

A main source of such difficulties is easy to identify. The normal framework for histories in the nineteenth century tradition was the territorially-bounded state; world-history was written, in alternative versions, from the same perspective. The dispersed Jewish people, which had no sovereign center of its own before the rise of the Israeli state, was an entity whose fitness to be a subject of history was obviously questionable within this accepted canon. What this kind of general history found interesting in the Jewish past was only what had immediate significance from the perspective of one or another nation-state or the world-history it perceived. Much of what was published by Jewish scholars was thus seen as parochial and irrelevant.

But whoever wished to present the Jewish past as a coherent narrative needed more than fragments selected as relevant to other histories. Particular developments that brought Jewish history into critical, but transient connection with general history did not make up a continuous, intelligible sequence of events. As for the apologetic catalogues of Jewish contributions to various nation-states, the mere

---

[11]Scholem, *Major Trends in Jewish Mysticism* (New York, 1946), pp. 317-320; cf. Scholem, *On the Kabbalah and Its Mysticism* (New York, 1965), pp. 5-31.
[12]Hannah Arendt, "Jewish History, Revised," *Jewish Frontier* (March, 1948), pp. 34-38; David Biale, *Gershom Scholem: Kabbalah and Counter-History* (Cambridge, MA and London, 1979).

collection of such records could still less be credited as constituting a coherent history. Indeed, what was memorable and made sense to Jews as their historical tradition was what could be abstracted from the special experience of each part of the Dispersion and communicated to Jews in other parts, sustaining their common identity.

Jews, moreover, could not readily take an approach recently adopted by some others who feel neglected by past historiography. The latest wave of revisionist "new history," which rejects the sexist, racist, Western-centered, bourgeois, or elitist bias of the nation-state histories of the past, may choose simply to ignore the principles of unity, of narrative continuity, and of purposive rationality required by the historicist canon. Their methodology can content itself with an anthropological or sociological, horizontal approach to history, confident that their focus on aspects of popular life and other areas not previously highlighted corrects a longstanding imbalance in the discipline. But Jewish historians could not dispense with a view of the past capable of meeting the challenge of traditional historiographical standards.

This was so, for one thing, because, owing to the scattering of the Jews, their collective identity did not rest on a particular habitat in the way normally presumed by descriptive ethnology. A thread of common identity for Jews could only be found in the dimension of time, in the collective development of a dispersed, intercommunicating people. The requirement of communication, moreover, ruled out another method by which revisionist histories are now being written: by compiling a cyclopedic roster of the experiences of a group suffering a common fate – women, colonized or colored people, or the blind, deaf or otherwise handicapped. The experience of such victimized groups, gathered from everywhere and all times indiscriminately, can be treated by the methods of the "new history" as significant in itself, whether or not the scattered subjects of the study are in effective communication and share a common program of aims and action (as some, to be sure, tend to do). Jews, who were always in communication and whose sense of a common destiny was precedent to their common fate, required an historical consciousness that not merely recorded their sufferings: it had to map a road from their past to a clearly envisaged, commonly-intended future.

Traditional Judaism laid out precisely such a road in its conception of Exile and Redemption. But this was a formulation that presented severe difficulties for modern historians. Moreover, the clear connection between antisemitism and the theological view of Jewish history caused many ideologues to wish to be rid of the dangerous "metamyth."[13] And if the theological schema were simply suppressed under the cover of an equivalent secularized version, it still remained an embarrassment for modern historians, since it bracketed a period of historical passivity (the Exile) between an initial and a terminal period – the covenanted Promise and the messianic Redemption – both transcending history. Furthermore, a special feature of this approach was to create a periodization of Jewish history (particularly in regard to its socio-political course) that was radically disjoined from the chronological structure of general history, and thus raised the question of the relevance of one to the other. These were some of the underlying concerns that, consciously or not, shaped the approach of major modern Jewish historians to their subject.

One should note, first of all, tendencies in recent Jewish historiography to apply models current in general history. Reference has been made to Scholem's rewriting of the historical role of Jewish mysticism on parallel lines with its function in the history of Christian Europe. Salo Baron's disparagement of the "lachrymose" approach to Jewish history is consonant with a general tendency in his work, to question a periodization that disjoins Jewish from general history, and to stress the coordination of the two disciplines. The product of such a mild revisionism is his monumental survey of the Jewish experience, region by region, country after country, whereby the subject is comprehensively organized, to be sure, but not in a way that provides a compelling sense of their identity for contemporary Jews. Another trend that should be mentioned is the Marxist approach to Jewish history – and to the definition of a Jewish social-political strategy – represented by Ber Borochov's ideological essays and the historical studies of Raphael Mahler, among others.

In all such cases, historians have encountered the limits restricting the assimilation of the Jewish experience to general historiographic models. Scholem's awareness of this, touched on in another connection, is shown also by his conscientious care in pointing out how Jewish mysticism, by its essentially communal orientation, differs from Christian and other parallels. So, too, the Jewish Marxist-nationalist historians have been at pains to give an account of the specificity of the Jewish case, leading them to produce revisions of Marxist theory as well as innovative analyses of pertinent historical problems.

Broader, more direct attacks on the problem of the disjunction of Jewish from general historiographic patterns have followed two

---

[13]Jacob Bernard Agus, *The Meaning of Jewish History* (London, New York, Toronto, 1963), pp. 1-3, 391; cf. Arthur A. Cohen, *The Myth of the Judeo-Christian Tradition* (New York and Evanston, 1970).

diverging paths. One, the Zionist approach of Ben-Zion Dinur, is a frank secularization of the traditional, theological schema. Jewish history is written as the saga of expulsion from the homeland, the long exile, and the ensuing process of return and restoration. The popular, ideological counterpart of this way of thinking is to depreciate the historical relevance of the intermediate period in exile, when Jews did not make history but suffered it. In historical works, the main technical feature of this approach is the unabashed assertion of a periodization confined to the bounds of the Jewish experience and quite detached from the guidelines of general history.

The alternative approach is that virtually fathered by Simon Dubnow. The ideological thrust and popular appeal of his work derives from its positive appreciation of the Diaspora experience – especially in the years before the breakdown of communal authority. Its focus on the adjustment to the lands where Jews lived (as in the still clearer case of Baron) favors a coordination of the space-time frame of reference of Jewish with that of general history. Yet, by conceiving of a succession of changing central and peripheral areas of Jewish creativity, Dubnow permits both the integration of Jewish with general historical perspectives and the intracommunal communication by which Jews sustained a common identity. The active centers of Jewish creativity could be thought of as rising and declining with the rise and fall of the major centers of human civilization, while the center-periphery relationship channeled the vital gains of each era in forms that Jews as a people could absorb.

Obviously, this schema, which enriches the Diaspora with a sense of its independent relevance, tends to downplay the traditional setting of Exile and Redemption. Yet, studies that adopt this approach, beginning with Dubnow's own work, show traces of their binding dependency on the old model. A prime topic of such histories is the story of Jewish communal authority and autonomy, conceived as an effective surrogate for the brief sovereignty Jews possessed in ancient Israel and Judea, and as proof that exile did not mean powerlessness, passivity, and historical irrelevance. This is a revision that is meaningful only through what it seeks to revise.

As a final note, it deserves mention that two cardinal events in recent Jewish history, the Holocaust and the rise of Israel, have sharply raised the salience and the perceived relevance of the Jewish experience for general historians. The first, cataclysmic event contributed decisively to the ecumenicist wave that, among other theological rapprochements, gained a hearing for the case against religious triumphalism and provided an audience for Jewish thinkers like Buber and Rosenzweig and for Jewish scholarship on biblical and postbiblical *Ideengeschichte*. The rise of Israel, with the widespread repercussions it has caused in international affairs, brought Jewish history into focus for a broad range of concerned observers. In this case, it was the idiosyncratic experience of the Jews that gained sharply in its perceived relevance as a subject of study by general social-political science, historians, and the public at large.

Part Two

JUDAIC LEARNING AND
THE LOCUS OF EDUCATION

2

Does Jewish Studies Belong in College?

William Scott Green
University of Rochester

Our setting is the university, not the seminary or the *yeshiva*. We see our work as integrally related to the larger context of university education, and we must determine the ways in which our subject is properly part of the university....We have the heavy responsibility of making the academy aware of the general significance of our Jewish materials. Our task is to engage neither in apologetics nor in a kind of chauvinistic expansionism. It is simply to make Jewish learning what it properly ought to be in the university, a valued partner in the common intellectual enterprise.

Marvin Fox (133)

I

American colleges and universities, and the faculty who teach in them, have lost their way. This is the grim and unavoidable conclusion of two recent and important national reviews of undergraduate education: the Association of American College's *Integrity in the Undergraduate Curriculum* (1985) and Ernest Boyer's Carnegie Foundation Report, *College: The Undergraduate Experience in America* (1987). The indictment in these two reports and the remedies they suggest pose serious challenges to Jewish Studies as a plausible subject in the American undergraduate curriculum.

The Boyer report depicts the current disarray of undergraduate learning:

Today's undergraduates are products of a society in which the call for individual gratification booms forth on every side while the claims of community are weak. No less influential are the claims of job training, even at the cost of education for citizenship....Colleges exacerbate this tendency toward self-preoccupation and social isolation....Colleges offer a smorgasbord of courses, and students pick and choose their way to graduation.

Too many campuses...are divided by narrow departmental interests that become obstacles to learning in the richer sense. Students and faculty, like passengers on an airplane, are members of a community of convenience. They are caught up in a journey with a procedural rather than a substantive agenda. Faculty agree on the number of credits for a baccalaureate degree, but not on the meaning of a college education. (83-84)

The *Integrity* report describes the fragmentation of the undergraduate curriculum:

There is so much confusion as to the mission of the American college and university that it is no longer possible to be sure why a student should take a particular program of courses. Is the curriculum an invitation to philosophic and intellectual growth or a quick exposure to the skills of a particular vocation? Or is it both? Certainty on such matters disappeared under the impact of new knowledge and electives in the late nineteenth century. The subsequent collapse of structure and control in the course of study has invited the intrusion of programs of ephemeral knowledge developed without concern for the criteria of self-discovery, critical thinking, and exploration of values that were so long central to the baccalaureate years. The curriculum has given way to a marketplace philosophy: it is a supermarket where students are shoppers and professors merchants of learning. Fads and fashions, the demands of popularity and success, enter where wisdom and experience should prevail. Does it make sense for a college to offer a thousand courses to a student who will take only 36?

The marketplace philosophy refuses to establish common expectations and norms....(2-3)

Concern about the negative consequences of specialization – whether in the form of narrow scholarly preoccupations or excessive careerism – is a powerful leitmotif in these criticisms of American undergraduate learning. The Boyer report decries the "fragmentation of knowledge, narrow departmentalism, and...intense vocationalism" that have become "the strongest characteristics of collegiate education" (7). The *Integrity* report holds the faculty itself responsible for this unprecedented curricular drift.

Central to the troubles and to the solution are the professors, for the development that overwhelmed the old curriculum and changed the entire nature of higher education was the transformation of the professors from teachers concerned with the characters and minds of their students to professionals, scholars with PhD degrees with an allegiance to academic disciplines stronger than their commitment to teaching or to the life of the institutions where they are employed. (Integrity:6)

As an antidote to this crisis of coherence in undergraduate studies, the Boyer report recommends an "integrated core" curriculum of seven "areas of inquiry" that highlights "themes that cut across the disciplines" and can "relate the curriculum to experiences common to all people." Its "framework for general education" consists of courses in the areas of language, art, heritage, institutions, science, work, identity. In addition, it advocates what it calls an "enriched major," which contains not only deep exploration of a particular field, but also sustained attention to the historical, social, and ethical implications of the field under study (92, 110).

The *Integrity* report renounces the idea that educational coherence "can be constructed from a set of required subjects or academic disciplines." Instead, it argues that undergraduates should experience nine "methods and processes, modes of access to understanding and judgment" (15). These "experiences" are: 1) Inquiry: abstract logical thinking, critical analysis; 2) Literacy: writing, reading, speaking; 3) Understanding numerical data; 4) Historical consciousness; 5) Science; 6) Values; 7) Art; 8) International and multicultural experiences; 9) Study in Depth. Perhaps the most radical of these recommendations – aside from the absence of foreign language study – is the notion of "study in depth," which means "comprehension, a decent understanding, and control" of a "complex structure of knowledge" (28), and may or may not be the conventional department-based major:

> A course of study that offers depth will almost invariably exhibit certain features. It will have a central core of method and theory that serves as an introduction to the explanatory power of the discipline, provides a basis for subsequent work, and unites all students who join in the study in a shared understanding of its character and aims. It will force students to experience the range of topics that the discipline addresses and the variety of analytic tools that it uses. It will have a sequence that presumes advancing sophistication. It will provide a means – a project or a thesis – by which the student's final mastery of its complexity, however modest or provisional, may be demonstrated and validated. (29)

In their advocacy of broad and balanced undergraduate learning, these reports advance the case for liberal education as essential preparation for citizenship and public responsibility in a democratic, pluralistic, and increasingly fractious American society. In their joint refusal to reduce college education to a prescribed body of culturally ratified knowledge, these reports affirm that the real aim of college is to equip students with the capacity to comprehend by themselves what is unknown or alien to them, to give students the skills to makes sense on their own of what they have not yet read, seen, heard, thought, or experienced. In their joint insistence that college should push students beyond careerism, self-preoccupation, and social isolation, these reports claim that the mark of an educated person is the ability to conceive and to understand lives we do not lead. The stakes in liberal learning are not trivial, "because our democratic way of life and perhaps our survival as a people rest on whether we can move beyond self interest and begin to understand better the realities of our dependence on each other" (Boyer:8).

These two reports reflect a national concern about the quality of American education. Their recommendations, along with comparable ones from other studies, have been taken seriously and have helped to generate in many colleges and universities moves to reenforce the goals of liberal education, revise general education requirements, and develop tighter and more coherent undergraduate curricula. In addition, they have prompted a national review of the liberal arts major. With support from the Fund for the Improvement of Postsecondary Education (FIPSE) and the Ford Foundation, the Association of American Colleges has convened task forces from fourteen learned societies to assess "study in depth" in their respective fields and to make recommendations for improvement. At the center of this three-year project will be questions about the intellectual purpose and coherence of concentrated study in particular fields, the presence of sequential learning and increasing complexity in the structure of the undergraduate major, the distinctions and interrelations among introductory, middle-range, and advanced intellectual work, and the ways study in depth enables students to make connections to other fields.

II

Jewish Studies has been both a principal beneficiary and a major victim of the curricular diversification, fragmentation, and lack of focus these two reports describe. During the past five years – precisely when the Boyer and *Integrity* reports were being written and published – Jewish Studies reached a peak in an explosion of openings – at least 35 – at major institutions. Senior positions – usually endowed chairs, some established, many new – opened at such institutions as Harvard, Yale, Stanford, Northwestern, Case Western Reserve, Duke, Syracuse, Tennessee at Chattanooga, South Carolina, Maryland, William and Mary, Wellesley, Mount Holyoke, George Washington, Chicago, Drew, Creighton, Florida, Columbia, SUNY Albany, California at San Diego,

NYU, Ohio State, Washington University, and Virginia. In the same period, there were junior openings at Boston University, Williams, Northwestern, University of Pennsylvania, Temple, Indiana, St. Lawrence, Wittenburg, Emory, SMU, Smith, and Georgia. Most of these positions were in departments of religion. This list does not include various openings at the rabbinical seminaries or in the area of Hebrew language and literature, so the total in Jewish Studies as a whole is even higher. It is unlikely that any other field, except perhaps Women's Studies, can boast such an impressive development.

But in two crucial respects this astounding expansion has not come without costs. The market environment that now dominates higher education has allowed Jewish Studies to grow too fast and not always for academic purposes. The context of curricular disarray has deprived Jewish Studies of viable educational models and made plausible a discourse of insular specialization in both teaching and scholarship. Let us examine these in turn.

First, although some institutions supply courses in Jewish Studies to give students a rounded picture of Western culture, it is a poorly kept secret that many programs and positions in Jewish Studies – especially those initiated by Jewish donors and paid for with Jewish money – are and have been added to college curricula and faculty rosters for reasons other than educational. Faced with shrinking enrollments and increased competition for students and finances, many college administrators feel that their institutions must offer courses in Jewish Studies to attract Jewish students, to encourage donations from local Jewish communities, to reengage alienated Jewish alumni who remember resentfully the lack of acceptance they experienced – as Jews – when they were undergraduates, or all three. Each time a university or college convenes a multi-departmental search committee for a post in Jewish Studies – a practice not typical of most other fields – it expresses a judgment that Jewish Studies can go anywhere, and hence belongs nowhere. When colleges or universities include donors or local community representatives on a Jewish Studies search committee – a practice unheard of in any other field – they announce that the curricular stakes in the position are lower than the communal or financial ones. Anecdotal evidence suggests that it is as rare for deans, presidents, and even department chairs to read the scholarship of their professors of Jewish Studies as it is common for them to invite these colleagues to maintain warm relations with alumni and the local Jewish community.

Second, unlike area studies or such cross-disciplinary fields as cognitive science or medieval studies, Jewish Studies is not an offshoot of an established discipline or the combination of two of them. And unlike Women's Studies or African-American Studies, its origins as an institutionalized field of learning lie outside of the university, in the *Wissenschaft des Judenthums*. The historical, philological, and textual researches of the *Wissenschaft*, which aimed at least to demonstrate the historical coherence and cultural worth of all Jewish experience, defined the scholarly bases on which all subsequent Jewish Studies are constructed. Thus, unlike other interdisciplinary fields, before Jewish Studies entered the curricula of American colleges and universities, it already possessed a scholarly tradition and discourse of its own, the goals of which were at least as political and apologetic as they were intellectual. With little constraint to adopt alternative educational or scholarly models, much of Jewish Studies continues to draw on the concepts and categories of the *Wissenschaft* – despite their nineteenth-century European provenance – for guidance in how to proceed.

With this context in mind, it is not captious to observe that – unlike Women's Studies, for example, which has developed a substantial literature of curricular and pedagogical theory – Jewish Studies as a field of learning has yet to devise for itself a contemporary educational rationale that fulfills what Marvin Fox calls "the heavy responsibility of making the academy aware of the general significance of our Jewish materials." In both teaching and scholarship, the academic fragmentation described by the Boyer and *Integrity* reports has allowed Jewish Studies to be treated, and to treat itself, with a kind of exceptionalism that identifies the field as in, but not necessarily of, the university. Deprived of models for connection or intersection, the field has been left, and has kept, largely to itself, shaped principally by its own scholarly tradition.

For example, what scant work there is on teaching Jewish Studies in college still tends to be more articulate on the importance of the field for Jewish purposes than for general educational ones. The most recent volume to appear on the subject, *Methodology in the Academic Teaching of Judaism*, edited by Zev Garber – which, despite its title, devotes more space to biblical studies and Hebrew language and literature than to Jewish religion – is a case in point. Garber's introduction not only recommends that Jewish Studies faculty be available outside of class as a "resource person" for Jewish students, it also urges that classroom exercises be constructed to enhance Jewish self-consciousness:

> Confronting Jewishness is an important task of a Jewish Studies professor; by varying the classroom procedure to a variety of learning experiences, one can help his/her students value and respect the rich tapestry of Jewish heritage within the context of world civilization. This widening of the Jewish consciousness through intense awareness and

pride of the Jewish psyche in all its manifestations is surely one of the
primary obligations of a teacher in Jewish Studies....(9)

It is difficult to imagine a programmatic statement on undergraduate
Jewish Studies less suited to the goals of liberal learning than this one.

Other papers in the book – particularly that of S. Daniel Breslauer
on the use of narrative as a way to teach about Judaism and the report
by Steven Lowenstein, Joel Rembaum, and David Stern on the Core
Curriculum in Jewish and Western Civilization at Lee College of the
University of Judaism – serve to balance Garber's insularity. In general,
however, the essays in the volume seem less engaged by the issue of
connecting Jewish Studies to the larger goals of liberal education than
by the chronic problem of the students' deficient background. This
problem, which appears to be the bane of Jewish Studies, raises
precisely the issue of specialization the Boyer and *Integrity* reports
underscore. If undergraduates appear consistently unprepared to learn
what Jewish Studies thinks it important to teach, then perhaps it is
time to reconceive the field's pedagogical agenda.

The persistence of the *Wissenschaft's* holistic conception of Jewish
experience and its impact on the problem of the "general significance"
of Jewish Studies emerge with special clarity in the area of graduate
studies, where teachers of Jewish Studies are trained. In a thoughtful
discussion of the "Three Academic Cultures of Graduate Education in
Jewish Studies," Ivan G. Marcus argues that there is a "tension between
disciplinary training and the inner logic of Jewish Studies," and
regards "extradisciplinary studies," "an in-depth knowledge of areas
and periods of Jewish Studies which lie outside the discipline one
pursues in the departmental culture" as necessary for "sound doctoral
training in Jewish Studies" (155). Marcus further suggests that "because
the establishment of American academe thinks in disciplinary terms
and is totally unfamiliar with the subject matter of most areas of
Jewish Studies," technical research in Jewish Studies will find a more
welcome home in Jewish scholarly journals than in disciplinary ones.
Only "general, comparative, and theoretical restatements" of Jewish
Studies research will find their way to the disciplinary publications
(156).

Although leading journals in history, near eastern studies, oriental
studies, and religion are rather more receptive to technical submissions
in Jewish Studies than Marcus suggests, his comments about the general
academic ignorance of Jewish materials surely reflect the experience of
many in the field. The larger issue is the assumption that the "inner
logic of Jewish Studies" is somehow in tension with major disciplinary
fields. If graduate education in Jewish Studies proceeds on such a basis,

is it any wonder that teachers of Jewish Studies find college students unready to learn?

Perhaps the most graphic illustration of the problems of connection and intersection that confront Jewish Studies emerges in *The Encyclopedia of Religion,* edited by the late Mircea Eliade, and recently published by MacMillan and the Free Press. If there is an academic field in which Jewish Studies has become a component rather than an appendage, it surely is the study of religion. The majority of college and university faculty positions in Jewish Studies are in religion departments, and – unlike history, literature, or languages – few in the study of religion would argue that a credible undergraduate program can exclude Jewish materials. But even after more than a quarter century of integration, the *Encyclopedia* reveals that the study of religion and Jewish Studies have yet to develop a shared discourse. The comparative entries on religious phenomena and scholarly categories and those assigned by Robert Seltzer, the editor for Judaism, reflect two different worlds that barely intersect.

In general, the *Encyclopedia's* entries in the categories of "Religious Phenomena," "Art, Science, and Society," and "Scholarly Terms" treat Judaism inappropriately in three ways. They either reduce it to the Hebrew Bible, ignore it when it is exemplary of their topic, or grossly misrepresent it. Some representative examples – listed, for convenience, alphabetically – illustrate.

The entry "Apostasy," in a section called "Apostasy in Jewish Ritual Law," observes as follows:

> Apostasy needed to be legally regulated. 'Whole Israel has a share in the world to come....And these don't have a share in the world to come: whoever says "There is no resurrection of the dead in the Torah" and "There is no Torah from heaven," and the Epicurean' (San. 10:1). About 100 C.E. the twelfth prayer of the so-called eighteen benedictions has been expanded by the *birkat ha-minim* ('the blessing over the heretics'): 'For apostates let there be no hope. The dominion of arrogance do thou speedily root out in our days. And let Christians and the sectarians be blotted out of the book of the living.' This amplification implies that apostates had earlier been cursed in Jewish divine service. Christian literature corroborates that after the fall of the temple Jews cursed Christians. (1:354)

There is not space here to correct all the mischief done by this paragraph. Perhaps it is enough to note that the rendering of Mishnah Sanhedrin 10:1 is both vulgar and inaccurate, *birkat ha-minim* does not mean "blessing over the heretics," the benediction cited is from the fourth century not the first, and the word in it translated here as "Christians" means something else. Jewish liturgical cursing of

Christians in antiquity is something John Chrysostom might have wished for, but there is scant evidence for it.

The entry on "Authority" discusses Buddhism, Christianity, and Islam as "founded religions," treats "Primitive" and "Archaic" religions, but ignores Judaism (and Hinduism). Although rabbinic Judaism made benedictions into a virtual art form, and although the first tractate of the Mishnah and both Talmuds is entitled "Blessings," the entry on "Blessing" discusses only the Hebrew Scriptures, Islam, and Christianity. Despite the extensive development of halakic codes in Judaism – all of which are listed in the entry "Halakah, History of" – the entry on "Codes and Codification," under a section amazingly entitled "Jewish Codes," discusses only the Book of the Covenant and the "legal parts of Deuteronomy."

The entry "Charity" gives an incomplete account of Maimonides on charity and then observes:

> ...notwithstanding occasional references to liberality toward the gentiles, in Jewish tradition 'charity begins at home,' and for many centuries the object of charity was the fellow Jew – the individual, the family circle, and the community. (3:222)

What this entry invidiously labels "occasional references to liberality toward the gentiles" is in fact an explicit Talmudic injunction to give charity to the gentile poor as to the Jewish poor (Babylonian Talmud, Gittin 61a). The article "Confession of Sins" bypasses Judaism, as does the long entry on the "Crusades," which has separate sections on Christian and Muslim "Perspectives." The entry on "Eschatology" discusses only the Bible and the Pseudepigrapha, and then moves on to Christianity. The entry on "Faith" mentions Judaism in a section called "Faith-as-Obedience," but refers only to 1 Sam. 15:22. It supplies detailed examples from Confucianism, Christianity, Buddhism, and Islam. (Ironically, the entry "Obedience" makes no mention of Judaism.)

The entry on "Knowledge and Ignorance" claims to examine "the various and conflicting conceptions of religious knowledge that have emerged in the major traditions through history." It discusses nearly every religion in the world, and some major philosophers, but ignores Judaism and the concept of Torah. Instead, it devotes 21 lines to "The Hebrews." The article on "Love" treats ancient Chinese traditions, Hinduism, Buddhism, Plato, Christianity, and even modern psychology. It ignores Judaism (and Islam). In a surprise, the sub-entry on "Magic in Greco-Roman Antiquity," in a section called "Jewish Magic," deals only with the Hebrew Bible. One wonders why the great Marcel Simon thought that in antiquity magic was "congenital" to Judaism.

Remarkably, Judaism finds no place in the entries on "Memorization," "Migration and Religion," and "Oral Tradition." This despite the facts that the Mishnah was written to be memorized, that migration, both forced and voluntary, accounts for many developments – and is a fundamental mythic theme – in Judaism, and the extensive literature about oral tradition in Judaism. Likewise, the major entry on "Poetry and Religion," which has separate sub-entries on Indian, Chinese, Japanese, Christian, and Islamic religions, makes no mention of Judaism. Surely a few pages could have been given over to a discussion at least of the Psalms in Judaic liturgy, the medieval *piyyutim*, Judah HaLevi, and the Nobel Prize winner Nelly Sachs.

One final example will conclude this sampling. The entry on "Revelation" observes:

> ...the Judaism of the scribes (beginning with Ezra, fourth cent. B.C.E.) shows a tendency to regard revelation as closed and to see the prophetic movement as now past. The Jewish tradition generally accepted these positions. Only Jewish mysticism...regarded not only the once-for-all historical act of divine revelation but also the repeated mystical expressions of God as revelatory; the function of the latter is to bring out the implications of the historical revelation and make it intelligible.

Even the slightest familiarity with some reliable secondary work on the theory of "oral Torah" in rabbinic Judaism would show how misleading this judgment is.

If the entries on religious phenomena and scholarly categories ignore the work of Jewish Studies, some of the major entries on Judaism ignore the study of religion and, as a result, illustrate what happens when the discourse of Jewish Studies becomes too disconnected from that of other fields.

For example, the main entry on Judaism, by Eugene Borowitz, entitled "An Overview," is impressive for its scope, erudition, and occasional eloquence, and it exhibits an admirable sensitivity to the varied positions of contemporary Jewish religious denominations. But its usefulness is severely diminished because it eschews the categories of the study of religion in favor of a different approach. Instead of supplying a critical definition or morphology of Judaism, which would have helped readers distinguish Jewish religion both from other religions and from other Jewish activities, the entry offers the following agenda:

> This article describes postbiblical Judaism in terms of the evolving expression of the Jewish people's covenant with God, understood in liberal religious terms. (8:129)

The entry does not define the key term "covenant" or explain the placement of it as a distinguishing variable of Jewish religion. (The *Encyclopedia's* entry on "Covenant" is no help. Ironically – but typically for the *Encyclopedia* – it discusses covenant in the "Old Testament," at Qumran and in the New Testament, and in Christian theology and church history, but ignores Judaism.) More important, the last clause of this programmatic sentence should have disqualified this entry as inappropriate for an encyclopedia of religion because "liberal religious terms" are normative rather than descriptive. They are terms of apology rather than analysis. Describing Judaism in "liberal religious terms" undermines the study of Judaism as a religion in two ways. First, it imposes on Judaism – especially ancient Judaism – anachronistic categories that highlight the religion's least distinctive traits and suppress its most distinctive ones. Second, particularly when discussing modern Judaism, it blurs the distinction between what is religion and what is not.

In a section entitled "Way of the Rabbis" the entry divides rabbinic Judaism into the categories of "Responsibility of the Individual," "Family in Rabbinic Judaism," and "Jewish Community and Jewish People." These may reflect the interests of contemporary liberal Judaism, but they seriously misrepresent the emphases of the rabbinic texts themselves. As a consequence, the entry ignores these prominent characteristics of rabbinic Judaism: purity/impurity, the transfer of women, the holiness of the Land of Israel, the Torah-scroll as a sacred object, the supernatural abilities of rabbis, the sage as "living Torah," the collectivity of rabbinic literature, the conflict between the authority of Scripture and that of reason, and the union of sanctification and salvation.

Instead of highlighting these, the entry begins its description of rabbinic Judaism with a discussion of androcentrism, which concludes:

> The rabbis did assign women a comparatively high personal and communal status. Nonetheless, by egalitarian standards, the differentiation of women's duties from those of men, which are viewed as the norm, imposes on women a loss of dignity and worth. (8:130)

By egalitarian standards, nearly every religion "imposes on women a loss of dignity and worth," so this observation, though correct, reveals nothing particular about rabbinism. More important, the facile condemnation of rabbinic sexism obscures a distinctive trait of rabbinic religion. The third Order of the Mishnah is entitled "Women" (*Nashim*), and in the Babylonian Talmud – rabbinism's most authoritative document – it occupies nearly one-fifth of the whole. The transfer of women is a self-declared preoccupation of rabbinic religion, but the rabbinic construction of gender and conception of gender relations – beyond a cursory nod to the conventional realms of home and family (8:131-132) – are overlooked in this entry. Surely, the issue of women reveals more about Judaism than the distinction between the "promise and problem" of liberal Judaism and the "promise and problems" of Orthodoxy (8:142,143). (Given the prominence of this issue here, it is ironic that the *Encyclopedia's* entry on "Androcentrism" neglects Judaism, save for a reference to the Shekhinah.)

The entry's second point about rabbinism is that it was democratic:

> The troubling issue of sexism aside, rabbinic Judaism is remarkably democratic. It calls all Jews to the same attainable virtues: righteousness in deed, piety of heart, and education of the mind....The sacred elite, the rabbinate, remains open to any man and recognizes no substantial barriers between rabbis and other Jews. (8:130)

Again the imposition of "liberal religious terms" yields an unilluminating description. Which religion calls its followers to unrighteousness, impiety, and ignorance? This depiction misses the ritual totalization – in action, speech, and thought – that defines rabbinic halakah. Moreover, it mistakes the absence of a religious hierarchy and central authority for democracy. Although in principle any Jewish male could join rabbinism's religious elite (as is the case in any religion without a caste system or dynastic priesthood), rabbis sharply differentiated themselves from the ordinary Jews among whom they lived – and thus objectified their claims to authority and leadership – by distinctive speech and dress, by supererogatory piety, and by assertions that their knowledge of Torah gave them supernatural powers. Finally, rabbis in no way constituted a "sacred" class. If they had, the barrier between them and other Jews would have been more than "substantial," it would have been, as in the case of the Israelite priesthood, absolute.

From the perspective of liberal religion it may appear that rabbinic Judaism was mainly a matter of "an ethnic group's unique covenant with God and its consequences for the lives of the individuals who constitute the group (8:131)" and that "...the rabbis exhibited a clear-cut sense of the unity and identity of the Jewish people, who were the sole recipients of God's law and thus bore unique witness to God" (8:133), but rabbinic literature shows these assessments to be oversimplifications. "The Jewish people" is a modern conception. Rabbinic literature speaks of "Israel," a social metaphor that rabbis themselves defined and circumscribed. Thus, rabbinic Judaism excluded from membership in "Israel," either in this world or the next, categories of people – from Samaritans to sectarians – who were not gentiles and whom we would regard, ethnically, to be Jews. It also included gentile proselytes in the category "Israel" and compared gentiles who fulfilled Torah to the high priest. Indeed, as the entry itself notes (8:135), some sages granted "righteous" gentiles a place in the "World to Come" (a view made normative by Maimonides) – the very redemption rabbinism denied to impious Jews. Religion and ethnicity were not coessential, and conformity to the sages' Torah was the ultimate arbiter.

To the liberal eye, Israelite religion and rabbinic Judaism appear equally un-liberal, so critical distinctions between them are difficult to discern. Although this entry speaks of rabbinism's "mix of continuity and creativity" (8:129) and acknowledges its "creative development" and its "reverent continuity with the past," the section on "Beliefs of the Rabbis" emphasizes "the primacy of continuity in rabbinic belief" (8:134), which yields the following judgment:

> ...the rabbis did not see the loss of the Temple as a disaster requiring major theological reconstruction; rather, they found it a confirmation of the Bible's teaching....Continuing the faith of the Bible as they understood it, the rabbis indomitably transcended profane history. (8:134)

It is correct that rabbinic Judaism saw the hand of God in the Temple's second destruction, which it could not regard as a gratuitous caprice. But after the debacle of the Bar Kokhba rebellion – which signalled precisely the enduring loss, not merely the temporary absence, of the Temple and its cult – rabbis generated the "major theological reconstruction" this statement denies. To take one obvious example, the Mishnah developed an unprecedented theology of sanctification, which located the power to effect holiness in the motivations and intentions of the ordinary Israelite – defined, of course, in rabbinic terms – to which God himself responded. Moreover, the claim that rabbis followed the Bible "as they understood it" is no argument for continuity. Church fathers did the same thing, with dramatically different results. At issue is *how* rabbis read scripture, *how* they understood it, and *how* they made it speak with a rabbinic voice – all of which the entry neglects.

In the entry's description of the impact of modernity on Judaism, the normativity and advocacy of its "liberal religious terms" are all too evident. If, in the entry's own terms, readers are to understand Judaism as the "evolving expression of the Jewish people's covenant *with God*" [italics supplied], how are they to comprehend secular Jewish activities – which by definition do not involve God – as manifestations of Jewish religion? How are they to make sense of the following claim?

> ...the interplay between Judaism and modernity can best be illustrated by the devotion of Jews to interpersonal relationships. American Jews today express the longstanding rabbinic commitment to family and community by their disproportionate involvement in the helping professions (such as teaching, social work, and psychotherapy) and their intense concern for family relationships. In these areas they demonstrate a dedication lacking in their observance of the halakic dietary laws and laws governing sexual relations between spouses. They seem now to believe that sanctifying life, their covenant goal, now requires giving these general human activities priority in Jewish duty. (8:141-142)

This argument seems to suggest that the career choices of modern Jews are somehow religiously determined. If so, shall we also see the hand of God in the disproportionate involvement of Jews in the American entertainment and movie industry, in the international diamond trade, and among the cabbies of London? Alternatively, the argument may mean to say that some values originally developed in Judaism persist in the modern secular Jewish community. Even if that be so – and it is notoriously difficult to demonstrate convincingly – by which analytic criterion do we classify the current expression of those values as religion? If, as the entry later suggests, "high culture" is the "'Torah' of secular Jews" (8:143), if "being politically informed and involved" is for Jews "the modern equivalent of a commandment" (8:144), what would count as not Torah, as not commandment? If secularity is evidence of religion, what can these terms mean?

The overarching difficulty with this Principle Article on Judaism is that it commits the bad habit of confusing religion with ethnicity. As a consequence, it vitiates religion, the very phenomenon the encyclopedia was constructed to explain.

A comparable problem is evident in Robert Seltzer's entry on "Jewish People," which discusses "the nature of Jewish corporate identity, from the biblical period to the present" (8:30). To begin with, this is a curious choice for a Principle Article on Jewish Religion. The authentic religious categories "Torah" or "Israel" – both of which are native to Judaic literature and liturgy of all regions, periods, and groups – would have been far superior choices. (Amazingly, the *Encyclopedia* has no article on "Israel" at all.) Because the entry fails to distinguish Judaic reflection on "Israel" from the social and political circumstances of the Jews, it lacks a consistent perspective. Thus, the qualified observation that "...medieval Judaism did not become a multinational *religion* in the sense that Christianity or Islam did" (8:36) [italics supplied] becomes, one paragraph later, a claim for the "mononational character of the Jewish people" and still later, for "the national unity of the Jews" (8:38) – a very different matter, which the entry's own listing of the "wide diversity of Jewish subcultures" in the Middle Ages renders doubtful. Again, the confusion of ethnicity with religion robs this entry of analytical coherence.

Regrettably, too many of the entries on Judaism describe their topics primarily within a Judaic framework and make no reference to the categories of the study of religion. This is unfortunate because in some cases the data and phenomena of Judaism constructively challenge the viability of those categories. For instance, the editors have classified the rites and practices of most religions into the categories of "Domestic Observances" and "Rites of Passage." For Judaism, however, this distinction is misleading because some rites of passage (circumcision, mourning practices) are or can be domestic observances as well.

The treatment of Judaism in *The Encyclopedia of Religion* illustrates how the character of American higher education, as described in the Boyer and *Integrity* reports, has allowed Jewish Studies and the study of religion to develop on parallel tracks. Neither field of study has been enriched by the experience.

III

The Boyer and Integrity reports make clear that the circumstances under which Jewish Studies entered and developed within American higher education are being altered. It was possible for all fields of study to impose their specialized discourses on the classroom because an overly diversified and market-driven curriculum required nothing more. But the rules of college learning are changing. As undergraduate studies in all fields come under closer scrutiny, as college and university faculties tighten and streamline their undergraduate curricula, and as fields of study reexamine and restructure their programs of "study in depth," it will be harder to justify the self-indulgent teaching practices of the past decades.

The extraordinary expansion of positions in Jewish Studies means that the field is now permanently established as a fixture in American college education. As colleges and universities seek to develop anew a common educational discourse, it will become more urgent for Jewish Studies – as a proper college subject – to confront the issues of curricular integration and teaching that the present context has enabled it to avoid. The call to common discourse does not mean that scholars and teachers of Jewish Studies should abandon specialization. After all, we cannot teach our students what we ourselves do not know very well. But knowing something well and teaching it well – so that it matters beyond itself, so that a college course has an educational purpose beyond the material it presents – are not the same thing. The idea that liberal education and Jewish Studies are in tension is a fiction. As a field, Jewish Studies has much to contribute to the current curricular debate, particularly in the area of interdisciplinarity, and much to learn from it as well. The degree to which the field will "belong in college" in the future will be a function not merely of its presence in the curriculum, but also of its engagement with the larger issues of liberal learning.[1]

References

Boyer, Ernest L.   *College: The Undergraduate Experience in*
1987   *America.* New York: Harper & Row.

Eliade, Mircea (ed.)   *The Encyclopedia of Religion.* New York:
1987   Macmillan Publishing Company.

Fox, Marvin   "Graduate Education in Jewish Philosophy." In
1984   *New Humanities and Academic Disciplines,*
                          pp. 121-134. Ed. by Jacob Neusner. Madison: the
                          University of Wisconsin Press.

Garber, Zev (ed.)   *Methodology in the Academic Teaching of*
1986   *Judaism.* Lanham, Md.: University Press of
                          America.

Integrity   *Integrity in the College Curriculum: A Report to*
1985   *the Academic Community.* Washington, D.C.:
                          The Association of American Colleges.

Marcus, Ivan   "The Three Academic Cultures of Graduate
1984   Education in Jewish Studies." In *New Human-*
                          ities and Academic Disciplines: The Case of
                          Jewish Studies, pp. 153-164. Ed. by Jacob
                          Neusner. Madison: The University of Wisconsin
                          Press.

---

[1] I am grateful to Professors Gary G. Porton and Abraham J. Karp for reviewing sections of this paper and helping me avoid obvious errors.

3

The University as a Locus for the Judaic Life of Intellect: Why the New Is Not Necessarily Better than the Old, but Only Different

Jacob Neusner
Brown University

In celebrating the great career of a scholar, all of us reflect on the lives we have led as part of his generation. What has distinctively characterized the life of Marvin Fox – and all of us privileged to share the age with him – has been the entry of Judaic learning into the academy. Only a handful of scholars of Judaic Studies before our own day spent their entire careers, without interruption or preliminary service elsewhere, in the academy. I am one of the earliest to claim these negatives: never served as a pulpit rabbi; never worked for a Jewish organization; never addressed a rabbinical body, local, regional, or national, or any other Jewish institution or organization in its national assembly; never taught in a Jewish primary or secondary school as my primary profession; never made my living as a professor in a rabbinical school or other center of Judaic learning under Jewish auspices. The only locus for my life of intellect has been the university. My sole reference group – people with whom I wish to conduct discourse – has been and remains other professors, they alone. In the millennial history of the traditions of Judaic learning, I believe I am the first to be able to make such a statement. It is perfectly clear that, for the near future, none of us is the last. Judaic Studies is a well established academic field in all universities that participate in Western civilization. That has happened in one generation, ours. What does it mean?

In this paper, which joins together originally separate messages to the University of Bologna on the occasion of receiving an honorary degree in celebration of that university's 900th year and to future scholars, I explain two things. The first is why the university does not stand in judgment upon, but rather stands under the judgment of, Judaic Studies, a much older and I think more enduring tradition of learning than the academic one. Second, after thirty years of service to the academy, I set forth the reasons why the university is not the best place for Judaic Studies (or any other field of learning), merely a possibly useful but today not terribly productive one. I can think of no more fitting tribute to Marvin Fox than honesty about the things that he and I have stood for, and to which we have given our lives. Here we celebrate a great life, a splendid career. In calling into question the worth of the place in which Marvin Fox and the rest of us have spent our lives, I mean only to underline what I see as his achievement: having made something of worth in difficult and unfriendly circumstances.

I. Why Universities Are Different from All Other Centers of Learning, and the Example of Judaism

What we celebrate, on the occasion of the 900th anniversary of the University of Bologna through the conferring of this degree requires definition.[1] The occasion, I think, draws us back to questions of philosophy concerning continuity and change, permanence and transience. A university as old as this one has changed many times over 900 years, so we reflect on what has lasted, amid time and change, to make us want to celebrate the long history of a distinguished center of learning. These questions are framed through the metaphor of the river. So we ask: what precisely do we mean by a river? For both Indian and Greek philosophy, and also, as a matter of fact, the rabbis of the Mishnah, want to find out whether the river is all the water all the time and everywhere? or merely the spot at which we stand? And when is the river the river? Is it when it flows from beginning to end, or just in the here and now? These profound questions of continuity and change, permanence and transience and essence and existence, capture our attention. For we have to find out what words mean in context, such words as learning and as university, for instance, and indeed we do well to undertake even the definition of context, address not only speculative

---

[1]Address at the University of Bologna on accepting the degree *Laurea ad Honorem in Science Politiche*, on March 17, 1988.

minds. We today participate in something entirely concrete and not abstract, namely, the celebration of 900 years of something. But precisely what is that? The answer to that question will give food for thought about the next 900 years of this ancient, properly celebrated foundation, this University of Bologna – and also about what animates that university and justifies its near millennial endurance, which is learning.

We do not celebrate these buildings, or even the place at which they stand, for the university originally had no fixed location. Lectures were given wherever they were given, in convents, for instance, until the Archiginnasio Palace was built in 1562. So for nearly 500 years, one could not point to the University of Bologna. But there was a University of Bologna. Nor do we celebrate what was taught in Bologna for 900 years. For the contents of learning changed, in the nature of things, but so too did the categories. The university in its day was famed for the study of law; in the twelfth and thirteen centuries, thousands came here to study Roman law. But the subject of law was only one, and other subjects, medicine and philosophy and science, joined the curriculum in due course. So we do not celebrate 900 years of the study of some one thing. We do not even celebrate the coming together of teachers of a certain kind and students of a certain kind. In the present age young women as well as men assemble. But in the early centuries, mature men – no women – came here, and these were officers of the church or the state, archdeacons, heads of schools, canons of cathedrals, for example. So the University of Bologna at that time may be compared not to the University of Bologna today but to a War College for colonels and brigadier generals, undertaking vast new responsibilities in the military, or to a business school for the training of advanced executives in industry. If, then, we ask ourselves where is the river, what is the river, and what makes up the river, that is this university, we cannot easily answer that question. There is more change than continuity, and the transient seems all there is. Yet if you give me a moment of patience, I shall propose an answer and identify what we celebrate.

Before identifying what we rightly celebrate, however, let me focus briefly on the selection of a specialist in the history of religion whose focus is on Judaism and ask about what, in 900 years past and even today, has prompted that particular choice. The sources on which I work, the ancient writings of Judaism in the first seven centuries A.D., have never been studied in this university, though they were long studied by major intellects in Italy, and they are just now beginning to find a place here. So as a matter of fact we do not celebrate something done here, or even the counterpart to a component of the faculty here.

And how I read these sources, which is as documents in the expression, by humanity, of its conception of the making of a world, a social world, hardly corresponds to any approach to the reading of any religious documents that has been taken in the 900 years of this university. True, the Talmuds and related writings form the counterpart, for Judaism, of the canon law and jurisprudence, studied with such remarkable distinction here by the noted jurists of Bologna Irnerius and Francesco Accursius (Accursio). Without a considerable labor of mediation by bilingual persons, they would have no more understood these writings than the succession of scholarly Talmudists would have understood the civil and canon law addressed so brilliantly in this place. But neither the famous Talmudists of Italy nor the celebrated canon lawyers of Italy will have understood the questions that I bring to the sources that, in one idiom or another, they studied. They wanted to know one thing, I something else, about the same thing.

The question now stands forth in stark clarity. We do not celebrate a place, however old. We do not celebrate a single tradition of learning, however deeply rooted in generations of successive masters and disciples. We do not in the person of this speaker celebrate a subject pursued at this university for endless centuries. Nor do we even mark a long-enduring subject, whether law, whether religion, though both law and religion form foci for distinguished intellectual effort in this place over a long period of time. Then what do these 900 years join together, which did not happen before, in this place, and did not happen somewhere outside of this place in the way that it happened here, within? And to these negatives I add the particular ones of the occasion at hand: we also do not celebrate a subject long taught here or even a reading of a kind of subject long undertaken here.

I may offer a particular way toward an answer to this question, what do we celebrate after 900 years of the University of Bologna that derives from my subject, and, if I am able to do so, then I shall have given toward commemorating the occasion something distinctive to myself. Such I conceive my task to be. I study books that celebrated their 900th anniversary when the University of Bologna (whatever we may mean by that) began. In 1088, the Mishnah, a philosophical statement in the form of a law code that bears comparison to Plato's Republic and Aristotle's Politics, was approximately 900 years old, having taken shape toward the end of the second century. So before you, and in celebration of your 900th anniversary, stands a representative of a tradition of learning that is twice the age of this ancient foundation. Not only so, but institutions in which the literature of ancient Judaism, beginning with the Mishnah, were studied enjoy a continuous history, if not in one place, alas, of nearly those same close to 2,000 years. My subject here is a very new one. But to that subject and its institutions, the University of Bologna, in its 900 years, is very new too, if no longer a mere parvenu. Consequently, you see me as a Judaic specialist as someone standing at the threshold of your palaces of learning, just as, with equal justice, you see me, as an American, as a new person, as indeed we Americans think that we are. But I see you, in the context of learning, as a chapter in a long story, a tale that began before, and that can continue afterward.

Nor is the story the one told by the Mishnah and its successor writings, which is not the only ongoing tradition of learning that, in the West, in Europe and in the Americas, finds its home, for the moment at least, in universities. There is, after all, philosophy. There is, after all, mathematics. There is, after all, music. The classics of ancient Greece and Rome may make the same statements in Greek and in Latin as I have in reference to writings in Hebrew and in Aramaic. Most of what we study here will see this new, this young, this scarcely-tried institution as a temporary home, this thing, this university, this Bologna. And, I should say, every professor of every subject may find roots to his or her subject of learning, however recent in its contemporary formulation, in the soil of remote antiquity. For mathematics, we now know, dictated the arrangement of the stones at Stonehenge, and the cave drawings in France and Spain, as much as the aboriginal wall-scratchings in Australia, as much as the ruins of the old cities of Africa, Zimbabwe, not to mention the remarkable Mayan monuments of the Yucatan and Aztecs of Middle America and of the Incas of the Andes – they all bespeak reflection, judgment, proportion, taste, composition: philosophy. And all these traditions of learning, each with its precision and its canons of rationality, every one of them flourished in intellect and in heart, but, for most of the history of humanity, not in universities.

When, therefore, we celebrate the 900th anniversary of this University of Bologna, our task is to remember not how old, but how new, this place really is: new, changing, transient, above all, transient – a river always flowing, always changing. Take the water out of the river and you have the banks, and they are, more or less, permanent. But then you have no river anymore. Everyone here, in every tradition of human knowledge, stands for something that humanity has pursued in other institutions than this type of institution, under other circumstances than this one, and in the service of different auspices from the ones that sustain and support universities as we know them and have known them for these 900 years of Bologna: church, state, industry, commerce, to name the more important auspices of learning today.

Learning transcends its auspices. Learning recognizes no limitations of an institutional sort. Learning is so natural to humanity as, in the end, to require nothing more than the intellect driven by curiosity and sustained by speculation. Accordingly, we have to ask ourselves what it is that marks as distinctive and as valuable the university as we have known it for the brief spell commencing nine hundred years ago in this place, among the ancestors of this people. Why is the university of the West, inclusive of the Americas, and now Africa and Asia as well, different from all other forms in which learning has found a home, in which, in more academic language, learning has been institutionalized in permanent and socially sanctioned form?

As I said, it is not because it is old, for it is young. It is not because the program of learning, the curriculum, is stable, because it is subject to change that, relative to the hundred thousand year history of humanity, happens every forty-five minutes. And it is not because the university is the best place in which to pursue curiosity and to sort things out, for that remains to be demonstrated. When we consider that nearly all of the great intellectual achievements in the history of humanity – by definition – took place outside of universities and were the accomplishments of persons who were not professors, paid to think great thoughts and write them down, we realize that fact. If we point to the formative intellects of the world as we know it, Darwin, Freud, Marx, to name only three, we must wonder who needs universities at all. For clearly, the great intellectual steps forward in the natural and social sciences were taken somewhere else, on the Beagle, or in the imagination of a despised Viennese Jew, or in the hall of the British Museum, open to a lowly foreign journalist.

What marks the university as different from all other modes of the institutionalization of learning? It is that as we have known universities from the very beginning, we assemble here to treat learning as shared, plural, open, diverse. The history of Bologna, with its greatness in law, is not the history of a law school but of a university, in which medicine, philosophy, natural and social science joined together. What we institutionalize in universities is the possibility of shared discourse and public exchange of knowledge among different people who know different things and seek to find a language common to those different things. What it means to study, in some one place, mathematics and botany, or sociology and religion, is that we judge it better to study these things in one place than in many places. And in the end, though not every day, that judgment addresses a deeper concern for explaining many things in a few ways. If chemistry did not speak to geology, or physics to mathematics, or economics to political science, then the premise of the university that learning many things helps us to understand them all in some cogent way proves flawed. But it is not flawed, for, as we know, economics without mathematics, and political science without history, and anthropology without psychology, are not possible. Learning flows across disciplinary lines, to the discomfort of the limited and the specialized, because humanity will not stay within bounds. The analytical mind, in mathematics, in times past turned to measure the dimensions of God. And so throughout: there are no limits to mind and imagination.

I do not think it will be difficult to identify the reason for that fact. It is this same quest to understand and make sense of things that is natural to our condition as human beings. And understanding, making sense, means putting many things together in some few ways. The mathematicians at Stonehenge had to make many observations indeed, gather accurate facts beyond number, to know how, at just one moment in the cycle of the solar year, light would enter one space, and not some other, and continue in one line, not some other. And those same mathematicians at Stonehenge had also to want to mark that moment, had to believe it mattered in so profound a way that the energies of an entire society, over a long period of time, could be invested in nothing better than the realization of that magic circle of stones that embodied the facts they put together. When we consider the caves in Ireland, the temples in Middle America, where, at some magic moment, the light over head strikes some one point, then but at no other time, when we contemplate the calculations in mathematics, the engineering skills, required to make a temple or dig a hole in such a way that, just then, things would be this way, not that, we realize what has always been at stake in learning. It is not the fact naked and celebrated in its raw state, but the fact explained by reference to some, indeed many other facts.

In universities we draw together many disciplines or fields of learning, *science* you say in Italian, in quest for not information but understanding. And by understanding, we mean, the capacity of many things to find explanation in some one way. What this means for those of us who study the particularities of a single human group, the Jews through time, or the Classics, or the anthropology of this tribe or the sociology of that class or locus, is simple. We all learn a great deal about some one thing. But only when we can intelligibly address others, who know a great deal about some other thing, are we able to join in that mode of discourse that marks the university as singular and, I think, unique. It is when we aim at facing problems in common, meaning at explaining many things in some few ways, that we join universities and belong nowhere but in universities. There the difference is to be explained, not (merely) celebrated. There the discourse is to be common, not (merely) distinctive and particular, whether to the discipline, whether to the data.

And how are we to do this? Let me close with a very simple answer. It is by treating the particular as exemplary, the unique as typical. So long as what we know we know only in its own terms and not by way of comparison, we celebrate the extraordinary and instead of explaining, simply paraphrase our sources. When we see what we know as suggestive, as data that serve as an example of a condition to be explored in diverse examples, and when we offer what we know as useful examples for the testing of hypotheses of common interest and concern, then we form universities. For how we treat knowledge indicates where we are, that, and not what the world calls us, or what we call ourselves. The entry of any subject requires displaying a passport: this is what I, knowing what I know, can teach you about you, knowing what you know – and therefore how I can learn from you as well.

What are those particular ranges of human experience that, in my judgment, the subject that I study illuminates in particular? The history and literature and religion of the Jews lay no credible claim to uniqueness in telling the story of humanity under stress, for Jews are not unique in suffering, nor in loyalty, nor in endurance, nor in hope, though they have special lessons to teach about the power of humanity to endure despite and against great adversity indeed. But there is something characteristic of the intellectual tradition of the Jews, the particular tradition to which I have devoted my life, that I think does have a distinctive contribution to make to public discourse in the university. It is an example of that very activity that, over all, the university is meant to nurture, seeing things whole, all together, and within a single, unifying field-theory of explanation. The very quest for connections, for the explanation of many things in some one way, that characterizes *le science* – all human learning – in the Italian sense, that is to say, all forms of learning, finds in the very canon of Judaism a stunning expression and exemplification. For that canon makes the effort to put together everything worth knowing and to explain it all in some one way. Providing an account of the formation of the world and the history of humanity, telling the story of everything in some one way, that remarkable canon, represented by the culminating statement of the Talmud of Babylonia, provides us with an example, in the form of a piece of writing, of what a university, an institution of persons, is meant to comprise and compose: everything put together, all at once, in a cogent way, in a single intelligible statement. In its odd context, that document and the writings that it holds together form a singular instance of what it means for learning to come together into a single system of understanding, for facts to yield a rationality, and for data all together and all at once to make sense.

Our work of learning in the particular kind of institution that we form in universities is different from the work of learning in all other settings for learning in that one way: the intent not merely to describe but to explain, and to explain not merely this and that, but everything, all together and all at once. True, appeals to the perennial philosophy and to encompassing explanations differ from here to there, with the result that there are, after all, diverse disciplines within the university, as there should be, and various things that form the object of study by those disciplines. The diversity of the university is as critical to the definition as the unity of learning in cogent explanation that marks the academic intellect but no other. No one can imagine that a single inherited system of holding things all together all at once and making sense of everything in some one way can yet serve. Nor do I suggest that we close all faculties at the University of Bologna and invite all the professors and students to study the Talmud.

But you have chosen to honor me in particular, and that means, a person who studies something you do not study here at all, and who studies in a way that is scarcely replicated anywhere else in which what I study is studied at all. So, in accepting this *Laurea ad Honorem in Science Politiche*, I do so only because I claim that the thing I study exemplifies in an interesting and suggestive way the things that all of us are meant to do together, in this kind of place and in no other, in the way in which we do it and in no other way: many things, in some one way. The framers of the Talmudic canon put together all knowledge, as they identified worthwhile knowledge, and they explained everything they knew in some one way. They produced not an encyclopaedia of knowledge but a single coherent and cogent statement of what they knew, set forth in a cogent and proportioned way. It was their theory of the whole, all together and all at once. When we can do that, we shall also have founded a tradition of learning that will endure, where it serves, as theirs has endured. I have meant only to make clear to the world within, to the Jewish people, and to the world beyond, to you, colleagues of Bologna, what these remarkable intellects accomplished in intellect, the seeing of many things in some one way, the explaining of everything in a system and a structure of balance, proportion, well-crafted composition. But then again, they claimed it came from God. And, I suppose, in context, knowing after all the source of our systems and our structures and our capacity to effect composition, we for ourselves can claim no less, if in different language.

II. Not Better, Only Different: What Has Gone Wrong in the Academy and Some Advice for the Next Generation

Along with Professor Marvin Fox, a whole generation of university professors now moves into the final decade of their careers. People who earned their doctorates in the 1950s and 1960s now reach their late 50s and 60s, and, it is clear, a dramatic change in the composition and character of university faculties will mark the beginning of the next century. We leave the universities considerably smaller and less consequential places than they were when we came on the scene. But I should claim that we have done our best. Let me explain, to a future generation of professors, how and why I believe we have wasted our lives in making the commitments that we made to the academy.

Professors were the earliest victims of the Cultural Revolution of the 1960s, but we went willingly to the barricades, being willing victims. We were the ones to make our peace with what we should have fought. Many of us from that time onward were to witness in our unfolding careers the transformation of the academic world from its gentle and intellectual character – women and men of curiosity, seeking understanding – to something quite different, rather more political and less engaged by learning and teaching.

We have seen the presidents and provosts and deans seek success not in education but in public relations, substituting for an academic vision of education an essentially instrumental program of public policy and the shaping of public opinion. We have witnessed the destruction of a beautiful and precious moment in the history of learning. What good has come from the ruin of the old I do not know. Ours was the transitional generation. We did our best to cope and accommodate, but we received from our masters universities that were better than those we hand on to our disciples – more humane, more intellectual, of a purer academic character. Our careers have spanned interesting times. But, at least, for good or ill, we always knew it. And, for my part, I always said so. At least the other side, from the Cultural Revolution onward, cannot say they did not know what they were doing: they knew precisely what they were doing, and they did it. But I say, Forgive them Lord, for knowing, they knew not. And forgive us too our incapacity to educate.

And yet, if truth be told – and I am a truth-teller, it being too costly to me not to tell the truth as I see it – all that has mattered in my life and career, excluding the life of home and family, is book writing. My advice to the next generation of scholars is that all that matters is the books you write, that alone. For intellect is shaped, where it is accessible, in books, there alone. And we live and strive for the life of mind, for that above all. I wasted much of my life by placing my highest priority upon teaching students and upon engagement with my university. I could have done much more had I understood what lasts and what matters and what makes a difference to the coming age and ages beyond counting, and it is only books, there alone: there alone is life. So I need not mourn the waste of a once precious organization, the university, nor do I mourn the destruction of a once vital institution of society, the one that pays my salary even now, nor do I look back with satisfaction on years given over to students and their nurture. All this is nothing. All that matters lies, now, in the reader's hand, or, at least, sits on the library shelf for readers to come. But that suffices to make this life, my life, worth having lived. Let me now spell out why I think the world has lost something of value, and something not very readily replaced.

We shaped our careers to serve three causes: scholarship, teaching, collegial citizenship. We deemed success the writing of books, the raising up of a new generation of thoughtful students, and the sharing of common responsibilities in the building of a campus community of intellect and heart. We measured success by our capacity to contribute to knowledge in some specific way, to share knowledge with others, both in writing and in the classroom, and to learn from others and join with others in a common life of intellect. We did not succeed all the time, or even very often. But these formed the royal way, the golden measure: scholarship and learning, teaching and sharing, citizenship and caring. It was a gracious ideal, a nourishing and giving and caring faith of the academy and in the academy. We formed that faith not within our own minds alone, but in what we saw in the generation that had brought us up.

If people today wish to conduct research and scholarship, in our day and society, most can do it only in universities or colleges. There is no living to be made outside of the academy in most academic fields. True, in engineering, many of the hard sciences and mathematics, you can hope to pursue research not supported by teaching – hence as a professor in a college – but supported in research institutes, corporations, government, and the like. In the social sciences, sociology, political science, and economics, for example, there are research institutes. But without inherited money, on a full-time, life-long basis one cannot study Greek and Roman literature, or medieval history, or English literature, or religion, or other of the humanities, without a Ph.D. and work as a college professor.

The things we thought mattered when our generation came on the scene – scholarship, publication, teaching in an engagement with students' minds, commitment to excellence in our campus – these no longer find a place on the campus. Universities have become places of privilege and self-indulgence, in which boredom – the cost of easy tenure based on considerations of politics, not accomplishment – reigns, and energy and commitment to learning defy the norm. Tenure marks not achievement but acceptability, and those who go along get along. The road to success is withdrawal and disengagement. As in prison, so in a professorial career you do your own time. But here our successors, like ourselves, locate themselves by choice – because it is where you can do things you think worth doing, and for that reason you accept the restrictions of the place.

When we came along, the things that mattered in the university were scholarship, teaching, collegiality. If, therefore, you wanted to teach, and also pursue scholarship, you were wise to follow a path to a professorship. You would not get rich, and not much, beyond learning, would ever be at stake. But you would learn and teach and enjoy the satisfactions of accomplishment in teaching others through both classroom engagement and also published scholarship, and those accomplishments would enjoy appreciation among colleagues. Today, the gentle virtues of learning give way to more robust values of politics and management. If young people want to teach, there are better places in which to do it than colleges. If they want to pursue scholarship as an exercise in ongoing curiosity, in many fields there are better opportunities, and more agreeable situations, than universities. It comes down to this: if you have to use universities in order to conduct a career of learning, then use them.

Today, for those who wish to sustain scholarship, universities offer one opportunity – and perhaps the only one. Universities two generations ago were not the main, or the only medium for scholarship, and many of the great discoveries in the humanities and sciences from the Enlightenment to our own century did not come from people who held professorships. People drawn by curiosity found ways to make a living – or lived on inherited wealth – and pursued their scholarship. Darwin and Freud – to name two of the greatest intellects we have known – pursued their research without university support. And many of the most important ideas that shape minds now came from people who made their living other than through university teaching – and some of them did not even have doctorates. Yet they made their discoveries and gained a hearing for their ideas. Today, much research, even when conducted in universities, finds support other than through students' tuition. That is the reason, the only reason, for seeking employment in colleges and universities as we now know them. For they have ceased to be communities, and they are in the main not very academic.

Why has it come to this? Let me explain how things were the way they were – and why they changed. We who began in the 1950s and saw the 1960s as assistant professors and the 1970s and 1980s as the senior faculty and now move toward our final decades of teaching and publishing research took over the dream of an earlier generation and lived through the nightmare of our own times. Our model of the university came to us as the gift of the generation of the Second World War, which brought America to a position of responsibility within the larger world. Universities took on the work of educating young Americans to address that great world beyond. Professors became scholars, not only teachers, responsible for learning more and more about many more things. To do our work, professors had both to learn new things and also to teach worthwhile ones, and students for their part had actually to study. Demanding, serious times awaited. No longer Mr. Chipps, benign but boring, saying over and over again the lessons he had learned from the Mr. Chipps who came before. And no more place for the cheering and the singing and the gentleman's C.

What changed? It was the entire configuration of higher education. Colleges became universities, and universities turned themselves into centers of research. Publication mattered. Tenure came to those who produced. Students studied, scholars taught, knowledge expanded and exploded, higher education in America set the standard for the world, as much as German universities had defined the golden measure a century earlier – and with good reason. From our universities came the science and the scientists, the social science, the humanities revived by fresh questions, the spirit of discovery, the compelling call of vivid curiosity.

At the age of eighteen I went to Harvard in 1950 because, so far as I then knew, it was the only university in which research went on. (Of course, I was wrong, but, for an adolescent intellectual in West Hartford, Connecticut, the choices were Harvard, Yale, and Brown, and among them, only Harvard seemed a place where people read books.) But ten years later, a dozen New England universities, and many score throughout the country, had gained that ambition to transform and transcend that in the aggregate formed the great leap forward of America's universities. A new definition of the calling of higher education took hold. We were partners, all of us on the campus, in an adventure of learning. That meant that students would study, not merely gain credentials. Scholars would publish, not merely speculate. Teachers would conduct the classroom as a realm of discovery, not merely as a stage for the rehearsal of other peoples' knowledge and the professor's opinions of that knowledge. Knowledge itself – the definition of what is to be learned for the degree of Bachelor of Arts or of Science – vastly changed. Old boundaries gave way. New subjects found entry.

That was the vision. Along with the best and the brightest I knew, I was drawn to a life of learning: reading and writing, studying and teaching, speculating and testing propositions: what if? and why? and why not? That was the life I chose, and, given the choice again and the years in which to carry it out, I should choose that same life again. But not for the same reasons, and not in the same realm of reality. Our tide flowed in, in the 1950s and 1960s. But it flowed out again. The ebb-tide came in the late 1960s and early 1970s. We who then were young, the legacy of the vision of the 1940s and 1950s, sustained the hope that others had given us, but confronted a world no one could earlier have conceived. The great presidents of the 1950s and 1960s were scholars, one and all. They also had the capacity to find the money they needed to build their universities by finding greatness in scholarship. They also were educators, who framed success by the criterion of the quality of mind – and, in the colleges, even the character and conscience – of the young people for whom, for four years, they and their faculties bore responsibility.

But in the trials of social revolution and political crisis, when the campus became the battlefield and the college students the shock-troops, the scholars and the educators failed and were replaced. What most of them could not, and did not, do was hold the center. They were educators, scholars and teachers, not politicians, not managers, not planners of budgets and manipulators of women and of men. And others came along – people thought they were needed – who could do those things. We still on the campus pay the price of the campus revolution of the 1960s and 1970s. And why not? Ours was the mistake, for we believed when we should have doubted, and we thought we could by an act of the faculty senate change human nature, reform society, and redeem the world. But we could not even save ourselves and our own ideals when the barbarians came. And come they surely did.

University leadership has now found its definition not in the particular requirements of the tasks of the academy: scholarship and research. Now what the campus needed was what other large institutions – deemed no different from the university in substance, but only in form – also needed. A person with political capacities could move from the cabinet or the House of Representatives to the campus. A general could turn himself into a college president. So could a chief executive officer of a large corporation. So could a fund-raiser, a foundation program officer, anybody who had shown capacities to control, manage, administer – and it did not matter what. These new types of academic office-holders were not chosen because of achievement in education and scholarship, and they did not value capacity to teach and to write – things they had never done and could not do. They were chosen to keep the peace and balance the budget, much as the Lord-Mayor of Johannesburg can keep the peace and balance the budget. And that is what they did.

The ideal of the builders of the 1940s and 1950s produced us, the professors of the 1960s into the twenty-first century. We received a vision and we lived by it. The vision discerned a different America and demanded of the academy a distinctive calling. But the academy can yet serve useful purposes, if not the cause of education and citizenship, community and civil discourse, reasoned argument about honorable alternatives. So use it for what it can give: the chance to do your work, that alone. The academy has no room any more for those who find themselves called to learning and to service. It is a place for careers – and careerists. It is not going to change very soon. So if the university serves your purpose, use it. Take your pay and do your job, just as you would in any other corporation, in a normal, utterly professional and impersonal transaction. More is not wanted.

But learning will go forward, if not on the campus, then elsewhere. For the curiosity of humanity draws us onward, and if this kind of institution does not nurture learning, some other will. The will to know, to ask why, and why not, and what if? – that never-to-be-satisfied hunger and thirst will never fail us but will always sustain us. It is what it means to be human. If I had to do it all over again, would I give my life of learning and teaching, sharing and building? Yes, I would do precisely what I did with my life: get learning, pursue learning. But I would do it for different reasons, and I would do it in a different way.

I would do it for one reason only, which is, as I said, because if you want to be a scholar, you have to make a living, and for many subjects you can make a living as a scholar only in a university. And I would do it not as I have done, giving half of my energy and commitment to students, and half to scholarship. I would give all of my energy and commitment to scholarship, and leave over only what I absolutely had to reserve for a minimal accomplishment of such tasks of teaching as I could not decently avoid.

So my best wisdom for the next generation, as just now it begins work for the Ph.D. and a life of learning:

[1] Scholarship, in published form, is all that matters in graduate school and in your career beyond. Pay no attention, now or later on, to issues of higher education and the larger setting of the university. These should not concern you.

[2] Do not think of yourself as an educator, let alone as a teacher, but only as a scholar. If you have to make a living in the academy, teach as little as you can, to as few students as you can, and avoid all engagement with students. And, for the rest, no committees, no politics, no involvements, just read and write.

[3] Take from the university what it has to give you, but give nothing more than your scholarship, which is to say, nothing the university wants or values. Leave the university to those who wish, today, to make of it what they will: the presidents, provosts, and deans, on the one side, and the students who come and go, on the other. They will do as they like, anyhow, so keep out of their way and do your work. Use them, as they use you, and you will have a useful career – for yourself and for your field of learning, and these are all that matter.

And – so I should claim – that forms the authentically Judaic message to the life of intellect, and that is what makes all the difference: the learning itself.

Part Three
ANCIENT ISRAEL AND
THE ANCIENT NEAR EAST

4

The Role of Inspiration Relative to Other Explanations of the Formation of the Hebrew Bible

Ernest S. Frerichs
Brown University

Particular topics of Biblical research rise and decline in scholarly attention for reasons often imperceptible to observers external to the field. A case in point is the current explosion of interest in issues centered in questions of scriptural canon. Explanations for the "process" of canonization, the definition of canon, the nature of canonicity, the role of canon in biblical interpretation – all these are suddenly of considerable attention in scholarly publication.[1] A part of this renewed discussion seeks to identify the role of inspiration in studies of canon

---

[1]See the bibliographies in B. Childs, *Introduction to the Old Testament as Scripture*, Philadelphia (1979), 46-49, and B. Metzger, *The Canon of the New Testament*, Oxford (1987), 11-38. Current works include S. Leiman, *The Canonization of Hebrew Scripture: the Talmudic and Midrashic Evidence* [*Transactions of the Connecticut Academy of Arts and Sciences*], Hamden,Conn (1976); J. Neusner, *Midrash in Context*, Philadelphia (1983), esp. ch 5; R. Beckwith, *The Old Testament Canon of the New Testament Church*, Grand Rapids, MI (1985); R. Beckwith, "Formation of the Hebrew Bible," 39-86, and E. Ellis, "The Old Testament Canon in the Early Church," 653-690, in M. Mulder, ed., *Mikra* [*Compendia Rerum Judaicarum ad Novum Testamentum*, Section 2, v. I], Philadelphia (1988); P. Miller, "Der Kanon in der gegenwaertigen Amerikanischen Diskussion," *Jahrbuch fuer Biblische Theologie*, v.3 (1988), 217-240; G. Coats and B. Long, eds., *Canon and Authority*, Philadelphia (1977); S. Leiman, ed., *The Canon and the Masorah of the Hebrew Bible*, New York (1974); J. Kaestli and O. Wermelinger, eds., *Le canon de l'Ancien Testament*, Geneva (1984).

and to argue for the conclusiveness of this attribute in distinguishing between what was finally included or excluded in the biblical canon.

This newer discussion of the role of inspiration can be distinguished from the views of canonical formation in early Jewish and Christian traditions (e.g., Josephus), as well as from the views of canon developed in the nineteenth century. The explanations of canon derived from extant ancient materials assumed that authenticity would be determined by authorship, the "purity" of the canonical formation by asserting an unbroken succession of biblical books, and the truth of the canonical works by declaring them to be divinely inspired.[2]

The discussion of this paper focuses upon the role of inspiration relative to other factors in the study of canon and limits the discussion to the formation of the Hebrew Bible understood as Jewish Scripture. The low level of attention to topics of canon and inspiration in Biblical scholarship from the end of the nineteenth century to the middle of the twentieth is apparent to all who review the titles of scholarly publications in biblical studies in the period in question. Although the nature of the German "Einleitung" insured that all introductory studies of the Hebrew Bible or Old Testament would contain discussions of canon, a review of those discussions reveals the genetic transmission of the "assured results of scholarship" with respect to questions of canon. One summary work, H. E. Ryle's *The Canon of the Old Testament* (1892), served as the standard work on the subject of canon for almost a century, though it was only the most popular of a number of works with similar titles and similar arguments.

Attention to questions of canon in the nineteenth century was partly a byproduct of the rise of historical Bible criticism and the forms of literary analysis which historical criticism fostered. Critical discussions on the history of the literature of ancient Israel and the process of literary formation produced new understandings of the origin and development of the Pentateuch. The relative triumph of Wellhausenism with respect to the explanations for the origins of the Pentateuch and the construction of ancient Israelite history provided a concomitant opportunity for newer theses explaining the creation of the Biblical canon. These newer understandings of canonical development coalesced into a fairly common view which was still evident in the critical Introductions produced through World War II.

As we approach the last decade of the twentieth century, however, it is clear that a shift has again occurred, both in the interest in this topic and in the character and quantity of the resulting publications. It is still the case that the majority of works written in the general field

---

[2]Childs, *Introduction*, 51.

of scriptural canon reflect a major interest in the role of canon in the Christian Church, no less so even when the primary or exclusive concern is for the Old Testament. It is also evident that the difference in understanding between the formation of the Hebrew Bible as Jewish Scripture and the formation of the Old Testament within the Christian Bible has often been obscured or misunderstood in scholarly discussion. The dominant interest in the Christian understanding of canon is even more evident when we review the publications of the past twenty years dealing with the role of scriptural inspiration in canon formation.[3] Scholarly interest in the role of inspiration in the formation of the canon of the Hebrew Bible has been less evident, however, in Jewish scholarship.[4]

A major contributor to the heightened interest in questions of canon has been the increased interaction in the twentieth century between Jewish and Christian scholars of Bible and the common sharing of research. The movement of various areas of Judaic scholarship from the Jewish institutions of learning to the arts and sciences faculties of both private (non-Jewish) and public colleges and universities has been a revolutionary move with multiple and permanent ramifications. A significant further factor in this newer discourse between Jewish and Christian scholars of Biblical studies has been the improved abilities of non-Jewish scholars to consult the primary materials of the Judaic tradition in their original languages. This has been accompanied by a burst of translations of traditional Jewish literature into English within the past decade.[5] Students external to the Jewish community, and often without requisite language abilities, suddenly found that they had access to large parts of the rabbinic corpus, if only in translation.

In addition to the enlarged discourse between Jewish and Christian Biblical scholars, the rise of Judaic and Jewish studies in non-Jewish

---

[3]See, e.g., P. Achtemeier, *The Inspiration of Scripture,* Philadelphia (1980); B. Vawter, *Biblical Inspiration,* Philadelphia (1972); A. Sundberg, "The Bible Canon and the Christian Doctrine of Inspiration," *Catholic Biblical Quarterly* 29 (1975), 352-371; P. Billerbeck, "Der Kanon des Alten Testaments und seine Inspiration," Excursus 16, *Kommentar zum Neuen Testament aus Talmud und Midrasch,* H. Strack and P. Billerbeck, Munich (1928), 415-451; J. Burtchaell, *Catholic Theories of Biblical Inspiration since 1810 ,* Cambridge (1969).

[4]See especially S. Leiman, *The Canonization of Hebrew Scripture* and S. Leiman, "Inspiration and Canonicity: Reflections on the Formation of the Biblical Canon, E. Sanders, et al., eds., *Jewish and Christian Self-Definition,* v.2, Philadelphia (1981), 56-63.

[5]See especially the extensive translation and publication of traditional rabbinic literature in English by Jacob Neusner.

institutions and the increased access of non-Jewish scholars to rabbinic materials, the growing interest in questions of canon and inspiration has been very much affected by the recovery of several major groups of primary materials unknown to earlier scholarship. Some of these bear more directly on the canon of the New Testament and the canon of the Christian Bible, but all of these materials play some role in the discussion of the formation of the Hebrew Bible. The materials in question would include the recovery in 1945 of the Nag Hammadi Coptic library of fourth century papyrus manuscripts consisting of twelve codices and eight leaves from a thirteenth codex – fifty-two separate tractates and forty-five titles. The almost simultaneous recovery in 1947 of the Qumran library of a Jewish sectarian group, presumably Essenes, with its examples of all Biblical texts (except Esther), of distinctive forms of commentaries on Biblical texts, and of non-Biblical documents of the preserving community has affected all areas of Biblical research in lasting ways. Septuagint research has also been radically altered by the Qumran materials and with that alteration has come a reassessment of questions of canon. Older views contrasting the Palestinian canon with the Alexandrian canon have been called into serious question. The Qumran Biblical texts have also resulted in a major recasting of the previously established ways of comparing the Masoretic Hebrew text with the Septuagint in textual criticism. No longer do scholars assert that the Septuagint was based on a late and unreliable Hebrew text and consequently less acceptable than the Masoretic Hebrew text.

In addition to the recovery of previously unknown materials from antiquity, there have been in the last quarter century a series of publications which have called into serious question the understanding of Hebrew Bible canonization and the role of inspiration as this was projected at the end of the last century.

Some explanation, e.g., was needed to explain the variations between the Jewish canon of antiquity and the Christian canon of the medieval church. The explanation commonly suggested was the explanation of an Alexandrian canon versus a Palestinian canon. Such an explanation had already been recognized in antiquity in the views of Augustine. Luther adopted Jerome's position and separated the writings of Jewish origin, but of debated inclusion in the Jewish canon of antiquity, placing them in an independent section, titled Apocrypha, following the Old Testament in the Luther Bible. It became common in subsequent Bible translations and editions of the Christian Bible to place these apocryphal works either between the Old and New Testaments (as in the New English Bible) or following the New Testament (as in the Revised Standard Version). Roman Catholics, believing these writings to be sacred and inspired by God (with the exception of 1st and 2nd Esdras and the Prayer of Manasseh) designated these works as deuterocanonical.

The explanation that these differences of inclusion and exclusion derived from the differences between an Alexandrian canon as over against a narrower Palestinian canon have been largely discarded. The work of Albert Sundberg in the late 1950s and early 1960s has made if difficult, if not impossible, to account for the differences in canon through the thesis of an Alexandrian/Palestinian canonical contrast.[6]

The work of Sundberg has been paralleled by the largely successful efforts of other contemporary scholars to dismantle or call into serious question other "assured results of scholarship" in the understanding of the formation of the Jewish Biblical canon. In Jewish antiquity the formation of the canon of the Hebrew Bible was variously attributed to Ezra (IV Ezra 14:38ff and Baba Bathra 14b) or to Nehemiah (Nehemiah 8-19; II Maccabees 2:13), or to the Men of the Great Assembly (Avot Rabbi Natan 1 or Baba Bathra 14b). In the modern discussion of this question in the 1870s by Heinrich Graetz, the argument was developed that the so-called Council of Jamnia or Yavneh at the end of the first century C.E. was the action which led to the final determination of the Jewish Biblical canon. This hypothesis of Graetz and others has been seriously contested in the work of several scholars in recent years, notably Jack P. Lewis and Sid Z. Leiman.[7]

Much use was also made of the Samaritan schism to support the thesis of three divisions of the Hebrew Bible and the creation of those divisions at distinct times in post-Exilic Israel. This schism was dated to the fifth century B.C.E. and coupled with the assumption that the Samarian Bible, limited to the Pentateuch, was a significant datum in determining the status at that time of the collected form of the Prophets and the Writings. James D. Purvis, writing in the late 1950s, used Dead Sea materials to show that the Samaritan schism and the Samaritan canon of the Pentateuch are better understood as occurrences well after the general period assigned to the formation of the prophetic canon. Purvis' argument was based on a study of the textual traditions of the Samaritan Pentateuch such as forms of writing and

---

[6]A. Sundberg, *The Old Testament of the Early Church* [*Harvard Theological Studies*, 20], Cambridge (1964).

[7]J.Lewis, "What do we mean by Jabneh," *Journal of Bible and Religion* 32 (1964), 125-132; S. Leiman, *The Canonization of Hebrew Scripture*. See the cautionary views of P. Schaefer, "Die sogenannte Synode von Jabne," *Judaica* 31 (1975), 54-64,116-124; Guenter Stemberger, "Jabne und der Kanon," *Jahrbuch fuer Biblische Theologie*, v.3 (1988), 163-174; G. Stemberger, "Synode von Jabne und das fruehe Christentum," *Kairos* 19 (1977), 14-21.

orthography to demonstrate their parallels with the Qumran materials. This view generally parallels that of Frank M. Cross and G. Ernest Wright.[8]

All of these major shifts in commonly accepted explanations for the process of "canonization" have taken place in the past quarter century. The stage is set for a new understanding and it is clear that newer arguments will be more carefully constructed when distinguishing between the canonizing of the Jewish Bible and that of the Christian Bible. Indeed the need to make such a distinction is an important outcome of the reconsiderations which have been put forward in recent scholarship.

One of the arguments recently advanced has been to underscore the decisive importance of inspiration in explaining the complex character of the inclusion or exclusion of materials in the Hebrew Bible. Sid Z. Leiman, in his earlier doctoral dissertation, *The Canonization of Hebrew Scripture: The Talmudic and Midrashic Evidence* (1976) argued this view. He has advanced the argument in his more recent essay, "Inspiration and Canonicity: Reflections on the Formation of the Biblical Canon."[9] Leiman's argument presupposes the possibility that the legal traditions of the Torah achieved an early "canonical" status and that there could have been important canonical understandings affecting more than Deuteronomy in the reign of King Josiah in the late seventh century B.C.E. The prophetic "canon" was largely determined between 500 and 450 and the "Writings" were canonized shortly after the activity of Judas Maccabee in the middle of the second century B.C.E.

Against this background, Leiman must define a canonical book and does so as follows: "A canonical book is a book accepted by Jews as authoritative for religious practice and/or doctrine, and whose authority is binding upon the Jewish people for all generations. Furthermore, such books are to be studied and expounded in private and in public."[10] This definition is carried further in a distinction Leiman uses between "inspired canonical literature" and "uninspired canonical literature."[11] Leiman recognized the problems inherent in these distinctions when he posed the question of what grounds would have

---

[8]J. Purvis, *The Samaritan Pentateuch and the Origin of the Samaritan Sect*, Cambridge (1968); G. E. Wright, *Schechem: Biography of a Biblical City*, New York (1965); F. Cross, " Aspects of Samaritan and Jewish History in Late Persian and Hellenistic Times," *Harvard Theological Review* 59 (1966), 201-211.

[9]S. Leiman, "Inspiration and Canonicity," 56-63.

[10]Leiman, *Canonization*, 14.

[11]Leiman, *ibid.*,14f.

been used to exclude Enoch and the Testaments of the Twelve Patriarchs from the biblical canon? The question carried with it the assumption that only inspired books would have been included in the biblical canon. In his more recent essay, Leiman has argued that "not every inspired utterance of the biblical authors was included in scripture. Only those inspired utterances whose message was necessary for all generations were included in the biblical canon."[12] Leiman immediately grants that the rabbis did not "clearly delineate" how they determined the inspired character of a biblical writing, nor how one determines that a book has a message for all generations. There is both a boldness about Leiman's assertions and a caution about the inconclusiveness of the evidence to support the basic theses. Guenter Stemberger has recently reviewed Leiman's work in the light of a study on Yavneh and the canon. He has questioned Leiman's use of rabbinical materials as historical sources and argued for the recognition that rabbinic sources reflect their own period and the conceptions of the period of their literary creation.[13]

The concept of inspiration is an ancient part of the discussions about books which were included in the Holy Scriptures of the Jewish community and has been used by Christians as well in the attempts to provide authority for the early Christian writings which would become known as the New Testament.[14] The reintroduction of inspiration as a decisive category in questions of canon is important at a time when a new construction of the canonical process is underway.[15] At the same time we cannot take this criterion and argue for its superior ability to explain the process of canonization. The following observations are pertinent to a judicious use of the category of inspiration which does not permit a single-factored explanation for the process of canonization:

1. All participants in the discussion of canon argue for a clarification of terms used in the discussion. Few readers of the literature in this field would not agree that confusion of terminology has increased the difficulties in canonical discussion. Despite the widespread use of the term "canon" in contemporary usage, it is not inappropriate to be reminded that the term "canon" was in its origins a Christian term and a relatively late term. The rabbinical material uses

---

[12]Leiman, "Inspiration and Canonicity," 56f.

[13]G. Stemberger, "Jabne und der Kanon," 166, fn 14.

[14]See P. Schaefer, *Die Vorstellung vom Heiligen Geist in der rabbinischen Literatur*, Munich (1972).

[15]See Beckwith's essay in *Mikra* as an an attempt to sketch a newer understanding of the canonical process.

a variety of terms to denote Jewish Scripture and no one of these is definitive in solving the problem of canonicity.[16] What is clear from the sources is that we cannot create a single definition of the concept of canon and that at various points the issue of "canonicity" may be related to "defiling the hands," or to its inspirational origin from the Holy Spirit, or to other factors. Despite the discussions across several centuries, it is clear that there is a need to reexamine certain equivalencies which can be found in the literature. The equation between inspiration and defiled hands has been too facile. Likewise, the view that the canonical status of a book is guaranteed by its defiling the hands must be reviewed.[17]

2.   In the current form of the discussion an equation is often drawn between the cessation of prophecy and the end of inspiration. Leiman, e.g., argues that "If the books were known to have been authored in the third century B.C.E. or later, They could not qualify for inclusion in the biblical canon because they were not inspired."[18] The issues of prophecy, its cessation and what that cessation means have received attention through the years.[19] While the argument used by Leiman makes easier the non-consideration for canonical status of large parts of the extra-canonical Jewish literature of the Tannaitic period (and increases the difficulty of Christian argument that New Testament writings are "inspired"), the sources are at least ambiguous on the relationship of the end of prophecy and inspiration.

3.   The difficulties of relying too heavily on the category of inspiration to explain inclusions and exclusions in the Jewish Scripture is shown in the example of the book of Ben Sira. This popular book produced various, and even contradictory, responses within the rabbinic tradition. As Menahem Haran has argued, the rabbis expound the sayings of Ben Sira and introduce their discussion of it with formulas such as "as it is said," or "as it is written," formulas characteristic of the rabbinical discussions of canonical materials. At other points in the rabbinic corpus, Ben Sira is classified as a work which does not "defile the hands," and is even classified with those works which should not be read. Haran argues that rabbinic opposition to Ben Sira was based on

---

[16]Beckwith, "Formation of the Hebrew Bible, " 39f., provides a broad variety of such terms from rabbinic and extra-rabbinic literature.

[17]Stemberger, "Jabne und der Kanon," 173f.

[18]Leiman, "Inspiration and Canonicity," 61.

[19]Most recently in F. Greenspahn, "Why Prophecy Ceased," *Journal of Biblical Literature* 108 (1989), 37-49; J. Blenkinsopp, *Prophecy and Canon*, Notre Dame (1977).

the absence of an attitude of holiness towards the book.[20] Leiman believes that opposition to Ben Sira came from its veneration by sectarian Jewish groups. He states that Ben Sira was excluded from the biblical canon "as part of a general rabbinic polemic against literature with biblical pretensions."[21] It is clear that inspiration is by no means the only factor involved in the exclusion of Ben Sira from the Jewish Scriptures.

The use of the category of inspiration in contemporary discussions of canon, especially by Leiman, is a healthy addition to earlier discussions dependent on a series of historical theses now shown to be in need of reconstruction. At the same time, inspiration has to be used with great caution as an historical explanation for complex events. It is clear, e.g., that there is a strong tendency for Jewish scholarship to look for a completed Scripture as early as possible. There is a similar desire on the part of Christian scholarship to seek as late a date as possible to make easier the argument for the continuation of scriptural definition and the creation of Christian Scriptures which include the New Testament. It is also clear that the variety of Judaisms in the Hellenistic and Roman periods defy simple arguments based on the notion that "the rabbis say."

Roger Beckwith is undoubtedly correct that we are moving into a new age with respect to our understanding of the formation of the Hebrew Bible. In that new construction we will undoubtedly find a role for a renewed understanding of the significance of inspiration in canonical formation, as Sid Leiman has argued. We will achieve these goals, however, only with a healthy appreciation of the multiple forms which Jewish life assumed during Hellenistic and Roman times. It is also true that an exclusive reliance on categories which do not yield easily to historical explanation, e.g. inspiration, will not provide a stronger foundation for the explanation of Biblical canon than the late nineteenth century arguments now being replaced.

---

[20]M. Haran, "Problems of the Canonization of Scripture," (Hebr.) *Tarbiz* 25 (1955), 245-271 [Reprinted in S. Leiman, ed., *Canon and Masorah*, 224-253.
[21]Leiman, "Inspiration and Canonicity," 62.

5

Genesis 21:33: A Study in the Development of a Biblical Text and its Rabbinic Transformation

Nahum M. Sarna
Brandeis University

Following the account of the pact that Abraham and King Abimelech concluded, as told in Genesis 22:32, it is recorded that the patriarch "planted a tamarisk at Beer-sheba, and invoked there the name of the Lord, the Everlasting God"[1] (v. 33). The Hebrew text reads as follows: ויטע אשל בבאר-שבע ויקרא שם בשם ה' אל עולם.

This notice, brief to the point of obscurity, contains several unusual features and raises numerous questions.[2]

First, there is the syntactical difficulty that the immediate antecedents in the plural – Abimelech and Pichol – cannot possibly be the subjects of the verbs in the singular found in this verse. Only the remote "Abraham" can govern the verbs ויטע and ויקרא. For the sake of clarity, the Samaritan recension and the ancient versions, the Septuagint, Peshitta and Vulgate, all felt constrained to insert [Abraham] into the text, and the English translations, including the Jewish ones, have traditionally followed this practice.

The syntactical anomaly gives the appearance of thematic disjunction between the present verse and the preceding narrative. Some medieval Jewish commentators attempted to sustain the organic unity

---

[1]Translations of biblical texts follow those of the new Jewish Publication Society's version (TANAKH).

[2]The documentary source attribution of v. 33 is quite irrelevant to the issues here discussed. In any event, modern commentators show no unanimity in assigning this particular verse.

of the entire chapter. Thus, Bekhor Shor (12th cent.) for instance, understood the purpose of the tree-planting to be commemorative of the aforementioned pact.[3] David Kimchi (1060?-1135?) supposes that the aborcultural act adjacent to the well at Beer-sheba was intended to exhibit undisputed assumption of sovereign possession of the facility.[4] In modern times, Benno Jacob's[5] explanation is similar to that of Bekhor Shor, while E. A. Speiser, despite the vagueness of his formulation, also seems to connect the tree-planting with the pact-making.[6]

The difficulty with these interpretations is that no analogous practice within a legal context is again to be found in the Bible, nor does anyone else plant a tree simply to memorialize some experience. Moreover, were Abraham's deed really the sequel to the preceding narrative, it might have been expected to have occurred before, not after, the departure of the two Philistines. Some explicit indication of the connection would surely have been forthcoming in the text. There seems no way of avoiding the conclusion that Genesis 21:33 belonged to an independent narrative, now thoroughly truncated,[7] that dealt with Abraham's tamarisk at Beer-sheba. This irresistible inference itself raises two problems: Why has the original story been so radically abridged? And why was the notice about the tree preserved at all? The answers to these questions are dependent upon a third one: What is the connection between the two parts of verse 33 – the act of tree-planting and the act of worshiping? This last issue must be addressed first since it provides the key to the understanding of the entire passage.

The straightforward implication of the text is that there exists an inextricable interconnection between the two clauses of the verse. That is to say, Abraham's planting of the tree is directly associated with his act of worship. Now it is well known that throughout the ancient Near East from Mesopotamia to Egypt, as well as in the Aegean and Minoan areas, the phenomenon of the sacred tree existed – not necessarily as an object of worship in itself, so much as the locus of a numinous presence. It was, therefore, an ideal place for theophany and worship. The tree served as a medium of oracles and revelation.[8]

---

[3]Ed. J. Gad, Jerusalem, 1956 *ad loc.* His comment is: אילן גדול להיות לזכרון על הברית.
[4]Ed. M. Kamelhaar, Jerusalem, Mosad Harav Kook, 1970, *ad loc.* His comment is: נטע שם נטיעה סמוך לבאר שהזיה לעדות כי נשארה הבאר בידו
[5]B. Jacob, *Das Erste Buch der Tora*, Berlin, Schocken, Verlag, 1934, (Reprint, Ktav, New York, s.d.), p. 489.
[6]E. A. Speiser, *Genesis* (Anchor Bible), Garden City, New York, 1964, p. 159.
[7]For examples of similarly truncated biblical narratives, cf. Gen. 9:20-27; 10:9-10 (cf. Micah 5:5); 35:22 (cf. 1 Chron. 5:1-2); Exod. 4:24-26.
[8]R. de Vaux, *Ancient Israel: Its Life and Institutions*, Translated by J. McHugh, New York, McGraw Hill, 1961, pp. 278f; C. L. Meyers, *The Tabernacle Menorah:*

Several biblical toponyms testify to the presence of many such sacred, arbored sites in Canaan. Genesis 12:6 records that "Abram passed through the land as far as the site of Shechem at the terebinth of Moreh." The term for "site" in Hebrew is *maqōm:* its combination with a city-name is unique in the Bible so that in the verse quoted it most likely carries the special meaning of "sacred site," just like Arabic *maqām,* as it does numerous times in biblical texts.[9] The name given to the terebinth is *'elon moreh* [plural in Deut. 11:30], which means "the terebinth of the teacher/oracle-giver." It was at this site that Abraham experienced a theophany and built an altar (v. 7). According to Joshua 24:26, the great military leader made a covenant with the people at Shechem, and "He took a great stone and set it up at the foot of the oak (Hebrew *'elah*) in the sacred precinct of the Lord." In the Book of Judges it is said that Abimelech was proclaimed king at "the terebinth (*'elon*) of the pillar at Shechem," and doubtless in the vicinity stood the "Diviners' Oak" (*'elon me'onenim,* 9:6, 37).[10] Earlier, Jacob had buried the pagan religious symbols possessed by the members of his entourage "under the terebinth (*'elah*) that was near Shechem" (Gen 35:4). Hebron too had its sacred trees, for Abraham had pitched his tent "at the terebinths of Mamre (*'elonei mamre*), which are in Hebron," and had "built an altar there to the Lord" (Gen. 13:18). It is quite probable that it was beneath one of these special trees that the patriarch entertained his three unexpected visitors, for the text repeatedly mentions "the tree," the definite article seeming to indicate one well known (*ibid.* 18:4, 8). "The Oak of Weeping" (*'allon bakhut*) was where Rebekah's nurse Deborah was laid to rest (*ibid.* 35:8), while the later prophetess of the same name "used to sit under the Palm of Deborah" to issue judicial decisions (Judg. 4:5), perhaps by oracular

---

A Synthetic Study of a Symbol from the Biblical Cult, ASOR Dissertation Series 2, Missoula, MT. Scholars Press, 1976, pp. 95, 133-156; cf. F. Matz in *The Cambridge Ancient History,* 3rd edition, II, 1. Cambridge, Cambridge University Press, 1978, p. 161.

[9]For *maqōm* as "sacred space," cf. Gen. 28:11, 17, 19; 35:7; Exod. 20:24; Deut. Ch. 12 *passim;* 14:23 ff; 15:20; Ch. 16 *passim;* 17:8, 10; 18:6; 23:17; 26:2; 31:11. In 1 Sam. 7:16 the term is used of the shrines of Bethel, Gilgal, and Mizpah; other examples are 1 Kings 8:6; Isa. 17:7; 26:21; 66:1; Jer. 7:12; Ezek. 3:12; 6:13; 43:7; Micah 1:2-3; Ps. 24:3; 26:8; 104:8; 132:5. In 1 Chron. 16:27 *maqōm* appears in place of *miqdash* in the parallel text in Ps. 96:6. Hebrew *maqōm* should probably also have the meaning of "sacred space" in Gen. 22:4, 9, 14; Num. 18:31; 23:27, and in Ezek. 3:12, a doxology parallel to that in Ps. 135:21 ("Zion").

[10]The meaning of the problematical *muṣṣab* here is immaterial to the issue at hand. A. B. Ehrlich, *Mikra' Ki-Pheshuto,* Berlin, M. Poppelauer, 1899, p. 59, points out that in 1 Sam. 22:6, as in 31:13, the definite article also indicates the special sacred character of the three.

means. "The Terebinth of Tabor" and "The Valley of the Oak" (I Sam. 10:3; 17:2) are two more sites bearing arboreal names that appear to indicate the presence of sacred trees. Finally, it is not without significance that it was from "under the terebinth at Ophrah" that Gideon experienced a theophany (Judg. 6:10-21).

The association of sacred trees with pagan cults, especially with fertility cults, made them anathema to the official religion of Israel. Canaanite cult sites established "under any luxuriant tree" were to be utterly destroyed and were not to be imitated even in the worship of the God of Israel (Deut. 12:2-4). The planting of "any kind of tree" beside the altar of the Lord was unequivocally proscribed (*ibid.* 16:21), and no wonder, for male prostitutes who were active in Judea in the days of Rehoboam son of Solomon were apparently connected with shrines built "under every leafy tree" (1 Kings 14:21-2). Hosea testifies to the practice of prostitution in the northern kingdom at shrines erected "under oaks, poplars, and terebinths" (4:13-14).[11]

In light of all the above, it is extraordinary that tradition should have recorded an association of Abraham with a tree in a cultic context. This in itself constitutes eloquent testimony to the great antiquity of that tradition, to its reliability, popularity, and persistence. It was not expunged from the Torah's record.

Further evidence for the antiquity of the tradition behind Genesis 21:33 lies in the divine epithet *'el 'olam.* This title never recurs in the Bible, although it has turned up in a fifteenth century B.C.E. inscription found at Serabit el-Khadem in Sinai. There it appears in the form of *'l d̠ 'lm* (*'l d̠u 'olam*).[12] Further, *'lm* as an epithet of a deity occurs in Ugaritic[13] text 2008:7, *špš 'lm;* in text 68:10, *mlk 'lm;*[14] and in text 52:1 *rpu mlk 'lm.* It also shows up in the eighth century B.C.E. Phoenician inscription from Karatepe as *šmš 'lm.*[15] Once again, the retention of the

---

[11]Cf. 2 Kings 16:4; 17:10: Isa. 57:5; Jer. 2:20; 3:6, 13; 17:2; Ezek. 6:13. On Hos. 4:13-14, see M. Weinfeld, *Deuteronomy and the Deuteronomic school,* Oxford, Clarendon Press, 1972, pp. 322, 336.

[12]F. M. Cross, Jr., "Yahweh and the God of the Patriarchs," *HTR,* 55 (1962), 225-59, esp. 233, n. 31; 238ff; *idem, Canaanite Myth and Hebrew Epic,* Cambridge, MA, Harvard University Press, 1973, pp. 17-22, 47-50.

[13]Cyrus H. Gordon, *Ugaritic Textbook,* Rome, Pontifical Biblical Institute, 1965.

[14]Cf. Jer. 10:10.

[15]H. Donner-W. Röllig, *Kanaanäische u. Aramäische Inschriften,* Wiesbaden, Otto Harrassowitz, 1962, I, No. 26, p. 6, III, 19. The title *špš 'lm* is equivalent to *Šamaš dārītum* in El Amarna 155.6, 47. It should be noted that the term *'lt 'lm* in the Arslan Tash inscription, translated by Albright as "goddess of eternity," *BASOR,* 76 (1939), 8, is now to be rendered "an eternal bond;" see Franz Rosenthal, *The Ancient Near East: Supplementary Texts,* ed. J. B. Pritchard, Princeton, New Jersey, 1969, p. 658; cf. E. Lipiński, *Near Eastern Religious Texts*

unique Hebrew divine title *'el 'olam* in Genesis 21:33 means that it must have belonged to the original, pre-pentateuchal form of the narrative. It is of great significance, however, that in the present narrative the divinity whom Abraham invoked has been carefully dissociated from any pagan deity by identifying *'el 'olam* with YHWH. This development is particularly meaningful because the other unusual divine titles compounded *'el* in Genesis are not generally so identified. *'El Shaddai* appears five times and is not once particularized as YHWH.[16] *'El 'Elyon* is invoked four times in Chapter 14, but is connected with YHWH only when it issues from the mouth of Abraham in addressing a non-Hebrew (v. 22). That text and ours in 21:33, therefore, may be said to exhibit special sensitivity to the possibility of mistaken identification of an exceptional divine title.

Further clue to the pre-history of the text may be recognized in another curious anomaly that, it seems to me, has not been sufficiently evaluated. The phrase *va-yiqra' be-shem YHWH* occurs thrice more in the patriarchal narratives: 12:8; 13:4, and 26:25. In each instance, it is accompanied by or associated with mention of an altar. The present citation constitutes the exception. The reverse situation is found: that is, mention of altar-building without the invocation of God – 12:7; 13:18; 33:20; 35:7 – but not the invocation of God without reference to an altar. The solitary omission of the altar in Genesis 21:33 would therefore appear to be deliberate. It must flow from a sensitivity to the association of Abraham with the planting of a tree and his act of worship at that spot.

The specific plant favored by the patriarch is designated an *'eshel*. James Barr has persuasively illustrated that already within the formative period of the Hebrew Bible this term occasioned embarrassment. Such is reflected in the Chronicler's change of *'eshel* in 1 Samuel 31:13 to *'elah* in the parallel passage in 1 Chronicles 10:12 in the story about the burial of King Saul and his sons "under the tamarisk tree in Jabesh." Barr has also pointed to the great variety of interpretation of this term *'eshel* exhibited by the ancient versions of Genesis 21:33, a phenomenon engendered, as he puts it, by "a name unpleasantly similar to that of the notorious idolatrous symbol, the *Asherah*."[17]

Relating to the Old Testament, Ed. W. Beyerlin, Philadelphia, Westminster Press, 1978, p. 248.

[16]Gen. 17:1; 28:3; 35:11; 43:14; 48:3.

[17]J. Barr, "Seeing the word for the Trees ? An Enigmatic Ancient Translation," *JSS* 13 (1968), 11-20, esp. p. 14. On the Asherah, see J. Day, "Asherah in the Hebrew Bible and Northwest Semitic Literature," *JBL*, 105 (1986), 385-408.

Abraham's *'eshel* at Beer-sheba is not again mentioned in the Bible. However, it is to be noted that Isaac traveled to Beer-sheba, received a theophany, built an altar, and "invoked the name of the Lord" (Gen. 26:23-25). The narrative does not identify the site with that of Abraham's *'eshel*, but it is to be noted that the theophany twice refers to Abraham by name. Jacob too visited Beer-sheba, on his way down to Egypt, offered sacrifices to "the God of Isaac his father," and also experienced a theophany at that site (*ibid.* 46:1-4). It is reasonable to assume that all three traditions relate to the same sacred locale.[18] Such a conclusion provides a convincing explanation for Judahite Beer-sheba remaining an attractive and popular cultic site even for the citizens of the northern kingdom long after the division of the country following the death of Solomon. The prophet Amos found it necessary to condemn the custom of northerners traveling to the cult-site at Beer-sheba (Amos 5:5; cf. 8:14).

In sum, it would be difficult to find a better explanation for the preservation of the statement about Abraham's activities found in Genesis 21:33 than that it is excerpted from an originally larger narrative describing the origins and founding of the famous cult-center at Beer-sheba. In consequence of the great popularity of that shrine as a place of pilgrimage, the story had become a classic, and reference to it could not be entirely omitted. Due to the obnoxious nature of the tree-cult in the folk religion, and to the possibility of mistakenly finding legitimacy for it through the patriarch's venture, only the skeleton outline of the ancient narrative was retained. The careful editing is evidenced by the exceptional absence of altar-building, and the identification of the unique epithet *'el 'olam* with YHWH, as well as by the exclusion of any mention of a theophany.

The sensitivity to the presence of the *'eshel* persisted beyond the period of the early Bible translations into the rabbinic age. A discussion about the term is reported in B. Sotah 10a, and in several midrashic sources.[19] R. Judah, followed by Resh Lakish, maintained that it meant an orchard (*pardes*). The popularity of this rendering is attested by its acceptance on the part of the Psuedo-Jonathan, the Yerushalmi, the Neofiti, and the Samaritan targums. According to R. Nehemiah, however, the *'eshel* was not something arboreal, but a

---

[18]See M. Haran, *Temples and Temple Service in Ancient Israel*, Oxford, Clarendon Press, 1978, p. 54ff.

[19]The midrash appears in various forms in Genesis R. 54:5, ed. J. Theodor and Ch. Albeck, [Reprint] Jerusalem, Wahrmann Books, 1965, p. 583; Midrash Tehillim, ed. S. Buber, Vilna, 1891, to Ps. 37:1 (p. 253); Ps. 110:1 (p. 465); cf. Yalkut Shimoni, para 95; Midrash Lekaḥ Tov, ed. S. Buber, Lemberg, 1884, p. 96.

"hospice" (*pundaq*, Greek *pandocheion*). Abraham is credited with providing wayfarers with food an shelter, thereby bringing them close to the true God. To add force to this transformational interpretation, *'eshel* is even taken to be an acronym formed from the initial letters of three words, *'akhilah, shetiyah, levayah,* "eating, drinking, and accompanying on the way."[20] Rabbinic exegesis has emptied the verse of its cultic content. An incident belonging to the realm of personal piety in a ritual context has been transformed so that it now exemplifies God's demands on man in a socio-moral context. At the same time, the provision of wayfarers and of the homeless has itself been elevated by the Rabbis to the status of a mode of divine worship. As the Talmud records in the name of Rab Judah who cited it in the name of Rab: "Hospitality to wayfarers is greater than welcoming the presence of the Shekhinah" (Shab. 127a).[21]

---

[20]Midrash Tehillim, *op. cit.*, to Ps. 37:1 (p. 253). See also the comment of Bahya ben Asher to Genesis 21:33, ed. C.B, Chavel, Jerusalem, 1962, p. 191, nn. 31-32.

[21]גדולה הכנסת אורחין מהקבלת פני שכינה

6

"He Should Continue to Bear the Penalty of that Case":

Some Observations on
Codex Ḥammurabi §§ 3-4 and § 13[1]

Tzvi Abusch
Brandeis University

The purpose of this paper is to suggest an explanation for *aran dīnim šuāti ittanašši in* §§ 4 and 13 of *Codex Ḥammurabi* (hereafter CH). More specifically, we wish to reconsider the function of the *-tan*-form of the G(rundstamm)tn durative *ittanašši (našû)* in § 4, and secondarily in § 13, and to reconstruct the legal situation, thought, and intent of the relevant legal cases. My concern here is to understand "the conceptual framework and moral standards implied in the normative prescriptions which these law collections explicitly set out."[2] I have paid little attention to the relationship of the relevant paragraphs to actual practice. This procedure is valid under any circumstance; it is especially valid since the nature of the "Code" has not yet been finally determined nor has it been decided whether the individual cases are statutory law, exemplary precedents or reforms, or scholastic

---

[1]A version of this paper was read before the 198th meeting of the American Oriental Society, Chicago, March, 1988. I have benefited from the questions and observations of several friends, most recently Marvin Fox and Stephen Kaufman. I am especially grateful to Kathryn Kravitz for her assistance and for a number of helpful suggestions.
[2]J. J. Finkelstein, *The Ox That Gored*, Transactions of the American Philosophical Society 71/2 (Philadelphia, 1981), p. 16.

speculation. Perhaps our reflections will provide further support for one or another position.

A study of the wording and thought of legal cases in a collection that forms an early part of a tradition that eventually included biblical and rabbinic legal collections is surely a fitting presentation in honor of the person and achievements of Professor Marvin Fox. For one of the areas nearest to his heart and central to his scholarship is the close reading of legal texts and the recovery of their underlying values and conceptions. Marvin has been a dear friend and respected colleague since we first met, and I take very great pleasure in dedicating this study to him on this occasion.

Introduction

The first part of the Code (§§ 1-5) sets out selected procedures to be followed by the courts. Opening the Code in this way seems to have been intentional, for such an introduction highlights the importance of proper judicial procedure for the administration of justice and suggests Ḫammurabi's concern for the rule of law. § 4 treats the testimony of a witness in a case involving a dispute over property, probably silver or barley loans. Actually, the division into paragraphs is modern,[3] and § 4 is not a separate unit. Rather, it is related to § 3 and forms the second segment of a unit comprising §§ 3 and 4. The text of §§ 3-4 reads:

(3) *šumma awīlum ina dīnim ana šibūt sarrātim ūṣiamma awāt iqbû lā uktīn*
     šumma dīnum šū dīn napištim awīlum šū iddâk
(4) *šumma ana šībūt še'im u kaspim ūṣiam aran dīnim šuāti ittanašši*

As we shall see, the protasis of § 4 is parallel to the opening protasis of § 3 and should be construed as if it read *šumma (awīlum ina dīnim) ana šibūt še'im u kaspim ūṣiam (ma awāt iqbû lā uktīn)*, "If he (a man) came forward (in a case) to bear witness to (a claim for) barley or silver, (but then has not proved the statement that he made)." But how shall we translate the apodosis: *aran dīnim šuāti ittanašši*, and what nuance of meaning does the /tan/ iterative lend to the verb?

G. R. Driver and J. C. Miles, *The Babylonian Laws*, vol. 2 (Oxford, 1955), pp. 15 and 19, have translated this phrase in §§ 4 and 13 as "he shall remain liable for the penalty for that suit."[4] Other scholars

---

[3]The designation of the text as a "code" is also modern. Cf., e.g., Finkelstein, *ibid.*, pp. 15 f., for the problems inherent in using this conventional designation as well as those inherent in the use of the modern division into paragraphs.

[4]Cf. *The Assyrian Dictionary of the Oriental Institute of the University of Chicago* (hereafter *CAD*) A/2, p. 298: CH § 13: "That man is guilty, he will remain liable for the penalty (involved in) that suit."

have been unwilling to work with the standard repetitive-habitual-continuous meaning for *ittanašši* here, perhaps because they felt that no sense was conveyed by this kind of iterative. Thus, while some have ignored the /tan/ here,[5] others have attributed a distributive meaning to it. A. Falkenstein in a review of Driver-Miles, *The Babylonian Laws*, vol. 1 (Oxford, 1952) correctly rejected the translation "he shall bear" for *ittanašši*, arguing that this translation "unterdrückt die hier vorliegende distributive Bedeutung der Gtn Form," and followed W. Eilers' earlier translation.[6] In his translation of the Code, Eilers rendered *aran dīnim šuāti ittanašši* as "so lädt er sich die jeweilige Strafe dieses Rechtsstreites auf."[7] A similar translation and analysis were accorded a somewhat authoritative status when W. von Soden, *Grundriss der akkadischen Grammatik*, Analecta Orientalia 33 (Rome, 1952) (hereafter *GAG*), § 91f, cited our passage as one of several examples of a distributive meaning for the /tan/.[8] And this understanding has been followed by others such as D. O. Edzard,[9] R. Borger,[10] and G. Steiner[11] in their grammatical studies and

---

[5]E.g., T. J. Meek, "The Code of Hammurabi," in J. B. Pritchard, ed., *Ancient Near Eastern Texts Relating to the Old Testament*, 3nd ed. (Princeton, 1955), p. 166, § 4: "he shall bear the penalty of that case."

[6]*Zeitschrift für Assyriologie* 51 (1955) 262.

[7]W. Eilers, *Gesetzesstele Chammurabis*, Der Alte Orient 31/3-4 (Leipzig, 1932), p. 17, § 4; p. 19, § 13.

[8]"Bisweilen haben Iterativstämme auch eine Art von distributiver Bedeutung, die am besten durch unser 'jeweils' wiedergegeben wird (z.B. aB *ittanašši* 'er trägt (die jeweils vorgesehene Strafe)' KH VI 5...."

[9]D. O. Edzard, "Die Stämme des altbabylonischen Verbums in ihrem Oppositionssystem," in *Studies in Honor of Benno Landsberger*, Assyriological Studies 16 (Chicago, 1965), p. 112, cites "*aran dīnim šuāti ittanašši*, 'er wird die für diese Rechtssache jeweils (vorgesehene) Strafe erleiden' (KH VI 3-5)," and notes that the Gtn "drückt hier das...distributiv gedachte...Vorkommen der durch G beschriebenen Handlung aus." It may not be irrelevant that in this instance Edzard deviates from his standard operating procedure of citing only Old Babylonian examples and draws on Middle Assyrian *inašši* as the example of a contrastive form to the Gtn.

[10]R. Borger, *Babylonisch-assyrische Lesestücke*, 1st. ed. (Rome, 1963), vol. 1, p. LXIX = 2nd ed., Analecta Orientalia 54 (Rome, 1979), vol. 2, p. 262 s.v. *našû* Gtn, translates "(die jeweils vorgesehene Strafe, *arnu*) tragen (KH §§ 4, 13)." This formulation appears as well in his contribution to R. Borger et al., *Rechtsbücher*, Texte aus der Umwelt des Alten Testaments 1/1, O. Kaiser, ed. (Gütersloh, 1982), p. 45, § 4: "muss er die jeweilige Strafe dieses Prozesses tragen." Cf. p. 46, § 13.

[11]G. Steiner, "Die sog. tan-Stämme des akkadischen Verbums und ihre semitischen Grundlagen," *Zeitschrift der Deutschen Morgenländischen Gesellschaft* 131 (1981) 24, notes that "bezeichnet die Präsensform der Iterativstämme...das Eintreten eines Vorgangs...unter verschiedenen

translations of the Code. Finally, another twist was given to the /tan/ form here by A. Finet in his translation of the Code. He translates *aran dīnim šuāti ittanašši* in §§ 4 and 13 as "il supportera dans sa totalité la peine de ce procès," and glosses the word "totalité" with the note that "C'est le sens exprimé ici par la forme à infixe -*tana*-."[12]

For awhile I, too, was content to accept the interpretation of the /tan/ in §§ 4 and 13 as a distributive largely because I had some difficulty imagining a situation that would suit a repetitive or habitual meaning. But, then, also the interpretation as a distributive seemed somewhat forced. In view of the limited number of alleged distributives and in response to a student's question, I decided to go back to the common basic meaning of /tan/ (*GAG*, § 91e: "Die Grundfunktion der *tan*-Stämme ist die eines Iterativs zu den zugehörigen einfachen Hauptstämmen....Nicht selten ist die Bedeutung der Iterativstämme zugleich habitativ...."), and see if I could make sense of the passage on the basis of the /tan/'s standard temporal meaning of repetition, habituality, continuity, permanence. What I should like to do here is to set out an alternative interpretation of *aran dīnim šuāti ittanašši* that satisfies, I believe, the philological and juristic requirements of the passage.

Analysis and Translation

Driver and Miles's translation assumes that /tan/ here operates within a temporal dimension and conveys a sense of continued or repeated action. In the philological commentary on § 4 (vol. 2, p. 149), Driver-Miles note as follows:

> ...the infixed -*tan*-...in *ittanašši* implies continued or repeated action...as the addition of *adi balṭat* elsewhere shows (CH. 148 81). Verbs denoting responsibility, such as *našû* and *apālu*, often take it to show that it continues so long as any actual or potential claims remain to be settled...especially so long as the person to whom they are due is alive or when the obligation is lifelong....

I do not know whether there is always a meaningful distinction between the G and Gtn of *apālu* and *našû;* that question remains to be investigated. But it is obvious from its uses elsewhere in the Code, for example in § 148, that in the Code the Gtn of *našû* conveys a standard temporal iterative meaning of repetition, regularity, and habit. True, *ittanašši* in §§ 4 and 13 could refer to bearing responsibility for all claims that might arise in the future. But this, too, is an insufficient

---

Umständen, z.B....*aran dīnim šuāti ita[t]na šši* 'er soll jeweils die entsprechende Strafe in diesem Rechtsfall auf sich nehmen'."

[12]*Le Code de Hammurapi* (Paris, 1973), pp. 45 f., § 4; pp. 48 f., § 13.

explanation of *aran dīnim šuāti ittanaššī,* because § 4 seems to be dealing not so much with real estate, which might require a permanent responsibility from the seller –*ītanappal*[13], but rather with a loan, or the like, whose claim can be settled with a one-time payment and need not require a life-long obligation. Surely, *aran dīnim šuāti ittanaššī* does not mean that he pays the amount of his fine repeatedly, or even more than just once. It seems, then, that standard situations do not convincingly or completely account for the iterative /tan/ form of the verb here.

Assuming that we are not dealing with a frozen form, we must wonder what specialized meaning or nuance of the standard sense of iteration or continuity is conveyed here by the /tan/ form of *našû* in combination with *arnu.* Why should someone be repeatedly or continuously penalized?

I, too, would now translate *aran dīnim šuāti ittanaššī* as "he shall continue to bear the penalty in that case," and would suggest that the iterative in § 4 conveys the notion that the witness always remains liable for testimony that he gave, that having paid the amount due in that case, he bears the guilt – for the duration of his life and even under changed circumstances – for not having been able to prove his testimony; the penalty will never be rescinded. Such absoluteness and irrevocability are compatible with the penalties stipulated in the apodoses of §§ 3 and 5: in § 3 the witness is to be killed – nothing is more absolute or irrevocable than death; in § 5 a guilty judge is to be expelled from his judge's seat in the assembly and may never resume that office. But the question remains: why should the witness of § 4 remain liable, and what can that mean?

Some scholars have understood the law as being directed against a lying witness who has come forward with false testimony. They have based this interpretation on the translation of *šībūt sarrātim* in § 3 as "false testimony"[14] and on the assumption that "false testimony"

---

[13]Cf., e.g., S. D. Simmons, "Early Old Babylonian Tablets from Harmal and Elsewhere," *Journal of Cuneiform Studies* 13 (1959) 91 f. and 14 (1960) 23, no. 46: 21-25.

[14]Cf., e.g., Eilers, p. 17: "Wenn ein Bürger vor Gericht zu falschem Zeugnis aufgetreten ist"; A. Pohl – R. Follett, *Codex Hammurabi* (Rome, 1950), p. 12: "Si (ali)quis pro tribunali ad testimonium falsitatis exierit"; Meek, p. 166: "If a seignior came forward with false testimony in a case"; W. J. Martin, "The Law Code of Hammurabi," in D. Winton Thomas, ed., *Documents from Old Testament Times* (Edinburgh/London, 1958), p. 29: "If a citizen in a case has borne false witness"; Finet, p. 45: "Si quelqu'un a paru dans un procès pour (porter) un faux témoignage"; Borger, *Rechtsbücher,* p. 45: "Wenn ein Bürger zu falschem Zeugnis auftritt." Our line is also treated this way in the dictionaries: W. von Soden, *Akkadisches Handwörterbuch* (Wiesbaden, 1959-

characterizes the nature of the testimony in both §§ 3 and 4.[15] I believe that this translation and interpretation are incorrect. The aforementioned translation and interpretation take for granted that the protasis at the beginning of § 3 serves as an overall introduction to both §§ 3 and 4, and that the second protasis and the apodosis of § 3 are parallel to § 4. But this construction is wrong. For neither is § 3b) *šumma dīnum šū dīn napištim*, "If that case is a capital case," the counterpart of § 4a) *šumma ana šībūt še'im u kaspim ūṣiam* "If he came forward to bear witness to (a claim for) barley or silver," nor does § 3a) *šumma awīlum ina dīnim ana šībūt sarrātim ūṣiamma*, "If a man came forward in a case to bear *šībūt sarrātim*," provide the common background of §§ 3 and 4.

To understand why this translation is incorrect and to grasp more fully the meaning of §§ 3 and 4, we must set out the structure of this text in a little more detail. *šumma awīlum ina dīnim ana šībūt sarrātim ūṣiamma* (§ 3a) introduces only § 3. § 3 contains a split protasis; *šumma dīnum šū dīn napištim* (§ 3b) forms a second delimiting protasis and presents the only – if most extreme – subcategory of *šībūt sarrātim* given in the text. § 3a) *šumma (...) ana šībūt sarrātim ūṣiamma* and § 4a) *šumma ana šībūt še'im u kaspim ūṣiam* are on the same syntactic and logical level, and each may serve as a replacement for the other. *ana šībūt sarrātim* and *ana šībūt še'im u kaspim* are parallel to each other. Thus, § 4a is functionally equivalent or parallel to § 3a. Thus, while §§ 3 and 4 are surely related, they are not a single integrated legal unit that opens with an introduction (§ 3a) laying out a common background, followed by two parallel sets (§ 3b-c, § 4) of subsidiary protases (§ 3b, § 4a) and concluding apodoses (§ 3c, § 4b). Rather, § 4 is parallel to § 3; they set forth two parallel but independent cases.

To understand why this must be so, we must take note of some of the different ways of setting out related laws that are used in the Code. For example, there are those adjoining cases for which the beginning portion of the text provides the initial situation that serves as the starting point for several possible cases; this background situation is not repeated as each case is described, and the individual case only consists of a secondary protasis with its apodosis, and therefore cannot stand on its own (e.g., §§ 9-11, §§ 17-20, §§ 138-140, §§ 163-166, §§ 229-231).

---

81) (hereafter *AHw*), p. 1031, s. *sartu* 4a ("falsches Zeugnis"); *CAD*, S, p. 179, s. *sarrātu* ("false testimony").

[15]E.g., Meek, p. 166: 3: "If a seignior came forward with false testimony in a case, and has not proved the word which he spoke, if that case was a case involving life, that seignior shall be put to death. 4: If he came forward with (false) testimony concerning grain or money, he shall bear the penalty of that case."

§§ 9-11, §§ 229-231, and §§ 17-20 provide very good examples of this type. The beginning of § 9 (VI 70-VII 17) lays out the situation that forms the common background for and introduces each of the three cases that follow. These three then examine various possibilities. Each one picks up at the point where the common background of § 9a ends, and, in each case, the first principal verb of the main clause is a perfect – not a preterite – form of the verb *wabālu: (lā) itbalam*. Thus, § 9a: 70-17 – (1) § 9b: 18-47 // (2) § 10: 48-61 // (3) § 11: 62-(VIII) 3. Less complicated and therefore perhaps more clear are §§ 229-231 and §§ 17-20. § 229: 64-70 describes a situation in which a house that a builder has built collapsed *(imqutma)*. This situation is then followed by three instances of different people being killed by the collapsing house. Each of the three alternative delimiting protases simply repeats the verb *uštamīt*, "has killed," in the perfect – not the preterite – form and is then followed by an apodosis. Thus, §§ 229a: 64-70 – (1) § 229b: 71-72 // (2) § 230: 73-76 // (3) § 231: 77-81. §§ 17-20 treat situations that arise from the capture of a runaway slave. § 17: 49-53 provides this background. This common protasis is followed by four separate protases presenting different situations that may then arise, each with its own apodosis: § 17a: 49-53 – (1) § 17b: 54-58 // (2) § 18: 59-67 // (3) § 19: 68-4 // (4) § 20: 5-13. In contrast to the preterite verb form of the common protasis *(iṣbatma*, "seized"), the verbs in each of the four delimiting protases are in the perfect form.

Different are adjoining legal cases that repeat from the initially stipulated legal situation all or most of the details that apply to the following cases and make whatever necessary change and insert whatever additional information is required (e.g., §§ 162-163). Each individual case contains a primary protasis and, on the whole, each case can stand on its own. §§ 3 and 4 are an example of this latter type of formulation. Actually, §§ 3-4 are part of a group comprising §§ 1-4, which group presents cases of unproved *(lā uktīn)* accusations (§§ 1-2) and testimony (§§ 3-4).

Having observed, moreover, that a subsidiary protasis, whether parallel to other subsidiary protases (as in the examples noted above) or as part of a single split protasis (e.g., § 136), would usually begin not with a preterite, but with a perfect form of the verb or its equivalent, we find therein additional support for our conclusion that § 4a *(šumma ana šībūt še'im u kaspim ūṣiam)* is not a subsection of § 3 that stands in parallelism with § 3b *(šumma dīnum šū dīn napištim)* but rather is itself a primary protasis that stands in parallelism to the previously occurring primary protasis § 3a *(šumma awīlum ina dīnim ana šībūt sarrātim ūṣiamma)*. For if § 4 were parallel to § 3b, it should have read *šumma ana šībūt še'im u kaspim *ittaṣi* (cf., e.g. § 136: 64 ff) rather than the attested *ūṣiam*. Hence, § 4 // § 3, and *šībūt sarrātim* and *šībūt še'im u kaspim* are parallel to each other.

And the relationship which obtains between §§ 4 and 3 is similar to that between §§ 2 and 1 (§ 4 : § 3 :: § 2 : § 1). As the first of the two legal cases dealing with accusation, § 1 gives a full version of its protasis; relying on § 1, § 2 can then state its protasis in a slightly abbreviated and less explicit form. Thus, where § 1 has the fuller text: *šumma awīlum awīlam ubbirma nērtam elišu iddima lā uktīnšu*, "If a man accused another man and charged him with murder but then has not proved it against him," § 2 states only: *šumma awīlum kišpī eli awīlim iddima lā uktīnšu*, "If a man charged another man with witchcraft but then has not proved it against him," and this is to be understood as an abbreviated form of **šumma awīlum awīlam ubbirma kišpī elišu iddima lā uktīnšu*, "If a man accused another man and charged him with witchcraft but then has not proved it against him." Similarly, § 4 is to be understood as if it read **šumma (awīlum ina dīnim) ana šībūt še'im u kaspim ūṣiam(ma awāt iqbû lā uktīn)*, "If a man came forward in a case to bear witness to a claim for barley or silver but then has not proved the statement that he made." The words *awīlum ina dīnim* and *-ma awāt iqbû lā uktīn* of § 3 are suppressed in § 4, but are surely implicit there.[16] The wording of § 3 that applies to both §§ 3 and 4 but is not repeated in § 4 is not *ana šībūt sarrātim*, but rather wording that need not be rendered explicit and can be abbreviated without loss.

sarrātu here in § 3 means "wrongdoing," "crime," or the like.[17] *šībūt še'im u kaspim* in § 4 presents a case comparable to the one involving the testimony about a crime *(šībūt sarrātim)*, but involving instead testimony about barley and silver. §§ 3-4 are to be translated:

> If a man came forward in a case to bear witness to a wrongdoing but then has not proved the statement that he made, if that case is a capital case, that man should be put to death.

---

[16]These abbreviations of §§ 2 and 4 are stylistic and should not be confused with what we find in those laws where the initial situation is set out only once at the beginning of a series of cases.

[17]The meaning "wrongdoing" or "crime" is certainly one of the meanings of *sarrātu*. For this meaning, see, e.g., *AHw*, p. 1031, s. *sartu*, "Falsches, Lüge, Verbrechen (italics mine)"; *CAD*, S, p. 187 f., s. *sartu* mng. 2, ("fraud, misdeed, criminal act"), p. 182, s. *sarru*, mng. 3 ("[in substantival use] criminal, thief, liar"). Note the translation of *šībūt sarrātim* of CH § 3 as "witness to a felony" in Driver-Miles, vol. 2, p. 15 (cf., p. 148) and *ad testimonium de crimine* in A. Deimel, *Codex Ḥammurabi* (Rome, 1930), cited Driver-Miles, vol. 2, p. 148.

If he came forward to bear witness to (a claim for) barley or silver (but then has not proved the statement that he made), he should continue to bear the penalty of that case.

§§ 3-4 take up the problem of unconfirmed testimony, with § 3 addressing this problem in legal cases involving wrongdoing, generally, and capital cases, specifically, and § 4 addressing this problem in cases involving disputes over contractual obligations, notably payment. The writer probably has in mind a situation such as that described in the Laws of Ur-Nammu § 26 where the witness to a lawsuit declined to testify on oath.[18] Both §§ 3 and 4 stipulate that the witness who is unable to substantiate his testimony by oath or the like is to suffer the same punishment or pay the same amount that would have been required of the accused. The principle of talion before the fact is applied. Thus, § 3 focuses on the extreme instance of wrongdoing, namely cases involving the death penalty, and stipulates that our witness should suffer the death penalty. § 4 requires of our witness that he pay the same amount that a party found liable would have been obliged to pay.

Many scholars have been deceived by the alleged falseness of the testimony and have treated false testimony as the central issue of §§ 3 and 4. Perhaps they defined the issue in this manner because they were influenced by such laws as Deut. 19:16-19, where, by contrast however,

---

[18]J. J. Finkelstein, "The Laws of Ur-Nammu," *Journal of Cuneiform Studies* 22 (1969) 70: 41-46; cf. O. R. Gurney and S. N. Kramer, "Two Fragments of Sumerian Laws," *Studies Landsberger*, p. 17. While I will not take up here in detail the relationship of the laws of Ur-Nammu §§ 25-26 and of Lipit-Ishtar § 17 to our laws, I would simply note that at least Ur-Nammu § 26 clearly supports my assumption that *lā uktīn* in CH §§ 3 (-4) means that the witness has refused to take an oath in support of his testimony rather than that he could not prove his testimony because it was a lie. The fact that the related law Lipit-Ishtar § 17 has -íl-e (and not íl-íl) may provide further support for our contention that the /tan/ of *našû* in CH § 4 was intentionally introduced and carries special meaning. W. F. Leemans, "Le faux témoin," *Revue d'assyriologie* 64 (1970) 65 f., also concludes that the witness in CH §§ 3-4 did not take the oath: "Dans ce cas aussi, il n'est pas dit que le témoin a juré son témoignage; il a simplement paru en portant témoignage devant les juges et n'a pas prouvé son témoignage, mais il ne l'a pas juré" (cf. Finkelstein, "The Laws of Ur-Nammu," pp. 79 f.). The death penalty stipulated in § 3, while probably theoretical (see below), may also have been intended to warn a witness in a capital case that if he were required to take the oath, he would not be able to refuse and pay a fine instead. For the oath, see S. E. Loewenstamm, "The Cumulative Oath of Witnesses and Parties in Mesopotamian Law," *Comparative Studies in Biblical and Ancient Oriental Literatures*, Alter Orient und Altes Testament, (Kevelaer/Neukirchen-Vluyn, 1980), pp. 341-345 (reference courtesy R. Westbrook).

the testimony is explicitly designated as a lie (v. 18). Even Driver and
Miles, who saw the parallelism of šībūt sarrātim and šībūt še'im u
kaspim, understood the meaning of sarrātim as wrongdoing or felony,
and correctly translated our text (vol. 1, pp. 66-67; vol. 2, p. 15),
persisted in seeing false evidence as the issue, and, distracted by the
supposed falseness of the testimony, interpreted *aran dīnim šuāti
ittanaššī* almost as if it did not contain an iterative:

> The distinction in §§ 3-4 is between giving false witness of which the
> subject is sarrātum and giving false evidence of which it is grain or
> silver (vol. 1, pp. 66 f.)....Here the phrase [scil. *aran dīnim šuāti ittanaššī*]
> means that the false witness must pay the penalty applicable to the
> case in which he has given the false evidence, and what this means is
> quite obvious: the principle is that he must suffer what he has tried by
> his false evidence to bring upon another person (*ibid.*, p. 68).

But as we have seen, šībūt sarrātim and šībūt še'im u kaspim a r e
parallel to each other, and šībūt sarrātim of § 3 denotes and connotes
false testimony no more than does šībūt še'im u kaspim of § 4. Here in
§ 3, sarrātu does not mean falsehood, and šībūt sarrātim does not mean
false testimony or perjury.[19] Certainly it does not mean false testimony

---

[19]While some scholars have understood šībūt sarrātim as explicitly denoting
"false testimony" (see above), several others have not translated the phrase this
way but still seem to have understood false testimony as the issue at stake (e.g.,
Driver-Miles, who seem to confuse the nature of the case under discussion
with the kind of testimony). Whether because of biblical and other legal
parallels or because of the associations of the word sartu/sarrātu (Hebr. šārā),
they seem to have equated unsubstantiated testimony with false testimony. As
stated, the issue is not falsehood but proof, not so much intent as objective
result. The failure of testimony to convince or convict may lead to the labelling
of that testimony as false – that is, unproved testimony may be regarded as
false testimony – but only after the fact and only as one limited way of
construing such testimony. But in the absence of very clear distinctions, such
reasoning in the study of CH and other Mesopotamian law collections only
serves to confuse the issues. (As an aside I should perhaps mention that Deut.
19:16 should probably not be translated "If a man appears against another to
testify maliciously and gives false testimony against him" [*Tanakh: A New
Translation* (Philadelphia, 1985)] but rather something like "If a witness [in a
case] of violence comes forward to testify against a man that he had committed
a crime.")

Not surprisingly, several scholars have noted correctly that the main issue in
CH §§ 1-4 was the absence of proof (though even here some equate absence of
proof with falseness): See A. Walther, *Das altbabylonische Gerichtswesen*
(Leipzig, 1917), p. 223, n. 1 on *l ā uktīn* in CH §§ 1-4 and 127: "...vielmehr ist der
einfache Grundsatz: wer etwas nicht beweist, hat Unrecht." M. San Nicolò,
"Anschuldigung, falsche," *Reallexikon der Assyriologie*, vol. 1 (1928), p. 112:
"Dem Anzeiger liegt der Wahrheitsbeweis ob, bei dessen Misslingen er
straffällig wird. Auf seinen eventuellen guten Glauben wird, wie auch nicht

that had been intentionally contrived. There is no unambiguous proof that the witness in §§ 3-4 intentionally lied. For the text of § 3a does not state that the witness has come forward intentionally for the purpose of giving false testimony, and in any case, § 4a and not § 3a provides the background for the apodosis in § 4b. In this connection and as regards *aran dīnim šuāti ittanaš̄ši*, I should note that properly speaking, a lying witness can do nothing but bear his penalty forever; hence, it seems gratuitous to use the Gtn when a simple G should have sufficed. The text states neither that the testimony is necessarily false nor that the witness has intentionally lied. Hence, the punishment of death in § 3 and the permanent liability in § 4 cannot be accounted for by the intentional giving of false testimony.

Meaning and Significance

We are dealing, here, not with false testimony but with unconfirmed testimony. What is at stake is not the absence of truth but the absence of proof. If §§ 3-4, then, are not dealing, explicitly at least, with falsehood or lies, why should the witness continue to bear the penalty? A correct translation of *aran dīnim šuāti ittanaš̄ši* must be connected with an appropriate situation. We must reformulate our understanding of these legal cases and derive therefrom an explanation or justification for the permanent liability of the witness in § 4.

The opening section of the Code constitutes an attempt to establish guidelines for the proper working of a just and orderly judicial process. The jurist's goal in §§ 3-4 is to define and discourage irresponsible or

---

anders zu erwarten, keine Rücksicht genommen." (Followed by H. P. H. Petschow, "Altorientalische Parallelen zur spätrömischen calumnia," *Zeitschrift der Savigny-Stiftung für Rechtsgeschichte* 103, Romanistische Abteilung 90 [1973] 18 f.; cf. idem, "Zur Systematik und Gesetzestechnik im Codex Hammurabi," *Zeitschrift für Assyriologie* 57 [1965] 148.) D. Nörr, "Zum Schuldgedanken im altbabylonischen Strafrecht," *Zeitschrift der Savigny-Stiftung für Rechtsgeschichte*, Romanistische Abteilung 75 (1958) 22: "§ 3 betrifft das falsche Zeugnis in Kapital-, § 4 dasselbe in Vermögenssachen. In keinem Falle wird auf das Wissen des Täters um die Unrichtigkeit seiner Anschuldigung oder seiner Zeugenaussage Rücksicht genommen. Kann er den Wahrheitsbeweis nicht führen, der ihm auferlegt ist, so wird er bestraft." C. H. Gordon, *Hammurapi's Code: Quaint or Forward-Looking?* (New York, 1957), p. 4: "The first law (§ 1) states that a man who accuses another of murder and cannot prove it shall be put to death. The code shows no interest in the possible sincerity of the accuser or in the possible guilt of the accused. Unprovable claims have no place in the code. Moreover, he who makes unprovable accusations must bear the penalty that he would impose on the accused. An unproved accusation entailing the death penalty means death for the accuser (§ 3); one entailing the payment of goods imposes that payment on the accuser (§ 4)."

improper testimony. Responsible testimony is testimony that can be
proved and upon which one can rely. Accordingly, the jurist stipulates
that a person may not voluntarily come forward in a judicial context for
the purpose of making a statement for which he is unable or unwilling
to provide confirmation (by means of an oath or the like), for such
behavior is of no utility and is actually harmful to all concerned.

The intention of the witness is of no consequence. The value or
assessment of the testimony is in no way dependent on whether the
witness himself believed the testimony or whether he fabricated it.
Nor are they dependent on his motivation – whether it be concern for
the public good or selfishness and malice. Our writer wishes to know
only whether the witness is able and willing to prove his accusation or
testimony. He is interested only in objective or external results, not in
the witness's reasons or intentions. Actually, whether or not the witness
is lying is of no interest whatsoever to the jurist. He does not even
assume that an irresponsible witness is necessarily falsifying
testimony. But irrespective of intentions, a witness must bear absolute
responsibility and liability for his acts and their results. And an
irresponsible witness must bear the responsibility for bringing unproven
testimony.

Accordingly, testimony for which the witness is penalized is not
necessarily untrue. It is simply unproven or unsubstantiated. And for
bringing this kind of testimony he is to be subjected to the punishment
that would have been meted out to the accused: death in capital cases,
payment in cases involving dispute over contractual obligations. *But if
the witness was not lying, his testimony would sometimes be true.* It is
important that we remember this, for herein lies the rub. For especially
in cases of unproven but true testimony, proof substantiating the
penalized witness's testimony may turn up at a later date. How should
the system react in the instance where evidence turns up subsequent to
the imposition of the penalty? Should the case be reopened and the
witness absolved and perhaps even rewarded? This is one of the
questions which the jurist wished to answer in §§ 3-4.

These two cases envision and address themselves to this
eventuality. They treat the very act of bringing unsubstantiated
testimony as an unqualified crime. They tell us that this act is and
remains a crime and that its penalty may not be revoked. In a capital
case, the witness is to be killed: capital punishment cannot be undone –
the witness perforce remains dead. In a case involving a dispute over
payment, the witness pays the appropriate penalty; and if afterwards,
evidence substantiating his testimony turns up, he remains liable for
the earlier act of bringing unconfirmed testimony and does not receive
restitution. Hence, *aran dīnim šuāti ittanašš*i and the use of the /tan/

form of the verb; he bears the liability for that case whenever and however the case comes up again.

Some may think it harsh of the jurist not to revoke a penalty that can be undone, especially when the penalized witness might actually have been telling the truth and acting in good faith. But in fairness to the writer, I must note, first of all, that such criticism is off the mark if the writer's concern is not actual practice but rather the formulation of legal principles. Our reading of § 4 provides further support for the idea that at least some of the laws in the Code are of a theoretical character. Along with B. L. Eichler and others, I would argue that some of the law cases in the Code are the result of scholastic activity and represent casuistic investigation and exposition of legal principles.[20] The writer presumably did not expect that the rules we have been examining would serve as actual judicial regulations. (Additionally, the death penalty in the Code should often be construed as meaning that the offender is deserving of death and not be taken literally. It is an evaluation of the act and not a judicial sentence.) In any case, our witness may well be a prosecuting witness, that is, an accuser, and not simply a bystander, and is therefore deserving of punishment for initiating a charge.

Moreover, to revoke the penalty or fine would be counterproductive from our writer's point of view, for it would subvert his purpose. The writer wishes to make clear the rule that a witness should not come forward except when he is able and willing to prove his testimony. He stipulates this rule because he believes that an accusation and testimony carry objective results; they adversely affect the accused regardless of later qualification or outcome. His purpose is not to penalize but rather to ensure that witnesses in judicial (and perhaps even in pre- or extra-judicial) settings give strong weight to the rules of evidence and only come forward with testimony *(ana šībūtim waṣû)*[21] when they can expect to prove it. By stipulating formal objective guidelines, the writer helps the court and the witness understand what

---

[20]See B. L. Eichler, "Literary Structure in The Laws of Eshnunna," in F. Rochberg-Halton, ed., *Language, Literature, and History: Philological and Historical Studies Presented to Erica Reiner*, American Oriental Series 67 (New Haven, 1987), pp. 71-84, and references there. Note especially the conclusions, pp. 81-84, regarding the scholastic nature of the laws of Eshnunna and Hammurabi. Cf. also my article "Hammurabi" in P. J. Achtemeier et al., eds., *Harper's Bible Dictionary* (San Francisco, 1985), pp. 370 f.

[21]I have in mind a witness who comes forward voluntarily in contrast to one who is summoned. Cf. A. Falkenstein, *Die neusumerischen Gerichtsurkunden*, vol. 1, Abhandlungen der Bayerischen Akademie der Wissenschaften NF 39 (Munich, 1956), pp. 68 f., n. 4.

it means to initiate or volunteer testimony. He wishes to discourage unfounded and possibly malicious accusations. Perhaps he wants to lay out these principles and guidelines in the belief that more objective procedures are needed by an urban society that is becoming increasingly less cohesive and more diverse and anonymous, a society in which people are less able to render judgment on the basis of personal knowledge and where the accused (even more perhaps than in a simpler society) is at the mercy of public declarations – formal or informal – made against him. To revoke the penalty and make restitution would effectively go against our jurist's belief that what is done in court has permanent effects and is, in some cases, absolute and irrevocable and would undercut the principle upon which he bases his reasoning: the absoluteness of the legal act. Neither the original action nor the outcome can be reversed: hence, the absoluteness and irrevocability of the actions described in the protases of §§ 3 and 5 and of the penalties of these cases. Similarly, by excluding restitution in § 4, the writer emphasizes this absoluteness and also conveys the idea that the legal act should be undertaken only with great care and assessed only on the basis of objective guidelines.

To revoke a punishment imposed originally to discourage unfounded testimony, when evidence later turns up confirming that testimony, would only serve to contradict and render useless the original purpose and act of imposing the punishment. Such an absolutist approach to testimony is especially valid in the present instance where the jurist is operating with a theoretical system of state sanctioned punishment and determining the nature of the punishment on the basis of the rule of talion. In § 3, it is actually true that what is done cannot be undone, for while this is always true to some extent, it is absolutely true in a capital case. The punishment in § 4 must remain in force to exemplify the insight and precept that what is done cannot be undone. To revoke would be tantamount to saying that one need not operate with care and according to objective criteria in the first place. Such a lack of care is undesirable in any case; it is unthinkable in a capital case.

In this context, I should mention yet another reason why the jurist should not allow the penalty to be revoked. He must exclude the return of property in order to protect the underlying principle of the rule of talion. In theory, at least, a system of talion that imposes penalties, such as capital punishment, that cannot be reversed or compensated may not revoke or undo others of its penalties that are capable of revocation. To do so would expose the system to major contradictions and to the possibility of breakdown. Our writer is a purist and holds to the principle. Both the act and the penalty cannot be undone. One can revoke a penalty no more than one can undo a legal act.

Confirmation: Variant Readings and § 13

aran dīnim šuāti ittanašši is a specific rule of jurisprudence and describes the situation as seen from the perspective of the judiciary. From that perspective, the liability is held to be permanent – *ittanašši*. This interpretation actually finds support in the variant reading *rugummānē [dīnim šuāt]i ippal*, "he shall pay the claims in that case," which replaces *aran dīnim šuāti ittanašši* in a late Old Babylonian copy of the Code.[22] J. J. Finkelstein, who published this text, was of the opinion that "Exactly the same sense is given by both versions, and there is no way of deciding which is the 'superior' text. It is likely that both readings were already current in Hammurapi's own time."[23] Here I must disagree with Finkelstein. There is a difference in meaning between the readings. The variant highlights the approach of the jurist who wrote *aran dīnim šuāti ittanašši;* it emphasizes that writer's courtroom orientation by showing us what happens once that orientation is changed and the penalty is looked at not from the point of view of the abstract judicial system but from the practical perspective of litigants who need to be satisfied. From the perspective of claimants, not permanent liability but actual payment is of interest; hence, the shift to a simple G durative of *apālu*.[24] Moreover, the reading *aran dīnim šuāti ittanašši* seems to be the better reading because it appears more consonant with the overall perspective and intention of these laws and their concrete expression of abstract principles of justice. While it is not easy to decide which is the more original of the two readings, I would favor *aran dīnim šuāti ittanašši*.

Further support for our understanding of *aran dīnim šuāti ittanašši* in § 4 is provided by § 13, where this phrase recurs. § 13 reads:

šumma awīlum šū šībūšu lā qerbū dayyānū adānam ana šeššet warḫī išakkanūšumma šumma ina šeššet warḫī šībīšu lā irde'am awīlum šū sār aran dīnim šuāti ittanašši.

If that man's witnesses are not at hand, the judges shall grant him a period of up to six months, and if he has not brought his witnesses

---

[22]J. J. Finkelstein, "A Late Old Babylonian Copy of the Laws of Hammurapi," *Journal of Cuneiform Studies* 21 (1967 [1969]) 44.

[23]*Ibid.*, p. 44.

[24]I would also note here the interesting shift of the notion of plurality from the verb (*ittanašši*) to the noun (*rugummānê* [cf. A. Poebel, *Studies in Akkadian Grammar*, Assyriological Studies 9 (Chicago, 1939), pp. xi f. and 140]). Also the shift from the objective *arnam našû* to the subjective *rugummānê apālu* is of interest.

hither within six months, that man is guilty; he should continue to bear
the penalty of that case.

The judges grant him an extension because they recognize that he may
be telling the truth but needs more time to produce his witnesses. He
does not produce his witnesses within six months. This fact, however,
does not in itself prove that he does not have witnesses or that he is a
criminal. He may still be telling the truth and be able to produce
witnesses in the future. Moreover, the judges who accorded him the
presumption of truthfulness in the first place may still even believe
him and accept the possibility that witnesses will eventually appear.
But the judges must bring the case to a close within a reasonable period.
The question of truth must be deemed irrelevant at some point because
an orderly judicial process requires limits and closure. A time period
must be designated and a decision made. And the ruling must remain
binding whether or not he brings witnesses. He is punished not because
he was lying but because he has not been able to produce the witnesses
who could confirm his claim. To overturn the decision were he to bring
witnesses after six months would not only contradict the rule of
responsibility but would, moreover, undercut the justice of using a time
period in the first place as a limit and as a basis for a legal decision.

This use of *aran dīnim šuāti ittanašši* in § 13 clarifies its meaning in
§ 4 and confirms our interpretation. By granting the man an extension,
the judges in § 13 indicate their belief that he may well be speaking
the truth and have witnesses. And by setting a limit of six months, they
indicate that, regardless of his truthfulness, they will have to impose
the penalty permanently should he not bring witnesses in the time
stipulated. Here, then, the judges impose a permanent penalty on a man
although he may be telling the truth, and here, the writer conveys this
by means of the formulation *aran dīnim šuāti ittanašši*. Similarly, *aran
dīnim šuāti ittanašši* in § 4 indicates that although the witness may be
telling the truth, he must permanently bear the penalty of the case.
Even if evidence is eventually produced in support of his testimony, he
remains liable because initially he was not able to prove his testimony.

Here, we should say a word about the identity of the *awīlum šū*,
"that man," of § 13, for his identity defines his place in the legal
situation (e.g., plaintiff vs. defendant) and determines the kind of
proof he is required to bring in support of his claim; his identity,
therefore, may allow us to understand better the connection between
§ 13 and § 4 and may even increase the usefulness of § 13 for an
understanding of *aran dīnim šuāti ittanašši*. Students of the Code have
puzzled over which of the parties to the suit is referred to by *awīlum
šū* and have come to different conclusions. For example, Driver-Miles

think that *awīlum šū* designates the original owner, seller, and purchaser of the lost property contested in §§ 9 ff.[25]; P. Koschaker[26] and A. Finet[27] think it the owner and purchaser; E. Szlechter[28] and R. Westbrook–C. Wilcke[29] think it the purchaser.

The very real confusion over the identity of *awīlum šū* of § 13 is due to the redactional history of §§ 9-13. Thus, we should be able to determine his identity by taking into account the history of the text. There can be no doubt that § 13 is some form of addition to this section. Koschaker suggested that § 12 is an early interpolation and that § 13 was a later accretion or addition to § 12.[30] But the subject of § 11 is the owner while the subject of § 12 is the buyer. § 13, on the other hand, seems to be a direct continuation of § 11 (cf., e.g., the use of *sār* [§ 11: 1; § 13: 21-22]) and, like § 11, only deals with witnesses. I would, therefore, suggest that § 13, not § 12, was added directly to § 11 (§ 12, which treats a problem related to § 10, would subsequently have been inserted between §§ 11 and 13[31]). Accordingly, the subject of § 13, like that of § 11, should also be the owner. Note that § 13 deals exclusively with witnesses and seems to make the outcome of the case dependent solely on their testimony; according to §§ 9 ff., the owner brings only witnesses for the confirmation of his claim, while the buyer brings the seller as well. Therefore, a case such as § 13 describes the situation of the original owner but not that of the buyer, and we conclude that the referent of *awīlum šū* is only the owner. The immediate unavailability of the witnesses in § 13 fits best with this identification, for the owner may well have gone in search of his lost property and found it in a community other than his own.

---

[25]Driver-Miles, vol. 1, pp. 101-104.

[26]*Rechtsvergleichende Studien zur Gesetzgebung Hammurapis, Königs von Babylon* (Leipzig, 1917), p. 99.

[27]Finet, p. 49, § 13, note c.

[28]"L'interprétation des lois babyloniennes," *Revue Internationale des Droits de l'Antiquité*, 3rd ser. 17 (1970) 103-106.

[29]"The Liability of an Innocent Purchaser of Stolen Goods in Early Mesopotamian Law," *Archiv für Orientforschung* 25 (1974-77) 113. In the context of our discussion of the theoretical character of the laws, see their remarks on pp. 118 f.

[30]Koschaker, pp. 98-100.

[31]Although § 12 was added to the text later than § 13, it was placed before § 13. This position may be explained as follows: whereas § 13 treats a problem related to the owner (= § 11), § 12 treats a problem related to the buyer (= § 10). It was not inserted immediately after § 10 because §§ 9-11 form a tight unit. § 12 was added after this unit, but before § 13 so as to maintain the relative order of topics in §§ 9-11. Cf., also, Finet, p. 49.

This identification of the referent of § 13 agrees with the nature of the act underlying and the penalty prescribed in that law and, thus, confirms and is supported by our understanding of the intent of *aran d īnim šuāti ittanašši*. The penalty – he shall permanently bear the liability – suggests that we regard the *awīlum* of § 13 as one who came forward of his own volition and initiated an accusation and proceedings, for such a penalty is imposed not on one who is summoned, but on one who voluntarily brought forward an accusation or testimony and who then could not prove his contention. Therefore, this party must bear absolute responsibility and permanent liability even if he should be telling the truth. Of the three possible referents – owner, seller, purchaser – only the owner may be regarded as one who came forward of his own free volition, without constraint, and volunteered an accusation or claim; the others are reacting directly or indirectly to the original owner's accusation.

Here we should follow up one further implication of our historical scheme. We note that the phrasing in § 12 (*rugummē*[32] *dīnim šuāti adi 5-šu ileqqe*) matches the aforementioned variant reading of § 4 and that also the phrasing of § 13 matches the reading *aran dīnim šuāti ittanašši* of § 4. Should the chronology that we have posited be correct (§§ 9-11 + § 13 + § 12), then *aran dīnim šuāti ittanašši* of § 13 would be earlier than *rugummē dīnim šuāti* of § 12. Perhaps this temporal sequence would explain the change in § 4 from *aran dīnim šuāti ittanašši* to *rugummānē dīnim šuāti ippal* and provide the additional evidence necessary to confirm the originality of *aran dīnim šuāti ittanašši* in § 4 and its priority over its later replacement *rugummānē d īnim šuāti ippal*. This reconstruction would confirm the connection of §§ 13 and 4,[33] insofar as both use the same terminology in similar situations, and both are affected by the same later development which carried with it both the addition of § 12 and the rewriting of § 4.

The connections between § 4 and § 13 are not unexpected if, as we have argued, the referent of § 13 is the party who initiated the accusation and the legal proceeding. In any case, this would explain why a permanent penalty is imposed on him – as on the witness of § 4 – for not producing his witnesses, for regardless of his truthfulness, it is the accuser and/or witness who came forward who must bear the burden

---

[32]Note that the Late Old Babylonian copy containing the variant *rugummānē*...in § 4 also reads here *ru-gu-um-ma-⌜né⌝(?)-⌜e⌝(?)* (see Borger, *Babylonisch-assyrische Lesestücke*, 2nd ed., vol. 1, p. 12).

[33]I am intrigued by the possibility that originally § 13 was the direct continuation of § 4. Both deal with procedure; note the similarity: *šumma awīlum šušībūšu lā qerbū...aran dīnim šuāti ittanašši // šumma (awīlum) ana šībūt...ūṣiam...aran dīnim šuāti ittanašši.*

of the principle of absolute legal responsibility. He remains liable even if witnesses confirming his claim eventually appear.

Conclusion

To conclude, then, *aran dīnim šuāti ittanaššī* means that the person who has initiated or supported a legal claim in a dispute over property but has not been able to prove his claim must bear his punishment permanently – a revocable penalty will not be revoked – regardless of whether his claim is eventually proved by the appearance of witnesses or of other kinds of proof. This provides at least part of the explanation for the use of the /tan/ form of *našû* in CH §§ 4 and 13.

We have observed the ancient Babylonian student as he worked out and applied his legal principles in a systematic way. It is especially revealing, I think, to study this reasoning when it operates in a manner that is both logical and impractical, when – divorced from reality – the scholar applies his understanding of justice to the formulation of basic rules for proper judicial procedure. As do other sections of the Code, §§ 3-4 represent a statement of a principle, and this principle is formulated in terms that are logical but seem, in practice, to contradict rules of fairness and common sense.

Rather than discuss other examples of this scholastic procedure in Mesopotamian legal collections,[34] I should prefer to conclude this study in honor of a scholar of mishnaic jurisprudence and ethics by citing a mishnaic parallel as a partial illustration of some of the themes that we have examined in §§ 3-4 and 13. I have in mind Sanhedrin, ch. 3, mishna 8.

Sanhedrin, ch. 3 sets out procedures of the court in commercial cases. Mishna 3, sections I-II read:

> I. So long as [a litigant] brings proof, he may reverse the ruling. [If] they had said to him, "All the evidence which you have, bring between this date and thirty days from now," [if] he found evidence during the thirty day period, he may reverse the ruling. [If he found evidence] after the thirty day period, he may not reverse the ruling. Said Rabban Simeon b. Gamaliel, "What should this party do, who could not find the evidence during the thirty day period, but found it after thirty days?"

> II. [If] they had said to him, "Bring witnesses," and he said, "I don't have witnesses," [if] they had said, "Bring proof," and he said, "I don't have proof" and after a time he brought proof, or he found witnesses – this is of no weight whatsoever. Said Rabban Simeon b. Gamaliel, "What should this party do, who did not even know that he had

---

[34]E. g., CH §§ 229-232; see Finkelstein, *The Ox That Gored*, pp. 33-35.

witnesses on his side, but found witnesses? Or who did not even know
that he had proof, but who found proof?"[35]

I have no intention of analyzing this text, but I would simply note
that in the first section of Sanh. 3.8, the unnamed jurist opines, like CH
§ 13, that evidence cannot be considered if it is brought after the
expiration of a time period set by the judges. And in the second section,
this mishna resembles CH § 4 (or, at least, our interpretation thereof)
insofar as this jurist stipulates that witnesses or proof that only appear
after the ruling should not be considered even if they had not been
brought forward originally because of the litigant's ignorance of their
existence. Notice here the objections of R. Simeon b. Gamaliel, whose
point of departure seems to be the apparent practical injustice of the
rulings. Cuneiform and Talmudic scholasticism may take different
literary forms but intellectually they are probably not very far apart.

---

[35]J. Neusner, *The Mishnah: A New Translation* (New Haven, 1988), p. 589. For
the sake of an unbroken reading, I have omitted the translator's sentence
designations.

7

Dealing with Fundamental Regime Change

The Biblical Paradigm of the Transition from Tribal Federation to Federal Monarchy under David

Daniel J. Elazar
Bar Ilan and Temple Universities

Long-lived polities are inevitably characterized by regime changes in the course of their political history. The Jewish polity has undergone at least twelve such changes in its over three thousand year history, (Figure 1) the first of which is discussed in this paper.[1] This paper focuses on the biblical account of David's ascension to the throne and his consolidation of the kingship in Israel, ending the nearly 300 year old regime of the tribal federation instituted by Moses and Joshua.

The biblical account of David's rise and reign and its consequences for subsequent Jewish history offers a paradigm of regime transition and the successful imposition of a new regime on a reluctant or ambivalent body politic. It describes and analyzes the struggle for succession, the steps taken by David to consolidate his power by gaining control of the several domains of authority operative in Israel, while at the same time preserving their forms so as to avoid excessive conflict with traditionalists. It examines David's establishment of Jerusalem as his capital on territory independent of any tribe, his transfer of Israel's major religious symbol to his capital as a first step towards centralizing worship under the aegis of the king, his establishment of a professional

---

[1]Daniel J. Elazar and Stuart A. Cohen, *The Jewish Polity* (Bloomington, Ind.: Indiana University Press, 1984).

military force, a court, and a bureaucracy dependent upon and responsible to him.

Figure 1
Constitutional Referents and Principal Regimes of the Jewish People

	Period	Dates BCE	Constitution	Founding Events	Climactic Events	Culminating Events
1.	Ha-Avot (The Forefathers)	c. 1850-1570	Abraham's Covenant	Abraham leaves Haran	Jacob becomes Israel	Descent to Egypt
2.	Avdut Mizrayim (Egyptian Bondage)	c. 1570-1280	Patriarchal covenant as reaffirmed	Settlement in Goshen	Egyptian slavery	Exodus
3.	Adat Bnei Yisrael (The Congregation of Israelites)	c. 1280-1004	Mosaic Torah	Sinai	Gideon rejects kingship	David accepted as king
4.	Brit Hamelukhah (The covenant of Kingship)	1004-721	Covenants of Kingship	David's kingship	Division of kingdom	Destruction of Israel
5.	Malkhut Yehuda (The Kingdom of Judah)	721-440	Deuteronomy	Judean rule consolidated	Josianic reform	Abortive restoration of monarchy
6.	Knesset Hagedolah (The Great Assembly)	440-145	Ezra/Nehemiah Covenant	Esra restoration	Shift to Hellenistic world	Hasmonean revolt
7.	Hever Hayehudim (The Jewish Commonwealth)	145 BCE-140 CE	Oral Tradition (Torah)	Hasmonean kingship	Destruction of Temple	Bar Kochba Rebellion
8.	Sanhedren Ve-Nesi'ut (The Sanhedrin and Patriarchate)	CE 140-429	Mishnah	Organization of Mishnah/Renewal of Exilarchate	Christian ascendancy established anti-Jewish policy	End of Patriarchate
9.	Yeshivot Ve-Rashei Hagolah (The Yeshivot & Exilarch)	429-748	Gemara	Completion of Gemara	Jews come under Islam	Reunification of Jews under Islamic rule
10.	Yeshivot Ve-Geonim (The Yeshivot & the Geonim)	749-1038	Talmud & Codes	Geonim and first codes	Last Israel-Babylonian controversy	End of Ganoate
11.	Hakehillot (The Communities)	1038-1348	Sefer HaHalakhot	Passage of hegemony to Europe	Kabbalah in Spain. Reestablishment of Jewish settlement in Jerusalem	Black Death massacres
12.	Vaadei Kehillot (Community Federations)	1348-1648	Arba'ah Turim	Polish Jewry's charters. Council of Aragonese community	Spanish expulsion and aftermath	Sabbatean movement
13.	Hitagduyot (Voluntary Associations)	1648-1948	Shulhan Arukh	Rise of Modernism	Emancipation	The Holocaust
14.	Medinah Ve-Am (State and People)	1948-	?	Establishment of Israel	?	?

The paper also examines David's politics, his use of personal charm, his claim to God's charisma, his appeals to the people over the heads of the established tribal leaders, and his personal image-building, as tools in his successful effort to consolidate power. It examines the way in which David dealt with opposition, both tribal and prophetic, through cooptation where possible and confrontation where necessary. The paper concludes by examining his provisions for the succession of his son Solomon as the final step in the consolidation of a dynastic rule.

The paper considers the Davidic paradigm as one of two competing paradigms of the classic regime in the Jewish political tradition, along with the previous Mosaic regime. Not only have the two become competing models of the ideal polity in the Jewish political tradition, but also in the European political tradition prior to the modern epoch when it was customary to turn to biblical paradigms for justification of current or proposed regimes.

While much can be learned from the biblical account from a strictly behavioral perspective, the Bible, as always, addresses the issues from a normative stance, emphasizing that regime legitimacy must be anchored in God's covenant with Israel.[2] Beyond that, covenantal politics is emphasized at every turn, expressing both an understanding of Israelite political culture and a set of normative political expectations which place political actors and actions under judgement.

This paper is in the way of a very preliminary explanation of some of these themes. Its emphasis is on the interworking of behavioral and normative themes within the covenantal tradition. All this is conveyed in an account of epical proportions – what has been referred to as Israel's equivalent of the *Illiad*, *The Pelleponesian Wars*, or *The Anabasis*.

The Political Discussion in the Former Prophets

The Former Prophets include six books: Joshua, Judges, I Samuel, II Samuel, I Kings, II Kings. A close reading suggests that among their other purposes each reflects and analyzes a particular form of regime as understood by the prophets, that is the *keter torah* of that time.

1) *Joshua* describes the classic polity envisaged in the Torah, headed by an *Eved Adonai* (God's prime minister), paralleled by a *Kohen Gadol* (high priest). The *Eved Adonai* is responsible for the civil rule of the *edah* (the classic Israelite federal republic – literally, assembly), what is later to become known as the function of the *keter malkhut* (the domain - literally crown - of civil rule) and the *Kohen Gadol* is responsible for linking the people to God, what are later to become known as the function of the *keter kehunah* (the domain of priesthood). Both share the task of interpreting the Torah-as-constitution, the function of the *keter torah* (the domain of

---

[2]Cf. Delbert R. Hillers, *Covenant: The History of a Biblical Idea* (Baltimore: Johns Hopkins Press, 1969), p. 171.

constitutional interpretation). Both leaders function within the framework of a very active tribal federation in which the tribal leadership plays a vital role. The regime is presented as generally successful and classic in its form.

2) *Judges* presents the tribal federation in its minimalist state – what happens when the federation becomes a loose confederation and "every man does what is right in his own eyes." Power has reverted to the tribal elders, assisted by *shofetim* (judges, who lead the tribes in battle and administer justice as much as or more than they adjudicate disputes), who share the *keter malkhut*. The *keter kehunah* is also handled by local priests and Levites while the *keter torah* exists principally in the abstract as a fundamental law with no separate institutional mechanism. While tending to a negative evaluation, it offers a mixed picture, by no means all negative – for example, the rejection of monarchy is portrayed as good. On balance, however, confederal anarchism is rejected as a suitable regime.

3) *I Samuel* presents a picture of a prophet-led regime, or at least an attempt to restore the tribal federation by eliminating confederal anarchy through institution of a prophet-led regime. It paints a very dynamic picture of a confederation whose principal federal office was a hereditary priesthood which is deposed in the period under discussion, the rise of a prophet who was trained within the *keter kehunah* but shifts to the *keter torah* and his introduction of a *nagid/melekh* (high commissioner/king) reluctantly and out of necessity, to head the *keter malkhut*, but be subordinate to the prophet. The discussion documents the failure of this regime to stand up to foreign military pressure.

4) *II Samuel*, in describing David's reign, presents the classic regime of kingship. The head of the *keter malkhut* becomes a king and not just a chief magistrate. He reaffirms the authority of the other two *ketarim*, but also subordinates them by bringing them into his court, and retains the form of a tribal federation while centralizing power through a standing army and bureaucracy. While this regime is portrayed as successful, its flaws are clearly pointed out as well.

5) *I Kings* portrays the regime of kingship in its ordinary or declining phases. In fact, it contrasts two forms of kingship – dynastic kingship in the regime of Judah and nondynastic kingship in the regime of Israel – showing the virtues and defects of both.

6) *II Kings* discusses ordinary dynastic kingship in a political union (rather than a federation), its strengths and weaknesses.

In addition, *I* and *II Chronicles* add texture to the historical discussion from the perspective of the *keter melkhut* of the time. They emphasize political and military affairs, government organization and the problem of balancing powers and interests. In our examination of

David and the establishment of kingship in Israel, it will be useful to keep these perspectives in mind.

The End of the Tribal Federation

By the end of the first epoch of the history of the twelve tribes of Israel, the general thrust of events was to bring the existing tribal system with its political structure into the framework of a national polity, comprehensive in character and designed to establish a regime capable of defending Israel against its enemies, especially the Philistines who had overrun the Israelite tribes and subjugated them.[3]

The Philistines, a sea people, assumed by scholars to be from the Greek isles (Crete?), had landed on the southern coast of Canaan at approximately the same time that the Israelites had entered the hill country from the east. Possessing an iron technology and sophisticated political organization, with a well developed military component, the Philistines captured the lowlands of Eretz Israel (the new Israelite name for Canaan), and established five cities – Gaza, Ashkelon, Ashdod, Ekron and Gath. In the eleventh century, they began to invade the highlands, actually capturing the Ark of the Covenant (I Samuel 4-6) at one point. The generally disorganized Israelite tribes were unable to concentrate sufficient power to restrain the invaders, hence their decision to seek a king to lead them to military victory over their powerful new foe.

Israel's fortunes had indeed been laid low. Not only were they soundly beaten at the battle of Aphek (ca. 1050 B.C.E.) and the Ark of the Covenant captured, but the Philistines proceeded to occupy the whole country and destroyed Shiloh, the seat of the tribal confederation. The leader of the tribal confederation, Samuel, the twelfth and last of the judges, was faced with an extremely difficult situation. The old confederation had virtually disintegrated. Shiloh, once destroyed, was never revived. The old regime, whose major national leaders were the priestly guardians of Shiloh and the judge of the time, was discredited. The family of Eli, the chief priest at Shiloh, was, for all intents and purposes, destroyed. Eli's sons, Hophni and Phinehas, were killed while bearing the Ark in battle and Eli died of shock after learning of the defeat. Since his family was already portrayed as corrupted, no heirs emerged to assume the high priesthood until David appointed Abiathar and Zadok two generations later.

---

[3]For a history of this period see Martin Noth, *The History of Israel* (New York: Harper and Row, 1958); W.F. Albright, "Tribal Rule and Charismatic Leaders" in *The Biblical Period from Abraham to Ezra* (New York, 1968), pp. 35-52.

(Indeed, the vacuum in the priesthood was to help David to consolidate his power in Jerusalem.)

Samuel, who was a prophet as well as a judge, was not a military leader. Nevertheless, he attempted to restore the administration of covenant law and to reestablish the shrine of the federation at Mitzpah. He moved from Shiloh to his ancestral home at Ramah from where he travelled on a regular circuit between Mitzpah, Gilgal and Beth El, three towns with sacred and historic associations. While the Israelites thus maintained a degree of autonomy and may even have remained independent in parts of the Galilee or Transjordan, as long as the Philistines continued to have a monopoly of iron, they were able to keep military control over the country. Nevertheless the Israelite will to resist remained strong, if ineffective.

Seeing that the old regime was ineffective if not dead, Samuel attempted to institute a constitutional reform of his own, one that would have strengthened the civil institutions of the old federation to give the regime sufficient authority, power and leadership to overthrow the Philistines and regain Israelite independence. Elsewhere I have suggested that the Book of Joshua as canonized in the Bible is the presentation of Samuel's ideal regime for the tribal federation, built around the argument that if that regime, properly constructed, was strong enough to conquer the country, if properly reconstructed along the same lines it would be strong enough to repel all enemies.[4]

For reasons not explicitly conveyed in the Bible, Samuel failed. According to the biblical account, as Samuel aged and his sons proved unworthy as his potential successors, the people demanded a king, Samuel opposed their demands, formally on the grounds that this was a rejection of God's kingship, the classic feature of the regime of the tribal federation whereby Moses and Joshua as God's prime ministers (*eved adonai*) and the subsequent twelve judges (*shofetim*) were simply His deputies, chosen charismatically to lead the people. God intervened to indicate that the people's request was to be met, at least in a limited way. Reading between the lines, it seems that Samuel's own personality played no small role in the failure of his plan. from the tone of the text it also seems that Samuel was personally jealous of a new and more powerful political leader. Larger political forces were also involved.

In an act of charismatic transfer, Samuel was forced to find an appropriate candidate for the kingship, give him God's blessing, and

---

[4]Daniel J. Elazar, "The Book of Joshua as a Political Classic," *Jewish Political Studies Review*, vol. 1., no. 1 (forthcoming).

then bring him before the people to be elected. Samuel fixed upon Saul, a decent, simple young man of great strength and courage, no doubt because he thought that Saul was suitable to be a military leader but would remain politically subordinate to him as prophet.

In an effort to preserve the spirit of the old regime, albeit within a new institution, Samuel exercised his primordial constitutional function to designate the first incumbent of the office as *nagid* (best translated as high commissioner), rather than *melekh* (king) (I Samuel 10:1). For the rest of the history of the monarchy the two terms appear parallel to one another, with God and His prophets referring to the rulers as *nagid* and the people referring to them as *melekh*. He also established a constitutional framework within which the *nagid* is required to function (I Sam. 10:25), specifying that Saul's principal function as *nagid* was to lead the *edah* in war. However, the people still had to elect Saul, which they do (I Sam. 11:15) and they proclaim him *melekh*.

Saul is presented as a charismatic leader: "The spirit of God came mightily upon him" (I Samuel 11:6), but his choice also had an internal political advantage since he was from one of the smallest tribes, located between powerful Judah and equally powerful Ephraim.

At the beginning, Saul performs as expected, but, a serious man, he takes his responsibilities as king seriously, too seriously for Samuel's taste. The two clash in a power struggle and Samuel publicly rejects him. Moreover, the complex responsibilities of kingship are too much for the bluff, unsophisticated Saul and he begins to deteriorate mentally, first as a result of Samuel's rejection and then in response to politics and intrigues in his developing court, which are exacerbated by the appearance of David as a fair-haired young hero whose popularity rapidly comes to outshine that of Saul. Nevertheless, as long as Samuel remains alive it appears that Saul stays more or less within the framework of a *nagid* and only after the death of the prophet does an institutionalized kingship begin to emerge, limited primarily by Saul's limitations. In the end those limitations are to destroy him and his chances for establishing a dynasty.

Saul's final defeat and death on Mt. Gilboa are as much a result of his psychological state, according to the Bible, as to the continued strength of the Philistines. Militarily, Saul and his son Jonathan continued their successful tactic that had brought them earlier victories, of luring the Philistines into the mountains where the terrain favored the Israelites. But this time Saul is convinced that he will be defeated because God has rejected him. And so it comes to pass.

The Constitutional Process of Regime Change

The Bible presents us with two parallel accounts of the establishment of the monarchy. One (I Samuel 8, 12) is bitterly hostile to the very idea, and the other, (I Samuel 9-10) tacitly accepts it. Together these are among the important political statements in the Bible whose impact has echoed through the generations. (The Book of Chronicles, on the other hand, ignores the process of instituting the monarchy, mentioning the death of Saul as a prelude to the enthronement of David. In general it seems to be a book designed to strengthen the claims of David and his house to the kingship, of which more below.) The importance of the regime change is reflected in the fact that the whole Book of Samuel, which has come down to us as two books, is devoted to the transition, covering a period of slightly over a century, from ca. 1070 to 950 B.C.E., the first book concentrating on the period from the military failure of the old confederation, Samuel's judgeship, the appointment and rule of Saul, down through Saul's death, and the second dealing with David's reign.

Constitutionally, the appointment of Saul seems to have followed a three-fold process. First the tribal elders travelled to Ramah and, in an informal meeting, called upon Samuel to change the constitution and institute kingship. After trying to resist them and warning them of the price of kingship, Samuel acquiesced – following God's instructions according to the biblical account – but not before he warned them of the likely political and social consequences of introducing kingship, all of which were in the direction of drastically reducing Israelite liberties. Samuel then proceeded to find a candidate for the position he advocated, that of *nagid,* which did not carry the powers or the hereditary element of kingship, and choosing Saul, anointed him in the name of God.

Following that, Samuel formally called the people together as a constituent assembly in Mitzpah, the new shrine, in the manner of the old constitutional assemblies of the *edah,* and formally presented the new constitution and the new *nagid* to them for their approval. The people then elected Saul their king, using the term *melekh* (king) in preference to *nagid.* Samuel concluded by promulgating the *mishpat hamelukhah* (the law of the kingdom), which he wrote down as the civil constitution of the new regime within the framework of the Torah, the general constitution of the Israelite polity, after which everyone including Saul returned home.[5]

---

[5] B. Halpern, *The Constitution of the Monarchy in Israel* (Harvard Semitic Monographs No. 25, 1981). The idea that the Torah should be understood as

In light of our knowledge of the role of covenants and covenant ideas in West Asia at the time, we can assume that the Israelite tribes were culturally attuned to this means of reconstitution. The civil covenantal process introduced by Samuel brought about a certain redesign of the political structure and created a basis for further redesign in later epochs of Jewish history, Biblical and post-Biblical. This was to be the limit of Samuel's political success as a constitutional reformer.[6]

In retrospect, the most important aspect of this redesign was the reaffirmation and strengthening of the division of powers within the *edah's* leadership, a division established by a special set of covenants. The initial division of functions or powers was between Moses, the Elders of the *Edah*, and Aaron. God covenanted with Moses as His minister (in the political sense) responsible for relaying and interpreting God's constitutional teaching (Torah) and judging the people. These functions were immediately subdivided per God's instructions so that the 70 elders (as in senate or board of aldermen) took on primary responsibilities for judging, i.e., functioned as a civil branch of government, while Moses himself retained the prophetic responsibility for interpreting God's teaching. The separation between these two divisions was later to be institutionalized by the end of the period of the Judges, with Samuel the last figure to attempt to straddle both. God made a parallel covenant with Aaron and his sons, giving them the priesthood with the authority to be the links between the people and God in ritual and sacerdotal matters. Thus, the basis for a tripartite division of authority between civil, priestly, and prophetic or constitutional interpretation functions was set down through

---

the constitution of the Jewish people is an old and oft-recurring one, expressed by traditional and modern thinkers, as diverse as Spinoza, who understood the Torah as a political constitution first and foremost, and Mendelsohn, who viewed the political dimension as utterly dispensable. See Benedict Spinoza, *Politico-Theologico Tractate*; Moses Mendelsohn, *Jerusalem*, and Eliezer Schweid, "The Attitude Toward the State in Modern Jewish Thought Before Zionism" in Elazar, ed., *op. cit.*

[6]Moshe Weinfeld, "From God's Edah to the Chosen Dynasty: The Transition from the Tribal Federation to the Monarchy," in Daniel J. Elazar, ed., *Kinship and Consent, The Jewish Political Tradition and its Contemporary Manifestations* (Ramat-Gan: Turtledove Publishing, 1981); Hayim Tadmor, "The People and the Kingship in Ancient Israel: The Role of Political Institutions in the Biblical Period," *Journal of World History* (1968), pp. 46-68.

subsidiary covenants early in the Biblical account of the history of Israel as a polity.[7]

A millennium later, during the time of the Second Commonwealth, this tripartite division came to be described as the division into three *ketarim* (literally, crowns), the labels they bear to this day. Those responsible for relating and interpreting God's teaching are described as belonging to the domain of *keter torah*. Those responsible for the civil governance of the *edah* represent the domain of *keter malkhut*, while those responsible for the links between the people and God in ritual and sacerdotal matters are described as being in the domain of the *keter kehunah*.

This tripartite system became more fully articulated with the introduction of the kingship. Prior to the regime change, Samuel as judge and prophet (his two official titles) continued in the line of Moses and Joshua and straddled the constitutional and civil authority. Moreover, because he was raised at Shiloh, the central shrine of the tribal federation, within the priestly family of Eli, he had close connections with the priesthood as well. There are hints in the Biblical text that, in his efforts to restore more effective framing institutions for the *edah* after so many generations of national weakness, he tried to encompass all three domains of authority within his own office. This was decisively rejected by the people and, apparently, by God as well, and is one of the precipitating causes for his failure to reform the old constitution on its own terms and the introduction of kingship as such.

Saul then proceeded to fall into the same trap that was the undoing of Samuel by seeking to encompass in his office the functions of all three domains. For that he is punished and his family is denied dynastic inheritance. In I Samuel 13:8-13, we find Saul usurping priestly functions, i.e., offering sacrifices, and in 15:7-9, he usurps prophetic functions of constitutional interpretation by allowing his army to retain certain spoils from a captured Canaanite city, against the proscriptions of the Torah. Thus the principle of tripartite division is firmly established and is made part of God's covenant with David which is then ratified by the people.

David, with all his power and his success at centralizing the powers of government in his court, did not attempt to abolish this tripartite division, only to bring it under his control. So, he brought the tabernacle to Jerusalem and appointed a new priestly family to tend it, one that would be beholden to him, but in so doing reaffirmed their

---

[7]Stuart A. Cohen, *The Concept of the Three Ketarim* (Ramat Gan: Bar Ilan University, 1986); J. Mailenberg, "The 'Office' of the Prophet in Ancient Israel" in J.P. Hyatt (ed.), *The Bible in Modern Scholarship* (1966), pp. 79-97.

priestly power. He brought the prophets into his court, reaffirming their powers, even allowing them to denounce him for transgressions, but again keeping them within his purview. In short, David's genius was to formally maintain the constitution while altering the distribution of powers within it. David's wisdom was to recognize that, once constitutionalized by covenant, the basic lines of authority had to be maintained but could be manipulated to serve his ends.

David Begins to Advance

David appears on the scene as a somewhat innocent young shepherd boy from Bethlehem, "somewhat innocent" because even the laudatory biblical account that we have suggests a more complex figure than subsequent legend had it. David first appears in three accounts contained in I Samuel, chapters 16 and 17. In the first, Samuel seeks out David the young shepherd under God's instructions to anoint him as king to replace Saul. In the second version Saul, plagued by the psychological terrors that are to be his undoing, seeks relief in music, a member of Saul's entourage remembers David as a young harpist, and Saul invites him to court where David's playing provides temporary relief. In the third version, David, as the youngest son of Jesse, is not yet mobilized in the tribal militia levees confronting the Philistines in the Valley of Elah, but he does go back and forth, bringing food to his mobilized brothers, until he seizes the opportunity to distinguish himself by fighting Goliath.

These three accounts are not necessarily contradictory, and their sequential placement may be accurate. What is important is that we see before us a young man, appropriately modest in his overt behavior, yet handsome and talented and capable of winning over powerful people and garnering their support; a young man of original ideas, good bearing and military prowess. All these are characteristics that will stay with David as he acquires political power. They will be used by him to gain and secure that power.

David's first signal triumph is to become part of Saul's entourage. In other words, he begins to move upward from within the "court" where he is able to acquire knowledge and experience in politics, and perhaps also in governing. Since he enters the entourage as a popular hero, he also has a public dimension which gets him into trouble with Saul but which also enables him to survive exile from the court.

Whether precisely accurate or not, the paradigm of a potential leader successfully pursuing power is complete. It is entirely possible, indeed likely, that David was a gifted musician and poet. The Goliath story, on the other hand, raises some questions. Elsewhere in the text there is a cryptic reference to Elhanan as the slayer of Goliath. Did David appropriate this story of mythic proportions? If so, when? If not, what is the textual reference? Did Elhanan adopt the throne name of David upon becoming king? This hint of something amiss is characteristic of the Bible which, whatever its literal truth in some matters, is not a book of myths but what we might call moral science, using history as its raw material. Written as it is for the broadest public, its general tone must be and is popular, but, for the careful reader, it often drops important hints of this kind.

Since the Bible is not a book of myths, it does not have David automatically ascend to the throne. Instead he has to pass through a period of trials which sharpen his already substantial leadership skills and test his moral qualities. During that period he displays a wide range of human qualities: generosity and opportunism, love and cunning, loyalty and treason, forthrightness and deviousness.

David's troubles begin with his popularity which exceeds that of the king (I Samuel 18:7). Nor is David an innocent victim here. He encourages public adulation. In an effort to be sly, Saul attempts to have David killed in battle by requiring him to deliver one hundred Philistine foreskins as the bride price for Michal, Saul's daughter, whom David seeks to wed. But poor Saul is never successful at slyness and David, instead of getting himself killed, brings back the hundred foreskins and the couple are married (I Samuel 18:17-29). Now David is not only of the court, but married into the royal family – another bond strengthening any future claim to the kingship he might advance. The marriage to Michal is to go badly and when David flees, Saul gives her to another, but David retrieves her after Saul's death and keeps her with him until he has consolidated his hold on the throne.

(Michal is Saul's second daughter, younger than Merab who was originally promised to David but given to another. She is presented as loving David and supporting him against her father. Did she hope to rise to the top through her husband rather than simply be a second daughter? Is her later disgust with David over his populism a reflection of her pretensions?)

David also develops a very special relationship with Jonathan, Saul's oldest son and heir apparent. Jonathan is the biblical model of the singularly noble man who sacrifices his own interests for his friend. The friendship is portrayed through a series of increasingly sad vignettes. David appears to be a good and magnanimous friend, but his friendship never gets in the way of his ambition, while Jonathan, a far more noble character, is forced to choose between filial loyalty to his increasingly mad father and the throne, on one hand, and David, on the other. When he makes his choice and it is described in the usual spare biblical style, we can palpably feel Jonathan's consciousness of what he is doing and the nobility attached to the act (I Samuel 20-21:1).

From Outlaw to King

David is forced to flee from Saul's court. He becomes a political refugee, drawing about him a band of outlaws who have nothing to lose in being with him, but who give him strength because of the kind of characters they are – "natural men" described by one biblical scholar as having "contempt for authority and settled communities." They are to stay with him as his most trusted men for the rest of his life. Meanwhile David's own kin stayed away from him.

David and his followers are given modest help by the priests of Nob, perhaps because the latter were descended from Eli and the priestly family which had officiated at Shiloh and had been dispossessed with the introduction of the new regime. Whatever the reason, Saul has them massacred (I Samuel 22:11-19), leading to the alienation of other priests from Saul's rule, one of whom, Abiathar, joins David's growing band, bringing with him religious objects which endow David with the beginnings of legitimacy.

One can assume that it was in this period that David's understanding of the importance of legitimacy, already evident from the very first moment that he appears on the scene, is strengthened. When he ascends to the throne, David is to resurrect the national priesthood which had fallen into desuetude for two generations, reestablishing the office of high priest and raising it to an honored position in Jerusalem where it is associated with the new central shrine, while at the same time assuring that his appointees, Abiathar and Zadok, and their families, are tied to the court.

It is at this point that David's military strength grows sufficiently to give him and his force a semi-legitimate mission within Israel, namely to serve as an irregular border guard that acts to protect villages and herds against the Philistines and other raiders (23:1-5, 25:1-42). David makes other efforts to strengthen his hand by making marriage alliances with leading families in the borderlands (25:42-43). Nevertheless Saul's pressure against him continues undiminished and David is finally forced to seek refuge with the Philistine king Achish of Gath (the two versions of this event are found in 21:10-15 and 27:2-12). He settles in Ziklag as a Philistine vassal who engages in near-treasonous acts against Israel.

The Philistines then go out for the major assault on Saul and the Israelites which ends in Saul's defeat and death (996-995 B.C.E.). Either deliberately or fortunately, David and his men are not called upon to join in the campaign and remain behind. David is able to memorialize Saul and Jonathan in perhaps the greatest of his poems, which seems to reflect true emotion but also establishes his magnanimity and his claim to leadership of Israel.

The story of David's ascension to the kingship and reign are told in the second book of Samuel which opens with David's elegy. Taking advantage of the vacuum created with Saul's death, David moves to Hebron, the seat of the government of the tribe of Judah, and its religious center. According to the Bible, he does so after asking God whether he should and receiving an affirmative answer. There the men of Judah anoint David king over "the house of Judah" (II Samuel 2:1-4). David was to be king of the house of Judah alone for seven years and six months.

In the meantime, Abner, the commander of Saul's army, who survived the battle, took Saul's surviving son (Ishbosheth in the Bible, apparently because his real name was the pagan Ishbaal) and made him king over all the Israelite tribes north of Judah. David tried to undermine the appointment by diplomacy and apparently by limited conflict. The decisive clash is at Gibeon where Abner and other members of Ishbosheth's court meet with Joab, the commander of David's army and others of David's court. In the ensuing battle, Abner kills Joab's brother Asahel and he and the Israelites are forced to flee.

The long war leads to dissension between Ishbaal and Abner, according to the Bible over one of Saul's concubines. Abner determines to abandon Ishbaal and make a deal with David. As a prelude to any arrangement, David insists on having Michal returned to him. Abner arranges it, after which David and Abner meet and agreement for a settlement is reached, making David king over all Israel. Abner departs, only to be pursued by Joab and his men and killed in revenge for Abner's killing of Joab's brother. David treats the killing as if it were against his orders, but unquestionably it aided him by eliminating a potential source of opposition.

With Abner dead, Ishbosheth's court falls apart. Saul's son is killed by his own courtiers who hope to win favor with David by bringing him the head of his rival. David's response is to punish the murderers with death, but again, since his rival is removed from the field, the last real obstacle was removed to his being chosen as king of all of Israel (chapter 5). All the tribes of Israel came to David in Hebron and, emphasizing the blood relationship among the tribes, covenant with David and make him king over Israel (c. 988 B.C.E.). The formula they use is important. First they indicate that they know that God has appointed him *nagid* in place of Saul. Then they anoint him *melekh*, thus preserving the dual constitutional formula of the *melekh* of the people being God's *nagid*.

David's New Regime

Now king over all Israel, the 30-year-old David was to reign 33 years in addition to the 7 1/2 years he reigned over Judah. He moved swiftly to consolidate his rule by attacking the Jebusites in Jerusalem, capturing the city and making it his capital. This had the dual effect of removing a Canaanite city-state that divided Judah and Israel geographically and giving the new federal monarchy a capital outside of the territory of any of the individual tribes, a federal district as it were. Officially the personal property of David, it became known as the City of David and literally was that.

There David established his court and began to build an appropriate capital city, building himself a grand "house" with imported cedar from Tyre, constructed by Tyrean carpenters and masons. There he settled his family and from there he marched against the Philistines who responded to David's growing strength by sending a force to reimpose their rule on a vassal state that they saw was growing too strong. In two battles at Baal Perazim and the Valley of Refaim, the Philistines are defeated by David.

With the Philistine threat substantially reduced, David assembles the tribal militias to bring the Ark of the Covenant to Jerusalem. His first effort is stopped by a tragic accident when the Ark almost falls off of the cart upon which it was placed and Uzza the man who saves it, drops dead. But several months later the task is completed. Amid joyous ceremonies the Ark is ensconced in Jerusalem, thereby further consolidating David's power by making his city the principal cultic center.

The story of the interrupted journey of the Ark of the Covenant as told in I Chronicles 14-15 suggests that a constitutional issue was involved here as well. David's first effort to bring up the Ark has the people of his army hauling it. After the death of Uzza, David concludes that none ought to carry the Ark of God but the Levites (15:2), so the second time he brings it up he restores the Ark to the custody of the Levites, making that custody permanent, thereby consolidating their support as he has consolidated that of the Priests and the Prophets. The culmination of the transfer of the Ark is described in Chronicles 16:4ff where David appoints certain of the Levites to permanently minister before the Ark of the Lord.

By this time David also has brought Nathan, the leading prophet of his generation, into his court as a personal consultant (II Samuel 7).

Wanting to build a proper house for the Ark, David asks Nathan for God's permission to do so and Nathan's immediate response is to grant it. But, according to the Bible, the word of the Lord comes to Nathan that night to indicate that David should not build such a house on the grounds that God does not need a house and indeed that it is a violation of the spirit of the Israelite religion to violate the simplicity of the tent of meeting. Nathan is instructed to bring this message to David but also to indicate to him that he and his descendants are to be God's *negidim*, God will assure the rule of his dynasty, and that later in the history of the dynasty his son will build the house.

This dream is the principal source of God's promise of permanent dominion to David and his heirs. The fact that it is communicated to Nathan the prophet *(keter torah)* lends it constitutional credibility. David's response in a prayer to God directly makes it a mutual promise or covenant. In his response, David fully assumes the posture of spokesman for his people.[8] While David was unable to build the Temple himself, he did choose the site that Solomon was later to use, purchased the land, had plans for the Temple drawn up and materials assembled before his death (I Chronicles 21:18-22).

In addition to recording and publicizing God's promise via Nathan, David left few if any stones unturned to establish his legitimacy. He kept Saul's daughter, Michal, on as his wife, even after she rejected him, brought Jonathan's son Mephibosheth (Mephibaal) to his court to "eat bread at David's table."

David accepts God's will with all humility and proceeds with the business of building his kingdom. Now it is his turn to attack the Philistines (II Samuel 8) and he reduces them to vassals although he does not annex their territory. The Canaanite enclaves in Israel's territory are reduced and annexed. He then turns to conquer Ammon and Moab which also become vassal states. Turning northward he conquers Zobah and Aram, extending his rule over the two states as far as the Euphrates. Amalek and Edom also come under his rule and on the south his kingdom is extended to below Etzion Geber on the Red Sea. Taking advantage of the weakness of both Egypt and Assyria, David creates a small but strong empire and his rule is acknowledged by his neighbors.

---

[8]J. Levenson, "The Davidic Covenant and its Modern Interpreters," *Catholic Bible Quarterly* 41(ii), 1979, pp. 205-219. God's covenant with David is emphasized in the Psalms (e.g., Psalms 89, 132), many of which are court poems designed to praise the king. Its first important prophetic endorsement is by Jeremiah (Jeremiah 33). See also S. Talmon "Kingship and Ideology of the State in *The World History of Jewish People*, vol. 4, part 2 (Jerusalem, 1979), pp. 3-26.

Only Phoenicia, whose king Hiram had entered into an alliance with David, remains unconquered.

David's military successes enable him to begin the construction of a state of the kind that the Israelites had not previously known. The Bible describes this step in II Samuel 8:15-17, immediately following the record of David's military conquests, listing David's principal officers in the following order: his military commander, Joab, son of

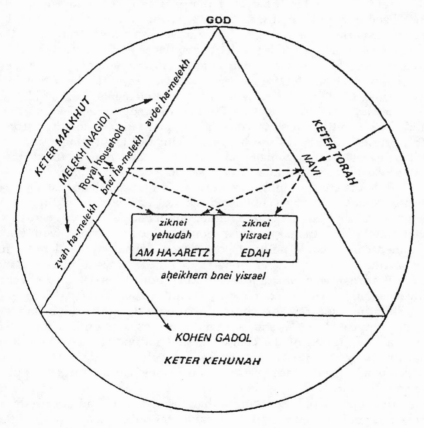

Zeruiah; *mazkir* (usually translated "recorder" but apparently more like its present use in the sense of "appointed manager") Jehosephat, son of Ahilud; two priests, Zadok, the son of Ahitub, and Ahimelekh, the son of Abiathar; *sofer* or secretary in the sense of keeper of the records, Seraiah; commander of the mercenaries, Beniaiah, son of Jehoiadaa; and David's loyal supporters (referred to as "sons of David"), heads of the various ministries. Thus we have a court and a cabinet, as well as the concentration of the three domains in David's court. Overall the new state structure can be described by the diagram on the preceding page:

Perhaps the most significant development here was the organization of a mercenary force loyal to the king himself. While wars were still conducted primarily through the tribal militias, organized in the traditional twelve divisions (I Chronicles 27:2-15), they remained under tribal leadership as reserves who were fully mobilized only in time of war. David's power position was secured by his mercenaries, a standing army who were to prove decisive in the various revolts against his rule, particularly in the great revolt of Absalom which came closest of any of them to succeeding.

The full scale of David's organizational effort is described in I Chronicles 23ff. The description has several elements. First of all, the bureaucracy provides offices for David's loyal supporters, his courtiers and their families, so as to consolidate their support for the throne. The priests and Levites are provided with full employment and the tribal levees are reorganized so that while they remain tribal, they can be easily mobilized into David's service.[9]

While the changes introduced by David brought the country peace and prosperity, they also completed the destruction of the old regime – but not entirely. David realized, either out of choice or out of necessity, that Israel had to remain a federation in which the tribal institutions retained considerable political power, hence what emerged from his reconstitution was a federal monarchy with the tribes in place but the overall thrust was inexorable centralization. This lead to several tribal revolts, often helped along by David's own sons who, because of interfamilial quarrels or sheer impatience to gain their father's throne, appealed to the "state's rights" concerns of the tribes. From the biblical description of the characters and individuals involved, it is hardly likely that this was more than a political ploy on their part which would have disappeared as soon as they had used tribal support to gain the throne. If anything, David was probably more sensitive to the virtues of the old constitution than his sons who had already been raised, if not born, into royalty. Certainly the subsequent history of the Judean monarchy suggests that was the case.

The greatest revolt was that of Absalom eleven years before David's death (II Samuel 15). Absalom had built up the revolt by appealing to the tribal elders on state's rights grounds and actually

---

[9]A. Malamat, "Organs of Statecraft in the Israelite Monarchy," *The Biblical Archeologist* 28 (2), 19656, pp. 34-50; Roland de Vaux, "The Administration of the Kingdom," in *Ancient Israel* (New York, 1965) vol. 1, pp. 133-142.

succeeded in capturing Jerusalem and causing David to flee. David defeated Absalom's tribal levees with his professional soldiers. Absalom was killed and David returned to Jerusalem with the nation rallying around him once again. A second revolt by an Israelite named Sheba ben Bichri was an effort to divide the kingdom through the secession of the northern tribes. David put this down as well and had Sheba killed (II Samuel 20).

Seven chapters (13-19) of II Samuel are devoted to Absalom and David, beginning with the personal conflict between Absalom and Amnon, another of David's sons, over Tamar, their sister, as a result of the rape of Tamar and Amnon's murder by Absalom, Joab's role in restoring Absalom to the court, Absalom's revolt and its repercussions, and David's restoration and its repercussions. In the story we see the power struggle among the king's sons, the crucial role of Joab in keeping David on the throne and his family and court together, the side intrigues of the various people in the court such as Mephibosheth's servant Ziba, who tries to curry favor with David and betray Mephibosheth, and various others. Finally after David's victory, there are the efforts of the leaders of the tribe of Judah and the tribes of Israel to get back on David's bandwagon.

One of the byproducts of Absalom's revolt was a stirring among the family and tribe of Saul, a testing of the waters to see if David's weakness could lead to their restoration to the throne. Mephibosheth may or may not have been linked to the conspiracy but he had to make an effort to get back into David's good graces after the latter's triumph. David bides his time and once the revolts of Absalom and Sheba are put down, uses the pretexts of compensating the Gibeonites for Saul's massacre of them years before to hand over most of the remaining descendants of Saul's family (not including Mephibosheth to whom he had promised permanent protection) for execution, thereby substantially reducing if not ending that threat. At the same time David has the bones of Saul and Jonathan reburied in their native soil of the tribe of Benjamin so as to distance himself from the execution.

David the King

One of the greatest characteristics of the Bible is that it portrays David "warts and all." His worst transgression in the eyes of the Bible was sending Uriah the Hittite to his death in the war against Ammon in order to take his wife Bathsheba. Considerable space is devoted to the incident (II Samuel 11-12) – to the story itself and to its prelude (II Samuel 10). In part, this is because the second product of the union of David and Bathsheba, Solomon, is to inherit David's throne and establish the dynastic principle. In part, it is part of the biblical teaching that even kings are under the judgement of God and his prophets. From another perspective it shows how David has consolidated his power by bringing the prophet into his court, but at the same time the price he must pay, namely within the framework of the court the prophet must be free to chastise him when necessary. The story also reveals David's character, how he could succumb to his passions, but how his own sensitivities developed and his rational faculties never departed from him.

David was not the only one prey to human weaknesses. The biblical account tells of the court intrigues, especially among his children, giving us a taste of what is to come as the result of kingship.

David's last days are described in chapters 1-2 of I Kings and 23-24 of I Chronicles. As his end grew near, the dynastic principle had still not been established and his son Adonijah attempted to seize the throne. Adonijah managed to secure the support of Joab and Aviatar, but Zadok, Beniaiah and Nathan lined up behind Solomon. Nathan became the decisive factor, mobilizing Bathsheba to intervene with the king to have him designate Solomon as his successor. In what is obviously an orchestrated move, Nathan joins Bathsheba in the presence of the king. Both make the point that if Adonijah is to become king, then their lives will be forfeit. This essentially forces David to designate Solomon as his heir.

In the process we have a new form of anointment instituted, whereby priest and prophet join together to proclaim which of David's sons is to be his heir to the throne, a proclamation which then is executed by one of the senior court officials. Again, all three *ketarim* are represented. Here, too, the formula used is both *melekh* and *nagid*. The proclamation must be public because the people must respond to it and assent.

David then personally and privately charges Solomon to maintain Israel's constitution as king, using the classic formula of the Torah, *hukotav, mitzvotav, umishpatav* (his statutes, his commandments and his ordinances) *ve'edotav kakatuv b'torat Moshe* (his covenant witnesses as written in the Torah of Moses). After that constitutional charge, he turns to more practical matters, directing Solomon to make sure that Joab is assassinated so that he cannot intrigue against David's chosen successor and that Shimi ben Gera of Saul's family who had cursed David when he fled Jerusalem during Absalom's revolt also be killed so as to keep the mystique of the monarchy intact and end any efforts on the part of the supporters of Saul to seize the throne. With that, David died.

According to I Chronicles 28-29, David himself assembled all the relevant actors to inform them of his designation of Solomon as his heir in a formal assembly (*vayakhel*, I Chronicles 28:1). These included, in order and by their titles listed: the ministers of Israel, the ministers of the tribes, the ministers of the departments that served the king, the officers of the regiments and companies, the officers responsible for the king's possessions, and David's personal bodyguard. In front of them he went through the appropriate constitutional litany with the addition of the promise to build a temple, and required all of them to pledge allegiance to Solomon.

The Role of Covenanting in a Constitutional Monarchy

The covenant with David and his house was not the first covenant of the *keter malkhut*. At the very least, the *mishpat hamelekh* (civil constitution) in Deuteronomy is the foundation of that *keter*, though, in fact, the foundation goes back earlier to the exodus itself. What is important about *mishpat hamelekh* is that the covenant of *keter malkhut* is not made with the king but is made with the people who are empowered to appoint a king if they so choose. Indeed, one can contrast the three covenants behind the three *ketarim*: the covenant for *keter torah* is made with the people through the mediation of the prophet Moses; the covenant with the priests is made with Aaron and his family and embraces the tribe of Levi in a subsidiary fashion; while the *keter malkhut* is made with the people without a king or equivalent leader being present. Only in a later epoch is an actual king introduced.

During the six centuries following the conquest of the land, the Israelite tribes attempted to build or rebuild their commonwealth through various internal political covenants based upon the overarching covenants with God established earlier. It has already been suggested that the Book of Joshua is the account of the initial effort in that direction. When the original tribal federation collapsed under external military pressure from the Philistines, Israel created a limited constitutional monarchy, bounded by the *mishpat hamelekh*, the covenant of civil rule, which was periodically reaffirmed through specific covenants between kings, the people, and God. The establishment of the office of *nagid/melekh* under Samuel with Saul as the first incumbent is described as a covenanting (I Samuel 9). The next major example, that of David, involves both bilateral and tripartite covenanting. First a relationship is established between God and David which gives David a theo-political status (I Sam. 16). Then that relationship is transformed into covenants between David and the people – with God acting as the guarantor (II Samuel 5:1-3):

> Then came all the tribes of Israel to David unto Hebron, and spoke, saying: "Behold, we are thy bone and thy flesh. In times past, when Saul was king over us, it was thou that didst lead out and bring in Israel; and the Lord said to thee: 'Thou shalt feed My people Israel, and thou shalt be prince over Israel.'" So all the elders of Israel came to Hebron; and King David made a covenant with them in Hebron before the Lord; and they anointed David king over Israel.

It seems that, despite the hereditary element introduced by David, his heirs had to be confirmed through covenants with the representatives of the people. Thus Solomon (965-928 B.C.E.) and the people covenanted with one another before God at the time of the transferring of the Ark of the Covenant to the Temple (I Kings 8). At least this was so after crises involving a previously reigning monarch who had violated the covenant and thereby cast doubt on the legitimacy of the Davidide house, as in the cases of Asa (908-867 B.C.E.), Joash (836-798 B.C.E.), Hezekiah (727-698 B.C.E.), and Josiah (639-609 B.C.E.). Table 1 lists these covenants.

Table 1
Covenants of Regime Change or Reinstitution

4.   Establishment of the Federal Magistery or Monarchy (I Samuel 8-12)
[Describes process of reconstitution]

4a.   Covenants with David (I Samuel 16:1-13, II Samuel 2:1-4; 3; 5:1-3; I Chronicles 11:1-3)
[Network of intertribal covenants with minimum Divine intervention]

4b.   David and the People Acknowledge and Reaffirm the Covenant of the Forefathers and God, in turn, Establishes the Davidic Dynasty (I Chronicles 16 and 17)

4c.   Solomon and the Elders of Israel Incorporate the Temple into the Sinai Covenant (I Kings 8-19; II Chronicles 5-7)

4d.   Asa and the People Renew the Sinai Covenant (II Chronicles 15)

4e.   Jehoiada the Priest Restores the Legitimate Monarchy (II Kings 11, II Chronicles 23)

4f.   Hezekiah Renews the Covenant with God in the Name of All Israel Through Religious Revival (II Chronicles 29) [Action in response to the fall of the northern kingdom]

4g.   Josiah Renews the Covenant and Restores the Book of the Covenant (II Kings 22-23:29; II Chronicles 34-35:19)

What was characteristic of the new regime is the combination of monarchic and tribal (or federal) institutions. David was elevated to the kingship by the tribal leadership speaking in the name of the people, Solomon was reaffirmed by that leadership, and Rehoboam was denied the kingship by ten of the tribes acting in concert when he went to them to establish a similar pact at the beginning of his reign (I Kings 12; II Chronicles 10). Considering his arrogant attitude toward the tribal leadership, it is clear that he was required to go before them by the constitution and did not do so of his own free will. Subsequently, while multi-tribal institutions disappeared from the southern kingdom because of the dominance of Judah (with the original federal institutions surviving only in the realm of local government), the northern kingdom maintained them until the very end of its existence.

The establishment of the federal monarchy under David required a complex network of covenants. God chose David to be his anointed one in a private conversation with Samuel, who proceeded to anoint David secretly (I Samuel 16:1-13). This made it possible for David to be chosen king by the people through their elders in a manner consistent with covenant tradition, a necessary second step. The people and elders of Judah did so (without any reference to God's earlier intervention) immediately upon the death of Saul (II Samuel 2:1-4) but the other tribes of Israel followed suit only after a civil war and protracted negotiations between Abner, the commander of the Israelite forces and real power in that regime (II Samuel 3:6) and David (3:12-21). The issue was complicated by Abner's murder at the hands of Joab, David's military commander (3:27-39) and the intrigues at the court of Ish-Bosheth, Saul's heir (3:6-11 and 4). Finally, the elders of Israel went to Hebron, the seat of David's government, and covenanted with the new ruler (II Samuel 5:1-3 and I Chronicles 11:1-3). This covenantal "package" includes several examples of different kinds of covenantal usages, e.g. for political alliances (Abner and David), for defining the relationship between rulers and ruled (David and the tribes of Israel), and establishing dynastic legitimacy (David and God), all of which find later echoes in Western political thought and behavior.

The establishment of the Davidic dynasty came only in the wake of the removal of the Ark of the Covenant to Jerusalem and the reaffirmation of the national covenant by David and the people at the time (II Samuel 6, I Chronicles 16 and 17). David was careful to make the transfer of the Ark a constitutional event since it was designed to recognize Jerusalem as Israel's capital and seat of God's providence as well as David's government. He carefully followed the right procedures (I Chronicles 13:1-7). After the Ark was settled in Jerusalem, Nathan, the first of the court-connected prophets (whose office emerges as a check on the new centralized executive), brought God's promise of dynastic succession to David (II Samuel 7, I Chronicles 18).

Implementation of the right of succession would come only when David's wife Bathsheba, Nathan, Zadok the High Priest, and various court figures engineered the appointment of Solomon to the throne by David in the latter's waning years, outmaneuvering Adonijah and David's other sons (I Kings 1). Upon Nathan's recommendation, David promised the succession to Solomon and ordered his decision proclaimed by the chief representatives of the three branches of the Israelite national government: the high priest, the prophet, and the steward of the royal court (1:32-37). This was done in a public ceremony to which the people responded by proclaiming Solomon king (1:38-40). The parallel account in I Chronicles 28 and 29 has David assembling the representatives of the people before the Ark of the Covenant to anoint and proclaim Solomon as God's chief magistrate.

Solomon himself reaffirms the covenant, along with the representatives of Israel's tribes, at the dedication of the Temple, in a manner parallel to David's reaffirmation on the occasion of the transfer of the Ark of the Covenant to Jerusalem (I Kings 8, II Chronicles 5). But David's son goes beyond his father to initiate what is, for all intents and purposes, a supplementary covenant with God designed to ground the Temple within the Israelite covenantal system. Since, by tradition, pacts between God and man must be initiated by God, Solomon presents his initiative in the form of a public prayer which he delivers at the dedication ceremony before the appropriate popular witnesses (8:1 – "The elders of Israel, all the heads of the tribes, representatives of the households of Israel" who are referred to collectively as *Kahal Yisrael*, the Congregation of Israel in 8:22).

The essence of Solomon's prayer consists of a series of practical proposals for including the Temple in the religio-legal-constitutional system of the nation. They are necessary because of the revolutionary implications of the Temple as a geographically fixed earthly locus for the Divine presence. Under the tribal federation, God explicitly abjured such a fixed dwelling place. God was free to locate and relocate His earthly presence. While He had commanded Israel to prepare the Ark of the Covenant and the Tent of Assembly, they were deliberately portable. This portability became a central element in ancient Israel's original theo-political ideology.

Solomon had the task of transforming that ideology into one which justified a permanent central worship site in Jerusalem, the city associated with the Davidides. His proposed covenant modification was a major step in that direction, one that followed upon his father's actions to constitutionalize the Davidic monarchy and preceded efforts of his heirs which continued for the duration of the kingdom. The Bible reflects Solomon's case; in I Kings 9:1-9 and II Chronicles 7:12-22, God is portrayed as responding favorably to Solomon's prayer, albeit to Solomon in private, in a dream, and with a clear warning that if he or his heirs should violate the original constitution, the Temple and the land shall be destroyed.

Throughout the years of the united kingdom, the strength of the tribes as constituents of the federation is clear. Despite the very real centralization which takes place under David and Solomon, the tribal institutions maintain much of their power and a serious role in the governance of the polity, a sure sign that the political covenant which united them under the monarchy remained a vital part of the Israelite constitution. Indeed, the Bible portrays the various revolts which punctured the period as reflecting conflicts over the federal character of the regime (e.g. II Samuel 15-19, II Samuel 20, I Kings 11).

A final demonstration of the importance of the political covenant came with the rupture of the kingdom after the death of Solomon. Despite the dynastic element which had been introduced into the constitution, every ascendant to the throne had to be accepted by the assembled people as represented by their tribal leaders. Rehoboam, Solomon's son, presented himself to the assembly as one who would increase the centralization of the kingdom (I Kings 12, II Chronicles 10). Already smarting under the royal court's encroachment on tribal liberties, the leaders of ten of the tribes proclaimed their secession by refusing to reaffirm their original pact with David. Thus the kingdom was divided into two states and remained divided for nearly 250 years until the Assyrian invaders destroyed one of them.

While the ten seceding tribes also organized themselves as a federal monarchy, keeping the name Israel, the dynastic principle never really took hold among them. At first, the assembly of tribal representatives elevated and deposed chief magistrates. Later, as Israel's polity degenerated, the changes were initiated through court intrigues or military coups but the basic principles were honored at least *pro forma* until the end.

Meanwhile, back in Judah, the southern kingdom, the House of David continued to reign on the basis of their founder's covenants at Hebron and Jerusalem for over 500 years, through the Babylonian exile until the Persians deposed the last of them. Those covenants were formally renewed at least three times, on each occasion as a response to a serious threat to the legitimacy of the Davidic house.

Not every monarchic succession required recovenanting. For the most part, they remained within the same constitutional framework, with each new king subject to affirmation of his legitimacy because the covenantal relationship required public acceptance of each new ruler.

Only after rulers had usurped power or done something to break the normal constitutional relationship between governors and governed was it necessary to go through some formal covenantal act in order to reestablish the principles upon which the relationship was built. Thus after Athaliah, the queen mother, usurped the Judean throne in 842 B.C.E. and murdered most of the royal family, responsibility for restoring the Davidic house fell to Jehoiada the Priest (II Kings 11 and II Chronicles 23). He proceeded to organize a rebellion against her (885 B.C.E.), mobilizing the people and using part of the palace guard, to restore the throne to its legitimate heir, Jehoash. The process by which he did so was significant. He simultaneously mobilized a segment of the palace guard and covenanted with them (11:4), mobilized the people through traditional institutions, simultaneously making the covenant with them (II Chronicles 23:2 and 3).

Other cases include Hezekiah's extension of his authority over the remnants of the northern kingdom; and Josiah's theo-political reform. In addition, Asa brought the people of all or parts of five tribes together in Jerusalem to renew the Sinai covenant (II Chronicles 15).

Of these, Hezekiah's covenant renewal marked both the restoration of the supremacy of the Davidides in all Israel, by default as it were, and the transition to a new epoch in Jewish political history. The Bible hails him as the most pious of all the kings who was rewarded by God accordingly. He saved Judah and Benjamin from Assyria and reunified what remained of the people, north and south (II Chronicles 30). His alliance with Isaiah (e.g. II Kings 19:20-26) restored the relationship between king and prophet which had been a feature of David's reign. On the other hand, he was the first to preside over an Israelite polity not constituted on a tribal basis (e.g. II Chronicles 29:20-30, 30:2). The tribes continued to exist, at least as sociological entities – the Bible mentions seven by name in connection with Hezekiah's reign (II Chronicles 30, 31) – and perhaps as local governing units as well, but they are not mentioned as participating in the national government.

The disappearance of the tribal federation as a reality after the fall of the northern kingdom in 722 B.C.E. can be said to mark the end of the original monarchic epoch in Jewish constitutional history, leading to a search for new political arrangements which culminated in the days of King Josiah when the Book of Deuteronomy became the constitutional basis for the regime (II Kings 22 and 23). The Josianic reform restored the idea that the Israelite polity was based on a tripartite covenant between God, Israel and the king, with God as sovereign and lawgiver represented in day-to-day matters by his prophets (II Chronicles 23:1-2,21; and 34:29-32). Coming as it did after the reconstitution of the Israelite regime on a non-tribal basis, the reform reaffirmed the essentially covenantal basis of the Israelite polity, just in time to strengthen the Jewish will to survive after the destruction of the first Temple (586 B.C.E.).

Israel: Monarchy or Theocracy?

All told, the Bible is quite ambivalent about the entire idea of monarchy and whether or not a monarchic regime is consistent with a covenantal system.[10] God's authorization of kingship in the Torah (Deuteronomy 17:14-20) is so ambiguous that traditional commentators and Biblical critics alike to this day argue over its meaning. Is the appointment of a king mandatory or a matter of human choice? To this writer, the text seems to take the latter position. What is clear is that the king must be subordinate to and bound by covenant *(brit)* and constitution *(Torah)* both. This is iterated and reiterated in the text from that first passage of authorization until the disappearance of the monarchy.

Throughout the period of the Judges, monarchy is rejected as a form of government consistent with God's covenant – by Gideon as the climactic figure among the Judges (Judges 8:22-23) who restates the

---

[10]See, for example, Martin A. Cohen, "The Role of the Shilohnite Priesthood in the United Monarchy of Ancient Israel" in *Hebrew Union College Annual* (Cincinnati: Hebrew Union College, 1965), Vol. XXXVI: Josephus's *Antiquities of the Jews;* Abravanel's commentary on Deuteronomy and Samuel; Martin Buber, *Kingship of God* (New York: Harper and Row, 1967); and Yehezkel Kaufman, "The Monarchy" in *The Religion of Israel* (Chicago, 1960) pp. 262-270. While Elijah has traditionally been considered an anti-monarchist, the Biblical portrayal of him shows him to have a more complex position, supporting Ahab as king but seeking to keep the monarchy tied to the Torah as mediated through the prophets. The reference here is to the tradition rather than to the more complex reality.

classic theory that only God rules over Israel and by the text in connection with usurpers (e.g. Abimelech in Judges 9). The actual adoption of a monarchy is portrayed in very negative terms (I Samuel 8). Samuel resists the change until God instructs him to capitulate to popular demand, telling him "they have not rejected thee, but they have rejected me that I should not be king over them" (8:7). Samuel's subsequent acquiescence is accompanied by dire warnings as to the consequences of a monarchical regime and, indeed, he spends the rest of his life trying to contain the new institution within an appropriate constitutional framework, including a special *mishpat hamelukhah* (law of the kingdom) and appropriate checks and balances.

In the last analysis, the text justifies human kingship only as a response to necessity – the deteriorated security situation of the tribal federation which is surrounded by powerful enemies and the deteriorated domestic situation as a result of the corruption of the priest Eli's and the prophet Samuel's sons. The federation needs stronger leadership to confront the first, while the collapse of its established institutions makes the change possible. The Bible is even reluctant to use the term *melekh*, or king, to describe the incumbents of the new institution, preferring the term *nagid*, best translated as high commissioner (of God) or chief magistrate.

The introduction of the major features of the monarchy are portrayed in the Bible as being of strictly human agency or as a result of God's private promises to the king. In the first category are the military and administrative innovations of David and Solomon, which lead to the establishment of Jerusalem, the private preserve and the Davidic house, as capital of Israel, the development of a standing army of non-Jewish mercenaries, and the emergence of a royal court with substantial administrative functions nationwide. In the second category is God's granting to David's family dynastic succession and Solomon's Temple in Jerusalem special status in the Jewish religious system. Both grants are made privately in dreams by the principal beneficiaries, unlike all other Divine covenants and dispensations after the age of the Patriarchs which are made publicly and, indeed, are pointedly public in character." Is the Bible asking us to read between the lines in connection with David and Solomon?

The reorganization of the priesthood, the transfer of the Ark of the Covenant to Jerusalem, and the building of the Temple partake of both human agency and Divine ratification on a private basis. All three involve major redistributions of power within the polity, leading to greater centralization of power in Jerusalem and a dominant role for the royal court. While all three are undertaken by David and Solomon, in fact the Bible indicates a continuing struggle over the full implementation of the intended goals throughout the history of the monarchy which ultimately ends in a compromise which preserves a polycentric system but integrates Jerusalem and the Temple within it.

The Federal Monarchy: A Case Study in Covenantal Adaptation

In a sense the biblical history of the monarchy is a history of how covenantal principles often must be adapted to necessity. While there are ambiguities involved, it is not unfair to suggest that the Bible portrays kingship as a second-best alternative, necessary because of external circumstances and internal corruptions whereby the success of external enemies bring people to lose faith in the classic regime of the tribal confederacy and exacerbate the Israelites' desire to be like all the other nations. The ultimate biblical confirmation of the Davidic house as a permanent dynasty does not contradict this since the Bible simply recognizes that the necessity also is likely to be long-lived. The way subsequent Jewish tradition elevates the Davidic house to messianic status, thereby eliminating the need to have living Davidides in kingly positions on earth, at least prior to the messianic age – and who knows when that will come – reflects the tenuousness of the tradition of kingship in the *edah*.

The problem was how to establish a legitimate monarchy within the covenant tradition. We have seen how that was resolved formally through covenants of kingship that had to be renewed even where the dynastic principle was observed. Three elements can be identified as part of that effort, all connected with the separation of powers into the three domains and all learned at the expense of Samuel's initiative with Saul.

First, the prophets are given a role as king-makers and critics but do not seek to rule. Second, kings can only rule by popular consent, meaning at very least the consent of the tribal leaders. Third, while the people may refer to their civil rulers as kings, the kings themselves are repeatedly reminded by the prophets that from God's point of view they are only *negidim* or high commissioners. This *nagid* tradition functions as a limiting factor on monarchic self-aggrandizement. Because of the separation of powers, within a relatively short time the high priest, although of the family originally installed by David, also acquires an active role in the process. Thus the king is tied to the constitution in three ways: (1) through the separation of powers into the three domains; (2) by having to have the confidence of the citizenry; and (3) through the limits of the constitutional tradition of God as Israel's real and only sovereign.

From the first there were differences between the ten northern tribes that became the Kingdom of Israel and the tribe of Judah with regard to dynastic succession, which succeeded so well in the Kingdom of Judah but never took root in Israel. Nevertheless, it seems that the prophets threw their weight behind dynastic succession in the southern kingdom, probably because they discovered that while any dynasty or kingship is likely to be corrupted, ordered continuity is a necessity for stable government and peace so that ordered continuity coupled with checks and balances to control the king was the lesser evil, again in an adaptation of a grand ideal to reality.

The prophetic role becomes three-fold. The prophets serve as king-makers, as critics, and if necessary as king-removers, and as definers of the ideal exercise of the rule (cf. Jeremiah 22:13-17), where the prophet denounces Jehoiakin on the grounds that the king must be implementer of justice and human rights.

The tribes play much the same role as the prophets, in tandem with them, joining the prophets as king-makers and king-removers, but playing less of a role as critics or definers of the royal ideal. This is evidenced in the various covenants between kings and people, as in II Samuel 3, 5; I Kings 12; II Chronicles 23 – all based on Deuteronomy 33:5.

David's Use of Psalms to Legitimate Covenant as Relationship

The Psalms echo this system of checks and balances. For example, Psalm 89 emphasizes the three-way covenant and Psalm 101, the king's covenant pledge. It seems that David's ascension to the kingship inaugurated a new form of scriptural literature associated with the *keter malkhut*. Biblical scholars have commented on how much of the *Torah* is associated with priestly matters – detailed descriptions of sacrifices, the role and function of priests and Levites. Indeed it has been suggested that the Torah was originally in the custody of the priests and hence was a national constitution skewed in the direction of priestly interests. According to the best scholarship, *Neviim*, the prophetic sections of the Bible date back at least to the time of Samuel and, while they represent a commentary on the kings, they have their own thrust connected with the *keter torah* in its prophetic form.

David as king begins the process of developing a literature associated with the *keter malkhut* which we have before us principally in the *Psalms* and the *Book of Chronicles*. First *Chronicles*, which covers the history of David's reign, is essentially a military and political history. Solomon carries on the tradition in *Proverbs*, *Song of Songs*, and *Ecclesiastes*. Other books that should be identified with this domain include *Job*, which describes the tribulations of an elder in some fictitious land; *Ruth,* which both glorifies life in the days of the tribal federation and also refers to David's ancestry; *Esther, Daniel* and *Nehemiah,* which deal with the bearers of this *keter* after the destruction of the First Commonwealth. All of these books are places in the third section of the *Tanach,* the Hebrew Scriptures, known as *Ketuvim.*

Psalms is a religio-political document designed to strengthen the kingship as a religious value and source of religious inspiration. One hundred and fifty Psalms are collected in the Book of Psalms. (There are some others found in other books including the long Psalm of David in I Samuel 2:1-10 and II Samuel 22:1-23:7.) The Psalms attributed to David include 3-32, 34-41, 51-65, 68-70, 86, 108-110, and 138-145. 71 and 72 are otherwise identified as Davidic. Indeed at the end of 72 it states, "the prayers of David, the son of Jesse, are ended," suggesting that this is where the book of Psalms originally ended. All told, 73 of the 150 Psalms are directly attributed to David by the oldest tradition.

What is important, however, is not the authorship but the function of the Psalms which emphasize national, monarchic and messianic themes, tying them together to establish or strengthen the links between the king and national religious aspirations. This is the overall thrust of the entire collection which seems to be divided into five books. The Midrash points out the parallel between this division and the Torah itself, stating that Moses wrote the five books of the Torah and David wrote the five books of the Psalms. While the statement represents tradition rather than historic fact, the parallelism suggested by the bearers of the *keter torah* is instructive.

We can surmise that the combination of David's artistic talents and the need for establishing the role of the king within the framework of Israelite religion combined to produce the Psalms and the religious poetic tradition they represent. The Psalms restate the covenantal dynamic, *habrit vehahesed* (the covenant with its loving obligations), in connection with such aspects of civil rule as *mishpat,* (covenant law,) and *shofet,* the judge engaged in judgement (often a reference to the king as the continuer of the role of the shofet in the previous regime) – often together as in Psalm 89. All this is embedded in literature of the highest order. The Psalms also offer explanations of the events chronicled elsewhere in the Bible, presented in poetic form to invoke a sense of God's greatness in the minds of the reader or listener and to identify Him with the king. Of the 150 Psalms collected in the book of Psalms, 75 contain directly covenantal references, half again (37) in relation to King David. Those references range from reflections on nature as a covenantal phenomenon to explanations of the shifts of political power within the Jewish polity *Adat B'nei Yisrael* to a probing of personal covenants linking individuals.

While the term *brit* appears in only 13 Psalms, *hesed* appears in 64 – in Psalm 136, 26 times. This modest quantitative measure suggests what a close reading of the Psalms reveals, namely that they are particularly concerned with covenantal dynamics, emphasizing God's sovereignty and kingdom, justice and judgement bound together by *brit* and *hesed*.

What is striking in reading the Psalms is the extensive and intensive use of political terminology. There is hardly a Psalm that does not use political metaphors even if it is not referring directly to political matters. These, along with the attribution of the Book of Psalms to King David and the fact that so many of the Psalms are labelled as his or written for him, make it reasonable to view the Book of Psalms as the voice of the *keter malkhut*. Hence the heavy emphasis on covenant and covenantal dynamics is doubly significant. Its theme is that God's covenant and pledge to His people is a reflection of the fact that we are all living within His kingdom under His sovereignty and judgement, that his judgement is based on righteousness and *hesed*. The latter in particular reflects the ways in which God shows favor to the one he has selected to bear the *keter malkhut* or the burdens of civil rule. The Psalms are the anthems of the kingdom of God designed to celebrate His justice and praise His covenant love.

The Psalm with the most extensive and comprehensive covenantal vocabulary is Psalm 89, ascribed to Ethan the Ezrachi (*ezrach* = citizen). It begins with a commitment to praise God's *hesed* over time and space (*olam* equalling space + time) from generation to generation because the universe is built on *hesed* and the heavens on covenant faithfulness. On this basis God has established His covenant with David and his heirs forever. The Psalm continues (verse 6ff.) describing how the heavenly hosts praise God who is their infinite superior. The former are described as the assembly of the holy ones and the council of the holy ones while God is described as the Lord of hosts.

Verse 10 begins a description of God's rule on earth, describing His rule at sea and how he crushed the mythical sea monster. In verse 12 the heavens and earth are described as God's possession because He founded and created them. Furthermore His throne is founded on four principals: justice and law, loving covenant obligation and truth (*tzedek u'mishpat, hesed v'emet*).

In verse 16 the Psalmist turns to describe how fortunate is the people that knows God's call and walks in the light of His continence. By rejoicing constantly in His name, they are exalted by His justice. In verse 18 this is applied to Israel and in verse 19 the Psalmist proclaims

God to be Israel's king. The next ten verses describe God's mandate to David, His anointed one, how He will strengthen him through his faithfulness in covenant love. The latter will be forever, along with His covenant, so long as the Davidides do not forsake God's Torah, laws, statutes and commandments. If they do forsake those commandments, they will be punished but the covenant will not be broken.

From verses 39 through to the end, the Psalmist apparently is writing after the transgression has occurred and the punishment is in progress. In those verses he addresses God, summarizing the punishment that has been meted out, asking God to end His wrath and restore His *hesed* toward the faithful. In short this Psalm integrates time and eternity, heaven and earth, nature and man, the nations and Israel, God's justice and wrath, punishment and redemption, all within the covenantal framework. This is the recurrent theme of the Psalms.

Conclusion

These Biblical paradigms and case studies are intrinsically important for what they tell us about the deeper structure of the Biblical text. They are at least equally important for their influence on subsequent political thought and behavior in the Western world. These are the paradigms and case studies which surface time and again in the literature of politics in the West to serve as the meat of political analysis. Prior to the age of empirical political research, they represent the closest thing to data used by students of and commentators on political affairs. In that context, the theory and practice of covenant naturally attracted attention as a vehicle for polity-building, constitution-making, and governance. Through the Bible, then, what was once a mere technical arrangement was transformed into a means for constituting new communities, and thereby, a seminal political idea, one which has had a signal influence on the history of human liberty.[11]

---

[11]Cf. Harold Fisch, *Jerusalem and Albion* (New York: Schocken Books, 1964) for an examination of the modern secularization of the covenant idea and John F. A. Taylor, *The Masks of Society, An Inquiry into the Covenants of Civilization* (New York: Appleton-Century-Crofts, 1966) for a contemporary American covenantal perspective. While this article seeks to expound and even shift our understanding of the covenant idea to include and emphasize its political dimension, it also uses theological terminology throughout because the Jewish political tradition of necessity has a philosophic base. Political theology has declined in importance in the West in recent generations, hence the usages may be somewhat unfamiliar to the reader, but it is nonetheless an old element in political science and legitimate in every respect.

Part Four
FORMATIVE CHRISTIANITY

8

The Transformation of Religious Documents: From Early Christian Writings to New Testament Canon

Mauro Pesce
University of Bologna

Introduction

The New Testament canon comes relatively late in the ancient church. Christianity had survived for more than one hundred years without it. It is true that the 27 texts which were included had been in existence for some considerable time and were used in the Christian communities, but there was no canonical collection, no New Testament canon. Each book was used alone, independently of the others and not as part of a collection of writings, a canon. Furthermore, the writings were often very different from one another, reflecting profoundly different phases of the birth of Christianity, written for different purposes and by groups which had to face up to different problems and situations and did so by means of different conceptual categories.

With their insertion into a canon of sacred writings, the New Testament, these early Christian writings changed their genre, and underwent a process of transformation. But this was not the only transformation that they experienced. These same writings had already undergone changes in genre over the varying phases of the history of the origins of Christianity. For transformation is a necessary law in the history of the origins of Christianity. The constitution of a canon of sacred Christian writings can perhaps be seen as the symbolic expression of the conclusion of this process of transformation which resulted in the existence of a clearly autonomous religion with regard to Judaism.

My aim here is to make a parallel between two series of facts: the transformation of early Christianity as a social realty (from Jesus to the church of the third century), and the transformation of the first Christian writings, from their first redaction to their inclusion into the Christian biblical canon. Both series of transformations, and the first one in particular, are widely known and have been extensively analyzed. Less usual, however, is the attempt to understand their relationship. J. Neusner has focused on the concept of canon in Jewish traditions and B. S. Childs has shown the effect of the canonical process on the literary shape and on the interpretation of New Testament writings.[1] In my opinion, the effect of canonization did transform early Christian writings much more than Childs is prepared to admit. I believe that the pattern of the two phases, that I have elsewhere advanced to interpret Pauline letters,[2] could contribute to the analysis and understanding of that transformation.

I. Transformation in early Christianity

One of the fundamental characteristics of the particular Jewish religious movement which would become ancient Christianity is that it was in constant transformation. Transformation was necessarily present in the very structure of its existence. Christianity was born out of Judaism. From being a form of Judaism, it became non-Judaism. It is

---

[1]B. S. Childs, *Introduction to the Old Testament as Scripture*, London 1979; *The New Testament as Canon. An Introduction*, London 1984; J. Neusner, *Systems and Their Contents: Canon as Inductive Category*, in: *Ancient Judaism and Modern Category-Formation. "Judaism," "Midrash," "Messianism" and Canon in the Past Quarter-Century*, Lanham/New York/London 1986, 3-120; Id., *Bavli vs. Bible. System and Imputed Tradition vs. Tradition and Imputed System*, in *The Formation of the Jewish Intellect*, Atlanta Georgia 1988, 151-171. For the relationship between canon and Christian religious systems in modern times cfr. my *Antropologia Biblica. Punto di riferimento o frutto del pensiero moderno?*, Annali di Storia dell'Esegesi 7(1990).

[2]M. Pesce, *L'apostolo di fronte alla crescita pneumatica dei Corinzi (1 Cor 12-14). Tentativo di un'analisi della funzione apostolica*, Cristianesimo nella storia 3 (1982) 1-39, also published in *Charisma und Agape (1 Kor 12-14)*, (ed. by L. De Lorenzi), Roma 1983, 51-125; *Funzione spazio dell'uso della Scrittura nell'attività apostolica paolina. Ipotesi di ricerca*, Annali di Storia dell'Esegesi 1 (1984) 96-108; *Ricostruzione del kerygma ai Tessalonicesi sulla base di 1Ts 1, 9-10*, Annali di Storia dell'esegesi 2 (1985) 36-37; *Problemi aperti nello studio della tradizione protocristiana*, in A. Cezesa Gastaldo (ed.), *Storia e preistoria dei Vangeli*, Genova 1988, 109-11; 119-120; cfr. *Christ did not send me to baptize, but to evangelize (1 Cor 1,17a)*, in *Paul de Tarse. Apôtre de notre temps*, Rome 1979, 339-363.

thanks to F. C. Baur that the development of primitive Christianity has been focused upon. The limits of his work, however, are perhaps that he saw this development above all as a dialectic at work within Christianity itself, whereas it was really above all an outcome of the dynamics of its early position within Judaism.

This transformation can be found in the different early Christian works which reflect the various stages of change in the post-Jesus movement, but it has been in some way removed from the New Testament canon, which by its very nature brought together differences and projected the final outcome of the transformation onto the initial stages of development. In fact, long before their incorporation into the canon, all the early Christian texts, from their very earliest formulation, show traces both of the transformation and of its removal. All the early Christian writings inevitably and unambiguously carry within them, although to greater or lesser degrees and in various different manners, this essential aspect of early Christianity as a phenomenon undergoing transformation. But at the same time they remove this aspect inasmuch as they are religious writings aspiring to convey a religious truth and not works of history describing change. Reference to the past is a constitutive feature of these works, but this past is reconsidered in the light of a contemporary rethinking which transforms it. Without references to the origin there would be no transformation. But the transformation is perceived as revelation of the profound truth of origins. Origin is thus no longer "past" but rather present. What the historian sees as the removal of difference, seems to the redactors of the Christian texts as a more profound understanding through the Spirit.

Jesus announced the imminent coming of the final reign of God.[3] This was the qualifying and generating principle behind his preaching. But later Christianity came to an exclusion of the imminence of this coming and to a religious system which hinged upon the present. An intermediate stage in this transformation was the conviction, held by a majority of the strata of the post-Jesus movement, that the eschaton had begun decisively with the resurrection of Jesus and with the presence of the Holy Spirit (the Spirit of God/of Christ[4]) in the ekklesia, which thus became the anticipation of the eschaton. This conviction led, although not without disputes, to the opening of the ekklesia to Gentiles. The moment, prophesied in the Bible, of the

---

[3]Cfr. R. Schnackenburg, *Gottesherrschaft und Reich*, Freiburg 1965[2]; J. Jeremias, *Neutestamentliche Theologie, I. Teil*, Gütersloh 1971; W. G. Kümmel, *Die Theologie des Neven Testaments*, Göttingen 1976,[3] Chapt. I.
[4]R. Penna, *Lo spirito di Cristo*, Brescia 1977.

eschatological conversion of the nations to the one God had arrived.[5] With the fall of the expectation of the imminence of the reign of God,[6] it was inevitable that the Church itself should come in the foreground, endowed with the gifts of God's Spirit, an anticipation of the eschaton which was indefinitely put back to a far distant future, and already able to bring together a new humanity which could go beyond the Gentile/Jew division. But by now, the separation from Judaism had become definitive. For the central element of the preaching of Jesus, which proposed to drag the whole of Israel towards the eschaton,[7] had long been abandoned.

A further element of transformation can be seen in the capacity of the post-Jesus communities to have recourse to a source of truth distinct from although complementary to Jesus: the Spirit. The fundamental element in post-Jesus preaching was not its reference to the past but its reference to, and possession of, a present truth, coming from the Spirit of God/of Christ/of the risen *kyrios*. This led to positions which differed subtly from one another. At the extremes, there were two positions which perhaps never actually existed in their most abstract and radical form. One affirmed the independence from the earthly Jesus (cfr. 2 Cor 5:16). The other presented itself only as spiritual rereading

---

[5]Cfr. M. Pesce, *La profezia cristiana come anticipazione del giudizio escatologico in 1 Cor 14, 24-25*, in *Testimonium Christi, Studi in onore di J. Dupont*, Brescia 1985, 379-438.

[6]Cfr. 2 Pt. 3, 8-10.

[7]There were three dimensions to the preaching of Jesus. One, centripetal, tended to set the whole religious system in motion in order to push it towards the future, to project it to the imminent day of judgement. Another, a horizontal critique, was aimed at elements within the system, judging them prophetically in the light of God's will. The two dimensions were closely linked but had different results. Jesus announced the imminent coming of the reign of God. His preaching was thus fully eschatological. But his strong emphasis on God and on his paternity, on the will of God and the radical need for conversion to God, at the moment of the imminent coming entered into conflict with the formulations, the practice and the understanding of his contemporaries. The third dimension was vertical: Jesus draws directly on God for his inspiration; he justifies himself in the name of God, through charismatic, pneumatic and revelational contact (but also through his gift of healing). Jesus comes from outside the official institutions, from the baptist movement, and later claims direct investiture by God. The pneumatic revelational dimension of post-Jesus Christianity is already present to a certain extent in Jesus (cfr. baptism and transfiguration). His appealing directly to God and the fact that his activity takes place outside the official religious institutions, together with the "prophetic" criticism that he makes with regard to certain aspects of religious practices and contemporary religious understanding are elements which lead the Jesus movement from the very beginning to have a dialectic of transformation with respect to Judaism.

and understanding of the words and acts of Jesus (cf. John 14:26; 16:12-15). There are only differences of emphasis. The Gospel of John gives an account of the words and actions of Jesus, but explicitly admits that the Spirit introduces new elements and the whole truth, whereas Paul, who essentially introduces his own apostolic authority willed by God (Gal. 1,1.11-12), does not entirely renounce either the words of Jesus (1 Cor 7:10; 9:14; Rom. 14:14), or tradition (1 Cor 11:23ss.; 15:3-5).

In the Gospel of John, we can find an explicit theory of the means by which the words and actions of Jesus have been handed down. There are two clear texts on this point:

John 14:25-26:

> These things have I spoken unto you, being yet present with you. But the comforter, which is the Holy Ghost, whom the Father will send in my name, he shall teach you all things, and bring all things to your remembrance, whatsoever I have said unto you.

John 16:12-15:

> I have yet many things to say unto you, but ye cannot bear them now. Howbeit when he, the Spirit of truth, is come, he will guide you into all truth: for he shall not speak of himself; but whatsoever he shall hear, that shall he speak: and he will shew you things to come. He shall glorify me: for he shall receive of mine, and shall shew it unto you.All things that the Father hath are mine: therefore said I, that he shall take of mine, and shall shew it unto you.

The Christian tradition that comes to expression in these texts is aware of a *transformation in understanding* of the meaning of the words and actions of Jesus. What the disciples had understood when they were with Jesus was not sufficient. The real meaning of his words and his acts were to be understood only when the disciples, after his death, received the "spirit of truth." But this was not all. The "spirit of truth" would complete what Jesus said, revealing the "whole truth." The transmission of the words and actions of Jesus brings with it necessarily a transformation in what is transmitted.[8]

This theory of the Gospel of John is common to all early Christianity. It was already in evidence in Chapter 2 of First Corinthians, where Paul speaks of a level of knowledge and understanding, of a *"sofia"* which can be reached only through the Spirit, and is attainable by "perfect" believers and not by those who

---

[8]This is true not only for the words and actions of Jesus but also for his very identity, for christology.

are still "carnal" or *"nepioi"* (1 Cor 2:6-3:4).[9] The whole of early Christianity is united in this. The conviction of being the addressee of the revelations of the Spirit is a universal characteristic of Christianity. Early Christian prophetism is *Sitz in Leben* of the formulation of the Gospels.[10]

The opening of preaching to Gentiles involved a transformation with respect to the preaching of Jesus which, precisely because it was aimed exclusively at the Jews, presupposed both belief in monotheism and the recognition of the moral principles of the Law. Jesus appealed constantly to conversion to God and to His will. With respect to the Gentiles, however, it was above all necessary to preach monotheism and a defence of Jewish morality. The Christian preachers thus drew spontaneously, in this case, upon their own Jewish tradition and not the words of Jesus.[11]

Finally, the outcome of this transformation can be seen in the process which allowed some of the necessary Jewish presuppositions or postulates of the preaching of Jesus and of the post-Jesus movement to be maintained, although they were now divorced from Jewish culture and religion. Later, at the end of the long process of separation from Judaism, Christianity was to keep the Jewish Holy Scriptures, monotheism, the ten commandments and the essential ethical positions of Jewish culture on women and the family.[12] It rejected, however, the ethnic basis, the political-religious institutions and culture of the Jews. That is was possible to appropriate the monotheistic ethical tradition of the Bible while rejecting the people and the culture that produced it was due to the Christians' conviction that they were in possession of an eschatological revelation of the Spirit of God and/or of Christ and that the risen Jesus had attained an extraordinary dignity.

---

[9]The same theory is presupposed in Philippians 3:15: "Let us therefore, as many as be perfect, be thus minded: and if in any thing ye be otherwise minded, God shall reveal even this unto you."

[10]E. Käsemann, *Die Anfänge christlichen Theologie*, in *Exegetische Versuche und Besinnungen II*, Göttingen 1964, 82-104; *Zur Thema der Urchristlichen Apokalyptik*, Ib., 105-131; G. Dautzenberg, *Urchristliche Prophetie: ihre Erforschung, ihre Voraussetzungen im Judentum und ihre Struktur im ersten Korintherbrief*, Stuttgart 1975; M. E. Boring, *Sayings of the Risen Jesus. Christian Prophecy in the Synoptic Tradition*, Cambridge 1982; M. Pesce, *La profezia cristiana come anticipazione del giudizio escatologico in 1 Cor 14:24-25*, in *Testimonium Christi, Studi in onore di J. Dupont*, Brescia 1985, 379-438.

[11]M. Pesce, *Ricostruzione del kerygma ai Tessalonicesi sulla base di 1Ts 1:9-10*, Annali di Storia dell'esegesi 2 (1985) 36-37; *Problemi aperti nello studio della tradizione protocristiana*, in *Storia e preistoria dei Vangeli*, Genova 1988, 109-11; 119-120.

[12]Cfr. the concern of Paul about *porneia* in 1 Thess. and 1 Cor.

Let us point at the fundamental phases in this transformation. The first transition is from a preaching of conversion within Judaism[13] in the light of the imminent coming of the reign of God,

> the time is fulfilled and the Kingdom of God is at hand; repent ye, and believe the gospel,
>
> Mk. 1:14

to a preaching with a Christological content with the same eschatological emphasis. This first transition is the fundamental one. It involved a move from an acceptance of the preaching of Jesus to the certainty of being the receivers of a spiritual revelation which saw itself as continuing, completing and going beyond the Jewish biblical tradition:

> This Jesus hath God raised up, whereof we all are witnesses. Therefore being by the right hand of God exalted, and having received of the father the promise of the Holy Ghost, he hath shed forth this, which ye now see and hear.
>
> Acts 2:32-33

Without this awareness on the part of the ancient Church, there would have been no New Testament. The next transition was towards a preaching with a *theological-Christological* content:

> How ye turned to God from idols to serve the living and true God; and to wait for his Son from heaven, whom he raised from the dead, Jesus which delivered us from the wrath to come
>
> 1 Thess. 1:9-10

still of an eschatological type and aimed at the Gentiles. The final transition was towards a theology and Christology deprived of the imminent coming of the reign of God and by now completely separate from Jewish culture and institutions:

> All power is given unto me in heaven and in earth. Go ye therefore, and teach all nations, baptizing them in the name of the Father, and of the Son and of the Holy Ghost: Teaching them to observe all things whatsoever I have commanded you: and, lo, I am with you alway, even unto the end of the world.
>
> Matthew 28:18-20

The protagonists of early Christianity were aware of the transformation but perceived it as willed by God, as a succession of events in a history which moved according to God's will.[14] They were aware of the transition from a preaching aimed at Jews alone to one

---

[13] Mt. 15, 24.
[14] John 16:12-15; 14:26; 1 Cor. 2:6-16.

aimed at Gentiles. They discussed this but they did not have any instructions from Jesus on the subject.[15] They realized that they were completing and reformulating the words of Jesus. They were aware of the novelty of abandoning entirely part of Jewish Law (such as circumcision or dietary laws).[16] With regard to this, too, they had long discussions. For Jesus had left no direct instructions, apart from some obscure *logion*.[17] They were aware of the transformation regarding the imminent coming of the reign of God. They were even more aware of the fundamental element in the transformation: the relationship with Judaism. The problem is at the heart of some of the most important documents of early Christianity: the Letter to the Romans, the Gospel of Matthew and the prologue of John. But the early Christian writings also testify to a lack of awareness of this transformation. They are also based on a removal of the transformation.

II. Early Christian Writings in the Transformation: the case of the Letters of Paul

At its very beginning, every early Christian text was closely tied to a particular group of the post-Jesus movement. But these groups belonged to different religious systems: a) to the Palestinian Jewish religious system before the destruction of the Temple and the disappearance of the Synedrion; b) to the Jewish religious system of the diaspora; c) to the religious system of the Christian communities outside Palestine, which were already separated from the various Jewish groups of the diaspora. It is true that the post-Jesus movement had a religious unity at the beginning, but this was essentially based only on mutual agreement amongst the itinerant preachers (Gal 2:1-10; 1 Cor 15:11) as to a nucleus of Christological-eschatological doctrine.

Let us take the case of Paul's letters, in particular the following five: the First Epistle to the Thessalonians, the First and Second to the Corinthians, Galatians and Romans.

---

[15]Gal. 2 and Acts 10 testify to the absence of instructions from Jesus on the question.

[16]It is not true that this abolition concerned only the Gentiles: the fact of eating together with Gentiles meant breaking Jewish law also for a Jewish preacher (cfr. Gal 2:11-14).

[17]Mc 7:18-19. 20-23/Mt 15:17-20; Rom 14:20. Lc 11:41; (cf. Atti 10:9-16); cf. R. Booth, *Jesus and the Laws of Purity. Tradition History and Legal History in Mark 7*, JSOT Press 1986; J. Neusner – B. D. Chilton, *Uncleanness: A Moral or an Ontological Category in the Early Centuries A.D.?*, (1988); J. Neusner, *"First Cleanse the Inside,"* in: *Method and Meaning in Ancient Judaism. Third Series*, Chico, CA, 1981, 155-164.

Paul's apostolic activity can be divided in two phases,[18] different in terms of aims, content and time. The first phase began with the preaching of the gospel and ended with the founding of a church and the departure of the apostle; the second consisted of the guidance, from a distance, of already founded communities. The structure of the second phase of Paul's apostolic activity[19] is characterized by a variety of means of communication between the apostle and the communities: a) visits by the apostle; b) visits by helpers sent by the apostle to the communities; c) the direct word of the apostle to emissaries of the communities who go to him to ask him about specific questions; d) the sending of letters.

The letters are thus not acts of evangelization. Their aim is not to introduce the gospel to those who do not know it and not even to provide fundamental instructions for the founding or the beginning of the life of a community. Neither do the letters constitute the entirety of the second phase of Paul's apostolic activity, but only a part of it. We must therefore conclude a) that the fundamental element, the evangelization (kerygma or gospel) and the founding of the community, is not expounded in the letters, unless it is necessary for the apostle to remind the community of points which may concern occasional problems of the community; and b) that this primary part, evangelization and foundation of the community, did really exist, but only orally and we have no direct historical information as it was never written down.

This has its importance in terms of the nature of the letters. They were interpreted on the basis of the oral kerygma and in the oral context of the second phase of Paul's apostolic activity. The criteria for their interpretation were oral.[20] When, though, they were included in a canon of writings which was normative for belief and action, the New Testament, the letters changed their nature. They would be interpreted in the context of all the other New Testament writings. On the other hand, as a part of the New Testament, they would tend to become normative for oral preaching and not vice versa. The relationship between oral and written was thus to be turned upside down.

---

[18]I have elsewhere proposed to adopt this pattern of the two phases to analyze the entirety of the Pauline missionary activity and its internal dynamics. Within this pattern the letters are to be conceived as functions of the Pauline missionary activity. That permits one to distinguish within the letters the literary forms and their socio-religious functions, cfr. note 2.

[19]Paul defines it as "caring (*merimna*) for all the churches" (2 Cor.11:28).

[20]1 Cor. 4:17: "For this cause have I sent unto you Timotheus, who is my beloved son, and faithful in the Lord, who shall bring you into remembrance of my ways which be in Christ, as I teach everywhere in every church."

It is possible that the original meaning of some documents can be understood outside the context in which they were written. But this is certainly not the case with the five letters we have chosen from Paul. They were written with precise reference to certain situations and people, and in particular moments of the evolution of the history of the communities and their relationship with the apostle. The context of the oral *kerygma* and the concrete situation of the communities is essential to the actual writing of the letters. In this case, text and context are inseparable. Once included in the canon, the five letters found themselves in a completely new context, one which was not that in which and for which Paul had thought them and written them.

III. The transformation of early Christian writings through the Canon

When the Christian biblical canon was created including the Old and the New Testament,[21] the early Christian writings in it ceased to be independent writings and became part of a single Christian religious system: that which produced the New Testament canon.

To understand the transformation undergone by the early Christian writings on their inclusion in the New Testament, it is necessary to understand what a canon of sacred writing is,[22] and what relationship it has to a religious system. A canon is not a simple collection of a variety of writings, it has a unity which transcends the individual writings that it encompasses. Its authority transcends that of the individual authors. Its author is not the same as the authors of the separate writings. Its literary and theological unity is the creation of a religious system on the basis of the criteria and principles upon which the system itself is based.

The religious system which created the New Testament contained structural elements which were different from and sometimes contrary to those of the initial system in which each of the writings which were included in the canon were produced. As the nature of a religious text is determined by the dialectic between its textual structure and the religious system which reads it, the transition from the initial system to the final system involves, for each text, or group of texts, a transformation which can in some cases be fundamental.

The letters of Paul were functional to a religious system characterized by a group of churches subordinate to the apostle, that is,

---

[21]R. Beckwith, *The Old testament Canon of the New Testament Church, and its Background in Early Judaism*, London 1985; M. Harl, G. Dorival, O. Munnich, *La Bible grecque des Septante. Du Judaïsme hellénistique au christianisme ancien*, Paris 1988.

[22]Cfr note 1.

to an itinerant leadership with no fixed base.[23] This system of Pauline churches was not an island without horizontal contacts with the rest of the post-Jesus movement, and was, however, in transformation. At the beginning, Pauline preaching came under the supervision of the community of Antioch, but then it became autonomous. At this point, Paul and other itinerant apostles were equals. The reference to the Church of Jerusalem was one of the cardinal points of the Pauline system. The Church of Jerusalem, in turn, was still part of the Palestine Judaic religious system. All the authentic letters of Paul were written when the Church of Jerusalem was still the center of the post-Jesus movement. The conflict between Paul and the Church of Jerusalem is explainable in terms of the diversity of the religious systems in which both found themselves. For the Church of Jerusalem, the post-Jesus movement was essentially part of Judaism and thus had to belong to the religious system of the Temple and of the synagogue, of the biblical tradition and of the traditional Jewish Law. The preaching of Paul, on the other hand, belonged to the system of the Christian communities which lived in close contact with the Jewish communities of the diaspora. It testifies to that crucial period in which the Christian communities tended to separate themselves from the Jewish community and thus tended to lose all contact with any sort of Jewish religious system.

The expectation of the imminent coming of the reign of God structures the whole of the Pauline religious system.[24] The very geographical movements of Paul are governed by this: only when he has preached to all the Gentiles, at the ends of the earth, will it be possible to think of the coming of the eschaton.[25] It determines also the attitude towards individual and public reality, that is, the attitude towards "this" world. The believer must live as if the reign of God was already present, and no longer find in this world the criteria for the choices he makes. He must behave to this world *as if* this world *no* longer existed, since "the ends of the world are come" (1 Cor. 10, 11). The expression "as if not" (ὡς μή) captures the precise essence of the whole of Pauline Christianity.[26]

---

[23]The apostle is surrounded by a group of itinerant collaborators who preach with him and go to and fro between him and the newly-founded communities. In their turn, the communities produce itinerant preachers who maintain contacts between the communities and the apostle.

[24]Cfr. not only classical texts like 1 Thess; 1 Cor 1:8; 7:29-31. 10:11, but also Rom 13:12.

[25]Rom 11:25-26.

[26]"But this I say, brethren, the time is short; it remaineth, that both they that have wives be as though they had none; and they that weep, as though they

The Pauline communities separate themselves from the Jewish communities of the diaspora without integrating themselves, however, into the religious-social systems in which they live. Their religious behavior, in any case, was based on living in this world *as if* this world did *not* exist. The project of "Christianizing" society is thus entirely absent in the Pauline religious system. The "Christianizing" of institutions, which was to become the great project of the church, was completely absent in Paul. The clearest expression of this awareness in Paul can perhaps be found in 1 Cor 5:12-13:

> For what have I to do to judge them also that are without? Do not ye judge them that are within? But them that are without God judgeth.

The jurisdiction of the apostle does not extend beyond the boundaries of the *ekklesia*, the congregation of worship, the community's only form of sociologically recognizable life.

The New Testament depends, on the contrary, on a religious system in which some of the fundamental elements of the Pauline system are now not only absent but contradicted. There is no more Church of Jerusalem as the central church. This means that the post-Jesus movement sees itself no more as being part of Judaism. It is in fact no longer a movement but a new religion. The fundamental institutions of Judaism, the Temple and the Synedrion no longer exist and those which substituted them, such as for example the Yavneh and Ushah academies and the patriarchate, were born after the formation of the post-Jesus movement and constitute no reference point for early Christianity. The expectation of the Reign of God, by now removed to a distant future, no longer structures behavior towards this world. Its attitude to this world swings rather like a pendulum between two opposing extremes: that of the complete separation from the world and that of the Christian transformation of social and political institutions. The Christian communities are no longer islands in a foreign socio-religious system. The idea of living ὡς μή, as if this world did not exist has been substituted by the words of Jesus in Matthew 28:18-20. It is the "Christianization" of society that will from now on determine behavior towards this world.

The five letters of Paul have been transmitted from the context of an original religious system to that of the church of the New Testament. They have changed from being single works to being

---

wept not; and they that rejoice, as though they rejoiced not; and they that buy, as though they possessed not; and they that use this world, as not abusing it; for the fashion of this world passeth away" (1 Cor. 7:29-31); cfr. M. Pesce, *Marginalità e sottomissione. La concezione escatologica del potere politico in Paolo*, in *Cristianesimo e potere*, Bologna 1986, 43-80.

inseparable parts of a canon. What was originally a means of communication between a sender and a receiver in the context of a specific religious system has become the word of God, valid universally and for all time. Let us look at the transformations which each element of these texts has undergone in this transition.

The *author* of the letters was that Paul who saw himself as an apostle and who claimed that the contents of these letters in any case came from the Spirit of God/of Christ,[27] but about whom some contested the apostolic nature and pneumatic authority. With their inclusion in the canon, the author of the letters became the Spirit of God itself. The works of the apostle, whose authority has by now been universally recognized within the church, are given the dignity of Holy Writings. The nature of the writings, which was precisely that of being the object of possible contestation, was transformed: they became the incontestable word of God.

The *receivers* of the letters were the communities evangelized by Paul. In the New Testament, however, the receivers are believers a) not evangelized by him; b) who did not know the Pauline *kerygma*; c) who did not know the problems of the original receivers; and d) who had different problems from them.

The *context* of the Pauline letters, the norm and criterion for understanding them, was the oral *kerygma* and that largely oral work of the guidance of the community both of which have by now been lost. The context now is a written context: that of the texts in the New Testament canon. Conceived as a single text, a unity, as a single sacred book, its various parts make up a whole and they are read each in the light of the others. The context of Paul's letters are now early Christian works which have not got a Pauline orientation and which are now conceived as being in theological harmony with the letters. The image of Paul in which the letters are read is now that of the Acts of the Apostles. And the historian of today knows that the Paul of the Acts and the Paul of the letters are different.[28]

While the Paul of the letters only looked for the eschatological end of the Judaic authorities who were opposed to Christ (1 Cor 2:6-8)[29]

---

[27] 1 Cor 2:6-3:4; 7:40; 14:37.

[28] This is true not only as regards the question of the so-called council of Jerusalem, or certain aspects of Paul's relationship with Peter, or the behavior of the emissaries of James towards him. It could be stressed also that the Paul of the letters was completely foreign to the baptist-Christian tradition, whereas the Paul of the Acts (13:16-43) preaches according to the typical model of the Synoptic Gospels, making the announcement of John the Baptist precede that of Jesus.

[29] Cfr. my *Paolo e gli Arconti a Corinto*, Brescia 1977.

and saw in the eschaton the acceptance of the Gospel on the part of the whole of Israel, on the basis of the received Jewish faith of Mishnah Sanhedrin (10.1),[30] the system of the New Testament clearly embraces the point of view of the Synoptic Gospels, which attribute to Jesus the prediction of the destruction of Jerusalem and/or the Temple. The Gospel of Matthew also attributes to Jesus the interpretation which sees in these two events God's punishment for having rejected and killed first the prophets and finally the Son. The Pauline letters were written in the context of links between the life of the Christian communities and the religious life of the synagogue (although these links had certainly become more tenuous with the passing of time). The great Jewish festivals of Pesah and Shavuot, for example, were the same Christian festivals. But the religious system which produced the New Testament now viewed the synagogues as places of cult belonging to another religion, as places of cult completely alien to itself. Christian festivals no longer have connections with Jewish festivals. The controversy within the church over the date of Easter is symptomatic.

IV. Unity of the canon, comprehension through the Spirit and discontinuity

The New Testament , as a constituent part of the Christian Bible, is not the simple sum of the parts which make up the whole: it is a unity. a) There is a textual unity which begins with the Gospel of Matthew and ends with the Revelation, a literary unity with an inner structure, as in any type of text. This inner structure is the product of a conscious, planned architecture. Whoever constructed the canon, even though it was based on previous collections, chose some books rather than others and decided to put them in a particular order. This is, in fact, what anyone who constructs a text must do: collect certain literary materials and put them together according to a conscious, planned architecture. This architecture is not that of the first redaction of the individual texts which contribute to the constitution of the canon. b) There is a theological unity in the canon which lies, in the final analysis, in the fact of being holy scripture, "word of God," and thus necessarily a unity.

A canon, like any other text, implies the context of a religious system in which it locates itself and an "author" who creates the text as an act of communication towards the receiver of the message. It also implies a project or strategy, on the part of the author of the canon, with regard to the receiver.

---

[30]Rom. 11:26; cfr. Mishnah Sanhedrin 10:1: "All Israel has part to the world to come."

It is true, however, that the creation of a canon is particular in that it consists, essentially, of the recognition of the fact that the texts included are the "word of God." And it is also true that the receivers of the canon are all those who belong to the religious system, including the "author," since, according to those who created the canon, it is God himself who speaks: the New Testament is Holy Scripture. Thus in the minds of those who formulated it, the canon consists of an act of recognition and of acceptance, not an act of literary invention or religious strategy. But this conviction cannot, however, dispose of the bare fact that someone chose the texts and organized them according to a specific literary architecture and had in mind a religious project with regard to a precise receiver of the message, thus qualifying himself for the title of "author" of this text, the canon. The creation of a new canon of holy Christian writings is, moreover, only possible and can only function on the basis of a particular religious system which operates according to particular theological principles.

The creation of the canon presupposes an hermeneutic. It presents 27 early Christian texts as valid for all time. This is possible only if it is believed that what was written in the *hic et nunc* is valid for all time and that what was understandable in the *hic et nunc* will always be understandable. In reality, whoever created the canon did not think in these terms. His conviction was that it was the Spirit of the risen Christ who spoke through the 27 texts and that this Spirit was consistent both with the ideas of God and the ideas of the Jesus who had actually lived in Palestine. Once again, we find that the creation of the New Testament was the fruit of the fundamental early Christian belief that the Spirit of God was present in the church and permitted a full understanding of the truth. As we have seen, all the early Christian writings, although they contain an absolutely essential reference to their origins, do not describe the origins. They do not include a historical representation of the origins. The origins remain in obscurity, implicit and not transmitted. They appear in the early Christian writings only as evocation and memory, as refraction and allusion, as an object of regret or debate. The early Christian writings are born out of the present, not the past. Their source is in the present. They are the result of the claim to the possession of a pneumatic wisdom, of a present, direct revelation on the part of the Spirit of God and/or of Christ. In some ways, this is no different from Josephus' belief that the biblical writings were faithful representations of historical events of the past because they were written by prophets who, having divine inspiration, had an exact knowledge also of the past.[31]

---

[31]Contra Apionem 1, 8.

The early church was aware of the transformation at the heart of early Christianity but it perceived it as the result of a deeper understanding through the Holy Spirit. To the historian, however, the transformation appears not only as evolution, but also as discontinuity. The early Christian writings are a product of different religious systems. Each of them represented and reformulated the origins and the previous phases in the light of specific moments of the transformation and of the religious system to which they belonged. These different transitions implicate discontinuities: from a form of Judaism to non-Judaism; from the Jesus movement to Christianity; from a movement embedded in Jewish culture to fusion with Hellenistic culture; from the expectation of the imminent reign of God to the reality of a church which embraced all peoples and which removed the final coming to a distant future. From living *as if* this world did *not* exist to the project of Christianization.

(translated by Patrick Leech)

9

Anti-Semitism in Saint John's Gospel

William A. Johnson
Brandeis University

One of the unanticipated benefits of teaching at Brandeis University is the almost daily opportunity to exchange ideas with Professor Marvin Fox. And because our philosophical and theological training has been somewhat similar, we have, upon several occasions, offered joint-courses, cross-listed in the Departments of Philosophy and Near Eastern and Jewish Studies. We have taught together a course entitled 20th Century Religious Thought (Jewish and Christian) and another time a seminar entitled Advanced Studies in the Philosophy of Religion (Theodicy and the Problem of Evil). It was in the context of the 20th Century Religious Thought course that Professor Fox referred in passing, in an almost incidental remark, to the anti-Semitism of the Christian Gospels. I had not thought of the Gospels from that perspective before, and was astonished that he could make that statement. But, of course, his remark was not only accurate but prescient. Contemporaneous with his comment there appeared a spate of books corroborating his contention, including Markus Barth, *Jesus the Jew* (1978); William D. Davies, *The Gospel and the Land: Early Christianity and Jewish Territorial Doctrine* (1974); Rosemary Ruether, *Faith and Fratricide: The Theological Roots of Anti-Semitism* (1974); E. P. Sanders, *Paul and Palestinian Judaism: A Comparison of Patterns of Religion* (1977); Samuel Sandmel, *Anti-Semitism in the New Testament?* (1978); Krister Stendahl, *Paul Among Jews and Gentiles* (1976); A. Davies (ed.) *Anti-Semitism and the Foundations of Christianity* (1979); John Koenig, *Jews and Christians in*

Dialogue (1979); G. Vermes, Jesus the Jew: A Historian's Reading of the Gospels (1981), et. al.

The essay which follows is a direct consequence of Professor Fox's comment on the anti-Semitism of the Christian Gospels.

An initial distinction must be made between anti-Judaism and anti-Semitism. Anti-Judasim may be defined as a set of beliefs asserting the inauthenticity of the spiritual and theological claims of Judaism; anti-Semitism is a combination of hostile beliefs and actions regarding the Jews.[1] To analyze properly the nature and extent of anti-Semitism in John's Gospel, I shall employ an exegetical method suggested first by Samuel Sandmel and E. P. Sanders.[2] They argue that given the conglomeration of material about Jesus in the early church one ought to begin one's study with what is "relatively secure," that is, the text itself. The exposition which follows is based upon the assumption that John's Gospel reflects the Christian side of the Jewish-Christian controversy at about A.D. 100. The exposition of John's Gospel provides the reader with a clarity and a precision regarding the character of anti-Semitism in the Gospel that one would not otherwise possess.

This paper will conclude with an analysis of the theological claims of the Gospel regarding "the Jews."

I. Exposition of the Text of the Gospel of John

In Matthew, Mark and Luke, the opponents of Jesus are the Pharisees, scribes, priests and elders. In John's Gospel, they are collectively and indiscriminately "the Jews." The phrase "the Jews" becomes a convenient term for the "unbelievers" and "the enemies of God," though it must be acknowledged that there is also some attempt to designate the Jews as a regional group, e.g., Judeans rather than Samaritans, and sometimes, though rarely, as the Jewish leaders rather than all of the Jews. Although the meaning may vary from passage to passage, the characterization of "the Jews" as the opponents of Jesus establishes John's Gospel as the most overtly anti-Semitic of the Gospels.

In the Synoptic Gospels Jesus' life reaches its climax in his death and resurrection. The controversies involved in his ministry are about

---

[1]John G. Gager, The Origins of Anti-Semitism, New York: Oxford University Press, 1985, Chapter 1, pp. 13-23; also Rosemary Ruether, Faith and Fratricide, New York: Seabury Press, 1973, who argues (p. 3f) that anti-Judaism constantly takes social expression in anti-Semitism.

[2]Samuel Sandmel, Anti-Semitism in the New Testament?, Philadelphia: Fortress Press, 1978; E.P. Sanders, Jesus and Judaism, Philadelphia: Fortress Press, 1985.

his actions, his teachings and his uncustomary manner of dealing with sinners and outcasts. In John's Gospel, one senses that he is already the resurrected Christ, and the controversies in the Gospel involve who he is, rather than what he has done or said. John asserts in the first chapter of the Gospel that Jesus is the Logos, the God who has come to earth in human form. Christians of that time (about the year A.D. 100) presumably are affirming that Jesus is both the Messiah and the Logos of God. The opponents of the Christians are those who contend that Jesus is neither the Messiah nor the eternal Logos. Therefore, some kind of replacement theory is operative within the Gospel of John in which the Jews have nothing but a negative status before God. "The Jews" reject Jesus because of their spiritual blindness and their failure to understand his divine nature. The anti-Judaism in the Gospel of John is nowhere stronger than in Chapter 8.

The Pharisees assert that they are the children of Abraham. Jesus replies as follows:

> You are of your father the devil, and your will is to do your father's desires. He was a murderer from the beginning, and has nothing to do with the truth, because there is no truth in him. When he lies, he speaks according to his own nature, for he is a liar and the father of lies. But, because I tell the truth, you do not believe me.
>
> 8:44, 45

This is an extreme statement: the contention is that the Jews have never worshipped God; their rejection of Jesus is indicative of their outcast status, their father is not God, but the devil. The Jews lack any valid religious insight because they have rejected the Christian contention about the Messianic and divine status of Jesus.

The prologue of the Gospel identifies Jesus as the Incarnate One; the divine Logos "became flesh" and "dwelt among us" (1:14). Jesus had come "to his own home, but his own people received him not" (1:11). The "law was given through Moses; grace and truth came through Jesus Christ" (1:17).

After the initial theological proclamation of the Gospel of John the narrative begins with the Jews sending priests to John to attempt to find out who he is. John the Baptist tells them that he is not the Christ nor Elijah, nor the prophet, but "the voice of one crying in the wilderness" (1:23a), and he adds, in a manner directly relating his remarks to the Jewish prophetic tradition "Make straight the way of the Lord, as the prophet Isaiah said" (1:23b). The Pharisees asked him why then was he baptizing, and he answered "I baptize with water; but among you stands one whom you do not know, even he who comes after me, the thong of whose sandal I am not worthy to untie" (1:26, 27).

Jesus is recognized by John as "the lamb of God who takes away the sin of the world" (1:29). John himself did not know him, but he came baptizing with water, "that he might be revealed to Israel" (1:31). Jesus will however baptize with the Holy Spirit, a mark of Jesus' character as the "Son of God" (1:34). Two disciples then left John the Baptist and became followers of Jesus. They called Jesus "Rabbi," and identified him as the Messiah (1:41). Philip, who came from Bethsaida, the same city as Andrew and Peter, told Nathaniel that "we have found him of whom Moses in the law and the prophets wrote, Jesus of Nazareth, the son of Joseph" (1:45). Nathaniel recognized Jesus as "Rabbi, you are the Son of God! You are the king of Israel" (1:49). Jesus promised Nathaniel that he would see greater things: "You will see heaven opened, and the angels of God ascending and descending upon the Son of man" (1:51).

The "greater things" are signs of Jesus' miraculous power, the first expression of which takes place at the marriage feast in Cana, in Galilee, where Jesus turned water into wine: "This, the first of his signs...manifested his glory, and his disciples believed in him" (2:11).

Jesus then went to Jerusalem to celebrate the passover. He drove the money-changers out of the temple (2:14-16), because he would not allow them to make his "Father's house a house of trade" (2:16). His disciples remembered the Psalmist's statement "Zeal for they house will consume me" (Psalm 69:9). The Jews sought for a sign about the temple, and Jesus told them "Destroy this temple, and in three days I will raise it up" (2:19). Many believed in Jesus because "of the signs which he did" when he was in Jerusalem at the Passover feast (2:23), "but Jesus did not trust himself to them (2:24) because he knew what was in man" (2:25).

Nicodemus, a man of the Pharisees, is introduced in Chapter 3. He sought for counsel from Jesus, whom he calls "Rabbi, a teacher sent from God." He acknowledged that "no one can do the signs you do, unless God is with you" (3:2). Jesus taught Nicodemus that the kingdom of God is dependent upon rebirth "unless one is born anew, he cannot enter the kingdom of God" (3:3). Nicodemus misunderstood what he meant by "rebirth," which prompted Jesus' answer "Truly, truly, I say to you, unless one is born of water and the Spirit, he cannot enter the kingdom of God" (3:5). Although Nicodemus was a teacher of Israel, he did not understand Jesus' teaching: "We speak of what we know, and bear witness to what we have seen; but you do not receive our testimony" (3:11). Jesus told him of heavenly things because he (the Son of man) has "descended from heaven" (3:13). Reference is made to Moses, who "lifted up the serpent in the wilderness"; the Son of man must also "be lifted up," (3:14) so "that whoever believes in him may have eternal life" (3:16). The reference to God's only Son in the oft-quoted passage in 3:16 makes it clear that the only way to God is through Jesus, "the only Son of God" Those who do not believe in Jesus are condemned; "he is condemned already" (3:18), the writer of the Gospel asserts.

John the Baptist recognized his subordinate position in relation to Jesus the Christ (3:28), and announced that "He must increase, but I must decrease" (3:30). John the Baptist then presents a sophisticated theological assertion about the relationship of God the Father to God the Son, in which he contends that "He who believes in the Son has eternal life; he who does not obey the Son shall not see life, but the wrath of God rests upon him" (3:36).

Jesus next passed through Samaria, a place of special animosity for the Jews. Jesus asked a Samaritan woman for a drink of water. She said to him, "How is it that you, a Jew, ask a drink of me, a woman of Samaria?" The writer of the Gospel explains that the "Jews have no dealings with Samaritans." Jesus replied, "If you knew...who it is that is asking of you, 'give me a drink,' you would have asked him, and he would have given you living water (4:10). Jesus explained that the water that he will give "will become...a spring of water welling up to eternal life" (4:14). Jesus goes on to announce to her that "the hour is coming when neither on this mountain (Mount Gerizim) nor in Jerusalem (Mount Zion) will you worship the Father" (4:21). Rather, "You worship what you do not know; we worship what we know" (4:22). The Messiah has come: "I who speak to you am he" (4:26).

The disciples then sought to get Jesus to eat something (4:31). But Jesus has another food to eat, "of which you do not know (4:32)...my food is to do the will of him who sent me, and to accomplish his works" (4:34). Many Samaritans thereupon believed Jesus to be "the Savior of the world" (4:43). When Jesus returned to Cana, in Galilee, he healed the ill son of an official from a distance (4:46-53), the second sign of Jesus' public ministry.

What follows in Chapter 5 is a Sabbath controversy. Jesus healed a man at the pool of Bethzatha who had been sick for thirty-eight years; this was the third sign of Jesus' ministry (5:2-9). The healed man immediately took up his pallet and walked. The Jews reminded him that it was not lawful to bear a burden on the Sabbath. The man did not know at first who had healed him (5:13) but Jesus found him in the temple, and said to him "See you are well, sin no more, that nothing worse befall you" (5:14). Then the man told the Jews who it was who had healed him. And it was because of this miracle of healing that "the Jews persecuted Jesus." Jesus said to them "My Father is working still, and I am working" (5:17), after which, the text tells us, the Jews sought even more to kill him, not only because he broke the laws of the

Sabbath, but also because he called God his father, "making himself equal with God" (5:18).

The identification of the Father and the Son is made extremely clear in the 5th Chapter of John's Gospel:

> The Son can do nothing of his own accord, but only what he sees the Father doing....As the Father raises the dead and gives them life, so also the Son gives life to whom he will. The Father judges no one, but has given all judgement to the Son, that all may honor the Son, even as they honor the Father. He who does not honor the Son does not honor the Father who sent him.
>
> 5:19-47

The sixth chapter begins with the account of Jesus feeding the five thousand, which took place at the time of the Passover, "the feast of the Jews" (6:1-14), which is the fourth sign of Jesus' miraculous ministry. The people responded to the sign which Jesus had done with the words "This is indeed the prophet who is to come into the world" (6:14). The people then wised to make Jesus king (6:15), which action prompted Jesus to withdraw to the hills. The author of the Gospel presumable attempts to deny that Jesus is a political figure. Jesus then is reported to walk on the water (6:16-21).

The people got into the boats and went to Capernaum, seeking Jesus, and asked him (addressing him as Rabbi), "when did you come here?" (6:25). Jesus' answer is in the form of a theological assertion:

> Truly, truly, I say to you, you seek me, not because you saw signs, but because you ate your fill of the loaves. Do not labor for the food which perishes, but for the food which endures to eternal life, which the Son of man will give to you, for on him has God the Father set his seal.
>
> 6:26, 27

The people ask him, "What must we do, to be doing the work of God?" (6:28). Jesus' response is again in the form of a theological affirmation: "This is the work of God, that you believe in him whom he has sent." They then asked him what sign he would do so that he would believe in him, such as the sign of the manna given by God in the wilderness (6:31). Jesus informed the people that it was not Moses who gave them the bread from heaven, but God, "my Father," as Jesus calls him, it is he who "gives you the true bread from heaven" (6:32). "For the bread of God is that which comes down from heaven, and gives life to the world" (6:33). Jesus then clarified his utterances for his audience: "I am the bread of life; he who comes to me shall not hunger, and he who believes in me shall never thirst" (6:35). His relationship to the Father is made even more intimate: "All that the Father gives me will come to me; and him who comes to me I will not cast out" (6:37). "For this is the will of my Father, that everyone who sees the Son and believes in him should have eternal life" (6:40).

"The Jews" are then provoked to wonder what Jesus meant when he said that he is "the bread which came down from heaven." They appeared to recognize him as the son of Joseph, and they reported that they knew his parents. Again, Jesus' response to their questionings is in the form of a theological affirmation: "No one can come to me unless the Father who sent him draws him" (6:44a) and "Everyone who has heard and learned from the Father comes to me" (6:45b). And the distinctions are drawn more sharply between the old and the new: "Your fathers ate the manna in the wilderness, and they died. This is the bread which comes down from heaven, that a man may eat of it and not die" (6:49, 50).

Again, "the Jews" are confused and ask how this man could give his flesh to eat. Jesus responded: "Truly, truly, I say to you, unless you eat the flesh of the Son of man and drink his blood, you have no life in you" (6:53). Some of his disciples left him at this time because they realized that the sayings of Jesus were "hard" and difficult to accept. Jesus recognized that there were some who did not believe in his mission in the world, and that there would be one who would betray him. (6:64.71). Jesus asked his twelve disciples if they too wished to leave him. Peter affirmed for them all that they believed and had come to recognize him as "the Holy One of God" (6:69).

Jesus decided to remain in Galilee and not to go to Judea "because the Jews (there) sought to kill him" (7:1). The Feast of Tabernacles was at hand. Jesus' brothers urged him to go to Judea so that his disciples might "see the works you are doing" (7:3). Jesus replied, "My time has not yet come...(the world) hates me because I testify of it that its works are evil" (7:6, 7). He remained in Galilee, but later went up to the feast, though he did so "not publicly, but privately" (7:10). "The Jews" were looking for him, and "for fear of the Jews no one spoke openly of him" (7:13).

About the middle of the Feast, Jesus went up to the Temple and taught. The Jews marveled at this saying, because he had not studied. Jesus responded "My teaching is not mine, but his who sent me" (7:17). And again, "Did not Moses give you the law? Yet none of you keeps the law. Why do you seek to kill me?" (7:19). The people answered, "You have a demon! Who is seeking to kill you?" (7:20). Jesus said, "I did one deed and you all marvel at it." He went on to assert that the Jews practiced circumcision even on the Sabbath, but that they are angry with him "because on the Sabbath I made a man's whole body well" (7:23).

Some of the people of Jerusalem wondered why the authorities did not kill Jesus because he was speaking openly in the Temple. Do the authorities believe that Jesus is really the Christ? (7:26). But they all know where he came from. The Christ would presumably be someone unknown. Jesus responded to this line of questionings by asserting (in the Temple) that "You know me, and you know where I come from. But I have not come of my own accord; he who sent me is true, and him you do not know" (7:28).

At that time an attempt was made to arrest him, but the arrest did not take place because "his hour had not yet come" (7:30). Many people believed in him, but they also wondered whether the Christ when he appeared will do more signs than this man (7:31).

The chief priests and the Pharisees sent officers to arrest him. Jesus then said "I shall be with you a little longer, and then I go to him who sent me" (7:33). The Jews did not understand where they would seek him and not find him, wondered aloud whether Jesus intended "to go to the Dispersion among the Greeks and teach the Greeks" (7:35).

On the last day of the feast, Jesus stood up and proclaimed that "If any one thirst, let him come to me and drink" (7:37). And he then promised that the Spirit will come when he himself is glorified (7:39).

Those words provoked a discussion among the people whether Jesus was a prophet or the Christ ("the Christ who is descended from David and comes from the village of Bethlehem"). The division among the people about the person of Jesus provoked some to want to arrest him. None of the officers laid hands on him, which prompted the chief priests and the Pharisees to rebuke them. The officers responded by saying that "No man ever spoke like this man" (7:40). The Pharisees replied "Are you led astray, you also? Have any of the authorities or of the Pharisees believed in him? But this crowd, who do not know the law, are accursed" (7:48, 49).

Nicodemus reappeared again at this point in the narrative, and protested that no man may be judged without a hearing. Their reply was that no prophet was to come from Galilee. (7:52).

(Chapter 8:1-11 is the account of the woman taken in adultery, which is omitted from the RSV and other modern translations of John's Gospel and put into a footnote. The normative text begins again at 8:12.)

Jesus announced "I am the light of the world, he who follows me will not walk in darkness, but will have the light of life" (8:12). The Pharisees replied, "You are bearing witness to yourself; your testimony is not true" (8:13). Jesus answered that he is bearing witness to himself, but his testimony is true, "for I know whence I have come and whither I am going, but you do not know whence I came or whither I am going" (8:14). And again, "In your law it is written that the testimony of two men is true" (the required number of valid witnesses), Jesus asserted that he had the requisite number, that is, Jesus and the God who sent Jesus: "In your law it is written that the testimony of two men is true; I bear witness to myself, and the Father who sent me bears witness to me" (8:18). They did not understand, "Where is your Father?" Jesus answered, "If you knew me, you would know my Father also" (8:19). He spoke these words in the treasure, as he taught in the temple. But no one arrested Jesus, because "his hour had not yet come" (8:20).

Jesus spoke again, "I go away, and you will seek me and die in your sin; where I am going you cannot come" (8:21). The Jews again did not understand him, thinking that he might be saying that he was going to kill himself. Jesus explained to them what he meant: "You are from below, I am from above; you are of the world, I am not of this world....You will die in your sins unless you believe that I am he" (8:23, 24). They asked him again, "Who are you?" He answered, "What I have told you from the beginning...he who sent me is true, and I declare to the world what I have heard from him" (8:25, 26). The author of the Gospel comments that they did not understand "that he spoke to them of the Father" (8:27). Jesus went on, "When you have lifted up the Son of man, then you will know that I am he and that I do nothing on my own authority, but speak thus as the Father taught me" (8:28). Many believed in him as a result of these words.

Jesus now addressed the Jews "who had believed in him": "If you continue in my word, you are truly my disciples and you will know the truth" (8:31, 32). They answered him in what would seem to be an appropriate way: "We are descendents of Abraham, and have never been in bondage to anyone" (8:33). He replied, "Everyone who commits a sin is a slave to sin....I know that you are descendents of Abraham; yet you seek to kill me....You do what you have heard from your father" (8:34-38). They responded to Jesus, "Abraham is our Father." He answered, "If you were Abraham's children, you would do what Abraham did, but now you seek to kill me, a man who has told you the truth which I heard from God (8:40). And then these astonishing words, "You are of your father the devil, and your will is to do your father's desires" (8:44).

The Jews believed that Jesus was either a Samaritan or possessed by a demon. Jesus answered, "I have not a demon; but I honor my Father, and you dishonor me...." (8:49). "If anyone keeps my word, he will never see death" (8:51b). The Jews responded by saying that Abraham had died, as had the prophets, therefore how could Jesus speak of never seeing death? Jesus answered by saying that they did not understand that is God who glorified him, the God who he knows (8:55). As well, Abraham rejoiced that "he was to see my day, he saw it and was glad"

(8:56). That saying confused the Jews even more because Jesus was not yet fifty years old and Abraham had lived hundreds of years earlier. The reply was "Truly, truly, I say to you, before Abraham was, I am" (8:58). As a consequence of this saying, they took up stones to throw at him; "but Jesus hid himself, and went out of the temple" (8:59).

Jesus proceeded to heal a blind man on the Sabbath, (9:1-17) which was the fifth sign. To heal on the Sabbath provoked a controversy, "This man is not from God, for he does not keep the Sabbath" (9:16a). Others were impressed with the signs that Jesus had done. "The Jews" did not believe that the man had been blind, and asked his parents: "Is this your son, who you say was born blind? How then does he now see?" The parents answered that this was indeed their blind son who could now see. But how it happened they did not know, "Nor do we know who opened his eyes" (9:21). The parents "feared the Jews," because "the Jews had already agreed that if any one should confess him to be the Christ he was to be put out of the synagogue" (9:22). They then went again to the man who had been blind and said to him, "Give God the praise, we know this man to be a sinner" (9:24). But the healed man affirmed that it was Jesus who had healed him, and remarked to the Jews: "Do you too want to become his disciples?" (9:27b). They reviled him saying: "You are his disciple, but we are disciples of Moses," and they added, "We know that God has spoken to Moses, but as for this man, we do not know where he comes from" (9:28, 29). The man replied: "Never since the world began has it been heard that anyone opened the eyes of a man born blind. If this man were not from God, he could do nothing" (9:32, 33). They answered him that he was born in sin and therefore was not in any condition to teach them; "and they cast him out" (9:34). Jesus heard that he had been cast out and asked him: "Do you believe in the Son of man?" He answered: "Who is he, sir, that I may believe in him?" Jesus said, "You have seen him, and it is he who speaks to you." The man said, "I believe," and he worshipped Jesus (9:35-38). Jesus said, "For judgment I came into this world, that those who do not see may see, and that those who see may become blind" (9:39).

The 10th Chapter of the Gospel of John begins with Jesus' teaching about the "sheepfold," or the true people of God. The true shepherd of the sheep enters by the door, and does not climb in another way (10:3-6). Jesus described himself as the "door of the sheep" (10:7), everyone who came before him were "thieves and robbers." Jesus is "the door," only those who enter by him will be saved (10:9). The thief came only to steal and kill and destroy. Jesus came so that they may have life. Jesus is "the good shepherd." The good shepherd lays down his life for the sheep (10:11). There are other sheep that are not of this fold (the

Gentiles); they too must be brought into the one fold, so that there will be one flock and one shepherds (10:16). Jesus then announced that the Father loved him "because I lay down my life, that I may take it again" (10:17). "...This charge I have received from my Father" (10:18b).

Once again these words provoked division among the Jews. Some thought that he was possessed of a demon, others said that a demon could not open the eyes of the blind (10:20, 21).

Next, there is the account of the Feast of the Dedication at Jerusalem in the winter. The Jews asked him, as Jesus was walking in the temple in the portico of Solomon (10:23) "How long will you keep us in suspense? If you are the Christ, tell us plainly" (10:24). Jesus answered, "I told you, and you do not believe...you do not believe, because you do not belong to my sheep" (10:26). And then what follows are the most astonishing words of all:

> My sheep hear my voice, and I know them, and they follow me; and I give them eternal life, and they shall never perish, and no one shall snatch them out of my hand. My Father, who has given them to me, is greater than all, and no one is able to snatch them out of my Father's hand. I and the Father are one.
>
> 10:27-30

The Jews again wanted to stone him. Jesus asked them for which of the many good works that he had done did they want to stone him? (10:32). They replied, "It is not for a good work that we stone you but for blasphemy; because you, being a man, make yourself God" (10:33). Jesus answered them that is it blasphemy for Jesus to assert that he is the Son of God if he was consecrated by the Father to do so (10:36)? He admonished them to believe the good works that he has done, "That you may know and understand that the Father is in me and I am in the Father (10:38). Again, the Jews tried to arrest him, but he escaped from their hands (10:39).

He retired to the place across the Jordan where John the Baptist had first baptized. Many there affirmed that everything that John the Baptist had said about Jesus was true, and many believed in him. (10:41, 42).

While Jesus was there, Lazarus became ill in Bethany which was near Jerusalem. Lazarus' sisters, Mary and Martha, sent word to Jesus that he ought to come to heal him. Jesus did not come immediately to Bethany, instead remained for two more days in Trans-Jordan. The Gospel reported that he knew that he (that is, the Son of God) would be "glorified" by Lazarus' death. After two days, he sent his disciples to Judea, but they were reluctant to go because "the Jews were but now seeking to stone you..." (11:10). Jesus attempted to assure his disciples by telling them that he would waken Lazarus from the sleep that he had fallen into (11:11). He told them that Lazarus was dead, and that he was prepared to go to him. When he arrived in Bethany, he discovered that Lazarus had been already dead and in his tomb for four days. Jesus assured Martha that her brother would rise again, not at the final resurrection, but soon. Jesus announced that he was "the resurrection and the life: he who believes in me, though he die, yet shall he live, and whoever lives and believes in me shall never die" (11:25, 26). Martha believed, and affirmed that Jesus was "the Christ, the Son of God, he who is coming into the world" (11:27).

Mary came to Jesus and fell at his feet saying that if Jesus (referring to him as Lord) had been here, her brother would not have died. Jesus saw that she was with "the Jews" who were there in the house, consoling her, and "he was deeply moved in spirit and troubled" (11:33). And he wept (11:35). Some of the Jews remarked that Jesus loved Lazarus greatly; others said "Could not he who opened the eyes of the blind man have kept Lazarus from dying?" (11:37).

At the tomb Jesus called Lazarus to come from the tomb, and the dead man came out, "his hands and feet bound with bandages, and his face wrapped with a cloth." Jesus commanded them to "unbind him, and let him go" (11:44). Lazarus' miraculous resurrection is the sixth sign that Jesus performed to the glory of God. The miracle took place so that the people standing by the tomb "may believe that thou didst send me" (11:42).

Now many more Jews believed in him (11:45). But the chief priests and the Pharisees were concerned what they should do and gathered together the council: "What are we to do? For this man performs many signs. For if we let him go on thus, every one will believe in him, and the Romans will come and destroy both our holy place and our nation" (11:47, 48). Caiaphas, the high priest, rebuked them, "You know nothing at all; you do not understand that it is expedient for you that one man should die for the people, and that the whole nation should not perish" (11:51). John commented on this profound passage, telling his readers that Jesus "should die for the nation, and not for the nation only, but to gather into one the children of God who are scattered abroad" (11:52). That cryptic affirmation of the role of Jesus was followed by the statement that from that day the Pharisees and the council "took counsel how to put him to death" (11:53). Jesus could no longer go openly among the Jews, but went with his disciples to a town called Ephraim, in the country near the wilderness.

The Passover of the Jews was again at hand. The Jews wondered whether he would come to the feast. The chief priests and the

Pharisees had given the order that "if any one knew where he was, he should let them know, so that they might arrest him" (11:57).

Six days before the Passover, Jesus came to Bethany, the city where he had raised Lazarus from the dead. There Mary anointed his feet, in the presence of Judas Iscariot, who protested against the cost of the ointment: "Why was this ointment not sold for three hundred denarii and given to the poor?" Judas apparently was an unsavory character who did not really care for the poor, and had himself stolen from the money box.

Many Jews came to Bethany to see Jesus and also Lazarus ("whom he had raised from the dead"). The chief priests planned to put Lazarus to death too, "because on account of him many of the Jews were going away and believing in Jesus" (12:11). On the next day, a great crowd heard that Jesus was coming to Jerusalem and they went out to meet him; "they heard that he had done this sign," (12:18), that is, the raising of Lazarus. The people took branches of palm trees and went out to meet Jesus crying: "Blessed be he who comes in the name of the Lord, even the King of Israel" (12:13). The Pharisees were perplexed, and said, "You see that you can do nothing; look the world has come after him" (12:19).

Jesus tells us that his soul is troubled (12:27). But he would not ask the Father to save him from this hour. Jesus acknowledged that it was "for this purpose" that this hour had come. A voice was heard from heaven, presumably that of an angel, a voice not for Jesus' benefit but rather for the crowd (12:30).

Jesus said: "Now is the judgment of this world, now shall the ruler of this world be cast out; and I, when I am lifted up from the earth, will draw all men to myself" (12:31, 32). The crowd responded that they "have heard from the law that the Christ remains forever. How can you say that the Son of man must be lifted up? Who is this Son of man?" (12:34). Jesus referred to himself as "the light" which is with you a little longer. "Walk while you have the light, lest the darkness overtake you" (12:35). Jesus then hid from them. And although he had done many signs before them, "yet they did not believe in him" (12:37). Reference is then made to the prophet Isaiah, referring to the lack of recognition of Jesus' Messiahship as the fulfillment of the passage in Isaiah 53: "Lord, who has believed our report, and to whom has the arm of the Lord been revealed?"

Many of the authorities now believed in him, "but for fear of the Pharisees they did not confess it, lest they should be put out of the synagogue: for they loved the praise of men more than the praise of God" (12:42, 43). Jesus cried out and said, "He who believes in me, believes not in me but in him who sent me. And he who sees me sees him who sent me" (12:44, 45).

The narrative of the Last Supper begins in the Thirteenth Chapter. John adds an account of the washing of the disciples' feet (13:3-11), and a discourse on humility (13:12-16). There follows the announcement that one would betray him, "he to whom I shall give this morsel when I have dipped it" (13:26). He gave it to Judas Iscariot; Satan entered into him, and he said to him, "What you are going to do, do quickly" (13:27).

The disciples were confused about what would happen to Jesus. Jesus ("the Son of man") will be glorified, and in him God will also be glorified (13:31). But he said to "the Jews," "where he is going they cannot come" (13:33). And he gave them a new commandment "to love one another; even as I have loved you, that you also love one another" (13:34). Simon Peter claimed that he was prepared to lay down his life for his Lord; Jesus told him that "the cock will not crow, till you have denied me three times" (13:38).

Chapters 14, 15, 16, and 17 are traditionally referred to as Jesus' "Farewell Discourses." Chapter 14 affirms that Jesus is "the way, the truth and the life," and that "no one comes to the Father" but by Jesus (14:6). The relationship between the Father and the Son has now been firmly established: "If you had known me, you would have known my Father also; henceforth you know him and have seen him" (14:7), and again: "Do you not believe that I am in the Father and the Father in me?" (15:10).

Jesus promised that the Counselor would come from the Father, who is the Spirit of truth, and the Spirit will dwell with you and in you (14:17). After Jesus' departure from this world, he will go to be with the Father: "In that day you will know that I am in my Father and you in me, and I in you" (14:20). The Counselor, the Holy Spirit, whom the Father will send in the name of Jesus, "will teach you all things" (14:26), and bring about an attitude of peace: "Peace I leave with you; my peace I give to you; not as the world gives do I give to you. Let not your hearts be troubled, neither let them be afraid" (14:27). The ruler of this world is coming, and Jesus must go away soon, confident that he had done "as the Father had commanded me" (14:31a).

The 15th Chapter begins with the discourse of "the true vine" which Jesus identifies with himself: "I am the vine, you are the branches. He who abides in me, and I in him, he it is that bears much fruit, for apart from me you can do nothing" (15:5). Jesus instructed his disciples to follow his commandments, and if one did so: "you will abide in my love" (15:10a). Anticipating his death, Jesus said, "Greater love has no man than this, that a man lay down his life for his friends" (15:13).

Jesus told his listeners that "the world may hate you," and that you may be persecuted "on my account, because they do not know him who sent me" (15:21). Therefore, any one who hates Jesus also hates the Father (15:23).

Chapter 16 continues the Farewell Discourse:

> I have said all this to you to keep you from falling away. They will put you out of the synagogues; indeed, the hour is coming when whoever kills you will think he is offering service to God. And they will do this because they have not known the Father, nor me.
>
> 16:1-3

The Counselor will come, but Jesus must depart from this world to allow him to come. "He will convince the world of sin and righteousness and of judgment" (16:8). The Spirit of truth will "guide you into all truth" (16:12). Jesus attempted to explain to his disciples why he must leave them. They did not understand that their initial sorrow would turn into joy (16:20). Jesus promised them that if they would ask anything of the Father, "he will give it to you in my name" (16:23). And he was confident that in the end all would be well: "In the world you will have tribulation; but be of good cheer, I have overcome the world" (16:33).

When Jesus spoke these words, he lifted up his eyes to heaven and said, "Father, the hour has come; glorify thy Son that the Son may glorify thee" (17:1). Jesus prayed for those people whom God had given him, "for they are thine; all mine are thine, and thine are mine, and I am glorified in them" (17:9,10). And he also prayed for those who will believe in him through the word of the disciples (17:20).

Jesus and his disciples then went across the Kidron Valley, where there was a garden, which they entered. Judas knew about the garden because Jesus often met there with his disciples. Judas procured a band of soldiers and some officers from the chief priests and the Pharisees, these carrying "lanterns and torches and weapons" (18:3). Jesus asked them, "Whom do you seek?" They answered, "Jesus of Nazareth." He said, "I am he." Some of them drew back and fell to the ground. Again he asked them, "Whom do you seek?" And again they said, "Jesus of Nazareth." He responded by saying that he had already told them that he was Jesus of Nazareth, and quickly added, "if you seek me, let these men go" (18:8). Simon Peter then cut off the ear of the slave of the high priest. Jesus recognized that the end was near: "shall I not drink the cup which the Father has given me?" (18:11).

The band of soldiers and their captain and the officers of the Jews seized and bound Jesus. They led him to Annas, the father-in-law of Caiaphas, the high priest that year (18:13). When Peter was in the courtyard, Annas questioned Jesus "about his disciples and his teaching" (18:19). Jesus replied, "I have spoken openly to the world; I have always taught in synagogues and in the temple, where all Jews come together; I have said nothing secretly" (18:20). One of the officers struck Jesus saying, "Is that how you answer the high priest?" Jesus answered, "If I have spoken wrongly, bear witness to the wrong; but if I have spoken rightly, why do you strike me?" (18:23). Annas then sent Jesus to Caiaphas, the high priest. (There follows the episode in which Peter denied Jesus). There is no reference to any exchange between Jesus and Caiaphas. He is then led to the praetorium, the official residence of the Roman governor. "They" do not enter the praetorium, "so that they might not be defiled, but might eat the Passover" (18:28). Pilate came out to them and asked, "What accusation do you bring against this man?" (18:29). They replied, "If this man were not an evil doer, we would not have handed him over." Pilate said, "Take him yourselves and judge him by your own law." The Jews then said, "It is not lawful for us to put any man to death," presumably to acknowledge that the Jews, a subject people within the Roman Empire, had no power to execute a criminal. But it is clear that the 18th Chapter of John's Gospel fixes the responsibility for Jesus' death with the Jews.

Pilate called Jesus into the praetorium. (18:33f). He asked him, "Are you the King of the Jews?" Jesus answered, "Do you say this of your own accord, or did others say it to you about me?" (18:34). Pilate replied, "Am I a Jew? Your own nation and the chief priests have handed you over to me. What have you done?" (18:35). Jesus answered, "My kingship is not of this world; if my kingship were of this world, my servants would fight, that I might not be handed over to the Jews; but my kingship is not from the world" (18:36). Pilate responded, "So you are a king?"; to which Jesus replied, "You say that I am a king. For this I was born, and for this I have come into the world, to bear witness to the truth." Pilate asked the immortal question, "What is truth?" (18:38).

Pilate went out to the Jews and told them that he could find no crime in Jesus: "But you have a custom that I should release one man for you at the Passover; will you have me release for you the King of the Jews?" They cried out, "Not this man, but Barabbas." Barabbas was identified as a thief. Pilate then scourged Jesus. The Roman soldiers plaited a crown of thorns and put it on his head. They dressed him in a purple robe, hailed him as "the King of the Jews," and beat him. Pilate again went out again to the Jews, saying, "See, I am bringing him out to you that you may know that I find no crime in him" (19:4). The chief priests and the officers saw him and cried out, "Crucify him; crucify him!" Pilate said, "Take him yourself and crucify him, for I find no crime in him" (19:6).

"The Jews" answered him, "We have a law, and by that law he ought to die, because he has made himself the Son of God" (19:7). Pilate was more afraid, he entered the praetorium and asked Jesus where he came from. But Jesus gave no answer. Angry and upset, Pilate said to Jesus, "You will not speak to me? Do you not know that I have power to release you, and power to crucify you?" (19:10). Jesus responded to the statement by saying, "You would have no power over me unless it had been given you from above; therefore he who delivered me to you has the greater sin" (19:11). Pilate again sought to release Jesus, but the Jews cried out, "If you release this man, you are not Caesar's friend; every one who makes himself a king sets himself against Caesar" (19:12).

Now it was the sixth hour on the day before the Passover. Pilate said, "Behold your King!" They cried out, "Away with him, away with him, crucify him!" Pilate said to them, "Shall I crucify your King?" The chief priests answered, "We have no King but Caesar." Then he handed him over to them to be crucified (19:14-16). They took Jesus to Golgotha and there they crucified him with two others (19:17, 18).

Pilate wrote a title which was placed on the cross, it read, "Jesus of Nazareth, the King of the Jews." Many of the Jews read this title for it was written in Hebrew, Latin, and Greek. The chief priests asked Pilate to change the title to "This man said, I am the King of the Jews," but Pilate refused (19:21, 22).

When the soldiers had crucified Jesus, they divided his clothes into four parts, one for each soldier. His tunic was without a seam, so the soldiers decided not to tear it, but to cast lots for it. This incident fulfilled a scriptural prophecy: "They parted my garments among them, and for my clothes they cast lots" (Exodus 28:32; Psalm 22:18).

John told the account of Mary, Jesus' mother, standing at the cross with the other women. The "beloved disciple" was also present. Jesus entrusted his mother to him. Then, Jesus, knowing that all was finished, said, (to fulfill the Scripture), "I thirst." He drank a spongefull of vinegar on hyssop. He said, "It is finished"; he bowed his head and gave up his spirit (19:29, 30).

"The Jews" asked Pilate that the legs of the three men crucified might be broken in order to prevent the bodies of the three from remaining on the cross into the Sabbath. The soldiers broke the legs of the two crucified with Jesus, but discovering that Jesus was already dead, they did not break his legs (19:31-33). Joseph of Arimathea, a disciple of Jesus, asked Pilate for the body of Jesus, "but secretly, for fear of the Jews" (19:38). Nicodemus aided him (19:39, 40). They laid Jesus in the tomb. (19:40-42).

Chapters 20 and 21 describe the resurrection of Jesus, and although that narrative is not directly related to our subject, it is clear that the supernatural sign of God raising Jesus from the dead is another "stumbling block" for the Jews.

II. Theological Conclusions in John's Gospel Regarding "the Jews"

1. The author of the Gospel of John uses the term "the Jews" almost exclusively throughout the Gospel. By the time of the writing of this Gospel, the distinctions made in the Gospel of Mark among the Jews, of Sadducees, Pharisees, scribes, and Herodians are largely meaningless. The scribes had given way to the Rabbis, the Sadducees had almost disappeared from the Judean scene, the Herodians were never of any importance. Memories of these groups remained within the Christian community, especially the dominant Pharisees. But the author of John's Gospel chooses, most of the time, to include all of the Jews together in one negative grouping, known simply and derisively as "the Jews." That "the Jews" are the enemies of the Christian Church reflects the environment of the author of the Gospel (cf. 2:18; 5:16ff; 6:41, 52; 7:15; 8:52-59; 10:31; 18:36; 20:19). Unlike the Synoptic Gospels within which Jesus is presented disputing the Pharisees, or vigorously opposing the Sadducees, or contradicting the scribes, in John's Gospel, it is "the Jews" which stand over against him and his mission. The term "the Jews," too, stands for such terms as "unbelievers" and the "enemies of God." It is not a part of the Jewish community that wants to kill him, for example, some of the priestly rulers, but "the Jews" in general (5:16ff). The Gospel writer clearly intended to establish a separation between Christians and Jews. This separation already can be seen in an explicit way in the Prologue in Chapter 1, in which the writer states that "He came to his own home, and his people received him not" (1:11).

2. "The Jews" no longer have any but a negative status before God. The Jews have rejected Jesus, but they have also rejected God. No other conclusion can be discovered from an attentive reading of the Gospel than this extreme one. "The Jews" are no longer God's elect; they have lost their status as God's chosen people. The Jewish past of patriarchs and prophets counts for nothing now that Jesus has come. A sampling of texts from the Gospel makes this point explicit: 1:17; 3:18; 5:37-45; 8:39-

47; 10:7-8; and the passage which can be considered as locus classicus for the replacement of "the Jews" by Jesus and his followers: 14:6, 7 (cf. 15:23-25).

3. The God of "the Jews" is now literally the devil. In the dialogue between Jesus and the Pharisees in Chapter 8 (which became dramatically the dialogue between Jesus and "the Jews"), in response to the assertion that they, the Jews, are the children of Abraham, Jesus replied, "You are of your father, the devil, and your will is to do your father's desires" (8:44a). According to this anti-Semitic sentiment, the Jews have never worshipped God. Their father, their God, is the devil. "The Jews'" rejection of Jesus is nothing more than a symptom of their apostate condition from the beginning: "He who is of God hears the words of God; the reason you do not hear them is that you are not of God" (8:47).

4. Jesus and those who love him come "from above"; Moses and his descendants come "from below" (3:5f, 31f). Jesus told Nicodemus of "heavenly things"; "the Jews" have been told "earthly things" and they did not believe them (3:12). No one has seen God but Jesus. The assertion is clear; Jesus had come from the divine realm, the Jews had been excluded from that realm. They do not know God. Only Jesus knows God: "No one has ever seen God; the only Son who is in the bosom of the Father, he has made him known" (1:18; cf. also 3:13). "Before Abraham was, I am" (8:58), Jesus proclaimed. He told his disciple Philip, "He who has seen me has seen the Father" (14:9).

5. Jesus and God are one. Those Jews who do not believe in the divine nature of Jesus do not know God. Jesus is the divine Logos incarnate (1:1-18). Furthermore, Jesus Christ is the Word who was always with God. Through him and only through him, all things have come into existence. The Word has become flesh in the person of Jesus. Throughout his earthly life Jesus is fully divine.

6. Jesus is "the way, the truth and the life," and no one may come to the Father except by Jesus Christ. (14:6, 7). This claim is an exclusivistic one, any association which may have existed between God the Father and "the Jews" is now abrogated. Jesus is now the sole means by which any one can know God; through Jesus Christ one knows God and "has seen him" (14:8). Jesus is "in the Father," and "the Father is in him" (14:10). Furthermore, the authority for the words of Jesus is not his own, but the authority of the Father who "dwells" in Jesus (14:10). Jesus asserted that he goes to prepare a place for those who believe in him (14:2b). But Jesus went further than that, not only does he provide a place, he also becomes the entrance to that place: "I am the door; if any one enters by me he will be saved" (10:9). To love Jesus means that the Father will love him and make his home with him. Jesus is

identified with that home: "If a man loves me, he will keep my word, and my Father will love him, and we will come to him and make our home with him" (14:23). Jesus is "the true vine" (15:1ff). If someone does not abide in Jesus, he is cast forth...thrown into the fire and burned. At this point in the Johannine text we find the most radical expression of the replacement motif; Jesus and his followers (the Church) constitute the final displacement of "the Jews" as the people of God. The Jews are cast off, they wither and die, and ultimately are burned.

The vine imagery is of greatest importance in the Johannine estimation of the Jews. In Paul's use of the vine imagery, Gentile believers were "grafted into a holy root" (Romans 11:16ff). But for John, Jesus is himself the holy root, and his followers are his true branches. Jesus' body, then, becomes the true temple, replacing the temple of the Jews in Jerusalem (2:19f).

7.   Jesus is the Messiah of Jewish expectations; there is no longer any need for the Jews to await the coming of the Messiah. All such anticipation is false. The earliest recorded recognition in the Gospel is of Jesus as the Messiah (1:41). God has sent Jesus to the world so that those who believe in him may have eternal life; (3:16), so that the world through him might be saved (3:17; cf. 17:1-3).

8.   The law of Christ supercedes the law of Moses, and makes it valueless. The Gospel does not admonish any one to obey the law of Moses, rather they are to obey the new law, the new commandment given by Jesus (13:34; 15:10f). No longer is the law given by God at Sinai of any meaning to the followers of Jesus.

9.   The "signs" that Jesus performed in the Gospel demonstrate his divine and supernatural nature. The seven miraculous deeds that Jesus performed in the Gospel confirmed for his followers the extreme supernaturalistic claims made for him. Supernatural deeds depend for their occurrence upon a supernatural figure. John's Gospel is not a narrative of ordinary and natural deeds, but rather of incredible deeds. The Jews who were skeptical about those deeds would also be skeptical about the supernatural claims made about Jesus himself.

10. Jesus is the fulfillment of the promises of Holy Scripture. John explicitly ties events in Jesus' life to passages in the Hebrew Bible. When Jesus entered Jerusalem, he "sat on a young ass," which seemed to refer to Zechariah 9:9 in which the reference is to the King who came "humble and riding on an ass." Other examples are found in 12:38 (Isaiah 53:1); 12:40 (Isaiah 6:10); 13:8 (Deuteronomy 12:12); 12:34 (Psalm 110:4, Isaiah 9:7); 15:1 (Isaiah 5:1-7, Ezekiel 19:10); 19:24 (Exodus 28:32), and so on.

There is an explicit bitterness towards the Jews throughout John's Gospel. Jesus was a Jew, he appeared to be the Messianic figure of ancient Jewish hope, and yet the Jews did not believe in him. Furthermore, Jesus preached in the synagogues and in the Temple. The Christians of John's Gospel appeared frustrated by the animosity of the Jews towards them.

Beyond the scope of this paper is the question of why the Gospel of John is so violently anti-Semitic. It seems clear from the text that the Gospel grew out of a local tension between the Christian community of John and the local synagogue. Professor J. L. Martyn in his *History and Theology of the Fourth Gospel* (1968) has argued that the Johannine community came into existence as a distinct Christian community only after being expelled from a Jewish community.

11. Jesus clearly stands overagainst the popular piety of the Jews. The details in the Gospel about the details of the chief Jewish feasts are an important factor to consider in the study of anti-Semitism. Early in Jesus' public ministry, Jesus cleansed the temple during the Passover holiday (2:13-23). The "bread of life" discourse is given in the synagogue at Capernaum just before the Passover season (6:24-59). The events leading to Jesus' passion in Jerusalem take place during Passover (11:55ff). Jesus addressed the Jews at the temple in Jerusalem at the feast of the Dedication (10:22f). Reference is also made to "the feast of the Jews" (5:1).

The Gospel assumes that the Jewish feasts are important for the life and ministry of Jesus. But Jesus stands overagainst these feasts by interpreting them in terms of himself and his unique role in the world. The feasts are mentioned either to provide a setting for Jesus' teaching (cf. 10:22f), or to exaggerate the differences between the Jewish festivals and Jesus' actions (especially the Passion which is reported in 8 chapters in the Gospel of John).

12. The Jews killed Jesus. The Jews are the ultimate villains, the Christ-killers. The responsibility for the death of Jesus is clearly indicated by John's Gospel. At the conclusion of the narrative of the interrogation of Jesus by Pilate, "the Jews" are singled out as the guilty party: "He (Pilate) said to the Jews, 'Here is your King.' They cried out, 'Away with him, away with him, crucify him!'" (19:14b-15a). After Jesus' death, it is Joseph of Arimathea, who "for fear of the Jews" who takes Jesus' body and lays it in the tomb (19:38-42).

I believe that the Gospel of John is unequivocal in its insistence that with the coming of Jesus, the people of God known as the Jews, have lost all of their ties with God. According to this Gospel the Jews are fully to blame for their apostate state. How different is the affection expressed by Paul towards the Jews in his letter to the Roman Christians, in which he refers to the Jews as "beloved of God for the sake of their forefathers" (Romans 11:28). Paul asserts that finally all of Israel will be saved and will enjoy the fullness of God's mercy (Romans 11:25-32). How much more salutary and Christian is this vision of the ultimate fate of the Jews. And when we accept that vision we can affirm with Paul "O the depth of the riches and wisdom and knowledge of God" (11:33).

10

The New Testament, the Early Church, and Anti-Semitism

John T. Townsend
Episcopal Divinity School

In the past few decades many have written about anti-Semitism[1] in the early Church, particularly as represented in the New Testament. Jewish authors on the subject include Jules Isaac,[2] who was not a New Testament scholar, and Samuel Sandmel,[3] who was. Turning to Christian writers, we immediately think of Rosemary Ruether's book, *Faith and Fratricide*, but we should not overlook the important sequel to her work, *Anti-Semitism and the Foundations of Christianity*, edited by Alan T. Davies.[4] Other writers on the subject include Gregory Baum,[5] John Koenig,[6] John Gager,[7] Lloyd Gaston,[8] Norman A. Beck.[9]

---

[1]It has become customary to distinguish between anti-Judaism and anti-Semitism. The first is supposed to denote hostility to Jews on religious grounds, and the second denotes that the hostility has a racial aspect. In practice, however, racial hostility was generally present to some extent from the time that the Church became predominantly gentile. In this essay, therefore, anti-Semitism denotes hostility to Jews and Judaism generally.

[2]*Jesus and Israel* (New York: Holt, Rinehart and Winston, 1971); *The Teaching of Contempt* (New York: Holt, Rinehart and Winston, 1964).

[3]*Anti-Semitism in the New Testament?* (Philadelphia: Fortress, 1978).

[4]*Faith and Fratricide* (New York: Seabury, 1974); *Anti-Semitism and the Foundations of Christianity* (New York: Paulist, 1979). While both works treat Christian anti-Semitism generally, they both have substantial sections on the New Testament.

[5]*The Jews and the Gospel* (London: Bloomsbury, 1961). For a slight revision of this book, see *Is the New Testament Anti-Semitic?* (New York: Paulist, 1964).

[6]*Jews and Christians in Dialogue: New Testament Foundations* (Philadelphia: Westminster, 1979).

Contributions by the present author include studies on John[10] and Luke-Acts.[11]

The modern study of the history of Christian anti-Semitism generally dates from before the Second World War, when James Parkes published *The Conflict of the Church and the Synagogue* in 1934.[12] Unfortunately Parkes was a lone voice crying for justice. More typical was the work of A. Lukyn Williams,[13] who covered the same material from a very different point of view. According to his introduction, "The origin of this book lies in some lectures given many years ago to a class of young men preparing for Christian work among the Jews." In the last few decades, however, several scholars have come to recognize anti-Semitism in the history of Christian literature for the evil that it is. They include, in addition to those mentioned above, Marcel Simon,[14] Edward H. Flannery,[15] and Shmuel Almog.[16] The most detailed treatment of the subject is *Kirche und Synagogue*, edited by K.H. Rengstorf and S. von Kortzfleisch.[17] The twenty-two specialists, who wrote this two-volume "Handbuch," represent Roman Catholics, Protestants, and Jews. Together they are comprehensive. They cover all Church-Synagogue relations until 1930 and even include special sections on early Syrian, Coptic, Armenian, and Ethiopian traditions.

---

[7]*The Origins of Anti-Semitism* (New York: Oxford, 1983).

[8]Gaston's articles on this subject are collected in *Paul and the Torah* (Vancover: University of British Columbia, 1987). His views are conveniently summarized in Gager, pp. 193-264.

[9]*Mature Christianity* (London: Associated University Presses, 1985).

[10]"The Gospel of John and the Jews," in *Anti-Semitism and the Foundations of Christianity*, pp. 72-97.

[11]"The Date of Luke-Acts," in *Luke-Acts: New Perspectives from the Society of Biblical Literature Seminar*, edited by Charles H. Talbert (New York: Crossroad, 1984), pp. 47-62.

[12]Reprinted by Atheneum (New York, 1985).

[13]*Adversus Judaeos: A Bird's Eye View of Christian Apologiae until the Renaissance* (Cambridge: Univ. Press, 1935).

[14]*Verus Israel: A Study of the Relations between Christians and Jews in the Roman Empire (135-425)*, translated by H. McKeating from the 1964 French edition (New York; Oxford for the Littman library, 1986).

[15]*The Anguish of the Jews: Twenty-Three Centuries of Anti-semitism*, revised and updated (New York: Paulist Press, 1985).

[16]*Antisemitism Through the Ages*, a collection of twenty-six essays edited by Almog and translated from the Hebrew by Nathan H. Reisner (Oxford: Pergamon, 1988).

[17]Stuttgart: Ernst Klett, 1968, 1970. Although the work is certainly scholarly, it occasionally betrays a Christian apologetic bias as in Wm. Mauer's treatment of Luther.

At present there is little need to argue that many parts of the New Testament, like most other early Christian writings, do in fact project an anti-Jewish bias in general and an anti-Pharisaic bias in particular.[18] Evidence for such a bias comes, not only from the study of the New Testament writings themselves, but also from their use throughout the history of the Church as a justification for persecuting Jews. Nor is there even a need to list passages of the New Testament which seem anti-Jewish. That task has already been completed, most recently by Beck. Rather this paper focuses on the following three specific areas:

1. The historical context of early Christian anti-Semitism, particularly in the New Testament.
2. The historical context in later times after Christians had gained political domination over Jews, with special reference to the influence of anti-Semitism in Biblical scholarship during the last two centuries.
3. Some efforts to ease the situation today.

The Rise of New Testament Anti-Semitism

New Testament and other early Christian anti-Jewish polemic falls into three major categories:[19]

1. The exaltation of Jesus toward equality with God together with an insistence that he fulfills Jewish messianic promises.
2. The assertion that Christianity has replaced Judaism.
3. Defamatory polemic, in particular the accusation that the Jews had crucified Jesus.

In regard to the first category of Christian polemic, i.e., the exaltation of Jesus, not everyone would treat it as anti-Jewish. Certainly Christians have a right to define their own beliefs. Even the Christian assertion that Jesus Christ is the equal of God, while totally unacceptable for most Jews, need not have been a conscious expression of hostility either against Judaism or against the Jewish people. There are, however, many who do understand this exaltation of Jesus as spawning Christian persecution of Jews.[20] Certainly many Jews have experienced the traditional Christian exaltation of Jesus in such a way. Here was a belief that few Jews could accept, but of which non-acceptance commonly meant persecution. While Christians may not be expected to alter their christologies, we should recognize that many

---

[18]It is interesting that the one New Testament writer who claims to have been a Pharisee (i.e., the Paul in Phil. 3:5) has nothing negative to say about Pharisees.
[19]See Beck, pp. 283-286.
[20]E.g., Ruether, especially pp. 246-251.

early Christians held what became unorthodox views on the person of Jesus, views that would have been quite unacceptable at any of the first six ecumenical councils, from Nicaea I (325) through Constantinople III (680-81). In particular, we should not assume that any New Testament writer exalted Jesus to equality with God. No New-Testament author ever did so.[21] In fact, the opposite is true. Against those who would accuse the Church of making such a claim (John 5:18), the Fourth Gospel stresses that Jesus only has the authority granted him by God (John 5:19, 30, 36f.; 8:54).[22] Nor is the Fourth Gospel exceptional. Paul clearly states that Christ must be subject to God as the one who shall be all in all (I Cor. 15:28).[23] Somewhat later, the deutero-Pauline epistle to the Colossians cites a hymn according to which Christ is "the first-born of all creation," i.e., a created being as Arius later claimed. Indeed, before the First Council of Nicaea (325) several major Christian writers, such as Justin Martyr, and Clement of Alexandria, Origen, and Hippolytus argued that Jesus, the Divine Word, was a somewhat lesser being than God. Nor did such interpretations of Jesus disappear in 325. Arian views of Jesus remained strong for many years after.[24]

Even the title "God" may not have exalted the risen Christ to a point that would necessarily have forced his followers out of the Jewish community. In the first place, those who wrote the New

---

[21]Later scribes corrected the oversight by adding the so-called Johannine comma, I John 5:7, according to which, "There are three who bear witness in heaven, the Father, the Son, and the Holy Spirit, and these three are one."

[22]Even the words of John 10:30, "I and my Father are one," must be seen in the light of John 17:21, which interprets this oneness as a mystical union like that between Christ and his followers. Against this view, see Jerome H. Neyrey, *John's Christology in Social-Science Perspective* (Philadelphia: Fortress, 1988). Neyrey begins by arguing on the basis of John 5:19-20 that Jesus is equal to God because God has shown Jesus *all* his works and because Jesus' own works therefore exhibit the power of God. Neyrey also argues that Jesus' power to raise the dead suggests equality with God. Within a Jewish context, however, such a conclusion need not have followed. Cf. the ninth-century *Tanhuma* (Buber), *Beha`alotekha*, 15, cited below, where God's sharing this power with Elijah hardly implies full equality with God. As for the assertion in John 5:19-20 that "the Son can do nothing on his own, but only what he sees the Father doing," this may actually imply that the Son is somewhat less than his Father.

[23]Cf. also the creedal formula in Rom. 1:3, according to which, Jesus was only "designated Son of God in power according to the Holy Spirit as a result of (*ex*) his resurrection from the dead."

[24]See George Williams, "Christology and Church-State Relations in the Fourth Century," *Church History*, 20(1951), no. 3, pp. 3-33; no. 4, pp. 3-25, who argues that the political interests of the emperor had more to do with the continuation of Arianism than strictly theological concerns.

Testament tended to avoid this title and used it rarely.[25] The reason may well lie in the nature of the Greek language. Since Greek has no indefinite article, one had two choices in using the title. One might either call Jesus "The God," and so identify him fully with the creator of heaven and earth, or else use "a god," which merely asserts that he is in some sense superhuman. It is the latter which appears in the Fourth Gospel. In the second place, such a usage need not have been anathema to all Jews.[26] In the first century Philo tended to use divine language of Moses; and Josephus, *Ant.* 3:180, referred to Moses as a "divine man" (*theios aner*).[27] Nor were such beliefs confined to Hellenists like Philo. In later times even Rabbinic writings could affirm in so many words that God shared the Divine Glory with Moses by addressing him as "God" (*Elohim*). Thus in the Buber *Tanhuma, Beha`alotekha,* 15, we read:

> What is the meaning (of Ps. 24:10): THE LORD OF HOSTS, HE IS THE KING OF GLORY? That he imparts some of his glory to those who fear him as befits his glory. How? Such a one is called "god" (*elohim*). Thus he called Moses "god," as stated (in Exod. 7:1): SEE, I HAVE SET YOU AS A GOD TO PHARAOH. The one who causes the dead to live imparted some of his glory to Elijah. Thus he caused the dead to live, as stated (in I Kings 17:23): AND ELIJAH SAID: SEE, YOUR SON IS ALIVE. Because the Holy One, Blessed be He, imparts some of his glory to those who fear him, he put his own clothing on the Messianic King, as stated (in Ps. 21:6): HONOR AND MAJESTY YOU SHALL LAY UPON HIM.[28]

Of course, such a passage hardly proves that referring to Jesus as "God" would never have offended Jewish readers; but it does show that quite traditional Jewish circles were able to regard certain humans, including the Messianic King, as sharing the glory of the Godhead. John 5:23 speaks of honoring "the Son, even as they honor the Father." How

---

[25]Probably only in John 1:1; 1:18 (according to good textual evidence, including p. 66, p. 75, S, B, C, L); and Heb. 1:8-9, (as part of a proof text). See R. Brown, "Does the New Testament Call Jesus God?" *Theol. Studies,* 26(1965), pp. 545-573.

[26]However, "The God" was applied to Jesus in the late second century. See Melito of Sardis, *Peri Pascha,* 96.

[27]See W. Meeks, "The Divine Agent and his Counterfeit in Philo and the Fourth Gospel," *Aspects of Religious Propaganda in Judaism and Early Christianity,* edited by E. Schuessler Fiorenza ("Univ. of Notre Dame Center for the Study of Judaism and Christianity in Antiquity," 2; Notre Dame: Univ. of Notre Dame, 1976), pp. 43-54; *idem, The Prophet-King* ("Supplements to Novum Testtamentum," 14; Leiden: Brill, 1967), pp. 138-162.

[28]There are parallel accounts in the traditional Tanhuma, Beha`alotekha, 9, and in Bemidbar Rabbah 15:13. See also Pesiqta deRav Kahana, 32:9 (= Suppl. 1:9); Midrash on Ps. 90:1.

much further does that statement go beyond the Rabbinic assertion that God imparted some of his glory to Moses by calling him "god"?

A second category of New-Testament, anti-Jewish polemic is the belief that the Church is a new Israel which has replaced the old. This view, however is not as wide-spread within the New Testament as might be expected. Recent work on Paul's epistles suggests that at least this Apostle saw Christ as the Savior who brings the gentiles into a covenantal relation with God, a relationship already enjoyed by Jews. The most important representative of this point of view is the pioneering theological work of Paul Van Buren.[29] In any case, it is quite clear from Rom. 11, that Paul the Apostle saw Jew and gentile receiving quite separate treatment. Here Paul argued that in the near future all, or almost all, humankind would enjoy salvation; yet he never specifically stated that the Jewish salvation was to be through some conversion to Christ. Indeed, Rom. 2:25 appears to affirm the saving effect of Jewish obedience to the Law.[30] Apart from Paul, however, it is quite clear that other New Testament writers do maintain that the Church has displaced Israel. The most notable example of such a view is found in the Epistle to the Hebrews, according to which Judaism is the mere shadow of the true religion inaugurated through Jesus. Then, once one accepts such a theology, it is easy to precede further and understand the end of the old Jewish way culminating with the destruction of Jerusalem (see, e.g., Matt. 22:7; cf. Matt. 27:51 // Mark 15:38). The New Testament also had Jesus prophesy this destruction by declaring, that not one stone there will remain upon another (Matt. 24:2 // Mark 13:2 // Luke 21:6). In time this prophecy took on special importance. While Jews were hoping for their eventual return to Jerusalem as promised by Isaiah 35:10 and Zechariah 14:10-12,[31]} Christians came to fear that such a return would prove Jesus Christ to be a false prophet. As evidence for the reality of this Christian apprehension, we need only scan the Christian reaction when the

---

[29]*Discerning the Way: A Theology of the Jewish-Christian Reality* (New York: Seabury, 1980); *A Christian Theology of the People of Israel:* Part II of *A Theology of the Jewish-Christian Reality* (New York: Seabury, 1983); *Christ in Context:* Part III of *A Theology of the Jewish-Christian Reality* (San Francisco: Harper and Row, 1988). These works are part of a four-volume systematic theology. Van Buren believes that Jesus is the Savior of the gentiles but not a Jewish Messiah.

[30]Gaston, pp. 138-150. This interpretation was first suggested by K. Stendahl, Paul among the Jews and Gentiles (Philadelphia: Fortress, 1976), p. 4.

[31]See Jerome's discussion of the matter in *Comm. in Zech.*, 14:10.

Emperor Julian attempted to rebuild the Jerusalem Temple in the spring of the year 363.[32]

It is the third kind of anti-Jewish polemic that has proved the most harmful throughout history, namely the various direct attacks on Jews and Judaism throughout the New Testament. Foremost among such slanders is the charge that it was the Jews who crucified Jesus (e.g., Acts 2:22, 36; 3:13-15; 4:10; 7:52; cf. John 19:12-16). In fact, the charge was quite untrue. A full presentation of the evidence would go beyond the limitations of this essay,[33] especially in view of the many critical problems surrounding the New-Testament gospels; but the following seems clear: The gospels maintain that Jesus died by a Roman form of punishment and that the only Jews who had anything to do with his death were the High Priest and those around him. In fact, the Pharisees almost entirely disappear from the gospel accounts of Jesus' trial and death.[34] Since it was the Roman governor who appointed Jewish High Priests,[35] High Priests were expected to support Roman interests. Moreover, the crime for which Jesus died was one which had drawn the wrath of Rome. In particular he had become known as the King of the Jews, and the Gospels all affirm that this was the accusation nailed to his Cross (Mark 15:25; Matt. 27:37; Luke 23:38; 19:19-22). As for what happened during any trial or inquest before the High Priest, the Gospels make clear that none of Jesus' followers were close enough to hear what went on. Therefore, any accounts of these proceedings must represent inferences of later Christians.

What the Gospels indicate about the death of Jesus finds confirmation in the much earlier writings of Paul. As one who had spent some time with the Apostle Peter and Jesus' brother James (Gal. 1:18-19; see 2:1-14), Paul certainly had access to reliable information about Jesus. Again and again Paul affirms that Jesus died on a cross and that he was known as "Christos," the Greek equivalent of the Hebrew *Meshiah*. In the Hebrew Bible *Meshiah*, or "Messiah," normally

---

[32]See Robert L. Wilken, *John Chrysostom and the Jews* (Berkeley: Univ. of California, 1983).

[33]For a short commentary on the trial and death of Jesus, see my study, *A Liturgical Interpretation of the Passion of Jesus Christ* (New York: NCCJ, 1985).

[34]The only exceptions are Matt. 27:62, with reference to a conversation with Pilate after Jesus' death, and John 18:3, which concerns Judas' betrayal. Mark, the earliest gospel, entirely dissociates the Pharisees from Jesus' death.

[35]The Caiaphas, the High Priest under whom Jesus was crucified, had been appointed by Valerius Gratus and retained by Pontius Pilate. So Josephus, *Antiquities*, 18:35.

designates a Jewish king,[36] but apart from the Bible the title occurs relatively rarely before the time of Jesus. In fact, there is no evidence that any Jewish messianic figure other than Jesus was ever called Messiah, at least before Bar Kokhba (132-135).[37] Jesus, therefore, would hardly have been called Messiah automatically, nor would he have given the title a new meaning. If Jesus or his followers had been uncomfortable with the title's royal implications, they could easily have chosen another. Therefore, if the title was applied to Jesus during his lifetime, it must have carried the biblical meaning of the "Lord's Anointed," namely "King of the Jews." This is what "Messiah" normally meant, and by itself the title would have invited condemnation by Rome. In other words, both Paul and the gospels provide evidence that those acting for Rome charged Jesus with claiming Jewish kingship and condemned him to a typically Roman form of execution.

After Jesus' crucifixion, when the various parts of the New Testament were written, Christians were in no position to oppose the Roman state. They could hardly admit that the Jesus whom they followed had been condemned by Rome for revolutionary activity. There was no denying that Jesus had died by a Roman crucifixion and that the charge was claiming kingship, but early Christians could and did maintain that he was innocent. The title Christ might have posed a problem, but Paul was turning it into a proper name,[38] and its significance as a Jewish royal title was forgotten.[39] In one instance (I Thess. 2:15) Paul may also have shifted the blame for Jesus' death from Roman to Jew, but the evidence on this point is questionable.[40]

---

[36]Typical of the thirty-nine biblical occurrences of the word are I Sam. 24:6, 10; II Sam. 22:51 // Ps. 18:50; Ps. 89:38. The only places where the title may not designate a Jewish king are Is. 45:1, where the title refers to the King Cyrus of Persia when that king ruled over Israel; Ps. 105:15, where it probably refers to the patriarchs; Hab. 3:13, where it denotes all Judah, and Dan. 9:25-26, where two uses of "anointed" probably designate ruling High Priests, although the "anointed prince" of vs. 25 may again denote Cyrus. The use of "anointed" in Lev. 4:3, 5, 16; 6:22, is adjectival and appears in the expression, "anointed priest."

[37]M. de Jonge, "The Use of the Word 'Anointed' in the Time of Jesus,' *Novum Testamentum*, 8(1966), pp. 132-148.

[38]The process was not yet complete. Out of sixty-seven occurrences of *Christos* in Romans, Paul still uses the word as a title (with the definite article) eight times.

[39]Cf. Suteonius, Claud. 25:4, who probably misunderstood *Christos* for *Chrestos*, which means "morally good" or "kind."

[40]Ever since 1830 several critics have argued that I Thess. 2:13-16 is an interpolation. So F.C. Baur *Paul the Apostle of Jesus Christ* (London, 1875), pp. 87-88. See B.A. Pearson, "I Thessalonians 2:13-16: A Deutero-Pauline

Whatever Paul might have believed about Jews and the crucifixion of Jesus, the Gospels clearly maintain that Jesus' condemnation under the Roman governor was due to Jewish pressure. Then after the apostolic age, Christian writers intensified what the Gospels had said about Jewish responsibility for Jesus' death. This shifting of blame from Roman to Jew continued for almost three centuries until Rome made its peace with Christianity in the so-called Edict of Milan of 313.[41]

Unfortunately, even untrue charges can sound convincing, and the charge that Jews were responsible for the crucifixion has been no exception. Within the New Testament the charge reached a climax at the condemnation of Jesus in Matt. 25:25 with "the people" of Israel shouting, "His blood be on us and on our children," and these words have been responsible for the slaughter of millions of Jews even before there were Nazis. After the New Testament era the specific charge that it was the Jews who had killed Jesus combined with an exalted Christology to justify the accusation of deicide,[42] a charge that gained wide credence in the centuries that followed.

Another reason for much anti-Jewish and anti-Pharisaic rhetoric in the New Testament has to do with the fact that the New Testament contains traditions from an earlier period, when Jesus and his followers were still very much part of that community. At that time there were indeed heated arguments between Jesus or his followers with other parts of the Jewish community, but such arguments took place within the Jewish family. They took on a different meaning, however, when Christians no longer saw themselves as Jews. Now these same arguments became invectives directed against the Jewish community. Members of a family or of a community tend to argue fiercely among themselves and use language that should not be repeated before outsiders. Moreover, people tend to argue with those with whom they have a lot in common. Therefore, the fact that gospels depict the Pharisees as the major opponents of Jesus may represent a situation that actually existed during his ministry, and may not simply reflect later controversies between Christians and Pharisees after the destruction of the Temple when these gospels were being written. In any case, Jesus' teaching as represented in the gospels seems closer to that of the Pharisees than to any other Jewish group, and where Jesus does differ

---

Interpolation," *HTR*, 64(1971), pp. 79-94; Beck, pp. 40-46, 90-92, etc. For a history of the controversy, see R.F. Collins, *Studies on the First Letter to the Thessalonians* (Louvain: Univ. Press, 1984), pp. 96-135, who himself argues in favor of the integrity of I Thess.

[41]For a study of this shift, see P. Winter, *On the Trial of Jesus*, rev. ed. by T.A. Burkill and G. Vermes (Berlin: Walter de Gruyter, 1974), pp. 70-89.

[42]For example, by Melito of Sardis, *Peri Pascha*, 96.

from them, the gospels often have Jesus present an argument that would have made sense to at least some Pharisees.[43] Thus it is quite possible that Jesus argued most fiercely with the Pharisees because the Pharisees were the one sect that came to hear him. In any case, Jesus and his earliest followers argued as Jews with other Jews; and some of the anti-Jewish sections of the gospels may well reflect such intra-Jewish disputes.[44]

A third reason for Christian polemic against Jews is proposed by Beck.[45] He suggests that, just as an adolescent breaking away from parents commonly expresses a certain hostility, so it is quite normal for a breaking-away religious sect to express hostility toward a parent religion. Such a child-parent hostility by a religious group may be found elsewhere. This type of hostility appears in the Hebrew Scriptures directed against the Canaanites (Gen. 9:10-27) and the worshippers of Baal (Deut. 12:1-3, 29-31). Fortunately such passages are no longer dangerous since they can hardly provoke harm against peoples who no longer exist; however, child-parent religious hostility also exists in various contemporary situations. The Koran, contains some polemic against Christians (Surah 5:15-16) and even more against Jews (5:82-83). The Book of Mormon also has invectives against the Jews and the Christian "church of the devil" (1 Nephi 14:10).[46] Similar attitudes may also be found among the Witnesses and the Moonies.

It is hardly surprising, therefore, that as the followers of Jesus gradually saw themselves to be a new sect, distinct and separate from the main stream of Jews, certain Christian writers addressed the separation with polemic. Paul, who wrote before the separation

---

[43]This statement must be understood with some caution because of the problems in determining both what Jesus taught and what the Pharisees stood for. Studies on the teaching of Jesus are too numerous to mention. There are also various theories concerning the Pharisees and their exact relation to early Rabbinic circles after the year 70. Especially important is the work of Neusner (e.g., *The Pharisees* "Studies in Ancient Judaism," 1; Hoboken, NJ: Ktav, 1985, a condensed edition of *The Rabbinic Traditions about the Pharisees before 70* 1971; *From Politics to Piety* [Englewood Cliffs, NJ: Prentice-Hall, 1973]). For other approaches, see Ellis Rivkin *A Hidden Revolution* (Nashville; Abingdon, 1978), who is important in defining the meaning of *Perushim* in Tannaitic literature, and Louis Finkelstein *The Pharisees* (Philadelphia; JPSA, 1962), who raises important sociological questions even though his answers are not always convincing. For a survey of the problem, see John Bowker, *Jesus and the Pharisees* (Cambridge Univ. Press, 1973).

[44]See, e.g., Baum, *The Jews and the Gospel*, especially pp. 42-46.

[45]Pp. 21-30; see also Ruether, p. 30.

[46]See also 1 Nephi 1:1-10:3, 11-14; 14; 2 Nephi 25:12-20; 28:3-6; 29:3-10; Mormon 8:32; Alma 33:14-17; Morani 8:19-21.

became final, showed little hostility toward non-Christian Jews (as distinct from gentile Judaizers);[47] but later writers (cf. Matt. 27:25) were not always so tolerant. Some New Testament books, such as the Fourth Gospel, display mixed attitudes toward Jews. In its early stages the Johannine community seems to have viewed Jews in a positive light, and the sections of John which stem from this period reflect such an attitude. Thus, John 4:22 declares that "salvation is of the Jews" (4:22). Then as the community became less and less Jewish, perhaps reflecting a situation presupposed by the *Birkat haMinim*,[48] later revisions of the Johannine Gospel depict "the Jews" as the enemies of Christ. Similarly Luke-Acts seems to reflect a situation in which Jewish Christians are being disassociated from the Synagogue.[49]

Early Anti-Jewish Polemic in a New Context

For three centuries Christian invective against Jews could do them little harm. Christianity was a relatively small and powerless sect, far smaller than the main body of Jews, who formed one of the major population groups in the empire. Silo Baron has estimated that every tenth Roman was a Jew and that east of Italy the population was twenty per cent Jewish.[50]

Even as late as the fourth century, when Chrysostom was giving his invectives against Jews in Antioch (the *Adversus Judaeos*), the Church still lacked power to inflict serious harm. Besides, people understood the context in which Chrysostom spoke. This golden-tongued preacher was concerned about members of his congregation adopting Jewish practices (I:5:7; 7:1; II:2:4; IV:4:2, 4-5; VII:4:5), attending synagogues during high holy days (I:1:3), and generally regarding these meeting places as more sanctified than the Christian church buildings (I:3:1, 3-5; 5:6, 8). He responded by attacking the Jews and their religion in eight sermons with all the venom that his rhetoric could muster. These "pitiful and miserable Jews" represent "a disease" (I:1:5; 2:3). They

---

[47]See Gaston, especially pp. 15-34; Gager, pp. 193-264.
[48]Since the story about this benediction in the yBerakhot 4:3 (8a) bar., appears to represent an earlier tradition than that of Berakhot 29a, the latter's dating of the benediction in the time of Gamaliel II is unreliable. However, the benediction was apparently in use by the middle of the second century. See Justin Martyr, Dial. 16;4; 96:2; also 47:4; 93:4; 198:31; 117:3; 137:2. For a detailed treatment of this whole approach to the Fourth Gospel, see my "The Gospel of John and the Jews."
[49]See my essay, "The Date of Luke-Acts."
[50]A Social and Religious History of the Jews, 2nd ed., revised and enlarged, Vol. I: *To the Beginning of the Christian Era* (Philadelphia: JPSA, 1952), p. 171. See Wilken, pp. 43-49.

share a kinship with dogs (I:2:1-2), and even their own prophets recognize their depraved condition (IV:3:6). Their fasting is a form of drunkenness (VIII:1:1). They are killers of Christ, our God (4:3:6), and so the synagogue is a house of demons (I:6:2, 6). It "is not only a brothel and a theater; it is also a den of robbers and a lodging for wild beasts" (I:3:1). Still, this virulent attack brought no immediate harm to Antiochene Jews. Not only were they secure in their numbers and power, but Chrysostom's audience recognized the standard oratorical idiom when they heard it. They took Chrysostom's extreme language about as seriously as most moderns would take the extravagant claims of a TV commercial.[51]

When Christians gained full power over the Graeco-Roman world, the anti-Semitism of the New Testament and of other early Christian writings took on a new meaning.[52] What had been written in one context for understandable historical and sociological reasons, now became the justification to persecute Jews, even more by the populous than by the officials of the Church. Church officials were often satisfied to see Jews as a second-class sojourners living as a testimony to the folly of rejecting Christ; but Christians generally were only too ready to proceed against Jews with destruction of property and life.

Chrysostom's sermons against the Jews took on a life of their own. They were copied and recopied for use as anti-Jewish propaganda.[53] Later writers cited them over and over again, and sections became part of the Byzantine liturgy for Holy Week. The sermons were translated into Russian during the eleventh century, just in time for the first pogrom of Russian history in the grand duchy of Kiev under Prince Vladimer.[54] Sermons that meant one thing in fourth-century Antioch, took on a new meaning in Medieval Europe, Byzantium, or Russia. And what was true of Chrysostom's sermons was even more true of the New Testament. The same anti-Jewish polemic, which in New-Testament times could do little practical harm, in later centuries became the justification for persecuting the Jewish people.

---

[51]W.A. Meeks and Wilken, *Jews and Christians in Antioch in the First Four Centuries of the Common Era* ("SBL Sources for Biblical Study," 13; Missoula: Scholars, 1978, pp. 30-36; Wilken, *John Chrysostom and the Jews*, pp. 95-127).

[52]For a study of Jewish reactions to this new Christian power, see Neusner, *Judaism in the Matrix of Christianity* (Philadelphia: Fortress, 1986).

[53]At present there are about two hundred known manuscripts of these works.

[54]See Wilken, *John Chrysostom and the Jews*, pp. 161-162.

By the nineteenth century such anti-Semitism was so pervasive that it was taken for granted throughout most of Europe.[55] It infected the world of Christian scholarship. Scholarly positions that seem quite "objective" take on a new meaning when we learn that their authors were active in the anti-Semitic parties of their day. It is well known that the New Testament scholar, Gerhardt Kittel, was a Nazi, but he is merely one representative of a more pervasive movement. Many well-known scholars were active anti-Semites. The rationalist theologian, Heinrich Eberhard Gottlob Paulus, argued that no Jew should have citizenship rights who did not abandon Judaism. The historian, Theodor Mommsen, saw ancient Jews as one reason for the decay of Roman society and their modern counterparts as too peculiar for integration into a united German nation. Other anti-Semitic scholars are well known from the pages of Albert Schweitzer's *Quest of the Historical Jesus*. They include David Friedrich Strauss,[56] Ernest Renan, and Bruno Bauer. Bauer was certainly no advocate of traditional Christianity; but he still preferred a mythical Jesus based on the philosopher Seneca to one who had been a Jew.

Others undertook to prove that Jesus was no Jew. In 1899 Houston Stewart Chamberlain published his argument that Jesus was certainly not Jewish and probably Aryan,[57] and again in 1918 R. Seeberg proposed the thesis that Jesus' mother was a gentile.[58] This view became quite fashionable in Nazi Germany, so that even the editor of *Zeitschrift fuer die altestestamentliche Wissenschaft* regarded the thesis as plausible.[59] Others ignored the purely racial argument and denied Jesus' Jewishness on religious and cultural grounds.[60] Unfortunately, such arguments unconsciously continue to the present among writers who would never regard themselves as anti-Jewish. Using what is known as the rule of dissimilarity, these scholars would begin their search for

---

[55]The situation is fully described in various works, but Jacob Katz, *From Prejudice to Destruction: Anti-Semitism, 1700-1933* (Cambridge, MA: Harvard, 1980), is a good place to begin.

[56]Even though Strauss became an avowed anti-Semite only after he had written his two lives of Jesus, it is difficult to believe that he was free from anti-Jewish feelings in his earlier years.

[57]*Foundations of the Nineteenth Century*, translated from the German by John Lees (New York: John Lane, 1913), vol. I, pp. 200-274.

[58]"Der Herkunft der Mutter Jesu," in Theologische Festschrift fuer G. Nathanael Bonwetsch zu siebzigsten Geburtstage, ed. H. Achelis *et al.* (Leipzig: Deichert, 1918), pp. 13-19.

[59]Johannes Hempel, "Der Synoptische Jesus und das Alte Testament," *ZAW* 15(1938), pp. 3-4.

[60]E.g., Johannes Leipoldt, Gegenwartsfragen in der testamentlichen Wissenschaft (Leipzig: Deichert, 1935), pp. 17-64.

the authentic teachings of Jesus in those elements which differ from the cultures of his day and in doing so denegate *a priori* whatever his teaching had in common with Jewish religion and culture.[61] Nor have the strictly racial arguments against Jesus' Jewishness disappeared. They have returned to bolster Arab hostility against Israel.[62] During the Nazi era and before, even those who opposed much of what the party stood for, could be sympathetic to its anti-Semitic stance and stress the dissimilarity between Jesus and Judaism. Thus, on January 14, 1933, just two weeks before Hitler assumed power, Karl Ludwig Schmidt, professor of New Testament Studies at Bonn and editor of the *Theologische Blatter*, publicly proclaimed in the presence of Martin Buber:

> We simply read [the Scripture] and allow it to tell us that Jesus of Nazareth had struggled against the contemporary Jewish church (*Judische Kirche*) in the name of the true church; that he included heathens in this church because he did not find such faith in Israel.... Jesus, the Messiah rejected by his people, prophesied the destruction of Jerusalem. Jerusalem has been destroyed, so that it will never come under Jewish rule. Until the present day, the Jewish diaspora has no center.[63]

Against such a background of anti-Semitism, questions arise about other accepted scholarly conventions in addition to the rule of dissimilarity mentioned above. Did anti-Semitism have anything to do with Adolf von Harnack's well known sympathy to Marcion,[64] a sympathy finding new life in Germany today?[65] Does anti-Semitism

---

[61]E.g., see Norman Perrin, *The New Testament: An Introduction*, p. 281: "Sayings and parables may be accepted as authentic if they can be shown to be dissimilar to characteristic emphases of both ancient Judaism and early Christianity."

[62]See Sarwat Anis Al-Assiouty, *Jesus le non-Juif* ("Recherches comparees sur le Christianisme Primitif et l'Islam Premier," 2; Paris: Letouzey & Ane, 1987), who argues that Jesus was born of an Egyptian mother and grew up speaking the language of that country.

[63]Cited in Paul-Mendes Flohr, *The Jew in the Modern World* (Oxford, 1980), pp. 159-160.

[64]*Marcion: Das Evangelium vom Fremden Gott* ("Texte und Untersuchungen...," Bd. 45 [3. Reihe, Bd. 15]; Leipzig: Hinirchs, 1924). For an English translation see, *Marcion: The Gospel of the Alien God*, trans. J.F. Steely & L.D. Bierma (Nurham, NC: Labyrinth, forthcoming).

[65]E.g., through Hanna Wolff, Neuer Wein – Alte Schlaeuche: Das Identitaetsproblem des Christentums im Lichte der Tiefenpsychologie (Stuttgart: Radius, 1981), pp. 7-15. Against her interpretations, see Werner Licharz (ed.), Michael Weinrich, Peter Winzeler, Pinchas Lapide, and Dieter Georgi, in *Nicht Du traegst die Wurze – die Wurzel traegt Dich* ("Arnoldshainer Texte," 30; Frankfurt am Main: Haag & Herchen, 1985).

have anything to do with the neglect of traditional Jewish sources for the study of the New Testament, a neglect that persists today in spite of the works of George Foot Moore, W. D. Davies, and more recently by E. P. Sanders, Lloyd Gaston, and Paul Van Buren? Why have major works on Judaism painted a picture that few Jewish scholars would recognize?[66] Did Rudolph Bultmann's relatively negative assessment of the Hebrew Scriptures[67] and his tendency to neglect later Jewish sources partly result from his dependence on Martin Heidegger, the philosopher who in his later years began his lectures with a "Heil Hitler"?[68]

The Situation Today

Although the anti-Semitism of the New Testament may well be understandable in historical and sociological terms, we must face the fact that such explanations have not prevented persecution of Jews in the past and are not likely to do so in the future. It should at least be possible to undo anti-Semitic aspects of New Testament where these aspects have been read into the New Testament by later exegetes. For example, Christians need to take more seriously those scholars who have begun to rediscover the Jewishness of Jesus and of various leaders in the early Church. Unfortunately, many aspects of our culture, such as passion plays,[69] are leaning in the opposite direction and are actually intensifying the anti-Semitism of the New Testament. Still, there will always be a sizable residue of anti-Semitism within the New Testament that is not due to insensitive interpretation. What should Christians do?

One answer comes from Norman Beck. He would rewrite the New Testament and remove anything anti-Semitic from the translations and to a certain extent from the Greek original. He points out that some anti-Semitism may be removed without violence to the text, but he

---

[66]E.g., Wm. Bousset, *Die Religion des Judentums in spaethellenistischen Zeitalter*, 4th ed. by H. Gressmann (Tuebingen: Mohr [Siebeck], 1926); Herman L. Strack and Paul Billerbeck, *Kommentar zum neuen Testament aus Talmud and Midrasch* (Munich: Beck, 1922-61). On the biased approach of these works and others, see Sanders, *Paul and Palestinian Judaism* (Philadelphia: Fortress, 1977), pp. 33-59. For an earlier period of scholarship, see the survey of Moore, "Christian Writers on Judaism," *HTR*, 14(1921), pp. 197-254.

[67]See his "The Significane of the Old Testament for the Christian Faith," in *The Old Testament and the Christian Faith*, ed. Bernard W. Anderson (London: SCM, 1963).

[68]Of course Bultmann also drew on E. Schuerer, Bousset, and Strack/Billerbeck.

[69]Since the new elections in Oberammergau, there may be a new sensitivity to the issue of anti-Semitism.

admits that further changes must be made. He is presently at work on such a project.

Perhaps a better suggestion is to make a distinction between the New Testament itself and what is publicly read in Christian liturgies. Most churches have always been selective about lectionary readings. Do Christians need to stress passages which in the past have been shown to arouse anti-Semitism? Unfortunately, there are times when it would be difficult for Churches to avoid such passages. It is hard to imagine Christian Holy Week rites without the reading of the Passion. Still there are ways around such difficulties. One solution has been to substitute the reading of a special liturgical passion narrative for Holy Week.[70] Such a liturgical passion narrative is no more radical than the special liturgical accounts of the Last Supper found in many Christian Eucharists.

A third approach is that of Paul Van Buren. He deals, not just with Scriptural texts, but with basic Christian theology. He argues that, while Jesus is a savior who brings non-Jews into a covenant relationship with God, Jews already enjoy such a covenant. In other words, he questions whether we Christians should understand our Gospel as the ultimate saving mechanism for all humankind. Such a position seems reasonable. If after almost two thousand years, a long time even in terms of *Heilsgeschichte*, only about twenty-two percent of the world is Christian; then perhaps it is time to question the Christian assumption that there exists a divine intention for all the world to follow Jesus Christ.

---

[70]See my version, *A Liturgical Interpretation in Narrative Form of the Passion of Jesus Christ.*

11

Four Christian Writers on Jews and Judaism in the Second Century

Robert MacLennan
Hitchcock Presbyterian Church

In 1974 Professor Markus Barth, while teaching a seminar on "Jesus and the Pharisees,"[1] explained that only in the twentieth century have Christian scholars not conversant with Hebrew or Aramaic become familiar with the primary sources of ancient Jewish literature. Barth continued by saying that this was due, in part, to the fact that the primary documents had previously not been accessible to Christian scholars: the large corpus of rabbinic literature of late antiquity known as the Mishnah and its commentary, the Talmud (225-450 C.E.), had only recently been translated by European scholars into French (M. Schwab, 1871-1890), German (L. Goldschmidt, 1929-1936) and English (I. Epstein 1935-1952, and H. Danby, 1933).

Professor Barth went on to tell his students that the study of the rabbinic literature had made it possible for Christian scholars to look at Jesus and the Pharisees in a new way. For example, no longer was it possible to describe the Pharisees in only negative terms, since most of the evidence discovered through a more thorough understanding of the rabbinic writings presented a positive view of the Pharisees.

Modern scholars are only starting the process of reevaluation of first- and second-century Judaism and Christianity. The causes of the conflicts between Jews and Christians in late antiquity are just

---

[1]This seminar took place in Gorwhil, Germany, near the Black Forest.

beginning to be reexamined.[2] It had always been known that there were tensions between two different peoples who were interested in establishing their place in the cities of the Greco-Roman world in which they lived. However, the precise nature of the conflicts and of the persecutions which sometimes resulted was still an unanswered question.

Questions about the circumstances surrounding the conflicts have led scholars to search for methodologies and new evidence that would enable them to find answers. My own search began with a reexamination of the approaches and interpretations proffered by other scholars (most prominently, S. Baron, L. W. Barnard, H. Chadwick, W. H. C. Frend, H. J. Leon, G. F. Moore, J. Parkes, M. Simon, and H. A. Wolfson,[3] among others) about the relationship between Jews and Christians in the first two centuries, and also with a critical look at the conclusions they drew from their readings of the early Christian and Jewish literature.

Many of these studies of early Christian and Jewish literature seemed to be limited to examinations of the texts themselves, ignoring almost entirely the contexts in which they were written. This was true even though biblical studies, especially Old Testament studies, for many decades, had insisted on studying texts in their context.[4]

But for some reason, early Christian and Jewish writings were examined by scholars who used the historical critical methodologies less rigorously. They did not pay enough attention to the context.

---

[2]See R. Ruether, *Faith and Fratricide, The Theological Roots of Anti-Semitism* (New York: Seabury, 1974) and J. Gager, *The Origins of Anti-Semitism* (Oxford: Oxford University Press, 1983).

[3]See, for example, S. Baron, *A Social and Religious History of the Jews*, vols. 1 and 2 (New York: Jewish Publication Society, 1937); L. W. Barnard, *Justin Martyr, His Life and Thought* (Cambridge, 1967); H. Chadwick, *Early Christian Thought and the Classical Tradition: Studies in Justin, Clement and Origen* (Oxford, 1966); W. H. C. Frend, *The Rise Of Christianity*, (Philadelphia: Fortress Press, 1984); H. J. Leon, *The Jews of Ancient Rome* (Philadelphia: Jewish Publication Society, 1960); G. F. Moore, *Judaism in the First Centuries of the Christian Era, The Age of the Tannaim*, 2 vols. 1927, reprint (New York: Schocken Books, 1971); J. Parkes, *The Conflict of Church and Synagogue: A Study in the Origins of Anti-Semitism*, 1934, reprint (Cleveland and Philadelphia, 1961); M. Simon, *Verus Israel: A Study of the relations between Christian and Jew in the Roman Empire* (135-435) [1964], translated by H. McKeating (Oxford: Oxford University Press, 1986) and H. A. Wolfson, *The Philosophy of the Church Fathers: Faith, Trinity, Incarnation*, 3d ed. (Cambridge, Massachusetts and London: Harvard University Press, 1956).

[4]For a summary of the critical study of the Bible see D. A. Knight and G. M. Tucker, eds. *The Hebrew Bible and Its Modern Interpreters*, (Philadelphia: Fortress Press and Chico, California: Scholars Press, 1985).

Further, most scholars seemed to read the ancient texts as if these ancient writers were describing, in a literal way, the events of their day. There appeared to be little concern for the nature of the literature being studied. Absent critical examination, any conclusions which these scholars drew relative to the relationship between Christians and Jews would always be suspect.

In 1974, I began to read through the rabbinic literature myself in English translation: the Mishnah, the Babylonian Talmud, Midrash, Tosefta, Mekilta and the Talmud of the Land of Israel. In the midst of this pursuit it became clear to me that teachings about Jews and Judaism by many Christian scholars had omitted many important details and distorted others.

For example, rabbis – those teachers, scholars and others who produced the corpus of literature listed above – devoted little of their works to discussions of Christians and Christianity. There were no extant anti-Christian documents composed by rabbis. There is no record in the texts themselves that rabbis argued with Christians over the meaning of the Bible, or over the assertion that Jesus was the Messiah, a central concern within Christianity. These rabbis seemed to be indifferent to issues that were so important to the Christian writers who were their contemporaries. Why was this?

An attempt to answer this question has come from those who study the structure and purpose of the rabbinic literature. Jacob Neusner has suggested through his approach to the rabbinic corpus and the reconstruction of early Christianity and Judaism of late antiquity that the issues in the rabbinic discussions were more about the life circumstances of their communities than the theological meaning of Judaism, much less Christianity.

Neusner introduced the thought that the Mishnah and other rabbinic literature were records of the way one thought about the mundane, and not so much about theological dogmatics.[5] Rabbis were concerned about such things as seeds, food, cloth, property, bodily functions, women, issues of blood, what was clean and unclean, issues that today are more the concerns of the cultural anthropologist than the theologian, the apologist, or the dogmatist.

---

[5]See, for example, J. Neusner, *Judaism, The Evidence of the Mishnah* (Chicago and London: The University of Chicago Press, 1981); *Method and Meaning in Ancient Judaism*, BJS 10 (Missoula: Scholars Press, 1979); *Formative Judaism: Religious, Historical and Literary Studies*, Third Series, *Torah, Pharisees, and Rabbis*, BJS 46 (Chico, California: Scholars Press, 1983) and *Ancient Judaism: Debates and Disputes*, BJS 64 (Chico, California: Scholars Press, 1984).

These insights from this approach to the study of rabbinic literature have led some scholars to attempt to reconstruct a more accurate picture of the relationship between Jews and Christians from a direct reading of early Christian or Jewish literary sources. The issue becomes one of the usefulness of these sources in understanding the conflicts. Could the Talmud (redacted finally in 450 C.E.), and the Christian writings, which were theological and polemical, alone be useful in reconstructing the relationship of Christians and Jews in the second century? What other data could be used to reconstruct the relationship between Jews and Christians? Something more than the texts themselves was needed.

New Testament scholars had already begun to use archaeological and epigraphic data in their study of the Bible, and so it made sense to others to study the early Christian and rabbinic writings using the same materials. Attempts have been made by students of late antiquity to do what the critical biblical scholars have done and apply those insights to the study of Christian and Jewish literature from late antiquity.

When the new methods and data are used on the biblical material as well as the early Christian writings, such as the Christian *adversus Judaeos* texts of the second century,[6] the subject of this article, some interesting results occur.[7]

Adversus Judaeos (against Jews) is the phrase traditionally used to describe early Christian writings of late antiquity which tried to prove that Christianity was superior to Judaism. Few modern scholars have questioned the intention of these early writings; in fact, most scholars until quite recently, have perpetuated the notion of the superiority of Christianity over Judaism.

---

[6]See J. Parkes, *The Conflict of Church and Synagogue* [1934] reprint (Cleveland and Philadelphia, 1961); A. L. Williams, *The Adversus Judaeos, A Bird's-Eye View of Christian Apologae Until the Renaissance* (Cambridge, 1935); R. Wilde, *The Treatment of the Jews in the Greek and Christian Writers of the First Three Centuries* (Washington D.C.: The Catholic University of American Press, 1949); H. Schreckenberg, *Die christlichen Adversus-Judaeos-Texte und ihr literarisches und historisches Umfled (1-11.Jh.)* (Frankfurt am Main and Bern: Peter Lang, 1982); J. Gager, *Origins* and R. Ruether, *Faith and Fratricide*.

[7]See W. A. Meeks, *The First Urban Christians, The Social World of the Apostle Paul* (New Haven: Yale University Press, 1983); G. Theissen, *Sociology of Early Palestinian Christianity*, translated by John Bowden (Philadelphia: Fortress Press, 1978); R. E. Brown, *The Community of the Beloved Disciple* (New York: Paulist Press, 1979) and B. Malina, *Christian Origins and Cultural Anthropology: Practical Models for Biblical Interpretation* (Atlanta: John Knox Press, 1986).

The earliest and most influential of the so-called *adversus Judaeos* texts include Barnabas' Epistle of Barnabas, Justin's Dialogue with Trypho the Jew, Melito's Paschal Homily and Tertullian's Answer to the Jews.[8]

These second century texts, written in various cities of the Mediterranean world, were very influential in the early and later Christian writings about Jews and Judaism. In fact, some would suggest that "[a]nti-Judaism, then, can be defined as what Tertullian says about Jews."[9]

This statement could also apply to the other writers as well: Justin, Barnabas and Melito have influenced the way Christian theologians and apologists throughout the centuries have thought about Jews and Judaism.

These texts are still used by the Church to define the questions which should be raised between Christians and Jews, even though much scholarly work has been done to present different questions and issues. For example, discussions on the floor of the General Assembly of the Presbyterian Church (USA) in Biloxi, Mississippi, as recently as June, 1987, with respect to a paper entitled "A Theological View of Christians and Jews" seemed to echo arguments presented in the *adversus Judaeos* writings of the second century.

A problem is created when the *adversus Judaeos* texts are used by modern Christians in ways that result, intentionally or not, in the propagation of prejudice or creation of false impressions about Jews and Judaism. In a similar fashion, the New Testament, an ancient first-second century text itself, has been wrongly used as a history book in the modern sense. Modern scholars still create the history of the Church from these texts.

Reading about the Jews through the lens of the New Testament or the second-century *adversus Judaeos* writings gives the reader an inadequate picture of the writers' view of Jews. Raising concerns about

---

[8]For studies of these texts see B. A. Pearson, "Earliest Christianity in Egypt: Some Observations" in *The Roots of Egyptian Christianity*, edited by B. A. Pearson and J. E. Goehring, (Philadelphia: Fortress Press, 1986): 132-160; H. Remus, "Justin Martyr's Argument with Judaism" in *Anti-Judaism in Early Christianity* 2, edited by S. G. Wilson (Waterloo, Ontario, Canada: Wilfrid Laurier University Press, 1986): 59-80; S. G. Hall, ed. and trans., *Melito of Sardis ON PASCHA and Fragments* (Oxford: Clarendon Press, 1979) and D. Efroymson, "Tertullian's Anti-Judaism and its Role in his Theology," Ph.D. Diss., (Temple University, 1976).

[9]See L. Gaston, "Retrospect" in *Anti-Judaism in Early Christianity* 2, *Separation and Polemic*, edited by S. G. Wilson (Waterloo, Ontario, Canada: Wilfrid Laurier University Press, 1986): 163.

the historical value of certain reports and seeking ways to understand the context in which the New Testament was written enables the reader to discover the original intent of the authors.

In a 1986 article in Biblical Archaeological Review, A. T. Kraabel and I made the following comment: "New Testament writers were not trying to tell their readers what they already knew, namely, the facts surrounding the events of the early Church. These writers were not trying to describe the events that had occurred. They were interested, rather, in interpreting the meaning of those events for their readers only. They wanted to tell why the church existed, what the Cross meant, why Jesus was the Messiah, why there was a split between the Jewish Christian movement and Jews. Their concern was not simply to give an account of what happened, but rather to provide an interpretive portrait in words of the events surrounding the origin of the Church. The New Testament is not so much a history book, in a modern sense, as a collection of early Christian sermons and letters."[10]

In light of the new archaeological evidence and approaches to ancient literature one must refrain from reading the *adversus Judaeos* writings as if they were designed to be understood universally. Rather, one must reconsider them in the light of the cities in which and to which they were written. The city of origin, then, becomes another text which, when examined from the perspective of archaeological and other evidence, reveals more clearly the intention of the second-century author of the writing.

We must ask straightforward questions about each city: What do we know about the city? How would the character of the city and the events in that city in the second century affect the author? What does the city tell us about the Jews and the Christians there? How large were the Jewish, Christian, or pagan populations in the city? Is there any information about the relationship between Christians and Jews in that city? What other information seems important for an understanding of how the author would feel or what he would think as a citizen of or visitor to that particular city?[11]

Examining a text in the light of the city as text is not new to biblical scholars. New Testament scholars have used this approach in considering the "life situation" of the text and examining the

---

[10]R. S. MacLennan and A. T. Kraabel, "The God-Fearers – A Literary and Theological Invention?" *BAR* 12.5 (1986): 51.

[11]See, for example, J. Neusner, "Anthropology and the Study of Talmudic Literature," in *Method and Meaning in Ancient Judaism*, BJS 10 (Ann Arbor: Scholars Press, 1979): 21-40 and W. A. Meeks, *The First Urban Christians* (New Haven: Yale University Press, 1983).

background to the questions raised in the Biblical texts. Some modern scholars have provided contextual studies, placing each letter of Paul, for example, more deeply into a city or region.[12] But for some reason these works have not made, until recently, an impact on those who study the early Christian and Jewish texts of late antiquity.

Problems are still not solved when one uses this approach. How, for example, does one allow a city to "speak?" How does one know that the questions are the right questions? Are the cities chosen as contexts for each text the right ones? How, for instance, can it be known that Barnabas was a native or resident of Alexandria, living there from 113 to 137 C.E., and not a resident of Yavneh, living there in 98 C.E.[13]

In my own study of the four representative *adversus Judaeos* texts, my reasons for matching the cities to the authors varied. I chose the cities I did on the basis of scholarly information and suggestions; the cities are the most plausible and useful. Even though it is not possible to establish absolutely the city in which a particular text was conceived of or written, much can be learned about the authors and their writings when one examines the city thought to be the context for the writings.

After identifying the cities which are the most plausible setting for the writings, then one can examine some of the characteristics of those cities and the evidence they provide for the presence of and relationship between Jews and Christians. The results are varied. Some are rich with information about the Jews and Pagans (Sardis);[14] others are not as complete (Neapolis).[15]

But what is clear and seems to be self-evident is that Barnabas, Justin, Melito and Tertullian wrote their *adversus Judaeos* to particular people in a specific time and place. They were not simply writing in a vacuum, about universal truths. Further, each of the writers was a leader in his community. It is reasonable to assume, then, that as a leader in the church, he had a congregation, those in his charge with

---

[12]See J. Neusner, "The Experience of the City in Late Antique Judaism" in *Approaches to Ancient Judaism, vol. V Studies in Judaism and Its Greco-Roman Context,* edited by W. S. Green, (Atlanta: Scholars Press, 1985) 37-52 and W. A. Meeks, *The First Urban Christians* (New Haven: Yale University Press, 1983).

[13]See M. B. Shukster and P. Richardson, "Temple and Bet Ha-midrash in the Epistle of Barnabas" in *Anti-Judaism in Early Christianity 2,* edited by S. G. Wilson (Waterloo, Ontario, Canada: Wilfrid Laurier University Press, 1986): 17-32.

[14]On Sardis see G. M. A. Hanfmann, *Sardis from Prehistoric to Roman Times: Results of the Archaeological Exploration of Sardis 1958-1975* (Cambridge, Massachusetts: Harvard University Press, 1983).

[15]See M. J. S. Chiat, *Handbook of Synagogue Architecture,* BJS 29 (Chico, California: Scholars Press, 1982).

whom he worked to discover what it meant to be a Christian. These writings, therefore, are not abstract dissertations, but purposeful statements written with passion.

The following is a summary of the meaning and purpose of four *adversus Judaeos* texts of the second century, derived by means of the new methodolgy and the use of new data.

Barnabas' Epistle

Barnabas worked and lived most of his life in Alexandria, Egypt. Even though there is much literary evidence about Alexandria in late antiquity, there is very little archaeological evidence about the Jews and Christians in that city until the late fourth century. Nevertheless, the city of Alexandria provided a very lively text for the study of the *Epistle.*

As I began to search for information about the Jews and Christians in Alexandria, I pieced together some of the trauma of that city in the early second century. Barnabas was faced with many disruptions during his time there. The cultural climate of early and mid-second century, as well as the social chaos of Alexandria, must have made an impression on him.

Also, Alexandria had a large Jewish population that was protected by the Roman *religio licita.* This status affected Jews differently. Not every citizen had the same legal status. This religious guarantee assured that Jews had a secure place in the city during the second century. Barnabas benefited from this legal status because as a Christian he was protected by the same law.[16]

The evidence indicates that the Jews were active in the cultural life of the city. Jews were found in every level of society. Inscriptions and papyri suggest that Jews made an impact on the city.[17]

The Jews were also fighting among themselves. As in every society and group, there were always factions struggling for position, status and power. Some were trying to assimilate into the culture of Alexandria; others tried to maintain their uniqueness. Some were caught up in

---

[16]See, for example, E. M. Smallwood, *The Jews Under Roman Rule. From Pompey to Diocletian. Studies in Judaism in Late Antiquity 20.* [1976] reprint (Leiden: E. J. Brill, 1981): 135-136.

[17]See, for example, *Corpus Papyrorum Judaicarum* 3 vols., edited by V. Tcherikover, A. Fuks and M. Stern (Cambridge, Massachusetts: Harvard University Press, 1957-1964); M. Stern, ed. and trans., *Greek and Latin Authors on Jews and Judaism* 3 vols. (Jerusalem: The Academy of Sciences and Humanities, 1976- 1984) and E. M. Smallwood, *The Jews Under Roman Rule. From Pompey to Diocletian. Studies in Judaism in Late Antiquity 20.* [1976] reprint (Leiden: Brill, 1981).

radical and fanatical movements in the city, while others hoped to go unnoticed.

In 115-117 and 134-135 C.E., tragedy struck the Jewish communities of Palestine and North Africa, including Alexandria. The revolt of Jews in Cyrenaica, and later in Palestine under Bar-Kokhba, proved devastating to Jews in those particular locations. Large numbers of Jews disappeared from the cities in North Africa where revolts took place.[18]

During this time some Jews, both in Palestine and other cities of the Diaspora, hoped for a messianic or military leader to restore their sole jurisdiction over their own land and to rebuild the Temple. R. Akiba, in Palestine, thought that Bar-Kokhba was one of those persons.[19] Jews continued to hope for the rebuilding of the Temple in Jerusalem. Alexandrian Jews were affected by this messianic excitement.

This evidence from Alexandria and the numbers and varieties of Jews in the city support the hypothesis that the occasion of the *Epistle* might have been Barnabas' reaction against an emerging "fanatical Jewish messianism," fanned by either the hope of rebuilding the Temple in Jerusalem (c.113) or the coming revolt in 115.

If this was the case, then Barnabas was trying to tell his readers, and perhaps some Jewish converts, that in these "evil days" (the days of fanaticism), God's people were followers of Jesus who did not allow themselves to swerve from the truth into the "wicked ways" of those who put their "hope on the building, and not on God."[20]

Barnabas believed that he was teaching a moderate kind of messianic Judaism which had been manifest in Jesus. Therefore, the *Epistle* was not so much an anti-Jewish writing as an anti-sectarian writing.

In other words, Barnabas was fighting for the life of emerging Christianity, which followed some early form of moderate messianic Jewish teaching. The Epistle, then, is evangelistic and apologetic – not anti-Jewish. It seeks to clarify and define Christianity as a moderate messianic form of Judaism rather than to degrade Jews.

---

[18]See E. M. Smallwood, *The Jews*, 409-412.

[19]See B. Z. Bokzer, "Justin Martyr and the Jews," *JQR* 64 (1973-1974): 97-122, 204-211.

[20]See *Barnabas*, translated by K. Lake, *The Apostolic Fathers*, vol. I, Loeb Classical Library (Cambridge, Massachusetts: Harvard University Press, 1925): 2.1, 9; 5.13; 10.10; 16.1.

Justin's Dialogue with Trypho the Jew

The second text, *The Dialogue with Trypho a Jew* is Justin's unique contribution to the *adversus Judaeos* corpus. The uniqueness is principally related to the fact that Justin had intimate contact with three cities: Neapolis in Samaria, Rome and Ephesus. It is necessary to look at each of the cities in turn so that one can gain from each of them what they have contributed as texts to Justin's view of himself, his Christian tradition, and his perspective on Jews and Judaism.

Most studies of Justin deal with the "Jewish" content of his writings. Many discuss only his biblical commentary and Christian ideas and leave out the fact that Justin was a cosmopolitan person. Each of these cities influenced his thinking.

Neapolis, a Roman diplomatic outpost in Palestine, provided a brief study of the Samaritan influence on Justin and his writings.[21] Many scholars have pointed out the "Samaritanisms" in his writings, but no one has suggested that Samaritan theology might have influenced the way he looked at or understood Jews and Judaism. The questions he asked and the feelings he had about the Jews, I suggest, are a result of his childhood experience with Samaritans.

Trypho, who is supposed to be a rabbi in the *Dialogue*, is not a typical rabbi. He was certainly not the one who followed Bar-Kokhba in the revolt against the Romans in 132-135, as R. Akiba did. He seems to be one of those moderates in the tradition of Johanan ben Zakkai (c. 70). I suggest that Trypho is portrayed this way because of Justin's childhood memories of rabbis or other Jewish leaders he and his family had known or possibly heard about from his neighbors in Neapolis.

Ephesus, like Sardis, had a large Jewish population.[22] This would certainly have affected Justin's view of Jews. It was a place with a long history of public lectures and debates in which teachers and philosophers discussed their ideas. It was a center for Greek culture and philosophy. It would make sense to write a *Dialogue* in a form that would appeal to the Ephesians.

---

[21]For a general comment about Neapolis see *The Archaeological Encyclopaedia of the Holy Land*, rev. and edited by A. Negev (Nashville: Thomas Nelson Publisher, 1986). See also J. D. Purvis, "The Samaritans and Judaism" in R. A. Kraft and G. W. E. Nickelsburg, ed., *Early Judaism and Its Modern Interpreters* (Atlanta: Scholars Press, 1986): 81-98.

[22]See C. Foss, *Ephesus After Antiquity: A late antique, Byzantine and Turkish City* (London and New York: Cambridge University Press, 1979).

The archaeological and historical evidence, which is abundant, suggests that Justin would have had much freedom to make his case in Ephesus. It is also a fact that there was no mention of Paul in any of Justin's writings. Ephesus was a place where Paul had visited and been jailed. Why does Justin not mention Paul? Perhaps Paul's way of relating to Jews did not make sense to Justin any longer. Perhaps the writings of Paul were not as influential among some Christian groups or as important to Justin's work. Or, it is possible that Christianity was far more diverse in the late first and mid-second century than some have thought.

The city of Rome,[23] where Justin taught and led a school, was another context that helped form his ideas about Jews and Judaism. The city was also host to a number of schools within the Christian movement and groups that did not always get along. The evidence demonstrates diversity among Jews and Judaism in Rome.[24] It is possible that the various Christian groups in Rome each had its own view of Jews and Judaism.

This diversity among the Jews and Christians in Rome certainly made an impact on Justin. How could he write a treatise or a dialogue about monolithic Christianity and Judaism when there were so many different kinds of Jews and Christians? The answer seems to be that Justin was concerned about those Christians and Jews he encountered in his travels, and not the many others who were wrestling with their own situation.

This would mean that he had to deal selectively with both groups. He had to set out his own definitions and limit his discussions to those parts of Judaism and Christianity which, in his view, were the most legitimate.

After examining the data of the three cities, I believe the *Dialogue* would best be described as an apologetic essay written to either a Christian school or a house church in which Justin participated as a teacher.

The *Dialogue* is best understood not as a hostile anti-Jewish writing, rather, as an essay dealing with a particular kind of Jew and Judaism known to Justin, possibly even created out of his own memory of Jews and Judaism in Samaria. It is with this phantom Jew, a composite of Jews from Rome, Ephesus and Neapolis, that Justin carries on his dialogue.

---

[23]See H. J. Leon, *The Jews of Ancient Rome* (Philadelphia: Jewish Publication Society, 1960) and E. R. Goodenough, *Jewish Symbols in the Greco-Roman Period* 13 vols. (New York: Pantheon Books, 1953-1968).
[24]See H. J. Leon, *The Jews*, 1-55.

Melito's Homily

The third *adversus Judaeos* writing is Melito's *Homily*. Sardis, the context in which the *Homily* was written, is rich in archaeological data but poor in literary evidence. Through archaeological studies, Sardis has opened the way for a fresh look at Jews and Judaism in the second century.[25] No longer is it possible to hold the view of the old consensus that Judaism was not vibrant during the second century. A new view of Jews and Judaism in the Diaspora has emerged as a result of the newly-gathered data from Sardis and other cities of late antiquity.

The Sardis evidence is helpful in establishing that the Jews maintained an impressive presence, at least at some locations, in the Diaspora. They did not assimilate completely into the culture. Neither did they separate themselves totally from the culture. They were a presence that had to be dealt with, and were often in the center of the town or taking some significant part in the life of the community. Jews were not ghettoized or hiding somewhere outside of the city. They were "at home" in Sardis.

The archaeological evidence from Sardis is that the Jews of Sardis were integrated into the Sardian culture.[26] They were seen as more than a religious group. Their synagogue was used for religious purposes, but it was not limited to that use. It is more precise to say that the synagogue was a community center in which a variety of activities took place, only one of which would be the reading and study of Torah. Therefore, those non-Jews who associated themselves with the synagogue were not necessarily there for religious reasons.

Very few Jews were rabbinic, nor were they all influenced by the rabbis of the Mishnah, even though many have thought they were. In the *adversus Judaeos* writings themselves, there are "other" Jewish influences present, including Jewish sectarians. Some have suggested that early rabbinic Judaism was itself a sectarian movement within the Jewish culture.[27] It is essential that we not think of all Jews as being influenced by or interested in the rabbinic form of Judaism.

---

[25]There is ample evidence for a lively Jewish community in Sardis presented in G. M. A. Hanfmann, *Sardis* (1983).

[26]See A. T. Kraabel, "Impact of the Discovery of the Sardis Synagogue" in *Sardis From Prehistory to the Roman Times*, edited by G. M. A. Hanfmann (Cambridge, Massachusetts: Harvard University Press, 1983): 178-190.

[27]See, for example, S. J. D. Cohen, "Yavneh Revisted: Pharisees, Rabbis and the End of Jewish Sectarianism," in *Seminar Papers* 1982, SBL, (Chico, California: Scholars Press, 1982): 45-61.

In the context of such a diverse and important movement as Judaism seemed to be in Sardis, it is understandable why Melito would be concerned in his *Homily* to distinguish Christianity from Judaism.

Therefore, it seems from the evidence that it would be appropriate to conclude that Melito wrote to plead the case for Christianity against a venerable Judaism. It is likely that the small and not well-developed Christian presence in Sardis would try to find something "evil" or "satanic" about such a powerful community in the town, for the purpose of its own survival as the "true" people of God.

Melito seems to be concerned to keep Christians out of the synagogues so that they would not convert to Judaism. Judaism was probably providing a rich spiritual resource for some Christians during the first and second century and this disturbed Melito and other leaders of the Church.

The New Testament, a first-second century document, consistently negates Judaism for its inadequacy. Scholars working in New Testament studies today demonstrate the reason for this polemic in the struggle of the early Christians (c.64-95 C.E.) with their own identity.[28] This struggle did not cease after the first century, but continued into the next four centuries, as the Church fought its way into existence.

In order for Melito to preserve his small community, he had to convince his constituency that they must beware of the enticements of the synagogue.

It becomes clear as one reads the *Homily* in the context of Sardis that this poetic masterpiece was really a sermon intended for a struggling community. Insofar as Melito argued for the survival of his Christian community against the Jews in Sardis, we can include the *Homily* within the category *adversus Judaeos* literature. But we must remember that it is not necessary to go from this to a generalization which suggests that the *Homily* condemns all Jews for all times. Melito was speaking to his Christian community in Sardis, attempting to present a rationale for his understanding of the Christian tradition. He had to state his case in the presence of a venerable and compelling form of Judaism.

Tertullian's Answer to the Jews

Tertullian, the fourth text I studied, presented special problems. His city was Carthage, North Africa. The evidence for the Christian and Jewish presence in second-century Carthage is mixed and difficult

---

[28]See R. E. Brown, "Not Jewish and Gentile Christianity but Types of Jewish/Gentile Christianity," *CBQ* 45.1 (1983): 74- 79.

to interpret. There is no archaeological data about the interaction of Christians and Jews in Carthage.[29]

It was not possible to determine the kind of Judaism that existed in Carthage during Tertullian's time. An obscure mention of the study of rabbinic sources in Carthage in the Talmud is hardly enough evidence to describe a particular kind of Judaism there.[30]

A study of the large necropolis leads to mixed conclusions. It seems that Christians and Jews were buried in the same area. If this can be proved, there was not a distinction between these two groups. It is difficult from this evidence, though, to establish exactly what significance this had for the two communities. I have to agree with recent analysis that all one can say is that there were large Jewish and Christian populations in the city, and they used the same area of the city to bury their dead. The literary sources and the presence of an established burial place indicate that there was a settled group of Jews and Christians in the city.[31]

The written evidence suggests that the two communities were quite diverse. Persecution is mentioned in the literary sources, which indicates tension in the city, but it is not possible from these writings to conclude that Jews persecuted Christians, or that Christians persecuted Jews there, or that there was any significant interaction between the two groups.[32]

The *Answer to the Jews* never speaks directly of contemporary Jews, instead it is speaking of Jews from biblical times. It was written mainly as a biblical commentary to be used as a resource by Christians in their own self-definition. The *Answer* describes Jews of the Bible, not Jews living in second-century Carthage. The concerns which the New Testament writers were interested in were the important issues for contemporary Jews, as far as Tertullian was concerned. This would rule out the old view that the *Answer* was influenced by some rabbinic teachings and writings. Marcion, a Christian teacher and leader and a heretic according to Tertullian, is probably the real enemy against whom Tertullian wrote. Jews in Carthage were not the problem for the

---

[29]See J. H. Humphrey ed., *Excavations at Carthage* 1975-1976, conducted by the University of Michigan, (Institut National d'Archaeologie et d'Art, and American School of Oriental Research) 1, (Tunis, 1976).

[30]See E. R. Goodenough, *Jewish Symbols in the Greco-Roman Period*, 2 (New York: Pantheon Books, 1953): 63-67.

[31]A. Ennabli, "North Africa Newsletter 3: Part 1. Tunsia 1956-1980," translated by J. H. Humphrey in *AJA* 87 (1983): 199 n. 28.

[32]See the discussion of these issues in D. M. Scholer, "Tertullian on Jewish Persecution of Christians," *SP* 17.2 (1982): 821-828.

Christian Church.[33] Jews and Judaism seem incidental in comparison to the real enemy, Marcion.[34]

Conclusion

As a result of this study of the four texts and their cities, several conclusions about the purpose and meaning of the early *adversus Judaeos* may be drawn:

(1) Each *adversus Judaeos* writing is unique and is a result of one writer's concern about the relationship between Christians and Jews in his own times or in the biblical times.

(2) Each is an attempt at Christian self-definition.

(3) Each writer deals with his own particular view of Judaism and speaks about Jews either as he is experiencing them in his particular place and time or as he portrays them as a "Bible-people." Curiously, the writers never seem to talk directly to or about Jews, unless the Jews are invented for a dialogue. There is no dialogue taking place between these two groups. Therefore, the authors did not intend for their writings to be universalized.

(4) It is unlikely that any of the authors I have studied knew anything first-hand about contemporary Judaism from a sustained relationship with the synagogue in his neighborhood.

There are many questions which remain and need further consideration. As one studies the new evidence on the cities and gains a more complete picture than is now available to us about Jews and Judaism in the second-century Diaspora, we will be able to draw a more accurate description about the relationship between Jews and Christians during that period.

Certainly Jews did not die out nor did Judaism become a sterile, legalistic religion during the emergence of the Christian Church in the second-century Roman Empire.

Jews were flourishing around the Mediterranean during the second century, and their creative contributions must have upset those Jewish Christians and non-Jewish Christians who believed that the Messiah

---

[33]See *Tertullian, Adversus Marcionem*, edited and translated by E. Evans, Oxford Early Christian Texts. 2 vols., (Oxford: Clarendon Press, 1972).

[34]See the discussion of these topics in D. Efroymson, "Tertullian's Anti-Judaism and its Role in his Theology," Ph.D. diss., (Temple University, 1976) and T. D. Barnes, *Tertullian, A Historical and Literary Study,* [1971] reprint (Oxford: Clarendon Press, 1985).

had come and the end of Israel was at hand. It must have been rather difficult for Christian writers to preach that message when Israel did not end after one hundred years of Christian missions. The evidence from the Diaspora synagogues encourages scholars to review their conclusions about the Jews of late antiquity. The discoveries tend to support the idea that Judaism and the Jews, as well as the Christians, were more diverse, less monolithic, and more complicated that we had previously thought.[35]

More study must be done on the nature and purpose of the ancient texts. The church saved these writings and preserved a certain point of view. The more we uncover evidence from the second century the more we will learn about the relationship between Jews and Christians.

More work needs to be done on the cities as texts. Wayne Meeks[36] and others have begun the task; still others need to develop further their work so that scholars can be more precise about the nature of the city as an interpretive tool in the study of ancient writings.

After examining the *adversus Judaeos* texts in light of the new archaeological and epigraphic evidence, reading them in a post-confessional way, and using the new approach to this literature as applied by J. Neusner and others, it seems clear that these texts were not written to create a hatred of Jews and Judaism. Nevertheless, anti-Judaism grew because third- and fourth-century readers and interpreters of Tertullian, Melito, Justin and Barnabas read them as literally degrading Jews.

One question remains: Can Christians define themselves in relation to the Jews without the supersessionistic or triumphalistic overtones? It has been the intention of this article to make a start in the direction of answering that question in the affirmative.

---

[35]See A. T. Kraabel, "The Roman Diaspora: Six Questionable Assumptions," (Yadin Festschrift) *JJS* 33.1-2 (1982): 445- 464.

[36]See, for example, W. A. Meeks, *The First Urban Christians*, (New Haven: Yale University Press, 1983).

Part Five
FORMATIVE JUDAISM: RELIGION

12

"Teach us to Count our Days": A Note on *Sefirat Haomer*

Harold Fisch
Bar-Ilan University

I

A famous Mishnah (*Menaḥot* 10:3) describes the ceremonial cutting of the barley-sheaf during the Festival of Passover and the great to-do (*'eseq gadol*) that was made by the officers of the bet-din at each stage of the ceremony as a way of demonstrating that theirs was the correct practice and that of the Boethusians was to be rejected. The argument related to when the fifty-day count referred to in Leviticus 23:15-16 should begin. On this would depend not merely the cutting of the *'omer* and with it the marketing of the new corn (*ibid.* verse 14) but also the timing of the festival of Shavuot. The Pharisaic view to which the Mishnah gives canonical authority was that the count should commence immediately after the first day of the Festival, i.e., on the 16th day of Nisan – an arrangement which yields a fixed date for Shavuot, i.e., the 6th day of Sivan – whilst the Boethusians, evidently following the Sadducees, began to count after the *Sabbath-day* of Passover which could be any of the intermediate days of the festival or even the last day. They contended that this was in accordance with the correct reading of Leviticus 23:15-16 which speaks of the "morrow of the Sabbath." The Pharisees understood the term "Sabbath" here to mean "festival" as in verse 32 of the same chapter and this could occur on any day of the week. The question of the proper interpretation of the disputed verses does not concern us here so much as the phenomenological differences between the two practices and their wider implications.

205

The Boethusian rule would clearly yield a wandering date in the lunar calendar for both the Cutting of the 'Omer and the festival of Shavuot – the latter could occur on any day from the 6th to the 12th of Sivan – but both events would always occur on a fixed day of the week, namely Sunday. The Pharisaic ruling resulted in a fixed date for both events in accordance with the lunar calendar but a wandering day of the week – for the two events could occur on any day including the Sabbath itself! On the Sabbath, the ceremony described in the Mishnah would take on a particular drama as the officer of the Bet-din, sickle in hand, cried out three times to the people, "On this Sabbath-day?" and they cried out, "Yes, yes, yes, on this Sabbath!" And then to make sure that they understood and approved, he cried out three times, "Shall I reap?" and they answered, "Yes, yes, yes, reap!"

Clearly, more is involved than the meaning of a particular verse or even than the authority of tradition. The evidence of the Septuagint and the Book of Jubilees as well as the practice of the Samaritans suggests that some of the traditions at least might have supported the Boethusians.[1] On the other side, linguistic evidence might be cited in support of the Pharisees, for šabbat can clearly bear other meanings than "the sabbath-day." In verse 15b *šeba' šabbatot temimot* clearly means "seven complete *weeks*" and, as already remarked, in verse 32 in reference to the Day of Atonement, the term signifies a particularly solemn day rather than the seventh day of the week. We thus do not have a simple confrontation between literalism and tradition – which is sometimes thought to be the ground of the controversy between the Sadducees and the Pharisees.[2]

The discussion of this Mishnah in the Babylonian Talmud (*Menaḥot* 65a-66a) helps to elucidate the underlying issues. A somewhat humorous piece of dialogue is cited as taking place between R. Yohanan ben Zakkai and an elderly member of the Boethusian sect. "Fools that you are," says R. Yohanan, "where do you get your notion from?" The old man babbled on at him (*mepaṭpeṭ kenegdo*) arguing that Moses being good-hearted, arranged that Shavuot would always fall on a Sunday, thus giving his people two days holiday in succession, i.e., a long-weekend for the Festival! Rabbi Yohanan, not to be outdone, retorts that if that was the motive how comes that Moses led his

---

[1]For discussion, see Hugo, Mantel, *The Men of the Great Synagogue* [Hebrew] (Tel-Aviv: Dvir, 1983), pp. 208-209, 218; R. H. Charles, ed., *The Book of Jubilees* (London: A. & C. Black, 1902), vi:22 and vi:32 and notes thereon. *The Book of Jubilees* evidently presupposes fixed days of the week for all the festivals.
[2]Cf. Josephus, *Antiquities of the Jews*, XIII:10 on the differences between the two sects.

people round the wilderness for forty years? After all, the text clearly says that it was only an eleven-day march from Horeb to Kadesh-Barnea (Deuteronomy 1:2). His opponent is taken aback by this *reductio ad absurdum*. Surely that is no argument. Indeed not, says R. Yohanan, but that is the only way to answer idle-talk. The real answer to the Boethusians he says involves an understanding of the balance the Torah seeks between days and weeks in the calculation of the time between Passover and Shavuot. One verse (15) emphasizes the "seven complete weeks" – this is ideally realized when the first day of Passover occurs on a Sabbath, and the count thus begins on the first day of the week. But another verse (16) says that we should "number fifty days" – this mode takes precedence when the Festival starts on a weekday and thus the weeks are not rounded off as "complete weeks." The Gemara takes up R. Yohanan's distinction between the two verses again at the end of the pericope but prefers the way in which a later teacher, Abaye, expounded them. He found in them a key to the form that the "Counting of the Omer" should take no matter on what day the festival might begin. There are two commands he says, "There is a command to count days and a command to count weeks." Both modes of counting are to be employed simultaneously. And this we are told was the practice of the School of R. Ashi. It is also that codified by Maimonides (*Mishneh Torah, Temidin*, ch. 7). He determines that "the command is to count the days together with the weeks." As a result, in the standard observance, we make the count by means of a particular and somewhat tautological formula, e.g., "Today is the sixteenth day of the Omer which are two weeks and two days."

It should be noted that if the command is, as Abaye insisted, a double command resting on two different verses of Scripture, the formula nevertheless emphatically brings the two units of time together. It seems that without combining the weeks and the days in this fashion we have not done our duty. This is also the sense of the language chosen by Maimonides who, unlike Abaye in the talmudic pericope, uses the term *mitzvah* only once, not "there is a command to count the days and a command to count the weeks" but "the command is to count the days together with the weeks." And in fact Maimonides in the *Sefer Hamitzvot* reckons the Counting of the Omer as a single positive command, not two, and develops a number of arguments to justify this.[3] There is thus a dialectic of oneness and separateness. Justice has to be done to both kinds of reckoning as signified in the two

---

[3]Number 161 in the classification of Maimonides. See *The Commandments*, ed. C. B. Chavel (London: Soncino, 1967), I, 171-72.

different verses of Scripture cited, but the two different modes must somehow be brought together. On that dialectic we may ponder.

II

We are of course concerned here with the very nature of time itself as Jews have striven to apprehend it. In the first place, Jews like all men experience time as natural process, measured in months, days and years. We are involved in the cycle of the seasons, dependent for our very existence on the winter rains and on the vivifying warmth of the spring that follows, bringing with it the ripening cereal crop. There is consolation in the thought of the regularity and assurance of this cycle but also fear lest some change or mishap should interrupt it. Primitive man (and less primitive man too for that matter) strove to assure the continuation of the cycle by means of ceremonies of propitiation, supplication and thanksgiving. Such ceremonies held at fixed times and seasons served to link human society itself to the natural cycle. Passover and Shavuot, like the other times and seasons of the Jewish year, are emphatically such ceremonies. Care has to be taken that Pesah coincides with the first ripening of the grain in the fields, i.e., the *'abib* (Exodus 23:15, 34:18). If there is no sign of the *'abib* as Nisan approaches, then an additional month has to be intercalated.[4] Similarly Shavuot has to coincide with the appearance of the first-fruits and of the ripened wheat which were to be brought to the Temple (Exodus 34:22).

It is this rhythm which accounts in the first instance for the necessity of counting days. The *'omer* is of course the sheaf of barley, the fifty days of the *'omer* marking the exact time-span dividing the beginning of the barley-harvest on the full moon of Nisan from the beginning of the wheat-harvest. Not only days but months and years are part of this rhythm. By means of the mechanism of intercalation the lunar calendar is linked to the solar year – a natural cycle which governs the seasons and with them the life of man and nature. This natural rhythm is not something that Biblical and later, Rabbinic Judaism hides away as a residue from the pagan fertility religions. We are bidden to heed and celebrate it. It conditions our existence as mortal men rooted in the organic world and seeking salvation in the blessings that that world yields. The first covenant formula indeed, that made with the survivors of the Flood, speaks of the promise and blessing of that natural order: "While the earth remains, seed time and harvest, and cold and heat, and summer and winter, and day and night shall not

---

[4]Cf. B. T. *Sanhedrin* 11b; *Midrash Haggadol on Deuteronomy*, ed. S. Fisch (Jerusalem: Mosad Harav Kook, 1972), pp. 348-49 (on Deut. 16:1).

cease" (Genesis 8:22). Far from rejecting the order of Nature as having significance only for men who are enclosed in the world of myth – as Rosenzweig might put it – such texts show us biblical man sanctifying the natural order itself, making it part of the poetry of the covenant.

Of course it is the special mark of the biblical religion, as Henri Frankfort and so many others have noted, that it sets limits to, and transcends the natural cycle of birth, copulation and death.[5] Ultimately, this rhythm fails to satisfy us; it leaves us in a deep sense frustrated. "All things are full of weariness; man cannot utter it" says Kohelet as he considers the cycle of nature and with it the myth of the eternal return of all things as day follows night in monotonous sequence – "the sun also rises, and the sun goes down, and hastens to its place where it rises again. The wind goes towards the south, and veers to the north; round and round goes the wind, and on its circuits the wind returns...and there is nothing new under the sun" (1:5-9).

Kohelet in this chapter calls attention to the emptiness and vanity of mere natural process; something else, it would seem, is needed, something "new under the sun." That something else, spelled out for us in other books and primarily in Genesis itself, is symbolized by the seven-days of Creation culminating in the Sabbath. Unlike Baal or Tammuz who are themselves functioning parts of the natural cycle, the Creator God of Genesis is capable of radical novelty. The "beginning" which he inaugurates is the beginning of an historical program which will be marked by revolutionary change. In that program Man will share. Having established the natural world and having symbolically "rested" or withdrawn himself from it, he then summons Man into fellowship with him. The sign of that fellowship is the Sabbath-day. Here we are in a different time-dimension, a time belonging to the Torah rather than the cosmos, to Man rather than to Nature. The seven-day cycle is not deduced from the natural movements of the sun, the moon or the tides and seasons: it is rather superimposed upon them, a mark of sanctity and purpose set upon time itself. As Eviatar Zerubavel has shown in a valuable anthropological study, "quasi weeks" are known in ancient Assyria and Mesopotamia but these on examination turn out to be irregular divisions of the lunar calendar; the true week, "a continuous seven-day cycle that runs throughout history paying no attention whatsoever to the moon and its phases is a distinctively Jewish invention." Zerubavel argues that the week is "a cultural artifact that rests on social convention alone...one of the first

---

[5]Cf. H. and H. A. Frankfort, *Before Philosophy* (Harmondsworth: Penguin Books, 1949), pp. 241-43; G. E. Wright, *The Old Testament Against its Environment* (London: SCM Press, 1950), pp. 22-27.

major attempts by humans to break away from being prisoners of nature."[6] The Rabbis, whilst they would have eagerly agreed with the importance accorded here to the sabbatical scheme, would most probably have demurred at this formulation on two grounds; first, because it is too anthropocentric; the week and with it the Sabbath were for them not a human invention but the gift of a covenanting God, calling man to share a space with him beyond that of mere nature. Second, as we have seen, this "Jewish invention" did not for them actually cut us off from the natural world but became the mark of sanctity and redemptive purpose imprinted upon that world. We are commanded to count the weeks but we are also commanded to count the days! What is more – and here is the extraordinary difficulty and challenge of the Jewish scheme – we are to see these two modes as ultimately and fundamentally one.

There are other halakhic paradigms which share the same deep-structure. The covenantal sign placed upon the flesh does not cut us off from the biological and instinctual life of the body, but aims at sanctifying it, integrating the lunar and the sabbatical, the physical and metaphysical. The word is circumcision rather than castration. We now begin to see the true nature of the argument on the Omer between R. Yohanan and the Pharisees on the one hand and the Boethusians and the Sadducees on the other. As Zerubavel puts it, "the Sadducean practice obviously reflects a strong desire to dissociate Jewish festivals from the lunar cycle."[7] One is reminded of the calendric system laid down in the Book of Jubilees which seems to have been followed also by the community of Qumran. This early text presupposes a 364 day calendar, i.e., a perfect multiple of seven with no remainder, making the week the "fundamental building block" and yielding a calendar which lacks a true accommodation to the lunar cycle and only a rough approximation to the solar cycle. The natural rhythm is denied and the Torah becomes a self-contained system separating its followers from the world. Using the semiotic model I have suggested, we could say that the Sadducean position here is that of castration rather than circumcision.

III

All this clearly places the dispute between the Pharisees and their opponents in an entirely different perspective from that suggested by Louis Finkelstein in his 1938 study. His basic thesis rests on what he

---

[6]Eviatar Zerubavel, *The Seven Day Circle* (New York: The Free Press, 1985), pp. 11, 8, 4.
[7]*Ibid.* pp. 72-73.

imagined to be the sociological differences between the two communities. The Pharisees he says were by and large "urban plebeians," i.e., town-dwellers and consumers; their typical setting was the market-place of Jerusalem.[8] As a result their emphasis was not on the agricultural aspect of the Festivals:

> The inhabitant of Jerusalem [i.e., the typical Pharisee] was not indifferent to the question of the harvest. But he viewed the harvest from a distance; he had not ploughed; he had not watched the stalks; nor had he waited for it. If Shavuot was to have any meaning for him and above all for his children, he had to find some meaning for it other than its agricultural associations.[9]

The emphasis for the Pharisees was on Shavuot as the Festival of the Giving of the Law, an event traditionally identified with the 6th of Sivan. The Sadducees denied this historical connection, claims Finkelstein; hence they had no interest in ensuring a fixed date for that festival. They were typically wealthy landowners, farmers, inhabitants of the coastal plain and the Jordan valley. Their interests were accordingly more agricultural. They were also suppliers rather than consumers; consequently, whilst a delay in the sale of the new barley might inconvenience the landless Pharisees, it could be profitable to the Sadducees.[10]

In the third edition of his work in 1962, Finkelstein reiterates his theory giving it some additional nuances. In particular, he speculates that the Sadducees and the Boethusians, belonging as they did to the priesthood, had an interest in fixing Shavuot for a Sunday – there were valuable emoluments for the Priests on all the pilgrim-festivals, but those which came their way on the Festival of First-Fruits were particularly attractive. The advantage of a Sunday was that the priests of the previous week's course would find it worth their while to stay on in Jerusalem for the extra day or two so as to enjoy these material benefits along with the priests of the new course. Thus everyone would be happy![11]

Finkelstein's theory based as it is on the flimsiest evidence, chiefly a phrase or two from Josephus,[12] seems to me high fantastical – a good

---

[8]*The Pharisees* (Philadelphia: Jewish Publication Society, [1938] 3rd revised edition 1962), II, 628.
[9]*Ibid.* I, 117.
[10]*Ibid.* II, 643-51.
[11]*Ibid.* II, 643.
[12]e.g., *Jewish Antiquities*, XIII:10 where Josephus speaks of the Sadducees having influence with the rich and the Pharisees drawing their support from the humbler sort; see also XVIII:1.

example of "over-interpretation."[13] It also ignores the clear theological overtones of the dispute, its momentousness and drama, as though nothing more was at stake than a few extra days for market manipulation or some extra perquisites for one of the priestly courses. Also it ignores the passion involved in what must have been one of the great fundamental controversies in the history of Judaism. That passion, conveyed in the Mishnah's dramatic account of how the Cutting of the Omer was conducted, is missing in Finkelstein's reconstruction. Moreover, if the Pharisees were so insensitive to the agricultural interest, how does it come about, one wonders, that they and not the Sadducees, emphasized the Water-Libation ceremony on the Intermediate days of Sukkot, a ceremony clearly inspired by anxiety about the autumn rainfall?[14] And again, who but the Pharisees developed the (non-biblical) solemnities of Hoshana-Rabba,[15] an occasion again designed to underscore the need for bounty and seasonal blessing as the dry season came to an end?

There is no escaping the conclusion that at bottom we have to do with two different ways of apprehending the nature of time itself. The Pharisees, whatever the sociological pattern of their constituency might have been, were alive to the rhythms of nature, whilst the Sadducean priesthood inherited a tradition according to which the life of the community was ordered predominantly by the sabbatical rhythm. In keeping with this emphasis, their forms of religion were to a great degree institutionalized, self-contained – almost on the way to a monastic ideal of Judaism.

It was against this monastic tendency that the Pharisaic teachers rebelled. The Torah for them was not the possession of a sect or a professional class; it was to be open to the world and the people. It is not in heaven, they might say, nor is it beyond the sea, nor is it locked up in the Temple. In the Counting of the Omer, the times of Nature and Torah are synchronized – hence the dialectical structure of the rules governing the Counting. Moreover, what is at stake is not just our understanding of time; there is also the question of our relation to the Land. After all, the pilgrim-festivals, divided as they are by a fixed number of days and months, celebrate the seasonal bounty of the Land. We are not merely mortals in that our lives are governed by the natural

---

[13]Cf. J. Neusner, *The Rabbinic Traditions About the Pharisees Before 70* (Leiden: E. J. Brill, 1971), III, 366, discussing far-fetched socio-economic interpretations of the debates between the Schools of Shammai and Hillel by Finkelstein and others.
[14]Cf. Mishnah, *Sukkah* 4:9.
[15]Cf. B. T. *Sukkah* 43b.

cycle, we are also earth-bound mortals – we have a terrestrial destiny. And yet we have a non-terrestrial destiny also. The sabbatical scheme serves to sanctify not only time but earthly space as well.

All this is underscored once again in the regulations governing the sabbatical year and the year of Jubilee as set out in Leviticus 25, i.e., only two chapters after the regulations for the Counting of the Omer and with obvious verbal echoes linking the two systems. Again we have the double time-scheme whereby the natural cycle of the year marked by sowing, growth and harvest is integrated into the non-natural cycle of the "sabbaths of years." The sabbatical year is of course emphatically the Sabbath of the Land when there was neither sowing nor harvest (Leviticus 25:4).[16] The same dialectic of belonging and yet not belonging obtains here in our relation to the Land. We belong to it and yet we are wanderers and strangers in the Land (25:23). The Land is ours and yet it is not ours; once every seven years it withdraws itself from our control. It is itself, so to speak, a covenanting partner, it keeps its sabbaths. When the sabbaths are violated, the Land of Israel becomes a witness for the prosecution – it "keeps its sabbaths" by turning into a desolation (Leviticus 26:34-35). The counting of the years is thus a matter of gravest consequence, the sabbatical year and the year of Jubilee being the covenantal sign placed on the earth itself from which we draw our sustenance, on which we dwell and to which our bodies will return. The years, like the days of the Omer, belong to the natural cycle, and they are to be counted! But the sabbaths of years like the weeks of the Omer have to be counted as well. The likeness of the language of Leviticus 25:8 ("And thou shalt number for thyself seven sabbaths of years, seven times seven years; and the space of the seven sabbaths of years shall be to thee forty nine years") to that of Leviticus 23:15-16 prompted the Rabbis in the *Sifra* to the same conclusion that Abaye reached in regard to the Counting of the Omer – viz. that the years as well as the sabbaths of years had to be counted.[17] Again, these are two commands which are one.

We noted that the rhythm of the week and the seven multiples of weeks introduced a sense of purpose into the measurement of time, the seven days of Creation representing the "beginning" of an historical program. We count the days towards the new thing that is to be

---

[16]On the link betwen the holiness of the Land of Israel and that of the Sabbath, see H. Y. Hadari, *Shabbatah shel Shevi'it* [Hebrew], (Jerusalem: Ministry of Education and Culture, 5740 [1980]), pp. 34-35, 93-99 (quoting Isaac Abravanel and Judah Loew of Prague).

[17]*Sifra*, "Behar" 2:2; *Yalkut Shimoni*, sect. 659; *Midrash Haggadol on Leviticus*, ed. A. Steinzaltz (Jerusalem: Mosad Harav Kook, 1976), p. 691 (on Lev. 25:8); and see Maimonides, *The Commandments*, ed. Chavel, I, 148-49.

revealed, awaiting a fulfilment, not a mere repetition of what was. That tension and alertness are of the essence of the Counting of the *'Omer*. They are caught in the verbal form *uqera'tem* "and you shall proclaim" – "and you shall proclaim on that self-same day, a holy assembly shall it be to you" (23:21). The Pharisaic tradition identified this holy assembly as the Festival of the Giving of the Law.[18] Creation leads to Revelation – that is the startling new thing that has to be proclaimed. Time has been fulfilled, redeemed; meaning has been given to history.

Now the same rousing term, *uqera'tem* repeats itself in the verses relating to the Jubilee year – "and you shall proclaim liberty throughout the Land to all its inhabitants...." (25:10). The fiftieth year would be a year of liberty marked by the sounding of the Shofar (the *yobel* or trumpet is what gives its name, of course, to the Jubilee) *proclaiming* the restoration of human dignity to slaves and the return of property to its owners. But the key word is of course *ge'ula* "redemption," repeated some sixteen times in this chapter – redemption for men and redemption for property. The counting of the sabbaths of years has brought us to the year of redemption – one looking back to the redemption from Egyptian bondage (verse 55) and forward – for thus the shofar was elsewhere understood (cf. Isaiah 27:13) – to a messianic redemption in which Man and Land would share. This is the promise and this is the historical task intimated in the long count of years to the Jubilee. The time of our lives is seen in the perspective of salvation-history.

IV

The counting itself, of course, is the important thing. Later traditions and associations attached themselves to the Omer making it a period of mourning, but this is not of the essence. What counts, we may say, is the counting. Accordingly, the command to count the sabbaths and days of the Omer, the sabbaths and years to the Jubilee, are positive commands in their own right to be distinguished from the commands governing the ceremonies with which the counting begins or ends. To learn to count our days and years is itself to learn something important, to experience time in a fully human fashion. That it seems is what the psalmist meant when he said: "Teach us to count our days aright, that we may gain a heart of wisdom" (Psalm 90:12). A man who has not "gained a heart of wisdom" experiences time as flux – he is swept onwards in the river of time, himself part of the natural process.

---

[18]B. T. *Shabbat* 86b; B. T. *Pesahim* 68b.

He does not look before and after, remembering where he has come from, preparing himself for what he will encounter at the next bend of the river. Nor does he truly experience the reality of the present moment; it passes him by, or rather, he is too much a part of it for him to apprehend it as something to be addressed before it is gone. As the psalmist phrases it: "thou dost sweep men away in a stream; they are like sleepers, like the short-lived grass in the morning. In the morning it flourishes and fades; by evening it is withered and dry" (*ibid.* 5-6).

In the imagery of these verses man and nature are undifferentiated; men share the same short time-span as the grass of the field; for both, the years and days fly away leaving nothing behind. This is one possible time-scheme for the life of natural man; its mark is an incredible fleetingness – *ki gaz ḥiš wanna'upa* – "it is soon gone and we fly away" (verse 10). The opening verses of the psalm emphasize the seemingly unbridgeable gap between this fleetingness of human life and time as it might apply to God:

> From everlasting to everlasting thou art God. Thou turnest man back to dust; and sayst, Return you children of men. For a thousand years in thy sight are but like yesterday when it is past, and like a watch in the night.

But there is a change as the psalm proceeds. Having gained a heart of wisdom, the speaker in the psalm can confidently turn to God and say: "let the pleasantness of the Lord be upon us; and establish for us the work of our hands" (17). No longer are his times and those of God separated by a great gulf. *No'am* here suggests not merely pleasantness but intimacy – Saul and Jonathan are "loving and pleasant [*ne'imim*] in their lives" (2 Samuel 1:23); and elsewhere it is "good and pleasant [*na'im*] for brothers to dwell together" (Ps 133:1). In short, the wisdom attained gives ground for the hope that God will now move closer to man, that he will truly become "our dwellingplace." The work of our hands will be established for, having learned to "count our days aright," we will come to share marvelously in God's own creative rhythm and purpose. We are still earthbound mortals, the days of our years being seventy or, at best, eighty; but now there is a change, for instead of flying away and leaving nothing behind, those days and years are filled with wealth and significance. Time has been redeemed:

> Satisfy us in the morning with thy steadfast love; that we may rejoice and be glad all our days.
>
> Ps 90:13

But natural time it would seem can present another aspect as intolerable as fleetingness, viz. tedium. Balancing the unbearably rapid passage of human life, we also know the equally unbearable monotony of what we might call the long-time scheme of natural man. It is to this that Kohelet had pointed in his first chapter. The wearying, monotonous revolutions of the sun and moon bringing with them nothing new arouse in us a mood of hopelessness, what in German is appropriately enough called *Langeweile*. There seems to be no end in sight. That is the other side of the same coin[19] – the unending sequence of yesterdays which in the end signify nothing. Kohelet considers one way of dealing with this tedium. It is to eat and drink and to pass the days as best we may; nowadays, we speak of killing time. But this too he concludes is vanity.

It would seem that according to the understanding both of the psalmist and the Rabbis, the true answer to both these modes – the brief and the tedious – of experiencing the natural time-rhythm is the counting; it is that which turns mere flux into history. In a thoughtful essay on *Time and Meaning in History*, Natan Rotenstreich notes that our awareness of the historical present requires us to be situated "on the borderline between structures and experiences."[20] In this connection, it may be suggested that the act of counting is a primary and fundamental means of structuring our experience of time. The first decisive act of Robinson Crusoe after being cast ashore on his desert island is to contrive a calendar and to begin to count the days and weeks – it is the first stage of his moral history:[21]

> After I had been there about ten or twelve days, it came into my thoughts that I should lose my reckoning of time for want of books, and pen and ink, and should even forget the Sabbath days.

To prevent this, he tells us, he set up a great post on the shore and after inscribing on it with his knife the date of his arrival on the island, he proceeds to mark the days and sabbaths and months and years as they pass:

> I cut every day a notch with my knife, and every seventh notch was as long again as the rest, and every first day of the month as long again as that long one; and thus I kept my calendar, or weekly, monthly, and yearly reckoning of time.

---

[19]Cf. N. Rotenstreich, *Time and Meaning in History*, Boston Studies in the Philosophy of Science, volume 101 (Dortrecht: D. Reidel, 1987), p. 159.

[20]*Ibid.* p. 160.

[21]On other biblical motifs in this novel, see by the present writer, "The Hermeneutic Quest in *Robinson Crusoe*" in *Midrash and Literature*, ed. G. H. Hartman and S. Budick (New Haven: Yale University Press, 1986), pp. 213-35.

Defoe has come near to an understanding of the biblical injunction to count our days not only as a way of attaining a heart of wisdom but as a key to survival in a world where in the end we are strangers and sojourners.

13

Are Women Property in the System of the Mishnah?

Paul Virgil McCracken Flesher
Northwestern University

The question, "are women property?" focuses on the issue of status. It assumes the broad question, "What is the status of women?" which it then qualifies by asking "Are they property?" Two methodological implications arise from this observation. First, to investigate a category's status is to search for its place in a hierarchy, that is, on a scale of social categories. The status of women cannot be determined without knowing their position relative to other classes of humanity, such as men, children and – in most ancient societies – slaves. To answer the specific question "are women property?" therefore, we must determine whether the position of women in the hierarchy equals that of property. Second, accurately determining the location of social groups in relationship to each other requires knowledge of the criteria that govern the placement of categories in the hierarchy. In other words, the scholar must understand not only a category's position, but also the basis for that position. To answer the question of whether women are property, we must discover the distinguishing characteristics of property and ascertain whether women possess them. The investigation of status thus entails the study of hierarchy – the relationship of rank among categories – and the analysis of classification – the delineation of categories and their distinguishing criteria.

The social world depicted in the Mishnah – a second-century Jewish law code – provides a particularly fruitful arena for studying the status of women, for the Mishnah's framers themselves focused their attention on problems of hierarchy and classification. Their discussions not only centered on distinguishing one category from another but they also provide a wealth of data concerning the relationship of these distinct groups. The Mishnah's very nature thus facilitates the investigation of status. Before I proceed with the analysis, let me briefly characterize the Mishnah. To begin with, the Mishnah can be compared to Plato's *Republic*. Although the *Republic* is philosophy and the Mishnah is a law code, both are products of systematic thought. The main difference is that Plato is interested in explicitly spelling out his system, while the Mishnah's framers assume a system and spend their energy discussing its problematic areas. Because of this interest, the framers' discussions are not free-ranging, but organized to make particular points about issues they consider important. Their discussions follow set principles, with the aim of enabling the Mishnah's laws to work together, rather than conflict with one another. Through this process of construction, the Mishnah's editors have necessarily formed clear and consistent conceptions of the categories of people and objects to which the laws apply. Their discussions, laws, and categories fit together into a single overarching, intellectual scheme – one portraying a cogent and coherent view of the world. The Mishnah's systemic nature therefore enables us rigorously to interrogate its social categories in general and the position of women in particular.

With this knowledge of the Mishnah's system, we can analyze the status of women in terms of both hierarchy and taxonomic classification. Since we want to answer a particular question – whether women are property – we do not need to analyze the Mishnah's entire scheme of status. Instead, we can directly compare the categories of women and property. Indeed, the Mishnah's framers have facilitated such a comparison, for their system contains a category of human property, namely, the slave.[1] By using this category as the indicator for the status of property, we solve two problems. First, we use a definition of property internal to the Mishnah, rather than anachronistically imposing a modern definition as some scholars have done.[2] Second, we need not even extrapolate the characteristics of property from non-human objects. The Mishnah's slave – which I call

---

[1]See pp. 67-77 of my book, *Oxen, Women, or Citizens? Slaves in the System of the Mishnah*, (Atlanta: Scholars Press, 1988) for a discussion of how the slave belongs to the category of property. This paper assumes and builds on the analysis done for the book.

[2]Judith R. Wegner, in her *Chattel or Person? The Status of Women in the Mishnah*, (New York: Oxford, 1988), defines her concept of "chattel" in accord with the modern notions of chattel found in American law and Common Law.

the bondman – thus constitutes an ideal category for determining whether the Mishnah's framers consider women to be property.

The comparison of women and bondmen must be performed for the questions of both hierarchy and classification. Restricting our comparison to matters of hierarchy alone – for example, by asking whether women and bondmen have the same rank in certain situations – will not necessarily provide us with an accurate assessment of women's status and can even lead in false directions. Ignoring the taxonomic criteria by which the Mishnah's framers determine those rankings can lead to seemingly obvious conclusions that are in fact wrong. Two examples should make this clear.

The Temple cult, which the Mishnah's framers treat as the central institution of Israelite society, provides the first context for comparison of women and bondmen. The norm for participation in the cult is set by the man, specifically, the free, adult, male Israelite. All adult males have cultic duties, that is, tasks and observances that they are required to perform. These are based on the man's caste status. Members of different castes must perform different duties. Priests officiate, for example, while Levites assist them and Israelites provide the animals, produce and other items necessary for the sacrificial rites. Our question is this: to what extent do women and slaves take part in these cultic observances? The answer is that they do not. Neither women nor bondmen have any caste-based duties.[3] At no point does their caste status require them to participate in Temple worship. If they wish, however, women and slaves may participate in some rites of worship. For example, they may bring animals to sacrifice and may even pay the Temple tax if they desire (M. Shek. 1:5). But their voluntary actions do not bring about the same results as would a man's performance of the same act. In fact, their offerings do not enter the same level of holiness as a man's. With regard to worship in the Temple cult, therefore, women and bondmen possess the same hierarchical position, one well beneath that of a free, adult, male Israelite. Can we term that position "property?" Before answering, let us study another example.

The Mishnah's depiction of the legal system provides a second context for comparing women and slaves. In the courts, adult males participate in different ways. For example, they occasionally serve as

---

[3] I have delineated the difference between caste-based cultic observances and cultic practices not based on the caste of the participant on pp. 112-134 of my book, *Oxen, Women, or Citizens?* In a nutshell, the distinction is that sacrifices having to do with cultic purity are not caste-based, while most other cultic duties are. Both women and bondmen must when necessary bring offerings to attain cultic purity, but they have no required tasks in Temple worship that stem from their caste status.

judges and officers, but most commonly appear as witnesses. Women and slaves never have any role among the court officials and rarely are permitted to testify. The limited circumstances in which they may witness, however, are revealing. The Mishnah's framers show women testifying about other women, slaves about other slaves, both about foreigners and – most significant for our purpose – women testify about slaves and vice versa. But the sages only portray women as testifying about male Israelites in cases concerning their relationship to their own husbands, and sages provide no case in which slaves witness about free men. Women and slaves can thus testify about individuals at their own status or lower, but not about the free, adult, male Israelites, who possess a higher status. Since they can testify about each other, women and slaves seem to be on the same level – one which we could argue is property.

So in two important social contexts – the Temple cult and the courts – the Mishnah's framers rank women nearly identical to bondmen. Does this hierarchical convergence permit us to conclude that the Mishnah's authorities treat women as human property? The answer is no. For we have shown only that the Mishnah's framers rank women and bondmen at the same level in certain situations, we have yet to investigate the classificatory factors for that similarity.[4]

To discover those factors, we must study how the Mishnah's framers identified and differentiated the categories of Israelite society, a task which they accomplished through the application of taxonomic principles of classification. Like the plants in a botanist's identification book, the Mishnah's categories of humanity conform to distinct criteria. These criteria furthermore show relationships among the categories and reveal how they form part of a structure that positions each category in relationship to all the others. Only by comparing women and bondmen within this structure can we accurately determine the place of women vis-à-vis the status of property. Let me describe these categories from a taxonomic perspective.

The Mishnah's authorities distinguish four main categories of Israelite society: householders, minor sons, women and bondmen. They accomplish this in what is logically a two-stage process. First, they establish the Israelite householder as the central category of Israelite society. The householder sets the standard of humanity. He represents the ideal human being, for he has both the full potential of a human being and the capacity fully to use that potential. Second, the

---

[4]In fact, although we have shown that the rank of women and bondmen in the two situations is lower than men, we have not shown that the lower position is one that can be properly termed "property."

Mishnah's framers define the other three types of people as counterparts to the householder; each class stands in opposition to or negation of one of his particular qualities. The capacity of reason, for example, distinguishes the minor son from the householder.[5] As adults, householders possess the capacity to reason, but minor sons lack this power. In terms of gender, women take the role of opposition; the householder is male, women are female. Bondmen, finally, oppose the householder in terms of freedom. The householder is free; no category of people can permanently dictate or interfere with his activities.[6] The bondman, by contrast, stands subject to the full control of his master.

We can furthermore restate each category's characteristics in terms of itself; each category is like the householder except where its defining attribute makes it different. Women are like householders except where their gender causes a distinction. Bondmen, similarly, possess the same characteristics as the householder except where their position as property makes them different. Finally, minor sons are like householders, except where their lack of reason causes a difference. To the Mishnah's authorities, therefore, all categories of people possess the same characteristics as the householder, except where the defining attribute of that category differentiates it.

This means of classification has important ramifications for determining the hierarchy of these categories. The problem can best be understood through an example. The Mishnah's authorities differentiate the classification of women in opposition to householders, but they do not delineate them with respect to bondmen or minor sons. Concomitantly, the framers rank the category of women vis-à-vis the householder, but not the other categories. It is thus impossible to accurately determine the rank of one category in relation to the others, because each category's rank relative to the householder stems from different factors. The minor son derives his rank from his lack of reason, the woman from her gender, the bondman from his lack of freedom. Each factor allows the members of a category to do certain things and forbids them from doing others. For instance, women can marry, while minor sons and bondmen cannot. In another example, bondmen serve as householders' agents – a task in which women are never depicted and minor sons are incapable of performing.[7] So although the ranks of each

---

[5]Minor daughters are classed, as we shall see, in the category of women. Their immaturity constitutes a secondary, although significant, issue.
[6]See pp. 159-167 of my *Oxen, Women, or Citizens?* for a full characterization of the householder's freedom.
[7]For a discussion of bondmen, women and agency, see pp. 127-131 of my *Oxen, Women, or Citizens?*

type of person are clear in relation to the householder, they cannot be accurately specified relative to each other. Status is a matter of positioning with respect to Israelite society's central category, not to all categories. Therefore, just because women and slaves are alike in one area, they will not necessarily be the same in another area. Or, more to the point, just because women and bondmen have the same status in the Temple cult and the courts, it does not necessarily mean that they are both property. To demonstrate that women are property, we must show that the framers *classify* them as property, not just identify a few situations in which the framers *rank* them at the same level as property.

Up to this point, we have treated the Mishnah's class of women as if it constituted a single, indivisible category. In fact, the Mishnah's authorities divide women into six sub-groups: minor daughters, adult daughters, wives, divorcees, widows, and levirate widows.[8] Sages arrange these categories into three pairs: minor and adult daughters, wives and divorcees, and widows and levirate widows. This has been clearly demonstrated by Judith Romney Wegner in her study, *Chattel or Person? The Status of Women in the Mishnah.*[9] We shall now describe these pairs of categories. The minor and the adult daughter comprise the first pair. A girl belongs to the category of minor daughter from birth to the age of twelve and a half.[10] She stands under her father's control. She has no property rights; any income that she earns and any object that she finds goes to him. The father has complete authority to arrange her marriage, either by betrothing her or by selling her as a concubine. A girl enters the category of adult daughter if she is not married at the age of twelve and a half. At this time, she becomes an independent woman possessing the right to acquire

---

[8]The names of the categories themselves derive from Scripture, but the taxonomic framework which we shall describe in a moment is designed by the Mishnah's framers themselves.

[9]This pairing of categories and the general description of them that follows is based on the work of Judith Romney Wegner in her *Chattel or Person? The Status of Women in the Mishnah.* Dr. Wegner delineated the pairing of categories in her work, I merely place them into the Mishnah's larger taxonomic system. See especially the section entitled "Mishnah's Taxonomy of Women" in Chapter One. I want to thank Dr. Wegner for sharing her manuscript with me prior to its publication.

[10]The Mishnah holds that the daughter belongs to an interstitial category for six months instead of passing directly from minor daughter to adult daughter. While in this category, the girl is called a *naarah*. During this period, she enters into some of the responsibilities and duties of an adult, but she retains some of the restrictions of the minor daughter. See M. Nid. 5:7 and Chapter Two of Wegner's *Chattel or Person?*

belongings and earnings independent of her father. Furthermore, she arranges her own marriage. The second pair consists of the wife and the divorcee. A wife stands under her husband's control. In this position, she has more rights than a minor daughter, but not as many as an adult daughter. For example, while she may own property, her husband has the usufruct of it. The divorcee, by contrast, is an independent woman who both owns and controls her own property. Her former husband has no power over her. The widow and the levirate widow constitute the third pair of women. Widows are independent women with rights similar to those of divorcees. But a wife enters the category of widow only if she has borne an heir for her deceased husband. If she has not, she instead becomes a levirate widow and enters the purview of her dead husband's brother.[11] A levirate widow is in a state of limbo. While she may take actions to maintain herself, including dealing in property, her brother-in-law controls her marital status. Sages, following Scripture, expect the brother-in-law to take her as a wife and produce sons in the name of the dead man. But he must choose to do so. If he refuses, then she performs a ceremony releasing herself from his control and becomes a normal widow. But until the dead man's brother decides which option he will take, the levirate widow stands in limbo, with her future under the control of her husband's brother.

The characteristics of these six categories of women actually derive from strict rules of taxonomic classification. The categories are distinguished by a two different taxonomic criteria. The genus of women is divided into three species – that is, the pairs – by the criterion of sexuality; specifically, the members of each pair share the same form of sexuality. (See the table below.) The sexuality of daughters is that of virginity. For wives and ex-wives, sexual activity comprises the operative form of sexuality. For widows, the important form is productivity, that is, whether or not they bore their dead husband an heir. At the second stage, sages apply the taxonomic criterion of the householder's control to distinguish one category from the other. For each pair of categories, the sexuality of one is subject to a householder's control, while that of the other stands free from such control. Thus, the minor daughter's virginity is controlled by her father, while that of the adult daughter is not. The wife's sexual activity is controlled by her husband, while the divorcee's is not. Finally, the parentage of the levirate widow's future offspring – that is, her future productivity – stands subject to her brother-in-law, while that of the ordinary widow does not. We therefore find that three categories of women – minor daughters, wives, and levirate widows – have their sexuality

---

[11]Of course, if the husband has no brothers, she becomes a normal widow.

controlled by the dominant householder in their lives, while three
categories stand independent of any control by a householder.

Sexuality

		Virginity	Activity	Productivity
Under a house-holder's control?	Controlled	Minor daughter	Wife	Levirite widow
	Not Controlled	Adult daughter	Divorcee	Widow

Figure 1

Knowing the classifications of women and their relationships can
help us see the misleading nature of our initial comparison of women
and bondmen in the context of the Temple cult and the courts. All six
categories have a low-level status in the two institutions. Sages do not
distinguish those whose sexuality is under a householder's control from
those who are totally independent from a man's power. Both groups of
categories belong at a low level of participation. Thus, the status of
women in these two arenas stems from the taxonomic criterion that
distinguishes the genus of women from that of men, namely, gender. The
secondary criterion of the householder's control of sexuality has no
affect on their general inability to participate in the Temple cult or the
courts. Similarly, the bondman's status stems from his taxonomic
criterion; but his criterion is that of property. Thus the Mishnah's
classification of persons does not classify women as property as it does
the bondman, even though in particular circumstances they may possess
the same status. As taxonomic criteria, gender and property exclude
each other.

At the primary level of the genus of women, then, we have shown
that women are not property. But there are three species at the
secondary level that are subject to a householder's control – minor
daughters, wives and levirate widows. Since the general definition of
property, including the bondman, is to be subject to a householder's full
control, it appears that these three categories of women may be
considered property at least in the areas where this control is
exercised. Perhaps this partial control over different categories of
women is equivalent to being partially in the status of property. To
avoid any suspense, let me reveal that this is not the case. Not even the
wife, whose husband has the most control over her, stands in the status

of property. But the answer is more easily stated than demonstrated. To support this claim, we must first investigate the forms of personal power held by the different categories of Israelite humanity and determine how the possession and exercise of that power is affected by their classification. Let us describe the Mishnah's concept of personal power, then study how the status of property affects the bondman's exercise of it and finally compare him to the dependent categories of women.

The householder provides the best focus for explaining personal power, for the Mishnah's framers use him as the norm for humanity. The householder possesses two forms of power relevent to our study; the first I call the power of acts that require the exercise of reason and the second I term the power exercised through relationships.[12] First, "acts requiring reason" are deeds that have legal consequences only if the performer has the capacity of reason. In order for the act to be considered legally effective, it must be performed by someone with the mental capacity to understand the act's implications. In sages' view, an adult Israelite meets these conditions. When such actions are performed by a person lacking the necessary mental ability – such as a minor – those acts have no recognized legal effect or standing. For example, if a householder injures his neighbor, he must pay compensation. The householder is culpable because he possesses reason and therefore understands the implications of his action. In contrast, if the householder's minor son – who lacks reason – injures the same neighbor, no compensation is paid. This is because the minor does not understand the ramifications of his deeds. Of course, there is some sort of physical effect, but that is of no legal consequence. Even if the neighbor has been physically hurt, the child bears no legal culpability because he lacks the requisite mental capacity.

Second, actions are not the only cause of legal effects; relationships may also produce them. These effects are continual, however, not momentary like those caused by actions. Wherein lies the difference? When a person performs a deed – for instance, he hits someone – all ensuing legal consequences stem from that single incident. The legal effects of a bond between two people, in contrast, begin with its establishment and continue as long as it exists. If the liason should end,

---

[12]There is a third type of personal power in the Mishnah's system, that of merely physical acts and bodily conditions. It includes sources of power such as sexual intercourse and cultic impurity. It is irrelevant to our investigation of whether women have the status of property because all four classes of Israelites – householders, minor sons, women and bondmen – have this power equally. For a further discussion of this matter, see pp. 84-90 and 131-134 of my *Oxen, Women, or Citizens?*

the effects likewise cease. Furthermore, relationships comprise another means through which one person can exercise power over another. For example, when a woman marries, she forms a tie to her husband. Through this link, the husband determines his wife's caste status. If the husband belongs to the caste of priests, she enters the caste of priests. If the husband should ever divorce her, thereby cutting the link between them, he ceases to determine her caste position. Thus, a relationship is a state of being; while a person remains in a particular state, the effects of that state persist.

The bondman's nature becomes evident when we investigate the effect of his status as property on his capacity to use these two powers effectively. Turning first to acts requiring reason, we discover that the Mishnah's sages grant the adult bondman the same potential to exercise such power as an adult householder. However, they complicate matters by denying him free use of his power; the bondman can achieve the intended purpose of an act only when his master allows. In other words, the householder determines whether his slave exercises his capacity of reason and thus dictates whether his slave's deeds bear legal consequences. When the bondman acts with his master's authorization, the deed has legal effects. But if he acts without his master's permission, then sages consider the act not to have legally happened and it therefore bears no legal consequences. For example, a householder can require his bondman to separate the offering of priestly rations from his harvested grain. The grain which the bondman designates enters the status of priestly rations. But if the householder changes his mind and removes his permission for the slave to do this task, any grain that the bondman then sets aside remains just grain (M. Ter. 3:4). This is because the bondman's actions were not authorized by his master and hence bear no legal effects.

Similarly, although the bondman has the potential to form relationships, his master denies him the capacity to do so. In fact, the master cancels all relationships that the slave possessed prior to enslavement; the slave has no kinship ties at all, neither of blood nor marriage. Furthermore, during the entire period of his enslavement, he is incapable of forming any new ties. Even if he cohabits with a slave of the opposite sex and produces offspring, no one is related to the others. The adults do not form any kinship bond, and there is no tie between mother and offspring. For a slave to be property, therefore, means (1) a total incapacity to form or hold relationships, and (2) that a master has complete control over the legal effects of the slave's acts requiring reason.

A comparison between the dependent categories of women and the bondman reveals that the householder's power over women is both quantitatively and qualitatively different from his power over his slave. By comparing the householder's control over the categories of women with his control over his bondmen, we can see the extent of these differences. We begin with the power exercised through relationships.

The three categories of women whose sexuality is controlled by a householder – minor daughters, wives and levirate widows – have the capacity to form and hold relationships. But the householder controls a woman's capacity to enter *new* relationships, in particular, marital or conjugal relationships. The householder dictates whom the woman may marry and with whom she may have sexual relations. The father of the minor daughter has full responsibility for and final say in choosing the man his daughter marries. A wife's husband automatically denies her the right to cohabit with any other man. The brother-in-law of a levirate widow has the right of first refusal to take the woman as his wife. To control a woman's sexuality, therefore, means to control her capacity to form new relationships.

When we compare a householder's control over the power of relationships held by these categories of women with his control over his bondman's power to maintain and enter relationships, we notice two important differences. First, the householder merely prevents these women from forming new relationships. By contrast, he not only prevents the bondman from forming new relationships, but also cancels old ones. Thus, the bondman is tied only to his master, whereas the women remain part of a whole network of kinship ties. The householder merely hinders the women's expansion of their network. Second, comparing the householder's control over the bondman with his control of his minor daughter, for example, shows that the form of prevention in the two cases is qualitatively different. Sages hold that the householder can prevent the minor daughter from forming a link to a man, but if the steps he takes to prevent that link fail, a relationship is formed. For example, if a minor daughter has sexual intercourse with a man and becomes pregnant, a relationship forms between the daughter and her offspring; her father can do nothing to alter that fact. This is not a problem with the bondman, by contrast, for the bondman simply cannot form relationships to anyone other than his master. His master's control cancels all attempts to establish new relationships. Thus, although the householder controls the power of relationships for three categories of women and for the bondman, he does not do so in the same manner. The control he exercises over the bondman applies to all relationships – past, present and future – and is insurmountable, while the power he exerts over the categories of women applies only to future relationships and even then it can be overcome.

Although the power of relationships directly corresponds to sexuality, we can also ask about the householder's control over the other form of power exercised by these categories of women – that of acts requiring reason. The three categories of dependent women differ with regard to their possession of this power and with regard to whether a householder controls their exercise of it. First, minor daughters possess no capacity of reason and thus cannot perform acts requiring reason. Consequently, the question of whether their father can control such acts is irrelevant. Second, the levirate widow possesses reason and hence can perform acts requiring it. Her brother-in-law, however, cannot control her exercise of this type of power. Until he actually takes her as his wife – thereby altering her classification – she is free to act as she pleases. For example, she can sell her inherited land as if she was a householder and all vows she takes are permanently binding and irreversible.[13] The only act requiring reason she cannot perform is marriage. Third, some acts requiring reason performed by the wife are subject to her husband's control. For example, a husband may annul many vows which his wife takes. He cannot annul every vow, however, only ones which impinge upon him and his marital rights.[14] If a wife vows to refrain from intercourse, for example, her husband can cancel the vow. The category of wife thus constitutes the only class of women for whom the householder can control any act requiring reason. She does not belong to the classification of property as does the bondman, for the householder exercises control over only some of her acts, while the same householder can control all of his bondman's acts requiring reason.

If we now ask the question, "in terms of their exercise of personal power, are women equivalent to slaves?" the answer is clearly no. The bondman is a chattel, while women appear more like a householder. Even though three categories of women are subject to a householder's control over some form of their power, that control is neither as extensive nor as effective as that over the bondman. This fact holds true for both forms of power we examined: that exercised through relationships and that exercised through acts requiring reason. The householder's control over his bondman's relationships is strong enough to cancel all the slave's relationships, whereas for minor daughters, wives, and levirate widows, the householder merely controls their

---

[13]See the insightful discussion of this matter in Wegner's *Chattel or Person?* in the sections entitled "Wife's Vows Inimical to Conjugal Relations," and "The Wife as a Owner of Property."

[14]This point has been clearly demonstrated by Wegner's *Chattel or Person?* in the section entitled "Wife's Vows Inimical to Conjugal Relations."

capacity to form new relationships. All past relationships remain valid in the present. Similarly, the householder's power over his bondman's acts requiring reason is all pervasive. He can cancel the legal effects of all his bondman's rational acts. By contrast, the wife – the only category of woman whose acts requiring reason are subject to a householder's control – can perform many acts outside her husband's control. He can cancel the effects only of those that interfere with his privileges.

We thus have a clear answer to the question, "Are women property in the Mishnah's System?" The results of this study reveal an unqualified "no." At the primary level of classification, the genus of women is distinguished by the taxonomic criterion of gender, not property. At the secondary level on which the six species of women are differentiated, we find three categories whose sexuality is controlled by a householder and three categories that stand independent of such control. But even the categories subject to such power are neither treated as equivalent to the slave nor classified as property.[*]

---

[*] The research for this article was supported by a grant from the Foundation for Future Generations.

14

Three Stages in the Development of Early Rabbinic Prayer

Tzvee Zahavy
University of Minnesota

A. The Difficulties of Using the Evidence of Mishnah and Tosefta Tractate Berakhot for an Account of the History of Early Jewish Prayer[1]

We face a variety of snares when we come to study traditional religious texts, such as the tractates Berakhot in Mishnah (M.) and Tosefta (T.). Since these are the first segments of authoritative rabbinic documents that were brought to their final form in Israel in the early part of the third century they are distant from us in space, time and culture. Ostensibly these legal and anecdotal statements represent valuable sets of data pertaining to some dimensions of the historical and intellectual life of the Jews of Israel of the first through third centuries. They appear to inform us of what some leading rabbis of that time thought about the world in which they lived, their philosophical concepts, their ideas and concerns on a variety of subjects.[2]

---

[1]This study follows many of the methods established in Jacob Neusner's studies of Mishnah and Tosefta and epitomized in *Judaism: The Evidence of Mishnah*, Chicago, 1981. I share many of the presuppositions of that work. However, on many specifics I seek angles of vision divergent from Neusner's. At times I take a more credulous approach to attributions of the texts. In some cases I seek a more reductive explanation for opinions and prescriptions.

[2]See my book *The Mishnaic Law of Blessings and Prayers: Tractate Berakhot*, Brown Judaic Studies: Scholars Press, Atlanta, 1987, for a systematic explanation of each pericope in M. and T. Berakhot.

But these are not simple texts. Rabbis of the third century edited them with great care to exclude the materials they found objectionable and to include only those very few teachings that for theological or political reasons they wished to propound. They did not tell us outright what if any comprehensive social or philosophical viewpoints underlie these texts. I do hope in this essay and in future studies to intuit and reconstruct some semblance of the rabbinic outlooks, even some dimensions of the ethics and metaphysics of the Judaic leadership that taught their disciples that in these documents were elements of the Oral Torah given to Moses on Mount Sinai.

The tractates of Berakhot in M. and T. dwell mainly on the subjects of prayer and blessings, and of mealtime commensality. As far as we know, some followers of the rabbis adhered to these rules. Some did not. They cared enough about the rules to dispute, debate, to catalogue and canonize them. Non-rabbinic Jews probably rejected or neglected most of the religious practices described in these short collections.

The rules deal with rituals, words and actions understood and accepted by a defined collective. What made these mannerisms and poetic declarations matter to the Jews of the rabbinic persuasion was their place within the political and social realities and relationships, amidst the complex struggle for leadership, dominance and control of the religious institutions and structures of an important religious community in Israel in that era.

Before I return to the historical motives of the rabbis, let me sketch out some of the basic background of this formative epoch. The age of early rabbinism spans three generations from the first through the third centuries C.E. Our texts contain declarations ascribed to rabbis of three generations prior to the age of the authoritative publication of the texts. A salient feature of the literary character of rabbinic teachings is the preservation of regulations in the traditional attributive form of discourse, in the name of a rabbi: "Rabbi X says" [followed by a ruling] or [a ruling followed by] "the words of Rabbi Y."

The rabbis named in Mishnah and Tosefta Berakhot lived in three somewhat disjointed periods in Jewish history. The latest, the Ushan masters, flourished mainly in the Lower Galilee in the middle to late second century after the defeat of the Bar Kokhba rebels in 135, and before the seat of rabbinic learning moved a short distance south to Bet Shearim at the end of the second century. That war severed many of their ties to the preceding generation, the Yavnean rabbis. In their centers on the coastal plain and elsewhere, these earlier masters thrived in a period of great turbulence from the traumatic destruction of the second Temple in Jerusalem in 70, the late first century, to the time of the equally disruptive Bar Kokhba war. The texts in Berakhot attribute several traditions to even earlier masters, the Houses of Hillel and Shammai, who were active in the early to middle first century in Jerusalem while the Temple was still standing.

The problem, to reiterate, is that because of the paucity of preserved teachings of each of these groups of masters, scattered selectively throughout the chapters of M. and T. in the process of redaction, I must proceed in stages to regain a historical perspective on the emergence of rabbinism.

Accordingly, I separate these strands of traditions attributed to masters of three generations and reassemble, reorganize and analyze them to get a better perspective on the contours of the gradual but distinct history and development of early Jewish prayer in the generations prior to the final closure of the Mishnaic corpus.[3]

Let me make a few observations on my critical procedures. Wherever there is a warrant, I raise the issue of the authenticity of the attributions. In a few cases there is reason to question the attribution of a ruling to a given master, as for instance where a ruling on a matter of concern to a later authority is anachronistically attributed to an earlier master. But, in the overwhelming majority of cases the attributions stand on their face value. I assume that the assigned rulings reflect the views of the rabbi to whom they are attributed, or at the very least to his school of immediate disciples or contemporaries. I give special attention to those ideas in earlier materials which are developed or refined further in traditions ascribed to masters in later generations because that form of attestation provides an additional argument for the earlier existence and authenticity of the attribution of a teaching.

These are some elements in my approach to using rabbinic evidence. Let me briefly describe now the main topics of the tractate. At the time of the formation of M. in the early third century, three major components made up the rabbinic system of blessings and prayers: the recitation in the morning and evening of the *Shema'* with its blessings before and after; the recitation three times each day of the Prayer of Eighteen Blessings; the recitation of blessings before and after eating a meal.

Each of these elements of the system has a distinct history. Evidence reveals that the formal ritual of reciting the *Shema'* goes back to the period before 70 C.E. when the Temple was standing in

---

[3]I review the Mishnah-redactor's perspective of the components of a system of rabbinic prayer by which he shaped the whole of the tractate in the process of the compilation of M. Berakhot in my study *The Mishnaic Law of Blessings and Prayers: Tractate Berakhot*, Atlanta, 1987, pp 2-17.

Jerusalem. From the data we observe that the institution of the recitation of the Prayer of Eighteen Blessings may be traced back to Yavnean times, the turbulent period between the wars of 70 and 135. Based on our sources we infer further that the structured system of blessings before and after the meal developed most dramatically in the late second century in the time of the Ushan masters. I hope to show that class and professional interests motivated the concern of those groups within rabbinism who sponsored these diverse religious practices.

By the third century I find postulated in tractate Berakhot *as a whole statement* a more fully articulated theory and theology. M.'s ultimate framers enunciated in the substantive selection and organization of early rabbinic rules for liturgical recitations, their own clear, structured early rabbinic definition of a system of prayer and blessings, and a theology of practical value for the individual Jew and of hope for the Jewish people.

B. The Formative Age: Berakhot Before 70

Before the destruction of the Temple in Jerusalem, scholars posit that three major social forces influenced the nascent formation of rabbinic Judaism: the priestly and aristocratic class, members of the scribal profession, and individuals within the class of householders who owned land and made substantive contributions to the economy of Judea and later to the Galilee and the Coastal Plain.

Neusner has argued that the early third century rabbinic compilations, Mishnah and Tosefta, including tractate Berakhot, derives from an amalgam of the interests of these three forces.[4] Neusner says, "There are these two social groups, not categorically symmetrical with one another, the priestly caste and the scribal profession, for whom the Mishnah makes self-evident statements....We must notice that the Mishnah, for its part, speaks for the program of topics important to the priests. It takes up the persona of the scribes, speaking through their voice and in their manner."[5]

Neusner rounds out this picture of the social components which speak through Mishnah with a third group, the class of householders, the audience for the document, the real and potential adherents at large of the religious system of the rabbis. This group he calls, "the

---

[4]See Jacob Neusner, *Judaism: the Evidence of the Mishnah*, Chicago, 1981, especially pages 232-256.
[5]*Op. Cit.*, p. 233.

basic productive unit of society, around which other economic activity is perceived to function."[6]

Mishnah in Neusner's view, turns out to be a cogent system uniting together the concerns and styles of discourse of its three constituents: scribes, priests and householders. The work of the ultimate redactor is so effective that "the Mishnah coalesces."[7] Not surprisingly, one of its main themes is the problem of mixtures. Having artificially combined the disparate views of competing social groups into one statement, the framers of Mishnah return repeatedly to their "prevailing motif" says Neusner, "the joining together of categories which are distinct."[8]

Thus, the rabbinic philosophers who framed Mishnah created in that book an artificial world where opposing forces come together as parts of a whole. These intellectuals shared with us little concerning what they deemed important about the real issues of village social structures or national politics. They instead gave us a stylized book which alternates between anonymous statements of unanimous assent and attributed rules cast within disputes or debates.

One "proof" that Mishnah's redactor's successfully camouflaged the social conflict between its constituent groups from its readers is evident in the very way Neusner himself chooses to describe the contributions of various factions to the composite. He speaks plainly, without any hint that he has chosen euphemisms, of "The Gift of the Scribes,"[9] "The Gift of the Priests,"[10] and "The Gift of the Householders."[11] Apparently Mishnah's seamless synthesis remains intact even under modern critical scrutiny and the centuries of internecine struggle which produced the cultural components of the system of Mishnah recede into the deep background of its ultimately successful interweaving of traditional laws, anecdotes, and interpretations originally spawned by varied and conflicting historical and social contexts.

Unfortunately, these texts provide us with exceedingly limited direct evidence about the origins and early development of Jewish prayer. The only explicitly attributed materials of any significance in the tractate for reconstructing the history of rabbinism before 70, when the Temple in Jerusalem was still standing, are the few lemmas ascribed to the Houses of Hillel and Shammai. These rules address but

---

[6]P. 236.
[7]P. 237.
[8]Pp. 238.
[9]Pp. 241 ff.
[10]Pp. 248 ff.
[11]Pp. 250 ff.

few liturgical subjects: the recitation of the *Shema'*, and the recitation of "blessings" on Sabbaths and festivals.

On this basis, the establishment of the recitation of the *Shema'* as a popular scribal rite may be traced to the time of the Houses of Hillel and Shammai, wisdom fellowships commonly thought of as the immediate precursors of some rabbinic associations of the late first century and thereafter. Diverse evidence of rabbinic traditions such as M. Ber. 1:3, associate rules and practices for reciting the *Shema'* with the Houses and so supports this supposition.

Early Christian evidence in Mark 12:29-30 depicts Jesus reciting the first two verses of the *Shema'* in the context of a debate with a group of scribes, and as an opponent of the Temple hierarchy. The scriptural verses of the *Shema'* appear in the earliest phylacteries found at Qumran.[12] Of course, some of the values promoted by the *Shema'* may be located further back in Israelite history in the wisdom movements of the Hellenistic age.[13] For centuries Israelite sages and scribes commonly emphasized Torah and commandments as primary motifs of religious life.[14]

Both the inclusions and exclusions of the contents of the standard text of the rabbinic liturgy clearly help us define its focus and original intent. The primary motifs of the national cult in Jerusalem are noticeably missing from both the *Shema'* and from the frame of blessings that surrounds it.[15] Such ideas and institutions as the Temple, the priesthood, Jerusalem, Davidic lineage, all prominent motifs in the Amidah, the Prayer of Eighteen Blessings, are of no concern to the framers of the *Shema'*.

Conspicuously, the Houses do not debate the rules for the Prayer of Eighteen Blessings. I believe this glaring omission, along with other positive warrants, strongly suggest that this liturgy becomes

---

[12]See Y. Yadin, *Tefillin from Qumran*, Jerusalem, 1969.

[13]The Nash Papyrus, c. 150 B.C.E., from Fayyum, contains the decalogue and the first two verses of the *Shema'*.

[14]See James Crenshaw, *Old Testament Wisdom*, Atlanta, 1981, pp. 27ff. for a discussion of some aspects of the sage as a member of a professional class. Crenshaw briefly reflects on the exodus motif in the Wisdom of Solomon. Also see his prolegomenon to *Studies in Old Testament Wisdom*, New York, 1977, where he deals with the importance of the theme of creation in the wisdom circles. I. Elbogen claims that the *Shema'* and its benedictions constituted the earliest form of the "synagogue service." See *Studien zur Geschichte des judischen Gottesdienstes*, Berlin, 1907, pp. 38-44.

[15]Even if we place the formalization of these blessings late in the second century, these expressions undoubtedly evoke the main themes of the earliest formulations of the *Shema'*.

institutionalized within rabbinism no earlier than the end of the first century. On this I shall have more to say below.

Most of the remaining traditions attributed to the Houses in our tractates of M. and T. not surprisingly relate in some way to rituals and blessings of the meal, or of the Sabbath, or to purity laws. Extensive recent research has shown that these topics dominate the interests of the rabbi-pharisees of the era before 70.[16]

Let me look more closely at the early references to the *Shema'*. M. 1:3A-F suggests that the accepted and proper ritual for the recitation of the *Shema'* is patterned on a Hillelite conception. Apparently, the entire first chapter of Mishnah Berakhot is based on an understanding attributed to the Hillelites. They said that the *Shema'* must be recited twice each day, morning and evening.

The recitation of the *Shema'*, according to the rule ascribed to the Hillelites, formed a main component of the rabbinic daily liturgy. Later Yavnean rabbis accepted the Hillelite opinion of the nature of the ritual and explicitly built their conception of prayer around it. They went so far as to promulgate a tradition to ridicule those who accepted the competing Shammaite view of the nature of the liturgy. M. Ber. 1:3 reports that Tarfon, who followed the Shammaite mode of practice, placed his life in jeopardy. He is portrayed as stating that he emulated the convention prescribed for the ritual by the Shammaites and thereby placed himself in danger of attack by bandits. The rabbis accordingly told him, "Fittingly, you have yourself to blame [for what might have befallen you]. For you violated the words of the House of Hillel" (M. 1:3H).

A second pericope attributed to the Houses deals with the number of blessings recited in the Sabbath liturgy. In T. 3:13 the Houses dispute the number of blessings one recites in the prayer of the New Year's day that coincides with the Sabbath and the procedure for reciting the prayer for the Festival that coincides with the Sabbath. The opinions are that one recites ten, nine, eight or seven blessings depending on the circumstance and authority. Noticeably, none of the alternatives suggests a liturgy of eighteen blessings.

One may question whether these disputes in T. are of any historical value, or are artificial and anachronistic units. On the one hand, a gloss to the unit, attributed to Rabbi, signifies that these pericopae may have been formulated at a late date. On the other hand, there is no reason to doubt that there were special prayers recited on the Sabbaths, Festivals, and New Year's days during Temple times, even if

---

[16]Jacob Neusner, *Rabbinic Traditions about the Pharisees Before 70 C.E.*, Vols. I-III, Leiden, 1972.

a more formalized requirement of regular *daily* recitation was widely instituted only after 70 C.E. At most then, these disputes in Tosefta reflect an early interest of the Houses in the regulation of liturgies for the special days of the year and they were revised at the time of the redaction of T. to reflect the practices of this later period.

The bulk of the Houses' materials in Berakhot, concentrated in chapter eight of M. and its corresponding units in T., present rules for the Sabbath and Festival dinner and other regulations which may apply to any dinner. The order of blessings a person must recite for the Prayer of Sanctification for the Sabbath day, and over the wine that one drinks at that occasion, is the subject of the first unit.[17]

Next, the Houses dispute the order of blessings for the Prayer of Division that was recited at the meal at the conclusion of the Sabbath.[18] These disputes presuppose that blessings were recited on periodic occasions, to sanctify the Sabbath at its start, and to divide it from the remainder of the week, at its conclusion.

Traditions ascribed to rabbis of later generations take for granted that a Jew must recite blessings before eating any foods. Surprisingly, only one early rule takes for granted that a person had to recite blessings before eating any fare at a meal. Two other units supply rules for the Prayer of Division service, which one could recite even apart from the meal.[19] Another dispute concerning a ritual practice at the meal deals with the use of spiced oil, a custom not developed any further in rules ascribed to subsequent generations.[20]

As I just suggested, the references to blessings recited at a meal should not be construed as evidence of an early first century practice of reciting blessings before consuming any foodstuff. The only food blessing mentioned in Berakhot ascribed to an authority who flourished before Ushan times is the blessing over wine debated in the Houses' disputes in M. Berakhot chapter eight. A later Yavnean master, Tarfon, speaks of a blessing over water in M. 6:8, although this likely refers to a blessing recited *after* drinking. The absence of sustained ascription to early rabbis of rules on these subjects supports the view that the concept and practice of a full-fledged system of food blessings, recited before eating, was institutionalized at the earliest by the Ushan rabbis, a century later.

A few traditions ascribed to pre-70 authorities do make reference to the blessings recited after a meal, not necessarily to the Sabbath meal.

---

[17]Cf. M. 8:1 and T. 5:25.
[18]M. 8:5 and T. 5:30.
[19]*Ibid.*
[20]T. 5:29.

Two of these deal with the special circumstances following the meal: what one does if he forgot to recite the meal blessing after eating, and what one does to recite the meal blessing over one cup of wine that he obtained after the meal.[21]

Three other pre-70 units speak to concerns of purity at the meal: how one is to keep clean his table and the utensils of his meal, the cup or the napkin, or how one avoids rendering unclean scraps of food left over from the meal.[22] Questions like these relating to rules of purity are less relevant in later generations once the whole system of ritual cleanness loses its pertinence after the destruction of the Temple.

One final Houses-unit transmits to us a fragment of a tradition pertaining to the meal. M. 6:5 attributes a cryptic gloss to the Shammaites ("Not even a potted dish"). Even in its full context, its meaning is difficult to ascertain and its import for our understanding of the overall character of this stratum of traditions relating to the meal and to blessings and prayers is therefore accordingly limited.

To sum up, the sayings in Berakhot attributed to the Houses reveal their interest in expected pharisaic-rabbinic concerns. They take up rules for the fellowship dinner and for the Sabbath meal in particular, and rules for ritual purity at the table. The Sabbath Prayers of Sanctification and Division are associated with these masters, as is the blessing one recites over wine and the blessings recited after the conclusion of the meal.

The regular recitation of the *Shema'* is closely associated with the Houses in the first century. Finally, there is a possible association of the Houses with liturgies for Sabbaths, festivals, and the New Year, though I suggested the connection of these rituals with the early masters may be anachronistic.

Several rules and subjects first mentioned here at this earliest stratum of the law are further developed and expanded in later periods as we shall see in greater detail below. At Yavneh, the rabbis developed formulary recitations for inaugurating and concluding the Sabbath and festivals, and for liturgical insertions into the prayers recited at those times. At Usha, the rabbis created a full-fledged system of blessings to be recited by the Jew before eating or drinking any foods or liquids. Such complex innovations of later authorities are built on simple prior notions associated with earlier masters such as the pre-70 convention that one recites a blessing before partaking the wine at the dinner.

---

[21]M. 8:7-8.

[22]M. 8:2 and T. 5:26, M. 8:3 and T. 5:27, M. 8:4 and T. 5:28.

While I have described the Jewish masters of the Houses of Hillel and Shammai as "Pharisee-rabbis," their main concerns stem from a scribal agendum: the use of standardized prayers and blessings in the village, the household at the table, and in the everyday life of the Jew. I now propose to show how such seemingly modest innovations in the first century serve as the firm basis for the more lavish articulation of rabbinic ritual in the subsequent generations.

C. The Age of Internal Conflicts, Self-definition and Transition: Berakhot at Yavneh

The Yavneans were less notable as systematizers of religious practices than would be their Ushan successors. They had to be more creative as innovators of new and modified religious institutions to come to grips with the demise of the Temple and its rites and with military and economic threats to their very existence. Yet they refused to completely submit to the limitations of external domination within the Roman Empire.

In the midst of their turmoil, Yavneans built the recitation of the *Shema* 'into a regular daily liturgy. They evolved through conflict and its resolution a requirement to recite daily the Prayer of Eighteen Blessings. Yavneans began to modify and institutionalize the formerly pharisaic fellowship meal into a rabbinic ritual. But for all that they did achieve, they remained preoccupied with maintaining their cultural independence and social vitality against the tremendous pressures of the forces around them. The Ushans in the subsequent period of relative calm, ultimately undertook to create a system out of the powerful but disjointed components of rabbinic life left to them by their more charismatic Yavnean teachers.

Direct and unambiguous accounts tell us that in the time of Yavnean sages major rifts occurred within rabbinism over liturgical issues. The Talmud reports that the rabbis overthrew the Patriarch Gamaliel II because of a dispute over the obligation to recite the Evening Prayer. Eleazar ben Azariah replaced him as interim Patriarch, and the rabbinic "academy" was opened to a broader constituency.[23] Reforms of many different issues were enacted "On that day," that is on the occasion of the rebellion against Patriarchal domination and the shift in power that ensued.[24]

---

[23]B. Ber. 27b-28a, y. Ber. 4:1.

[24]See J. N. Epstein, *Prolegomena ad Literas Tannaiticus*, Jerusalem, 1957, pp. 422-25. Epstein is skeptical about whether to give credence to those sources associating many of the decisions with "that day."

The Deposition narrative merits close scrutiny because, as I said, it centers on the struggle between first-century factions over the imposition of a liturgical ritual as obligatory. According to this narrative, Gamaliel was deposed from the Patriarchate because he insisted that the rabbis recite the Amidah at night.

Goldenberg questions whether we should dismiss the ostensible issue of liturgical reform as merely an excuse for the turmoil depicted in the narrative. He notes the, "Striking triviality of the dispute over the evening prayer."[25] However, there is reason enough to believe that the pivotal issue over which the Patriarch was deposed is just as stated, the question of whether the recitation of the evening prayer of eighteen blessings was optional or compulsory.

Institutionalization of the performance of the Amidah-ritual at night must have been seen as a move to displace the *Shema'* from its place of liturgical primacy. It was in short a direct challenge by patriarchal and priestly politicians to the authority of the scribal factions within rabbinism.

To be fair, Goldenberg's conclusion alludes to political struggle, but does not associate such conflict with the legislation of liturgical reform:

> The Patriarchal regime was just beginning to consolidate its power. The rabbinic conclave in general must have resented this. At least two rival groups, the priests and Yohanan's circle, are likely to have had aspirations of their own. The stakes in the struggle – control over the remnant of Jewish autonomy in Palestine – were large.[26]

Goldenberg fails to perceive that the promulgation of public prayers, the stated issue of the conflict he discusses, is a primary and effective means of exercising influence, dominance and control over a community of the faithful.

A review of the two versions of this deposition-narrative with reference to some of their substantive variants will help to better illustrate my view. In the version of the narrative in Yerushalmi Berakhot 4:1, the action begins in the Beit Va'ad (Gathering Hall) and continues in the Yeshivah. In the main action of the story, Eleazar b. Azariah, a priest descended from a scribe, and himself an aristocrat, takes the place of Gamaliel after he is overthrown.

Eleazar, despite his aristocratic pedigree, elsewhere in rabbinic traditions upholds a value of the scribal agendum, avowing that he understands why the exodus must be mentioned at night. Eleazar

---

[25]Robert Goldenberg, "The Deposition of Rabban Gamaliel II," in *Persons and Institutions in Early Rabbinic Judaism*, Missoula, 1977, p. 37.
[26]Goldenberg, p. 38

thereby accepted and promoted practices of the scribes.[27] His statement, takes on a dual application. The rabbis applied it as justification for both the mention of the exodus in the evening *Shema'* and inserted the same tradition in the Seder to warrant the retelling of the Exodus in the evening, and accordingly to justify the Seder ritual itself.

The deposition-narrative emphasizes that Eleazar served as the interim Patriarch as the scribes seized control from the Patriarchal aristocracy. He was described as a priest who supported the ideals of the scribes, a pragmatic political figure. Aqiba, who was rejected as the compromise candidate for the Patriarchate, is portrayed as lacking the practical ability to mediate between factions as an active politician. Tradition tells us that this political extremist supported the messianic rebellion of Bar Kokhba and suffered martyrdom at the hands of the Romans.

The Bavli-editor in another version of the deposition narrative makes several additions at Berakhot 27b-28a. First he locates all the action in the rabbinized study hall. He depicts a guard of shield bearers supporting the Patriarch. In Bavli, the reform of the patriarchal court is effectuated by packing the membership of the house of study, by "adding benches." The deposition in Bavli's version was followed by a reconciliation wherein Gamaliel reclaims the patriarchate, bowing to the new realities and the change in the balance of power in the leadership of rabbinic Israelite society. As part of this process the patriarch visits the scribe's house and suffers debasing humiliation, to counterbalance Gamaliel's earlier humiliation of Joshua.[28] Once the deal has been cut to restore Gamaliel, Eleazar is informed in priestly metaphor that he must yield his position back to the legitimate heir.

The deposition-narrative compresses into stylized rabbinic form an account of events which probably stretched over a longer period of social unrest and instability within rabbinic society itself.[29] Without

---

[27]M. Ber. 1:5.

[28]In a touch of irony, M. Ber. 1:1, cited above, starts the primary rabbinic legal compendium by linking the *Shema'* with the Temple and continues with Gamaliel's sons mocking him by telling him, as an excuse for their late return home from the "banquet hall," that they did not recite the *Shema'*. Instead of chastising them, Gamaliel is portrayed as reciting a ruling to them permitting them to recite the liturgy. Echoes of division and transition reverberate in this and other compressed narrative references to the liturgy.

[29]In Bavli's version of the deposition narrative the anonymous student responsible for the destabilization of the status quo to begin with is Simeon b. Yohai, the mystic apocalyptic – a force of instability in society.

doubt, the underlying struggle for dominance within the nascent rabbinic community may be understood ultimately in light of all the political, social and economic consequences of the conflict. Regardless we must not lose sight of the overt facts represented by the traditions in our possession. The leadership of ancient Israel fought bitterly over liturgy because of its powerful potential impact within the community of the faithful. Numerous sources indicate historical tension in the development of the Amidah.[30] I cannot agree therefore with Goldenberg that the liturgical issue central to the narrative was just a trivial excuse for a broader conflict.

I argue that liturgical development closely mirrors political and social growth of rabbinism throughout its formative years in several discernable stages. During the initial transition after the destruction of the Temple, from about 70-90 C.E., the priests promulgated the Amidah to reinforce their authority and the scribes promoted the *Shema'*. At this time it would have been natural for the scribes to claim the *Shema'* was once part of the Temple Service, as we shall see.

In the second phase of development, from about 90-155 C.E., the patriarchate sponsored the Amidah to counter a growing scribal faction within the rabbinic movement. Scribes countered by rallying popular support, deposed Gamaliel, and effectuated a lasting compromise. Both liturgies were adopted in tandem and made obligatory rabbinic rituals.

The rabbis in succeeding years further consolidated the compromise. This led in the era from about 155-220 C.E. to the shaping of the composite rabbinic service that survives down to the present day. The leadership within Rabbinism amalgamated *Shema'* and Amidah into a compound liturgy with varied rules and prescribed mannerisms.

Some specific results of this process of internal conflict were lasting liturgical innovations such as the revision of the *Shema'* to include the theme of Kingship. As a permanent social outcome of the era the Priests in this era were relegated to figurehead status in rabbinic communities. Politically, the Patriarch continued to observe the conventional boundaries of his authority established after the deposition, and was excluded from internal rabbinic affairs.

In effect the scribal faction came to dominate the local communities of rabbinic Jews in the aftermath of the major crises of the internal rabbinic power struggle. This historical evolution fully divorced Rabbinic ritual from national political power structures.

---

[30]M. Ber. 4:3 for example, gives a dispute between Gamaliel and Joshua over the formalization of the Amidah. T. Ber. 3:12 makes an explicit comparison between the Amidah and the rituals of the Jerusalem Temple.

Let me review some of the evidence of how in a short span of sixty-five years, between the end of first war in 70 C.E. and the defeat in the second rebellion in 135 C.E., the rabbis transformed and constricted many aspects of Judaism. Whereas at the outset of this era Jewish religious life was centered around special meals in the home and the national cultic procedures of the Temple, by the close of this era it had changed. The rabbinic system of religious practices limited its practical regulatory focus to the major aspects of the life of the late antique Jew, in his town or village and its related personal experiences.

Naturally, the dominant concerns of the rabbis at Yavneh such as they were, reflected some primary issues of late antique religion and society in general within an imperialist Roman setting. A primary issue at the outset of the Yavnean age was, in a word, local survival. The rabbinic leadership struggled to assert some authority against the forces of foreign political domination. Rabbinic Jews, like many other subservient subordinate populations were essentially powerless and accordingly indigent. Day after day the people had to struggle against the elemental forces of nature for rudimentary sustenance.

The rabbis turned their attention where they could. They espoused that through their knowledge and religious virtuosity a Jew could help fend off the powers of nature, protect himself from the harm of the elements and of the unknown, of sickness, and of the dangers which lurked throughout the world inside of the village.[31]

The rabbis in the age of Yavneh afforded the Jews means to control the immediate vicissitudes of nature. Through their teachings and practices, through the rabbinic Torah, and mainly through prayer, the masters of this time postulated that they could for instance bring rain, or stop the rain. They could avert the dangers of the natural world or the likelihood of attack by bandits or other potential human enemies. They offered the people a way to cure their diseases, or at least to foretell the outcome of sicknesses. In the Yavnean period after the fall of the Temple, the rabbi who employed prayer and engaged in the study of Torah evolved by the necessity of the context in which he thrived into the local holy man par excellence of Judaic life.

As the rabbis took control of more of the religious life of the Jews they advanced the transfer of the locus of holiness from its former center, the Temple in Jerusalem, to the domain of the rabbis, their places of congregation, and to the study hall where the rabbis taught

---

[31]On the spirit of the age in general see, P. Brown, *The World of Late Antiquity*, London, 1971. A more intense examination of the imperial setting is to be found in Richard Horsely, *Jesus and the Spiral of Violence: Popular Jewish Resistance in Roman Palestine*, San Francisco, 1987.

their disciples the Torah. An isolated ruling in M. Berakhot 4:2 clearly reflects this major shift in religious authority from the Temple to the study hall and from priestly rituals of sacrifice to rabbinic practices of prayer:

A   R. Nehuniah b. Haqanah used to recite a short prayer when he entered the study hall and when he exited.
B.   They said to him, "What is the nature of this prayer?"
C   He said to them, "When I enter I pray that I will cause no offense and when I exit I give thanks for my portion."

Nehuniah's prayer asks for protection lest the student or teacher make an error in studying, misinterpret the tradition and thereby improperly unleash the forces of the holy. In the view of this Yavnean tradition, the study hall was the primary precinct of the sacred. One employed special prayers to defend himself from any spiritual or physical danger he might face as he would enter and exit this location.

A related source reports that the rabbis of the time also relied on prayer to protect and preserve them from more explicit tangible dangers they faced when they entered the study hall to congregate. To the governing Roman forces, a congregation of religious leaders was a potentially seditious mob and could have constituted an overt threat to the authority of Roman rule. When the rabbis called together crowds of followers, they were monitored by guards to restrain the temptation to activism. A pericope in T. 2:13 shows how prayer was associated with the kind of power that afforded religious leaders the ability to strengthen social solidarity and mount a challenge against external control:

E.   Said R. Meir, "One time we were sitting in the House of Study in front of R. Aqiba and we were reciting the *Shema'* to ourselves [i.e., silently]
F.   "because a quaestor [a Roman guard] was sitting in the doorway."
G.   They said to him, "One cannot derive a precedent [of law] from [an incident in] a time of danger."

Other traditions ascribed to Yavneans reflect the tenor of the imperial situation of these late antique times in Judaic circles. The attitude to prayers conveyed in the materials reflects a fundamental concern with the need for protection against both danger from natural forces and threats from within society itself. Some of the materials explain quite directly how via rabbinic practices one may protect himself. According to the explicit ruling in M. 4:4, a person recites a short prayer in a place of danger to protect himself from physical harm.

B. R. Joshua says, "One who goes through a dangerous place should recite a short prayer, [an abstract of eighteen].

C. "And he should say, 'God save your people Israel. In all their crises let their needs come before you. Blessed art Thou, O Lord who hears our prayers and supplications.'"

A tradition in M. 9:4 proposes that prayers serve to protect man from the dangers of the wilderness beyond the civilization of the village, and a concise liturgy serves to express one's thanks for returning safely to home after a dangerous journey abroad.

A. One who enters a town recites two prayers, one upon his arrival and one upon his departure.

B. B. Azzai says, "[He recites] four [prayers], two upon his arrival and two upon his departure.

C. "He gives thanks for the past and cries out for the future."

For the rabbinic Jew of the village, brief prayers protected a person from less ominous, hazards. In their towns the heat and vapors of a bathhouse could cleanse and even cure, but could also when out of control, cause injury or death. According to T. 6:17 a visit to this place merited the recitation of special formulae.

Within the range of rabbinic circles variation existed in the type and intensity of sanctity and power ascribed to the holy rabbis. When a great virtuoso in prayer, according to one tradition, was engaged in recitation he was protected from harm. Prayer prevented Haninah ben Dosa from the injury of a potentially lethal bite of a poisonous lizard. A story narrates how Ben Dosa was protected and the lizard died after biting him. "Woe to the person who is bitten by the lizard. Woe to the lizard which R. Hanina bit Ben Dosa," Tosefta 3:20 reports.

Haninah also had the power through prayer to peer into the future. His recitations served as a kind of omen for the destiny of a sick person, as M. 5:5 indicates. By virtue of his prayer for the sick, Haninah could tell, "who would live and who would die."

For the Yavneans then, prayer had the power to protect the individual in the village. Through prayer a master might also gain the power of precognition of the future and a better perception of a person's present state.[32]

Out of this understanding of the power of prayer in the life of the Jew, the Yavnean rabbis began to transform the practice of reciting prayers into a regular daily institution. Evidence suggests, as we saw,

---

[32]Additional Yavnean traditions emphasizing the centrality of prayer are found in T. Ber. 3:3-4.

that Jews were reciting the *Shema'* even before the Temple was destroyed. Yavnean masters further ritualized this practice.

Formalization of the most prominent rabbinic liturgy of prayer, the liturgy of eighteen blessings, took hold as we argued earlier in the era of Yavneh. We see this process articulated indirectly in our sources in M. and T. Berakhot, as I shall show later.

Several late rabbinic traditions in the Talmud make this point more explicit. Consider the following [T. Babli Meg. 17b]:

A.   When did the Prayer [of Eighteen Blessings originate]?

B.   It was taught: Simeon of Paqoli established the order of the [Prayer of] Eighteen Blessings before R. Gamaliel at Yavneh.

C.   [The Talmud continues with an apparently contradictory tradition:] Said R. Yohanan, and it was also stated as a Tannaitic teaching:

D.   It was taught: One hundred and twenty elders, and among them [were] several prophets, ordained the order of the [Prayer of] Eighteen Blessings.

The Talmud subsequently harmonizes the two conflicting traditions [Babli Meg. 18a]:

A.   If "One hundred and twenty elders, and among them [were] several prophets, ordained the order of the Eighteen Blessings," why then did Simeon of Paqoli have to establish [the order of the Prayer also]?

B.   [Because the Jews] forgot the [blessings of the Prayer] and he came and established them again.

This tradition and other evidence indicates that the later Talmudic authorities believed that Yavnean rabbis sought to institute the regular standardized liturgy of the Prayer of Eighteen Blessings. I earlier surmised that this came about after serious struggle and conflict between rabbinic factions.

In the evidence of Mishnah we find several signs that some rabbis of the period resisted the formalization and institutionalization of prayer, claiming that regularization, *qeba'*, diminished the power of the liturgy. R. Eliezer says in M. 4:4, "One who fixes [the recitation of] his prayer, his prayer is not supplication."

This brief remark reflects the fluidity, the instability and the effervescence of the time. While some authorities sought to establish the best means to formalize prayer as a daily ritual, to further various motives, others resisted, seeking to maintain the more impromptu character of prayer.

Yavnean masters such as Gamaliel, Joshua and Aqiba, developed rules and practices for the recitation of new prayers as we see for instance in M. 4:4-5. Rabbis of this era also further extended the existing practice of reciting the *Shema'* as a regular liturgy twice daily. Yavneans ruled in M. 1:2 on the proper times for the recitation of the *Shema'*.

In the context of their rules for the standardization of this liturgy, the Yavnean attitude towards prayer was that the proper recitation of the *Shema'* affords protection to an individual and, the converse of this claim, one who recites the wrong way, risks exposing himself to danger. Tarfon faced danger when he followed the Shammaite ritual for the recitation of the *Shema'* in the passage at M. 1:3G-H.[33]

The Yavnean sources clearly indicate that the recitation of both prayers and the *Shema'* in accord with the directives of the rabbis will protect a villager from danger and from harm. Needless to say, the rabbis maintained that power of the words of the prayers derived from God, the ultimate source of protection. God was the source of immediate safety and the fountain of final redemption, for the Jew of the towns. They were more imprecise about national salvation. After all, the religious leaders of this age witnessed the defeat of their people in two tragic wars fought by those who strove to gain freedom from Roman rule, under the banner of leaders who believed they could hasten the coming of the age of the messiah for the Jewish people.

The texts do make a link between the recitation of the *Shema'* and the quest for redemption in several Yavnean traditions in Berakhot, but the connection remains vague at best. In M. 1:5, the rabbis direct that the exodus from Egypt be mentioned in the *Shema'*. This suggestion of the bond between the liturgy and ultimate redemption is carried forward in T. 1:10-15, linking the recitation of the *Shema'* with the messianic age.

I have argued that the Yavnean masters were preoccupied with the dangers lurking around the village, and accordingly with providing the Jews of the time with the means to withstand them. Their rules regarding the recitation of the liturgy pay little attention to the internal state of mind of the person who recites the liturgy. The Yavnean rules for reciting the *Shema'*, for instance, mainly focus on external aspects of the recitation.[34]

In this era of transition under Roman domination the rabbis sought to establish some stability and shelter in their local communities by

---

[33]There is a further hint of the protective powers of the recitation of the *Shema'* in T. 1:4. One might see the reference in that pericope to the 'destroyers' as an indication of a potential source of harm. But this is far from certain since the term is obscure.

[34]See M. 2:3. The tradition concerning Gamaliel's wedding, M. 2:5, is an exception.

means of prayer and ritual. Not surprisingly Yavnean rulings provide us with no coherent attitudes towards public prayer, merely several isolated, independent rules.

Two of these rules are preserved in the name of the Ushan tradent Judah, who is associated with a particular Ushan attitude towards public prayer. The later Ushans legislated more openly and confidently on all aspects of public prayer, as we shall discuss below. Judah's traditions about the practices of the Yavneans primarily serve to express his own Ushan interests. Hence this further limits their value for reconstructing the development of rules for prayer at Yavneh.

One of these traditions at T. 3:5 about Aqiba, claims that he prayed differently in public and in private, underlining the virtuosity of Aqiba in prayer. In M. 4:7, Eleazar ben Azariah says that the Additional Service on festivals and new moons is only to be recited with the congregation of the village. While we presume that this means the liturgy may only be said in a public setting, references to the congregation of the village elsewhere in our tractate or in rabbinic literature in general has been suppressed. As a result this isolated tradition is of limited value to us in reconstructing a broader picture of the dynamics of the development of the phenomena of public Jewish prayer in this period.

The same may be said of the institution of the synagogue. One of the few explicit references to the synagogue in our early material, M. 7:3, alludes to the practices of reciting prayer in the synagogue. The call to prayer is fixed in the synagogue, Aqiba says, regardless of how many people are there. Lacking a fuller context of several traditions on the same subject, this pericope is of restricted value in the reconstruction of the history of the Yavnean ideas and practices relating to prayer and the synagogue.

To recapitulate, Yavneans emphasized that prayer can protect the Jews. They instituted regular daily prayers. They did not completely formulate a system of regular public prayer. Their views on the matter and rules for the synagogue are either lacking or suppressed.

Finally, I see several secondary trends in the development of liturgical ritual in this era. Yavnean materials rule that some rituals, formerly associated solely with the table fellowship, may be integrated into the regular recitation of prayers. So for example, the Prayer of Division, the recitation of formulae for the close of the Sabbath, or the Prayer of Sanctification, blessings for the inauguration of the Sabbath, may be recited as part of the regular prayer liturgy.[35]

---

[35]M. 5:2, T. 3:10, T. 3:11.

Yavneans propose that another short liturgy, the prayer for rain, which may have been previously recited as a separate rite, may also be integrated into the regular recitation of the Prayer of Eighteen.[36]

On the basis of these examples, we may conclude that once Yavneans more firmly established the daily recitation of prayer as a recurring ritual, it dominated the liturgical life of the Jews and began to absorb into it other, formerly independent practices.

The Yavnean traditions convey a sense of the late antique quality of rabbinic notions of prayer in this period under imperial domination. The rabbis of this era emphasized that prayer can protect a person from the dangers around him, be they natural danger, or the dangers inside or outside the village. In this period the rabbis acknowledged the power of the recitation of formal prayers. At Yavneh we find accordingly, the beginnings of the formalization of regular daily liturgies of new prayers, and most prominently, the establishment of the recitation of the Prayer of Eighteen Blessings as a routine religious obligation.

As rabbinic ritual matured, the fellowship meal became an occasion of note for recitation of prayers and blessings. Yet from the traditions taken as a whole, it appears that the Yavneans placed the fellowship meal at the periphery of their concerns, it never became a dominant issue of religious life.[37]

Linked to Yavneans are a few questions on the subject: how many individuals comprise a minimum for a collective meal, and what formula of invitation does one use to call the group together to recite the blessings after the meal (M. 7:3).

Yavnean names are associated with only a few rules regarding the blessings for foods and other rules for the meal. A Yavnean is associated with a ruling regarding the traditional blessing over wine. Ben Zoma explains in T. 4:12, one of M.'s rules about the recitation of the blessing over the wine that one drinks during the meal. This wine-blessing is associated in a tradition concerning the recitation of the blessing (M. 8:1), with the earlier masters of the first century, the Houses of Hillel and Shammai. A Yavnean master merely carries forward a previously articulated issue.

---

[36]See M. 5:2 above, T. 3:9.

[37]Naturally, it could also be that the conceptions developed at Usha and fostered by the redactors of M. and T. so dominated in the selection of prior rulings for inclusion in M. and T., as even to preclude the mention of Yavnean apperceptions of modes of practicing commensality. Whatever the reason, only the most basic issues of the fellowship meal are associated with Yavnean names.

Another tradition about wine ascribed to Yavneans discusses the nature of the substance itself. If one tastes it before one dilutes it to its normal strength for drinking, must he recite a blessing?[38]

Yavneans are also associated with concerns for recitation of blessings after a meal. Indeed one issue is what foods make up a meal as we see in M. 6:8:

A   "If one ate figs or grapes or pomegranates [as the main dish of his meal] he recites over them [after eating] three blessings," the words of Rabban Gamaliel.

B.   And sages say, "[He recites] one blessing [embodying three]."

C.   R. Aqiba says, "Even if one ate cooked vegetables and that was [the main dish of] his meal, he recites over them [after eating] three blessings."

D.   One who drinks water to quench his thirst says, "For all came into being by his word."

E.   R. Tarfon says he recites, "Creator of many souls and their needs."

The sense from this tradition and other material ascribed to masters of this age taken together, is that Yavneans are interested in the blessings one recites at the conclusion of the meal (see T. 1:7). But they have no strong systematic conception of a formal fellowship meal. Their laws, and Aqiba's regarding vegetables in particular, apply more to the setting of the average villager, rather than to a patrician or member of the upper-class, to the basic subsistence consumption of a society on the edge of survival, not to the concerns of national leadership.

If the Yavneans addressed themselves to the concerns of those who were overwhelmed by their struggle to survive, and thus deal with the aspects of daily life that buffet their existence, as we suspect, then that explains why they did not have the motivation or the luxury to develop a detailed etiquette for the comfortable institution of the formal fellowship meal.

The Yavneans could not fully articulate some of the institutions within their group because they had directed their rulings to the villager whose energies went to fend off the daily pressures of external imperial rulership. Several sources like T. 2:6, on different subjects tend to indicate that Yavneans gave priority to external political events over religious obligations. We are told by Meir, in T. 2:13, that one may in fact alter the performance of a ritual in order to avoid severe persecution, to survive against countervailing pressures.

While this may have been a practical response to external political and social domination, at least one short lemma in our

---

[38]M. 7:5D, T. 4:3A-E.

tractate indicates that other attitudes might have been prevalent among the Yavnean masters. One should give his soul for the commandments, Ben Azzai remarks at T. 6:7.

In sum, the repertoire of Yavnean traditions provide us with strong evidence of some of the concerns of the era. These second century masters were preoccupied with survival in an imperial world, with a struggle against the elements of nature and the forces of political dominance. In their rules concerning prayers we saw repeated concerns for protection for the villager from local danger and from harm.

There emerged in this era some tendencies to formalize and regularize prayer. But, on the whole, the institution appears to have remained fluid and effervescent, reflecting the conflicting internal forces within rabbinic life of the time and the external pressures faced by followers of the rabbis.

Finally, in their rules concerning the fellowship meal and blessings for foods the Yavneans also do not far advance the formalization of these practices. One view has Rabbis at Yavneh consider even cooked vegetables, even dates, as substance enough to constitute the main food for a collective meal.[39]

As I next discuss, from the rulings ascribed to the masters of the generation at Usha, a different picture emerges. The rabbis of that age take a dissimilar approach to defining the meal. Under more flexible historical conditions, they develop an apparently original fully-developed system of blessings to be recited before one eats any foods. They systematize the life of the rabbinic Jew through rigorously delineating and applying a scheme of ritual, especially of prayers, to daily life.

D. The Age of Standardization and Systematization: Mishnah and Tosefta Berakhot at Usha

The period following the unsuccessful Bar Kokhba revolt brought relative political and social stability to the Jewish centers of learning, then located mainly in Usha in the Lower Galilee. Unlike the previous two generations from 70 to 135 marked by wars and rebellions, this period returned rabbinic social and cultural life to a more serene routine with few major disruptions for the an entire generation and for several more to follow.

One of the fruits of peace and stability was the significant stabilization and restraint of the intellectual and social life of rabbinism at Usha resulting in part in rabbinic work on the

---

[39]M. 6:8, T. 4:15.

organization, systematization, and development of the Jewish laws that emerged out of the turbulence of the prior two generations.

At Usha the rabbinic masters gathered, arranged and canonized their own teachings, and the received instruction from the masters of the past. They systematically assembled in formulaic compilations those rules and regulations, stories and anecdotes which best expressed their understanding of themselves and of the world. The canonical tractates of Mishnah and Tosefta emerged in the generation that followed the Ushan era, as a direct result of their contributions towards the organization of rabbinic knowledge.

Just as their work reveals an intense interest in the structure and organization of ideas and traditions of past teachers, their desire to systematize is reflected directly in those materials that they themselves authored. From the numerous rules attributed to Ushans one gets an even more unmistakable impression that this period was a time of structuring, building and organizing within rabbinic society at large.

Let me illustrate this with a few remarks in the Ushan materials related to prayer and correlative rituals that manifest the idea of rank and hierarchy within the social order.

A tradition attributed to Meir, a leading Ushan, best conveys the temper of the process of transformation of rabbinic traditions on prayer from a corpus of scattered rabbinic rules into a system of liturgical regulations:

> R. Meir used to say, 'There is no person in Israel who does not perform one hundred commandments each day [and recite blessings for them]. One recites the *Shema'* and recites blessings before and after it. One eats his bread and recites blessings before and after. And one recites the Prayer of Eighteen blessings three times. And one performs all the other commandments and recites blessings over them.'
>
> T. 6:24F-G

In the view of this Ushan master, all of a person's prayers, meals and other religious obligations comprise *parts of a larger system.*

The recitation of variations of liturgical formulae, the blessings, associated with each religious event, connects these disparate phenomena together. Within this conception the many rabbinic practices of prayer and blessings form part of a distinctive and coherent religious system of liturgy.

Further examination of the materials in our texts attributed to the Ushan masters, illustrates how they reflect contention within Jewish life in the late second century for control over the community of the faithful through two major realms of religious activity: public prayer and table fellowship.

The struggle for political and social dominance over communal activity, such as liturgical practice, may be evident in a pericope attributed to an Ushan rabbi that deals with the proper recitation of the *Shema'*. The text reads:

> Rabbi Simeon b. Gamaliel says, 'Not all who wish to take [the liberty to recite] the name [of God in the *Shema'* and its blessings] may do so.'
>
> M. 2:8

This statement implies that those who wish to invoke God's name in prayer may do so only in accord with the regulations of the rabbis who alone sanction the recitation of prayers in Judaic life. Another tradition underlines an additional social ramification of liturgical recitations:

> From a man's blessings one can tell whether he is a boor or a disciple of the sages
>
> T. 1:6

According to this brief unattributed lemma on liturgical formulae, reciting the correct or incorrect words signifies one's social status, i.e., that one belongs within one defined group or another. An Ushan lemma makes another closely related point. One must recite each day three blessings which reinforce the social distinctions of the group: Blessed art Thou O Lord our God who did not make me...a Gentile, a boor, or a woman (T. 6:18). Through blessings then, one may express some of the basic rabbinic notions of social stratification and division.

Several of the Ushan regulations governing the recitation of the *Shema'* and of the Prayer of Eighteen communicate directly or obliquely how these rabbis sought to establish their dominance in their fraternity within the study hall, the unquestioned domain of the sages, and over the synagogue, the popular province of the common folk, and in this way to control public prayer.[40]

Aside from the more direct social aspects, Ushans showed further interest in the regulation of other particulars of the liturgy. They extend the regulations of the time for the *Shema'* enunciated earlier by the Houses and developed at Yavneh. Simeon, for instance points out an anomaly in the rules governing the times of the recitation of the

---

[40]On the basis of relevant literary and material evidence one must conclude that the rabbis ordinarily were not the dominant figures in the governance of the synagogues in Israel in the first through third centuries. In face of this the rabbis attempted to maintain their authority over prayer, and by promulgating their dicta they sought to weaken the authority of other forces governing the hierarchy of the synagogues.

Shema', "Sometimes one recites the *Shema'* [twice in one night]" (T. 1:1).

Judah, tells a story about two Yavnean masters who recited the *Shema'* late in the morning in T. 1:2. Interestingly, in Judah's story the rabbis are portrayed reciting the *Shema'*, "On the road." While in several traditions we find Ushan regulations for the time of recitation, they ordinarily evince little concern with rules regarding the place of recitation. One can recite on the road, or in any location for that matter [which is not unclean]. The overt implication of several Ushan rulings is that one need not enter a specific place, e.g., a synagogue, in order to recite one's prayers.

Previously I discussed the friction and compromise among Yavneans leading to the acceptance of a requirement for reciting the Prayer of Eighteen three times each day. Ushans, according to the data, then established the more specific timetable for the daily recitation of this liturgy. Judah glosses the primary Mishnaic pericope on this subject in M 4:1, "The Morning Prayer [may be recited] until midday. R. Judah says, 'Until the fourth hour, etc.'" This unit most likely was formulated at the time it was glossed, in Usha. Other evidence at T. 3:12 suggests that the masters of Usha sought to regulate the form of the prayers.

The Ushans introduced several new conceptions in their formulation of the requirements for the performance of the rituals by expanding and further regulating the existing religious practices of prayer. Analogy between prayer and Temple law was one such idea developed at Usha, as I outlined above. Another primary Ushan interest was the role of a person's intentions while reciting prayer.

Because it is difficult to directly define in a few words the nature of the concentration needed to properly perform this ritual, the rabbinic prescription specifies how, during the recitation, one must alter his relationship to the external distractions of the world around him, so that, he may properly direct his internal consciousness.

Judah in T. 2:2 said that one who recites the *Shema'* must have the proper frame of mind. Judah and Meir debated in M. 2:1-2 the definition of the frame of mind that one must have for reciting the *Shema'*. They agreed that one must limit his social discourse during the recitation. But they disagreed over the means of doing this.

Judah and Meir disagree concerning the propriety of extending or returning a greeting while reciting the *Shema'*. According to both rabbis one may vary his level of concentration during one's recitation. Meir (D-E) says that between paragraphs one may relax his concentration and extend a normal greeting out of respect as in ordinary discourse. But while in the midst of reciting a paragraph, one may not lapse into an ordinary state of mind to extend or respond to a greeting unless he fears the consequences of ignoring some important person close by.

Judah is more lenient. While reciting a paragraph one may certainly extend a greeting to a person of authority whom he fears and one may respond even to a person deserving respect. Between sections of the *Shema'*, one may exchange common greetings. He may greet a person he respects and answer the greeting of any ordinary person.

Both rabbis agree that one's concentration on the recitation of the *Shema'* establishes a state of mind which requires a person to modify his relation to other people nearby. Their dispute concerns the intensity of this change in ordinary social interaction necessary during the heightened consciousness of the recitation of the *Shema'*.

In a more subtle way, another tradition reflects Judah's concern with the need for a person to direct his intention during the performance of a ritual. Those who attend a funeral may or may not participate in the recitation of the *Shema'*. It all depends on the extent of their involvement in the rites of the funeral. Onlookers who are not directly engaged in the procedures of the funeral, may be able to concentrate and hence may recite. Participants involved directly in the funeral are presumed by T. 2:11 to be too distracted to properly recite the *Shema'*.

Another Ushan, Abba Saul, provides a scriptural basis from Psalms 10:17 for the general requirement that one must concentrate for the recitation of the Prayer. The only prayer that God hears, says this master at T. 3:4, is one recited by an individual who concentrates.

Related to the concept of intention is the idea of meditation, that is of "silent recitation" of prayer. This notion is associated with Ushans at M. 3:4. Judah's gloss in M. links this unit with the Ushan era. T. 2:12 more directly links this notion to Yosé. Meditation is a subtle process. It is quite a daring idea to think that one may concentrate on a text without reciting it in order to fulfill the requirement of the religious obligation to pray.

So the traditions attributed to Ushans indicate two ways the masters of this era regulated the actual performance of the rituals of prayers. They controlled the timetable for recitation and they legislated regarding the kind of intention or concentration needed for an individual's recitation of the prayers.

In other ways too, the rabbis of this period sought to exercise their supervision of the institutions of the recitation of prayers in private or informally, and formally, in public. As cited above, one Ushan unit makes the simple point that all recitations of blessings and prayers must be sanctioned by the rabbis: "Rabban Simeon B. Gamaliel says, 'Not all who wish to take [the liberty to recite] the name may do so'"

(M. 2:8). Certain rules in particular were directed towards the regulation of more formal gatherings for public prayer. In T. 1:9 Judah indicates how the participants in the public service must recite the blessings that followed the *Shema'* liturgy along with the leaders of the service.

In another unit, T. 3:5, Judah conveys an anecdote about the way Aqiba would restrain himself to conform to the conventions of public prayer. The message of that pericope is that Aqiba, virtuoso of the rabbis, conformed to the rules of conduct for public prayer by not bowing overly much. The ordinary rabbinic Jew then surely must follow the regulations of the rabbis for ceremonial public prayer.

In M. 4:7, Judah proposes a compromise between the views of Eleazar b. Azariah and sages on the public recitation of the Additional Service. The basic notion that an individual may indeed recite on behalf of the congregation or group, is implied elsewhere in sources associated with Judah (T. 2:12). He says that one who was unclean by virtue of a rabbinic decree may not recite the liturgy. He thereby limits the role of such an individual in the public recitation of prayer.

Even within the systematic treatment of Ushan legislation, several major issues remain vague. From our data we cannot tell whether at Usha the recitation of the *Shema'* was to be practiced as a public liturgical ritual of the community, or a private rite of individuals, or both.

One rule refers to the recitation of the *Shema'* in the synagogue. The rule itself is anonymous and its reference to the *Shema'* is only implicit from the context of the rule: "One who entered the synagogue and found that [the congregation] had [already] recited half [of the *Shema'*] and he completed it with them...."(T. 2:4). But in general the Ushan regulations in M. do not take into account any distinction between the public or private recitation of the *Shema'*, as we see at M. 2:3. Such issues cannot be resolved based on the limited sources we have.

Ushans contributed to the tightening formalization of the literal content of prayer. One unit attributes to Yosé an interest in the formulation of the liturgy: "If one did not mention the covenant in the blessing of the land [i.e., the third blessing in the grace after meals], they make him begin [the recitation] again" (T. 3:9).

In their rulings for the food and meal blessings Ushan masters maintain a similar scope of activity and interest. Through their rulings the Ushans solidify and extend rabbinic dominance over two major areas of the life of their community: the institution of collective public prayer, as shown, and the practice of commensality, that is, the collective fellowship meal.

In addition to the many rules they promulgated for reciting liturgies and prayers, the Ushans created an intricate system of blessings to be recited before eating any foods. The rabbis justified the idea of requiring preliminary food blessings in a creative anonymous rabbinic tradition as follows:

> One may not taste anything until he recites a blessing. For it says, 'The Earth and all therein is the Lord's' (Psalms 24:1). One who derives benefit from the world without first reciting a blessing has committed a sacrilege. [It is as if he ate sanctified Temple produce.] [One may not derive any benefit] until [he fulfills all the obligations] which permit him [to derive benefit, i.e., recites the proper blessings].
>
> T. 4:1

The analogy of food blessings with Temple taboo served as a strong polemical basis for the legitimacy of these rituals. Through the blessings-system the rabbis could regulate the consumption of foods and thereby the institutions of the commensual meal or the table fellowship, much as the priests in the Temple could exercise their dominance over the production and distribution of foods in a past era when the Temple in Jerusalem was standing. So to foster this analogy the rabbis promulgated their bold dictum: one who eats any foods without following the rules of the rabbis commits a sin as severe as the ancient transgression of sacrilege against the priest and their Temple property.

Accordingly, by requiring all Jews to recite the rabbinic blessings before eating, to follow the rabbinic rules of commensality, rabbis could directly govern a main affair of the daily life of every Jew.

The first Ushan unit of the tractate more subtly illustrates this connection. In T. 1:1, Meir parallels the time for reciting the *Shema'* with the time for eating the Sabbath fellowship meal. Recall also that the earlier Yavneans in M. 1:1 had explicitly compared the timetable for the *Shema'* with the schedule of the Temple.

Other Ushan statements regarding the system of food blessings express a basic categorization of the natural world and of the edible produce of a second century cultural context [M. 6:1], reminiscent of the systematic priestly taxonomies of earlier ages.

The regulation of membership in the table fellowship, control of the institution of the meal, is an ongoing Ushan concern. In M. 7:2 Judah rules on the minimum one must eat to be included in the quorum for the recitation of the blessings after eating the meal.

The Ushan conception is that the fellowship dinner is a formal full-course affair, not a meal of just vegetables or dates.[41] In this context advice on table etiquette is appropriate.[42] Simply by propounding rules of etiquette, the rabbis could not fully regulate, guide, or control a complex institution like the collective meal. Much more is involved in governing this complex institution. The Pharisaic leaders, for instance, regulated the table fellowship of their era by promulgating purity laws for foods and agricultural taboos, especially the laws of tithes for produce.[43]

The rabbis of Usha did not reaffirm these rules as a means of directing the obligations of the collective meal in their era. There was no Temple, no active priesthood. So there was no gain in extending the rules of purity and uncleanness to the Jews of the second century and no way to justify the system of agricultural offerings and tithes.

Accordingly, the Ushan rabbis exercised control over the fellowship meal of their time by establishing a system of blessings to be recited before and after eating foods both at the formal dinner, and by extension, even outside of the formal structures of the fellowship meal. As noted earlier, these authorities proclaimed that the whole world and all of its contents were sacred. To eat from the fruit of the land was a sacrilege unless one performed the proper religious actions. For the rabbinic Jew of the late second century, the rituals that permitted a person to consume the foods of the earth were not the sacrifices of animals at the Temple, or the offerings of meal, or the separation from one's produce the gifts for the priests and levites. The Jew had to recite the proper formal blessing before eating, and then he could proceed to benefit from the produce of the land.

The rabbis provided little additional justification to gain support for their innovations. The few Biblical precedents for such ideas or practices are limited to at best remote hints of the practice of reciting blessings at a meal, such as in Deut. 8:10, "And you shall eat, and you shall be satisfied, and you shall bless the Lord...."

The Temple, the locus of holiness in the world of the Jew in Israel, had been destroyed more than a generation earlier. The Yavneans learned through tragedy and trauma that the Temple would not be

---

[41]This is a sharp contrast to the conception of the meal underlying the story in which Aqiba and the rabbis are portrayed eating dates in Jericho (T. 4:15).

[42]T. 4:14. Other anonymous units on the formal etiquette of the dinner may be associated with the Ushan stratum of traditions, including T. 4:8-9, T. 5:5-6, M. 6:6-7.

[43]See J. Neusner, *Rabbinic Traditions About the Pharisees Before 70 C.E.*, vol. 3, Leiden, 1972.

rebuilt in their times. The rabbis at Usha knew in their own historical experiences only of a life of piety without a centralized place of holiness. Out of necessity, they refined and developed the Pharisaic and early rabbinic notion that holiness could be centered around the household and sacrality focused at the table of the ordinary villager.

Liturgy thus understood had some undeniably "rabbinic" facets. By the late second century, the rabbis were, more than anything else, a group of sages whose major concern was the study and formulation of their traditions. Accordingly one of their major preoccupations was the mastery and recitation of the traditions that later became the basis for the canonical documents of M. and T., highly formulaic documents made up of short lemmas in formalized diction. The recitation of blessings comprised of brief, fixed formulae to express their conceptions of religious order and meaning at the formal setting of the dinner was definitely a ritual that reflected elements of the basic character of rabbinic culture.

Admittedly the primary notion that one recites a blessing over a food was not an original conception of the Ushan masters. As shown above, the Houses of Hillel and Shammai in their first century rules speak of the blessings over wine and refer to the recitation of other formulae (viz. chapter eight of M.). Rules concerning the recitation of the blessings after the meal were ascribed to Yavneans. Indeed, the Yavneans are said to have developed the formal daily prayer liturgy comprised of eighteen formulaic blessings.

But in the era when rabbinism was centered at Usha the rabbis developed their complex system of blessings to be recited by the Jew before eating any food. As we have shown, this deceptively simple taxonomy of foods and their blessings of M. 6:1 enunciates the essence of the rabbinic scheme of blessings and makes a powerful statement.[44] To eat of any food, the sancta of the earth, one must first carry out his religious obligation, recitation of the formula of the appropriate rabbinic blessing.

Within the development of this system of religious practice at Usha, there emerged the dominant system of blessings expressed in the pericopae of Mishnah Berakhot. Alternative expanded categories and formulae were also proposed by rabbis of the era, as indicated by rulings attributed to Judah, Meir and Yosé in Tosefta 4:4-5.

The establishment of a system of different blessings for various foods, and of the requirement to recite these blessings before eating any food gave rise to a complex set of real and potential questions. For

---

[44]On the basis of Judah's gloss we may associate that entire tradition with the Ushan period.

instance, when one ate more than one kind of food at the same meal, did he recite a blessing over each food? Did he recite a blessing over one food before he recited a blessing over another food? In other words, was there a hierarchy or rules for precedence within the system of food blessings? If so, by what criteria did one establish the rank and order of importance of foods?

Ushan units respond to these issues. Judah suggests that one may seek guidance regarding the issue of priority from a familiar source, Scripture. The seven types of foods mentioned in Deuteronomy 8:8 take precedence over other foods (M. 6:4). An alternative means of establishing hierarchy among foods based on the quality of the food, is suggested elsewhere.[45]

Within the framework of the meal, the consensus is that one does not need to recite a blessing over each food one eats. One recites a blessing over the primary food of the meal, usually bread, and other foods are exempt. Certain special foods, like salted relishes or desert cakes, are exceptions to this practice.[46] One needs to recite a separate set of blessings for these items.

The complexity of the rules creates a whole host of problems for the rabbis to solve. The nature of the principles makes it essential for the rabbis to establish a detailed set of governing priorities to guide the implementation of the system of blessings in the everyday life of the rabbinic Jew. Through this system of blessings the rabbis are able to guide and to govern the institution of the table fellowship, and to regulate the consumption of all foods.

This naturally engenders the circumstances in which the rabbi plays a central and indispensable role. He must be consulted to solve any new enigmas generated by the principles that govern the system of rules for reciting the food blessings. No one else has the expertise to make the decisions. So, by means of this system of blessings, the rabbis made themselves essential to the daily life of the Jew.

In the final analysis I have contended that one of the great contributions of the masters of the Ushan period was their successful systematization of rules and regulations for disparate phenomena, for the basic rituals and concepts of rabbinic Judaism. The Ushans took the scattered traditions of a group of charismatic holy men [the Yavneans] and transformed the independent rules of individual teachers into a systematic tradition, a Torah. The Ushans believed that all religious obligations were parts of the same Torah, and were to be governed under the authority of the rabbis.

---

[45]See T. 4:15, Judah's version of the dispute between Gamaliel and sages.
[46]See T. 4:14, T. 5:12.

Meir accounted for this succinctly, as illustrated above (T. 6:24-5): Each day a person recites one hundred blessings. The *Shema'*, the mealtime blessings, the recitation of the prayers are indeed, in Meir's view, all part of the same system as those basic scriptural obligations of the adult male Israelite, i.e., wearing tefillin, and fringes, and placing a mezuzah on his doorpost.

Such thoughts leave open issues of precedence within the system. Consider the impact of the *Shema'* and its blessings on the theology of early rabbinic Judaism. The ritual of the recitation of the *Shema'* expressed a powerful basic underlying theological message. Scriptural obligations of the each Jew [such as the use of tefillin, mezuzah and ṣiṣit] are equal parts of the same system as the rabbinic practices incumbent on the individual and practiced in fellowship with other Jews [the recitation of the *Shema'*, the recitation of other blessings and prayers, the meals in the home]. Are they equal or is one practice and symbol more crucial than another?

Once the Ushans had established the notion of a system of religious obligations for the Jew, the inevitable issue to be raised is the question of priorities. When there is a clash between two commandments, which one takes precedence? Some examples of this process of clarification of priorities are to be found in traditions ascribed to Ushans. One matter at T. 2:6 is: do scribes stop writing their sacred scrolls in order to recite the *Shema'* and the prayer? Another concern at T. 5:1-4 is: what takes priority, prayer in the study hall or the Sabbath eve meal?

Furthermore, may one who is unclean by virtue of a rabbinic form of uncleanness still fulfill the obligations established on the authority of the rabbis? May he still recite the blessings of the meal and of the *Shema'*?[47] A related question: do social responsibilities take precedence over the requirements of religious obligations? Must the processes of public administration be halted for the recitation of the *Shema'* and the Prayer (T. 2:6)? Ushan rulings close and settle some issues, leave others open ended and allow for multiple responses to some. These options established at Usha pave the way for the fuller Talmudic analysis of generations to come.

To close this review of the Ushan contributions, consider the precepts for several miscellaneous practices associated with them. One must recite blessings for unusual natural events, and when visiting national shrines or other special places, and for good or bad fortune. Through rules such as these requiring the recitation of blessings at various occasions, the rabbis consolidate even popular, personal,

---

[47]See M. 3:4, and T. 2:13.

occasional prayers into their system of worship and religious practice.[48]

In sum, the data in Berakhot demonstrates that Usha was a period in which the rabbis advanced their control over their followers through regulation of religious practice. They are credited with rulings concerning the control of the time of prayer. Their materials show interests in governing the intention of the individual during his recitation of prayer. They make statements that indicate their concern with the public recitation of prayer.

In all of these traditions we find little to indicate that Ushans legislated rules for the synagogue. A conclusion one may draw from this lack of evidence is that rabbis did not have much influence over synagogue practice. It may be that the synagogue was yet to be sufficiently institutionalized in Israel by the end of the second century. Or it may be that rabbis could simply not manage and direct the ritual processes of that institution. By contrast, they did seek to direct the institution of the common dinner.

We do find that they issued rulings concerning blessings recited at fellowship meals. Other rules effectively attempt to link a person's status within the rabbinic group with his virtuosity in rabbinic religious practice and his mastery of rabbinic thought.

Above all, the Ushans saw all religious obligations, based on both rabbinic and scriptural authority, as parts of a larger system. One may say that at Usha we find the beginnings of the idea of a "halakhah" or integrated system of laws that governs all of life's activities. The creativity of the Ushans in this regard undoubtedly paved the way for the formation of the canon of the Mishnah in the next generation and thereby for the genesis of the Talmuds of the centuries thereafter and the forms of Judaism associated with those corpora.

---

[48]See M. 9:1-2, T. 6:2A-C, T. 6:6C-D.

15

Architecture and Law: The Temple and Its Courtyards in the *Temple Scroll*[1]

Lawrence H. Schiffman
New York University

Sometime in the second half of the reign of John Hyrcanus (134-104 B.C.E.) the author/redactor of the *Temple Scroll* (11QT) sought to propound his plan for a total reformation of the Hasmonean order.[2] Although his demands for reform included the restructuring of the political system as well, his primary emphasis was on the reorganization of the Temple and its worship to conform to those interpretations of the Torah embodied in the *Temple Scroll*. Among those aspects most important to the author/redactor of the scroll was the reconstruction of the Jerusalem Temple in accord with a thorough plan which is probably to be seen as the centerpiece of the scroll. At the outset it needs to be emphasized that this plan is not intended for a Messianic Temple but rather for a Temple to serve until the coming of the end of days when a new one will be substituted.[3]

---

[1]I wish to thank my New York University colleagues, Professors Baruch A. Levine, Elliot R. Wolfson and Robert Chazan for their help in preparing this study. I wish to thank the Israel Exploration society for permission to adapt the Temple Plan from that prepared by Professor Y. Yadin.

[2]See L. H. Schiffman, "The King, His Guard, and the Royal Council in the *Temple Scroll*," *PAAJR* 54 (1987), pp. 237-59.

[3]Y. Yadin, *The Temple Scroll* (Jerusalem: Israel Exploration Society, 1983), vol. I, pp. 182-5. Contrast B. Z. Wacholder, *The Dawn of Qumran* (Cincinnati: Hebrew Union College Press, 1983), pp. 21-30. Wacholder cannot be correct since his view requires the translation of Hebrew *'ad* as "during," a meaning otherwise unattested. The so-called New Jerusalem fragments describe the city plan and

This Temple plan was not simply an attempt to provide a larger or more beautiful sanctuary for the God of Israel. Sanctuaries invariably reflect the views of their builders on a variety of significant issues relating to ideas of sanctity and holiness, approaches to worship, and what we have come in the modern west to call theology.[4] This is certainly the case with the Israelite temples known from archaeological research or from literary sources.[5] The architect of the Temple plan of the *Temple Scroll* certainly intended his plan to convey such messages. The present study seeks to investigate the architecture of his plan to uncover the conceptual universe which lies behind it. In doing so, it is hoped that this study will once again confirm that the various systems of ancient Jewish thought must be recovered through careful study of the legal and exegetical materials preserved for us.

In the *Temple Scroll* as presently constituted, the Temple plan begins with detailed instructions for the construction of the Temple building itself. Thereafter, complete descriptions of the furnishings of the Temple appear. At this point, the sacrificial festival calendar, originally a separate source, has been included by the redactor.[6] When this calendar reaches its conclusion, the text turns to description of the actual Temple precincts. Continuing from its earlier discussion of the Temple building, it precedes outward to consider the three courts which surround the Temple and which together constitute the *temenos*.

There is considerable evidence pointing to the existence of this Temple plan before the redaction of the scroll. Among the fragments which Yadin identified as representing manuscripts of the *Temple Scroll* is Rockefeller 43.366. This fragment includes much of the Temple plan discussed below. Yadin dated this fragment to the last quarter of the second century B.C.E., basing himself on the examination by N.

---

aspects of the Temple plan of Jerusalem, and are to some extent based on Ezekiel's plan, especially as regards the measurements of the city. See M. Baillet, J. T. Milik, R. de Vaux, *Les 'petites grottes' de Qumran, Texte* (Oxford: Clarendon Press, 1962), pp. 184-6. The text does not seem to parallel that of the Temple Scroll. (For parallels, see Yadin II, p. 480.) For texts and bibliography, see J. A. Fitzmyer, D. J. Harrington, *A Manual of Palestinian Aramaic Texts* (Rome: Biblical Institute Press, 1978), pp. 46-64 and 198f.; K. Beyer, *Die aramäischen Texte vom Toten Meer* (Göttingen: Vandenhoeck & Ruprecht, 1984), pp. 214-22. This text does require twelve gates for the city (5Q15 frag. 1, col. i:10).

[4]B. A. Levine, "Biblical Temple," *Encyclopedia of Religion* 2, 211-14.

[5]See M. Haran, *Temples and Temple Service in Ancient Israel* (Winona Lake, Indiana: Eisenbrauns,1985), pp. 13-57.

[6]See L. H. Schiffman, "The Sacrificial System of the *Temple Scroll* and the *Book of Jubilees*," *Society of Biblical Literature 1985 Seminar Papers*, ed. K. H. Richards (Atlanta: Scholars Press, 1985), pp. 217-33.

Avigad.[7] In fact, J. Strugnell has noted that this fragment is not part of a manuscript of the *Temple Scroll*, but rather belongs to an expanded Torah scroll, a Pentateuch with non-biblical additions.[8] If so, such scrolls served as sources for the author/redactor of the complete scroll, or of some predecessor who may have combined the ritual calendar with the Temple plan. In any case, this fragment proves that the Temple plan of our text pre-dates the complete *Temple Scroll*.[9]

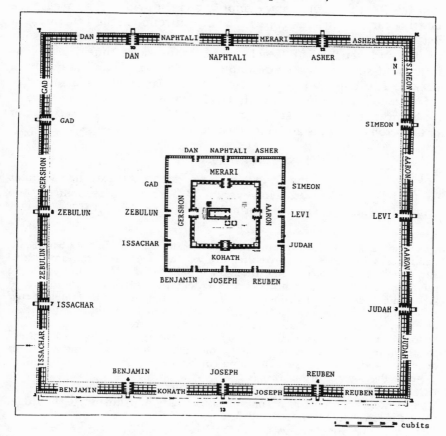

cubits

The Temple Plan according to the Temple Scroll

---

[7]Yadin I, p. 20.

[8]In Wacholder, Dawn, p. 206. Cf. F. García Martínez, "Estudios Qumranicos 1975-1985: Panorama Critico (II)," *Estudios Biblicos* 45 (1987), pp. 365f.

[9]Cf. A. M. Wilson, L. Wills, "Literary Sources in the Temple Scroll," *HTR* 75 (1982), pp. 275-88.

The *Temple Scroll* is providing for a Temple of very different plan and proportions from that which had existed in First Temple times, or that which existed at the time of the architect and the author/redactor.[10] This new Temple plan would be characterized by the enclosure of the sanctuary itself within three concentric courtyards. While this Temple plan embodies some aspects of earlier designs, it is unique in many ways. Our detailed discussion of its elements will show that this Temple plan is an attempt to recreate within the *temenos* the Israelite camp of the desert period which surrounded the Tabernacle. It was this period which the architect saw as representing the pristine purity and sanctity of Israel.[11] Yet, at the same time, our text is influenced strongly by the description of the Temple and holy city in Ezekiel. This paper will seek to set forth the nature of this plan and to understand the ideal which underlies it. We will see that the nature of his Temple reveals much about the conceptual universe of the redactor of the scroll and of the author of this section or his source.[12]

I. The Inner Court

The beginning of the *Temple Scroll's* commands regarding the Inner Court is not preserved. However, it is possible to reconstruct the dimensions and plan of this court. The scroll provides (11QT 36:3-7):[13]

---

[10]See, however, the forthcoming study of J. Maier, "The Temple Scroll and Tendencies in the Cultic Architecture of the Second Commonwealth," *Archaeology and History in the Dead Sea Scrolls*, ed. L. H. Schiffman, to be published by the American Schools of Oriental Research and the Sheffield Academic Press. Maier argues that the Temple plan of the *Temple Scroll* reflects not the independent, utopian vision of its author, but rather "ideal norms which to a remarkable extent correspond to tendencies attested in the history of the Jerusalem sanctuary" which were part of a living architectural tradition. In particular, Maier seeks to trace the pattern of concentric squares in earlier traditions. Yet he evinces no convincing proof that these traditions pre-date the sources of the *Temple Scroll*.

[11]Cf. S. Talmon, "The 'Desert Motif' in the Bible and in Qumran Literature," *Biblical Motifs, Origins and Transformations*, ed. A. Altmann (Cambridge: Harvard University Press, 1966), pp. 31-63.

[12]For an alternative analysis, see C. Koester, *The Dwelling of God*, to be published in *CBQ Monograph Series* in 1989.

[13]For restorations and philological notes, see Yadin II, pp. 152-3, and J. Maier, *The Temple Scroll, An Introduction, Translation & Commentary* (Sheffield: University of Sheffield, 1985), pp. 96f. Lines 1 and 2 are too fragmentary to be satisfactorily translated. All *Temple Scroll* translations in this article are mine. Maier presents a complete discussion of the Inner Court on pp. 91-96. Our study indicates that the reconstruction of the Temple plan by Yadin is much more in consonance with the text of the scroll than is that of Maier. The discussion below, therefore, follows Yadin.

...] from the angle [...] [to the corner][14] of the gat[e one hundred and twenty cubits. The gate shall be forty [cubits] wide. For each and every side[15] [this should be its dimensions.] [The wi]dth of [its] wa[ll] (shall be) seven cubits, [and] its hei[ght] (shall be) [forty-]five [cubits up to the cei]ling of [its] roof. [The wid]th of [its] ch[ambers] shall be twenty-six cubits from angle to angle.

The text now turns to the gates of the Inner Court (11QT 36:7-9):[16]

And (as to) the ga[t]es through which they enter and [g]o out, the width of each gate (shall be) four[tee]n cubits, and their height (shall be) [tw]enty-eight cubits from the threshold to the lintel.

The text again returns to the overall dimensions (11QT 36:12-14):[17]

From the corner of the gate to the second angle of the court (shall be) one hundred twenty cubits. This shall be the dimension of all these gates of the Inner Court. And the gates (shall) enter into the court....[18]

From these texts it is possible to determine the plan of the Inner Court and its size. The text specifies an Inner Court the inside measurements of which, when the length of the sections between the gates (120 x 2) and the gates themselves (40) are taken together, is 280 cubits square. With the thickness of the walls (2 x 7), the total outside dimension of the Inner Court is 294 cubits square.[19]

The gates of the Inner Court are located one on each of the four sides. These gates, as can be determined by comparison with the apportionment of chambers on the outside wall of the Outer Court, represented the four groups of the tribe of Levi: the Aaronide priests on the east, and the Levites of Kohath on the south, Gershon on the west and Merari on the north. This arrangement corresponds exactly to the pattern of the desert camp as described in Num. 3:14-39.

---

[14]"Angle" *(miqsoa ')* designates the inside of the intersection of two lines, whereas "corner" *(pinnah)* refers to the outside (Yadin II, p. 153, commentary to line 4).

[15]E. Qimron, "Le-Nushah shel Megillat Ha-Miqdash," *Leshonenu* 42 (1978), p. 144 reads *ruhotaw* instead of *ruah wa-ruah* (line 5) which would require a translation "all its sides."

[16]See Yadin II, pp. 154f. and Maier, p. 96.

[17]See Yadin II, pp. 155f.

[18]For the restoration of the continuation, see Yadin II, p. 156.

[19]Yadin I, p. 204. Contrast the Middle and Outer Courts for which outside dimensions (including the thickness of the walls) are given.

II. The Middle Court

After describing the furnishings of the Inner Court,[20] the scroll turns to the discussion of the Middle Court (11QT 38:12-15):[21]

> And you shall make a second [c]ourt ar[ou]nd the Inn[er Court,][22] separated by one hundred cubits.[23] The length on the east side (shall be) four hundred eighty cubits. This shall be the width and length on all its sides, to the south, the west and the north. The thickness of its wall (shall be) [fo]ur cubits. Its height shall be twenty-eigh[t] cubits. Cells shall be made in the wall on the outside,[24] and (the distance) from one chamber to the next (shall be) three and a half cubits.[25]

The dimensions of these gates are discussed in 11QT 39:13-16:[26]

> Between the gates, the dimension (shall be): From the northeastern corner to the gate of Simeon, ninety-nine cubits; and the gate (itself) twenty-eight cubits. From this gate (marginal correction indicates: "From the gate of Simeon")[27] to the gate of Levi, ninety-nine cubits; and the gate (itself) twenty-eight cubits. From the gate of Levi to the gate of Judah, [ninety-nine cubits; and the gate (itself) twenty-eight cubits.][28]

The Middle Court is to be concentric (if this can be said of a square) with the Inner Court, surrounding it on all four sides, and located 100 cubits further out. Here the measurements are outside measurements. Included in the 480 cubits is the width of the walls (4 cubits). 99 cubits were to be between each of the three gates on each side (4 x 99=396).

---

[20]See Yadin II, pp. 207-41.

[21]For restorations and philological notes, see Yadin II, pp. 163f. and Maier, p. 101. Maier discusses the Middle Court on pp. 98-101.

[22]Yadin read *sav[i]v la-[ḥaṣer ha-pen]imit]*. E. Qimron, "New Readings in the Temple Scroll," *IEJ* 28 (1978), p. 165 reads *sovevet 'et he-ḥaṣer ha-penimit* ("which surrounds the Inner Court") which he says is "easily legible."

[23]Literally, "at a width of one hundred cubits." Cf. Yadin II, p. 163. Cf. also 11QT 40:5-11.

[24]Qimron, "New Readings," p. 165 reads *ba-ḥuṣ*, which he says seems to have been corrected to *mi-ḥuṣ*.

[25]Restoring with Yadin II, p. 164, commentary to line 15. 11QT 39:1-3 dealt with the construction of the gates of the Middle Court (Yadin II, p. 165).

[26]See Yadin II, pp. 167f. and Maier, p. 102.

[27]Qimron, p. 166 indicates that the word "Simeon" is not visible on the photographs, and that *ha-zeh* was inserted by the scribe as a correction.

[28]Restored with Yadin II, p. 169 who points out that the space is not sufficient on the top of col. 40 (lines 01-07) for a full catalogue of all the gates and dimensions. At some point the author must have abbreviated his description in some way.

The gates were 28 cubits wide (x 3=84). This yields a total length of 480 (396+84) cubits measured from the outside.[29]

The names and locations of the gates of the Middle Court are described in 11QT 39:11-13:[30]

> The nam[es of the ga]tes of this [c]ourt [shall] be according to the names of the sons of Is[r]ael: Simeon, Levi and Judah to the east; [R]euben, Joseph and Benjamin to the south; Issachar, Zebulun and Gad to the west; Dan, Naphtali and Asher to the north.

We will return below to the distribution of the gates. Suffice it to say at present that the twelve gates were apportioned to each of the twelve sons of Jacob, a pattern repeated in the gates of the Outer Court as well.[31]

III. The Outer Court

The command to build the Outer Court appears in 11QT 40:5-11:[32]

> You shall make a thi[r]d court...[separ]ated from[33] the Middle Court [by sixty-five cubits].[34]...in length, approximately one thousand six [hundred] cubits from corner to corner. For each and every direction this shall be the dimension, to the east, south, west and n[or]th. The width of the wall (shall be) seven cubits, and the height, forty-nine cubits. Chambers (shall be) constructed between its gates, on the outside against the foundation, up to its crenellations(?).

The Outer Court is again located at a distance from the Middle, arranged also concentrically. Again the measurements given in the scroll are outside measurements, including the width of the walls. The sides are each "about 1600" cubits long. The actual dimension is 1590 cubits, or, including the outward extension of the gates from the outer wall, 1604 cubits.

The gates of the Outer Court are described in 11QT 40:11-13:

> There (shall be) three gates in [it] in the east, three in the south, three in the west, and three in the north. The width of the gates (shall be)

---

[29]The 100 cubits from the Inner to the Middle Court is apparently measured from the inside of the wall of the Inner Court to the outside of that of the Middle Court.

[30]See Yadin II, p. 167 and Maier, p. 101.

[31]Cf. J. M. Baumgarten, *Studies in Qumran Law* (Leiden: E. J. Brill, 1977), pp. 145-71, first published as "The Duodecimal Courts of Qumran, Revelation, and the Sanhedrin," *JBL* 95 (1976), pp. 59-78.

[32]See Yadin II, pp. 170f. and Maier, pp. 110-11 for restorations and commentary. Detailed discussion of the Outer Court appears in Maier, pp. 103-10.

[33]Literally: "[wi]de around the..." (so Yadin II, p. 170).

[34]Restoring with Yadin II, p. 170, commentary to line 7.

fifty cubits, and their height seventy cubits. From gate to gate shall be a [dimension of] three hundred sixty cubits.

Each section of the wall is 360 cubits and each gate is 50. This yields a total of 4 sections of wall and three gates equalling 1590 cubits. 14 cubits may be added, since the gates I each side protrude 7 cubits according to 11QT 41:12 (1590+14=1604).[35]

These gates are to be constructed as follows (11QT 41:12-17):[36]

The gates (shall) protrude from the wall of the courtyard outward seven cubits. Inside, they shall extend (inwards) from the wall of the courtyard thirty-six cubits. The width of the openings of the gates shall be fourteen cubits, and their height (shall be) twenty-eight cubits up to the lintel. They shall be roofed with beams of cedar wood overlaid with gold. Their doors (shall be) overlaid with pure gold.

The scroll spells out the exact location of the respective gates for each tribe (11QT 40:13-41:11):[37]

From the corner to the gate of Simeon is three hundred and sixty cubits; from the gate of Simeon to the gate of Levi, the same dimension. From the gat[e] of Levi to the gate of Judah, the same dimension, three [hundred and] sixty cubits.[38] [From the gate of Judah to the southern corner, the same dimension, is three hundred and sixty cubits. From this corner to the gate of Reuben is three hundred and sixty cubits. From the gate of Reuben to the gate of Joseph, the same dimension, is three hundred and sixty cubits. From the gate of Joseph to the gate of Benjamin is three hundred and sixty cubits. From the gate of Benjamin to the we]st[ern corner is three hundred and sixty cubits. And thus from] this [corner] to the ga[te of Issachar is three hundred and sixty] cubits. From the gate of Issachar [to the gate of Zebulun is three] hundred [and sixty] cubits. From the gate of Zebulun to the gate of Gad is three hundred six[ty] cubits. From the ga[te] of Gad [to the northern corner] is three hundred and sixty cubits. From this corner to the gate of Dan is three hundred and sixty cubits. And thus from the gate of Dan to the gate of Naphtali is three hundred and sixty cubits. From the gate of Naphtali to the gate of Asher is three hundred and sixty cubits. From the gate of Asher to the eastern corner is three hundred and sixty cubits.

This account of the distribution of the gates of the Outer Court corresponds exactly with that of the Middle Court. Both descriptions

---

[35]Yadin I, pp. 253f.

[36]See Yadin II, pp. 175f. and, for a thorough discussion, Yadin I, pp. 253-5 and Maier, pp. 111-12.

[37]For restorations and commentary, see Yadin II, pp. 171-4.

[38]From this point the restoration is extensive, since the top of col. 41 is not preserved. Yet it is virtually certain. From line 5 the text of 11QT corresponds to that of Rockefeller 43.366 which has aided greatly in confirming the restoration.

list the sons of Jacob and proceed from the northeastern corner southwards.[39]

Especially significant is the requirement that a series of chambers be constructed in the inner wall of the Outer Court, facing inward (11QT41:17-42:6):[40]

> Between one gate and another, you shall construct inside (the wall) chambers, [rooms and stoas]. The width of the room (shall be) ten cubits, its length twenty cubits, and its height fou[rteen cubits. It shall be roofed with beams] of cedar wood. The thickness of the wall (shall be) two cubits. Outside of it shall be the chambers. [The width of each chamber shall be ten cubits, the length] twenty cubits, the wall a thickness of two cubits, [and its height fourteen cubits] up to the lintel. Its entrance (shall be) three cubits wide. [Thus you shall construct] all the chambers and [their] rooms, and the[ir] stoa[s all shall be of a wi]dth[41] of ten cubits. Between one gate and another, [you shall construct eight]een, and their rooms, eight[een....]

Three distinct structures are envisaged here. As one approached the outer wall, one first entered the stoas, then proceeded further into the "rooms," and then entered the inner "chambers."[42] The rooms and chambers each measure 10 cubits wide, 20 long and 14 high. For the chambers, we learn of 3 cubits wide entrances. In the case of the stoas, the width is 10 cubits and the height 14, but there are no room divisions. According to these measurements, there is space for 18 chambers and their rooms on each side.[43] On top of the bottom story were two more stories of these chambers, reached by stairways, and the upper level was then set aside for *sukkot* (booths) which were to be 8 cubits high (11QT 42:7-12). The total height of these structures was to be 50 cubits.

In 11QT 44:3-45:2 we learn of the relationship of the chambers to the various gates:[44]

> You shall apportion [the chambers and their rooms. From the gate of Simeo]n to the gate of Judah shall be for the priests [the sons of

---

[39]Yadin I, pp. 247, 255.

[40]See the commentary of Yadin II, pp. 176-8.

[41]Restoring with Yadin's commentary, II, p. 178.

[42]See Fig. 16 in Yadin I, p. 258 and the reconstruction in Y. Yadin, *The Temple Scroll, The Hidden Law of the Dead Sea Sect* (New York: Random House, 1985), p. 141.

[43]The length of 20 cubits includes the thickness of the walls (2 cubits) so that the inside measurement was 18. Specific details are not exact in these measurements. See Yadin I, pp. 256-61.

[44]See Yadin II, pp. 185-90 and Maier, pp. 113-15.

Aaron].[45] And the en[tire] right side of the gate of Levi and its left side, you shall apportion to the sons of Aaron, your brother:[46] one hundred eight chambers and their rooms, and their two *sukkot* which are above the roof. For the sons of Judah (you shall apportion) from the gate of Judah to the corner, fifty-four chambers and their rooms and the *sukkah* which is upon them. For the sons of Simeon, from the gate of Simeon to the second corner, their chambers, rooms and *sukkot*. For the sons of Reuben, from the angle next to the sons of Judah to the gate of Reuben, fifty-two chambers, and their rooms and *sukkot*. From the gate of Reuben to the gate of Joseph, for the sons of Joseph, for Ephraim and Menasseh. From the gate of Joseph to the gate of Benjamin, for the sons of Kohath, of the sons of the Levites. From the gate of Benjamin to the western corner, for the sons of Benjamin. From this corner to the gate of Issachar, for the sons of Issachar. From the gate of [Issachar to the gate of Zebulun, for the sons of Zebulun. From the gate of Zebulun to the gate of Gad, for the sons of Gershon of the Levites. From the gate of Gad to the northern corner, for the sons of Gad. From this corner to the gate of Dan, for the sons of Dan. From the gate of Dan to the gate of Naphtali, for the sons of Naphtali. From the gate of Naphtali to the gate of Asher, for the sons of Merari of the Levites.] From the ga[te of Asher to the eastern corner, for the sons of Asher. All the chambers (apportioned) for the tribe of Levi] are [two hundred and] seventy [chambers. For the Israelites, five hundred and eighty-six chambers].[47]

Here we see the total of 16 sets of chambers and rooms, of three stories, with the *sukkot* on top, apportioned to the eleven sons of Jacob other than Levi, with five sections going two to Aaron and one each to the Levitical clans. The apportionment of a double portion to Aaron raises the possibility that in a ritual sense Aaron holds the birthright among the sons of Jacob.

The pattern of distribution of chambers corresponds to the distribution of the gates. The twelve sons each receive the chambers closest to their gates into the Outer and Middle Courts, and the four Levitical clans receive chambers between those assigned to their brothers, opposite their gates to the Inner Court. Much energy has been expended in attempting to explain how and why the order of the sons of Jacob and their placement differ from that in the various biblical

---

[45]Following the first suggestion of Yadin II, p. 186, commentary to line 5. His second suggestion, the restoration of *bene ṣadoq*, "the sons of Zadok," is extremely unlikely since the Zadokites play no role in the *Temple Scroll*. This is but another small piece of evidence for the incongruity of the *Temple Scroll* with the writings of the Qumran sectarians.

[46]This is the only reference, albeit indirect, to Moses in the *Temple Scroll*. Otherwise, the author/redactor adapted the Torah so that his scroll would appear to be the direct revelation of God, with no intermediation.

[47]11QT 45:1-2 is restored with the commentary of Yadin, II, p. 190.

lists.[48] We remain unconvinced of the explanations but still cannot offer a better alternative.

IV. Comparison with Other Temple Plans

In order to highlight the uniqueness of the Temple plan of the *Temple Scroll*, it is useful to compare its general scheme to the plans for the Solomonic Temple, the Temple of Ezekiel 40-48, Josephus's descriptions, and Tannaitic sources.[49] These comparisons will show that although some sense of concentricity existed in other plans, it was not complete. Further, the addition of the extra courtyard (the outer) was a unique proposal of the *Temple Scroll*. Finally, we will see that the scroll's approach is not to be compared to the existing Second Temple in some misguided search for equivalence. Our author calls for radical changes in the order of the day; he does not describe contemporary reality.

The earliest structure for which detailed accounts are given is, of course, the Tabernacle of the desert wandering period. For our purposes it is not important if the descriptions of the Pentateuchal accounts are to be considered historical. Rather, what is significant is that for the designer of the Temple of our scroll, these texts set forth the "original" plan for an approved Israelite shrine. This Tabernacle was itself a rectangular tent shrine set in a rectangular courtyard.[50]

While the structures within the Inner Court, especially the Temple building itself, must remain beyond the scope of the present study, it should be emphasized that restoration of the design of the Temple and the various installations of the Inner Court in the *Temple Scroll* leads to the conclusion that the Temple was rectangular in this plan, and it and its accompanying furnishings fit within a rectangle. In this respect the architect was guided by the plan of the desert Tabernacle. The area in which the rituals took place was set within the Inner Court such that free space of the court surrounded it on all four sides.[51] This itself

---

[48]Yadin I, 255f.

[49]Cf. also the Temple descriptions of Hecateus of Abdera (M. Stern, *Greek and Latin Authors on Jews and Judaism*, vol. I [Jerusalem: Israel Academy of Sciences and Humanities, 1976], p. 39, quoted from *Apion* §§198-9); Letter of Aristeas 83-104; Eupolemus, Fragment 2, 35 (trans. F. Fallon, *The Old Testament Pseudepigrapha*, ed. J. H. Charlesworth, vol. II [Garden City, New York: Doubleday, 1985], pp. 34f.).

[50]S. Loewenstamm, "Mishqan," *Enṣiqlopedyah Miqra'it* 5, cols. 536-41, Haran, pp. 149-64.

[51]Yadin I, pp. 205-7 and Fig. 5, p. 206. Yadin, based on 11QT 37:9, suggests that the plan included an inner wall surrounding the Temple building and the ritual installations of the Inner Court.

represents a major innovation on the part of the scroll. In the case of Solomon's Temple there is no definitive evidence regarding the exact placement of the Temple within the courtyard. In Ezekiel's Temple, the structure is placed against the western side of the enclosure such that a western gate cannot be constructed. Josephus appears to describe Solomon's Temple such that the Temple was placed against the western side of the court,[52] although he has been interpreted as describing a design similar to that of our scroll.[53] The tannaim describe a gate on the western side,[54] yet the Temple building is still placed close to the western side of the Temple Mount,[55] not in the middle of the enclosure.

One would have expected our scroll to attempt to reproduce the Solomonic Temple as a model. Yet this is not the case. Solomon's Temple was itself not an independent structure; it was part of a complex which included the royal palace and other royal installations. The Temple building itself was surrounded by a courtyard in which the various rituals were undertaken. This inner court was itself surrounded by a second court which, however, included also the royal installations.[56] Solomon's outer court cannot be seen as a Temple court, since it did not wall off the sanctified area from incursion by any forbidden class. This, in practice, is the purpose of such courts in Israelite Temples. This outer court had no connection to the sanctity of the enclosed precincts since the royal area in First Temple times was open to all, Israelites and others, regardless of ritual purity or impurity. Solomon's Temple was a rectangular structure surrounded by one rectangular court. This plan is similar to the general plan of the Tabernacle, itself walled off within a courtyard and separated from the less sanctified areas which surrounded it.

The court around the Tabernacle was entered only from the east. The court surrounding the Temple of Solomon had three gates, on the east, north and south sides; access from the west was probably not possible. In neither of these structures is there a sense of concentricity. In fact, they give the impression, especially when the Temple building itself is examined, of entering into a further and further series of rooms, all closer and closer to the eventual holy of holies (*devir*). These plans

---

[52]*Ant.* VIII, §§95-98.

[53]Yadin I, pp. 192-4. Yadin finds in Josephus's description the three concentric courts of the *Temple Scroll*, but §95 seems to be describing a wall within the Court of the Priests, not a separate court.

[54]M. Middot 1:3.

[55]M. Middot 5:1.

[56]See I. Yeivin, "Miqdash Shelomoh," *Enṣiqlopedyah Miqra'it* 5, cols. 328-47. See also the plan in *Atlas of Israel* (Jerusalem: Survey of Israel, 1970), IX/5, B.

offer only partial parallels to the Temple of the *Temple Scroll* and differ from it in its most distinct characteristic, its three concentric courts.

In the Temple plan of Ezekiel 40-48 the situation is different. Here, for the first time, in Ezekiel's ideal construct, we encounter a Temple plan with two courts, an inner and an outer. The Inner Court surrounds the Temple building and the altar and furnishings, and the outer encloses an even wider area. Whereas only (Zadokite?)[57] priests may enter the Inner Court, Israelites may enter the Outer Court. The altar is in the middle of the Inner Court,[58] and the Temple building itself lies towards the west. The Inner and Outer Courts each have three gates, on the east, north and south.[59] Again, the notion here is not concentric. The concept is one of entering further and further into more and more sanctified precincts.[60]

Perhaps more significant for our purposes is the plan of the Temple which appears in the Mishnah.[61] It is usually claimed that this Temple plan is that of the Herodian Temple, and that the previous "Second Temple" was of considerably smaller dimensions.[62] Elsewhere we have questioned this assumption, based on a careful reading of the descriptions of Josephus.[63] Our view is that the Mishnaic description indicates that already in the pre-Herodian Second Commonwealth the Temple precincts included most of the present day Temple Mount.[64] Indeed, Josephus, when read correctly, attributes the construction of the

---

[57]Ezek. 44:15-17. Cf. L. H. Schiffman, *The Halakhah at Qumran* (Leiden: E. J. Brill, 1975), pp. 72-5.

[58]J. Milgrom, "Studies in the Temple Scroll," *JBL* 97 (1978), p. 520 who notes that this is not the case in the plan of the *Temple Scroll*.

[59]M. Haran, "Miqdash Yeḥezqel," *Enṣiqlopedyah Miqra'it* 5, cols. 346-56. Cf. J. Maier, "Die Hofanlagen im Tempel-Entwurf des Ezechiel im Licht der 'Tempelrolle' von Qumran," *Prophecy: Essays Presented to Georg Fohrer on his Sixty-fifth Birthday, 6 September, 1980*, ed. J. A. Emerton (Berlin and New York: Walter de Gruyter, 1980), pp. 55-67.

[60]Ezekiel's plan calls for Temple precincts to be located in an area devoted to no tribe, a sort of no man's land called the *terumah*. The author of these chapters envisaged the Temple as separated from the city.

[61]For a detailed reconstruction, see M. Avi-Yonah, "Bet Ha-Miqdash Ha-Sheni," *Sepher Yerushalayim*, ed. M. Avi-Yonah (Jerusalem and Tel Aviv: Bialik Institute and Dvir Publishing House, 1956), pp. 396-418. This restoration depends on the harmonization of the evidence of Josephus, the Mishnah and archaeological data and as such must remain tentative.

[62]H. Albeck, *Shishah Sidre Mishnah, Seder Qodashim* (Jerusalem: Bialik Institute, Tel Aviv: Dvir, 1958), p. 313.

[63]L. H. Schiffman, "Exclusion from the Sanctuary and the City of the Sanctuary," *HAR* 9 (1985), pp. 315-17.

[64]Cf. B. Z. Luria, "Teḥume Har Ha-Bayit," *Bet Miqra'* 13 (1967/68), pp. 3-14.

Temple Mount to Solomon.[65] In any case, the Temple Mount certainly was regarded by Josephus as ancient and pre-dating Herod.

This Temple plan, as reconstructed with some help from Josephus' descriptions of the Herodian structures, envisages a Temple building placed within a Court of the Priests, which itself opens into a further Court of Women. (The Court of Israel is only a small area in the priests' court into which Israelites were permitted to enter to perform certain ritual acts.) These two courts are in turn surrounded by the boundaries of the Temple Mount. Again, there is no sense of concentricity here. The central precinct with its adjoining courts is bounded on all sides by the boundaries of the Temple Mount to which it is affixed at the western side.

It is important, however, that the size of the Mishnaic Temple Mount is 500 x 500 cubits,[66] which is smaller than the platform for Herod's Temple known to us as the present day Temple Mount. This is due to Herod's shoring up of and expansion of the precincts which he did for architectural and topographic reasons.[67] Yet in the *Temple Scroll* we have noted that the dimensions of the Middle Court are to be only slightly smaller, 480 x 480 cubits (outside measurement). This means that the designer of the plan for the Temple in our scroll intended to expand his Temple by adding the additional surrounding courtyard. In doing so, he would have extended the Temple way beyond its original *temenos* to new, gargantuan dimensions which virtually encompassed the entire settled area of Jerusalem.[68] This entire area was to be cleared of its population and to become part of the *temenos*.[69]

V. The Temple and the Desert Camp

How can the unique Temple plan of the *Temple Scroll* be explained? What message did the architect of this plan seek to convey about the sanctity of the Temple and its relation to the people of Israel in his ideal view? The purpose of this Temple plan is to represent the fundamental aspects of the layout of the Tabernacle with the desert

---

[65]*Ant.* XV, xi, 2 (§§397-400), *War* V, v, 1 (§§184-189).

[66]M. Middot 2:1.

[67]Josephus (*War* I, xxi, 1 [§401]) says that Herod doubled the size of the Temple Mount.

[68]Cf. M. Broshi, "The Gigantic Dimensions of the Visionary Temple in the Temple Scroll," *BAR* 13, no. 6 (November/December, 1987), pp. 36f. who did not see my discussion in "Exclusion," p. 317.

[69]Contrast the view of Yadin I, pp. 277-81 and passim, that the "Temple City" represents the inhabited area of the city of Jerusalem. Cf. B. Levine, "The Temple Scroll: Aspects of its Historical Provenance and Literary Character," *BASOR* 232 (1978), pp. 14-17, and Yadin I, p. 415.

encampment of the Israelites which had surrounded the shrine during the period of wandering in the desert. The various prohibitions on entry into the three courts of the precincts of the sanctuary of the *Temple Scroll* have been shown to be based on the very same distinctions of the three camps found in tannaitic literature.[70] The Inner Court corresponded to the tannaitic Camp of the Divine Presence, the Middle Court to the Camp of the Levites, and the Outer Court to the Camp of Israel. Further, in characteristic manner, our scroll in certain cases imposed an additional stringency, permitting those allowed onto the Temple Mount in tannaitic *halakhah*, which is the camp of the Levites, only into the Outer Court, and not the Middle Court. Such a set of distinctions regarding the sanctity of the Temple precincts was in effect in the days of the architect of the scroll's Temple plan. He sought to place the camp of Israel within the expanded *temenos*, hence he created a Temple structure that made access for the tribes, and even symbolic dwelling places for them, a basic principle of his design.

Yet it must be asked why the architect chose to pattern his Temple after the desert camp, and exactly how he saw the structure and function of that camp. To these issues we now turn.

The architect of the *Temple Scroll's* plan has a schematic concept of how the Land of Israel is to be settled. Like Ezekiel before him, he sees the sanctuary as being the center around which all the tribes of Israel are to dwell.[71] Our author, however, goes further, in that he assumes the land to be a perfect square. The tribes are to be apportioned territory in the area surrounding the sanctuary. The sanctuary itself is an idealized microcosm of the Land of Israel. All its gates are oriented inward. Each gate is named for those who may go through it in order to enter into the next level of sanctity in the concentric Temple structure.

Each of the twelve sons has a gate leading into the Outer Court. The author must have assumed that each tribe would live outside that gate, in his imagined, idealized square country. Each tribe was assumed to enter the *temenos* and then to proceed initially into its chambers. From there, all members of the tribe or clan could circulate in the Outer Court. Those excluded even from the Outer Court, those impure from seminal emission, the blind, those afflicted with gonorrhea, *ṣara'at*, or

---

[70]Schiffman, "Exclusion," pp. 301-20.

[71]See M. Greenberg, "Idealism and Practicality in Numbers 35:4-5 and Ezekiel 48," *Essays in Memory of E. A. Speiser*, American Oriental Series 53, ed. W. W. Hallo (New Haven: American Oriental Society, 1968), pp. 63-6. Ezekiel does not propose a symmetrical distribution of the tribes in the Land of Israel, as does our author. His intention is to provide each tribe with a parcel of land including each of the geographic regions of the country. Hence, he arranges the distribution in strips running east-west.

the impurity of the dead,[72] are to be stopped at the gate of the Outer Court. Those allowed into the Middle Court, from which proselytes until the fourth generation, women and young boys were excluded, could then proceed through the respective second set of gates into that court, beyond which they were prohibited from going. Only unblemished priests in their vestments and, apparently, Levites, were permitted to enter even further, hence their gates which proceed into the Inner Court, where the Temple itself and the various ritual furnishings were located.

What we have here is a set of concentric squares of holiness and sanctity through which one proceeds until reaching the highest permissible point. The Israelite, in the perfect society and sacrificial system of the *Temple Scroll*, is to seek to enter the holy precincts as far as is permissible. Sanctity is experienced by entering the place God has chosen, the City of the Sanctuary. There one symbolically dwells in the Israelite desert camp, and experiences the supreme holiness which is enshrined there.

This explanation, like so much of our research on this question, shows that the City of the Sanctuary is not a name for Jerusalem. It is a term for the *temenos*, including all three courts. It was the ideal of the author, in planning his pre-Messianic Temple, that the expanded *temenos* would include areas corresponding to all the three camps of the desert. The entire desert camp with its special sanctity was to be included symbolically in the *temenos*. The places of residence for the tribes of Israel were to be located in the hinterland outside of the respective gates to the Outer Court. Yet the ideal of the scroll required that the tribes have a symbolic residence in the Temple. This is the purpose of the chambers, rooms and even *sukkot*.[73]

VI. Later Reflections

The Temple plan of the *Temple Scroll*, like so much else in the Dead Sea Scrolls, has later parallels and echoes. As is usually the case, these parallels cannot be connected historically to the Qumran manuscripts. Nonetheless, they help us to understand the Second Temple materials and show how later approaches to Judaism made use of similar motifs.

The Temple of our scroll is to be entered from twelve gates, each of which is designated for a particular one of the sons of Jacob. This notion must be derived from Ezekiel 48:31-34 where twelve such gates provide

---

[72]Schiffman, "Exclusion," pp. 306-14.
[73]On the use of the *sukkot*, cf. 11QT 42:12-17.

access to the city which is described as adjacent to the Temple structure. Rev. 21:12-14 has a similar description of the new Jerusalem, adding names of angels for each gate as well as twelve foundations, each bearing the name of an apostle, indicating the identification of the new Jerusalem with the church. The *Temple Scroll* expects those seeking sanctity to enter from these gates into the Outer Court of the Temple.

A depiction of the Israelite camp arranged around the sanctuary is found in a painting from Dura Europus.[74] Each tribe is shown as a tent, grouped around the Tabernacle, in front of which is a well with twelve rivers leading from the center into the twelve tents. In front of the well stands Moses, holding his staff. This well is that of Num. 21:16-18.[75] Yet there is an additional aspect. Num. 21:18 is interpreted to refer to Moses, who appears as the lawgiver with his staff. From the well of the Tabernacle, water, symbolic of sanctity, flows to the tribes of Israel in twelve streams.

A very similar idea appears in the *Sefer Ha-Bahir* where twelve "pipes," each named for one of the tribes of Israel, extend from a central spring and carry the divine effulgence to the people of Israel.[76] This image again appears in the *Zohar* where it is stated that the Divine Presence is itself surrounded by four camps of three tribes each, just as the altar below was surrounded by the twelve tribes. Each of the tribes receives its divine blessing through one of the twelve gates of the heavenly Jerusalem.[77] These gates presumably correspond to the twelve portals of earthly Jerusalem as expected by Ezekiel. We can further identify these twelve gates with the twelve windows of the Heavenly synagogue, a motif which serves as the source of the requirement that synagogues have twelve windows.[78]

---

[74]Panel WB I, in C. H. Kraeling, *The Synagogue*, The Excavations at Dura-Europus, Final Report VIII, Part I (New York: Ktav, 1979), Plate LIX, and pp. 118-25.

[75]For the aggadic basis of this painting, cf. T. Sukkah 3:10-13 and S. Lieberman, *Tosefta Kifshutah* IV (New York: Jewish Theological Seminary, 1962), pp. 876-8.

[76]*Sefer Ha-Bahir* 113 (ed. R. Margaliot, Jerusalem: Mosad Harav Kook, 1977/8, pp. 50-51. Here the twelve pipes serve as an alternative to the system of ten *sefirot* also found in the *Bahir*. On this system of twelve, see also *Bahir* 94-95 (ed. Margaliot, pp. 40-42), and the parallel in *Sefer Yesirah* 5:1 (Jerusalem: Lewin-Epstein, 1967/8), pp. 51a-b and the commentary attributed to Rabad (actually by Joseph ben Shalom Ashkenazi), *ad loc.* Cf. M. Idel, *Kabbalah, New Perspectives* (New Haven: Yale University Press, 1988), pp. 122f.

[77]*Zohar* I, 251b. The same idea appears in Mordecai ben Joseph of Avignon, *Sefer Maḥaziq 'Emunah*, MS Vat. 271, fol. 17, which will be published in R. Chazan, "Chapter Thirteen of the Maḥazik Emunah," to appear in *Michael* 12.

[78]*Zohar* II, 252a.

This motif goes through one final transformation in the Middle Ages. Isaac Luria uses this notion of twelve different entrances to Heavenly Jerusalem to explain the multiplicity of versions of the prayer book. He maintains that each of the tribes had its own rite which was directed especially towards one of the gates to the Heavenly city described by Ezekiel.[79]

Are these ideas reflections of the *Temple Scroll?* Most probably not. What we have here is a series of interrelated motifs. The artists of Dura-Europus understood the Temple as a source from which sanctity flows to the twelve tribes of Israel. In similar manner, the *Sefer Ha-Bahir* saw twelve different conduits for divine blessing and for Israel's praise. The Kabbalah of the *Zohar* amalgamated the camp of Numbers with the twelve city gates of Ezekiel's new Jerusalem to place the tribes in a square around the Temple, a square with a gate or window for each tribe.

These parallels, from totally different manifestations of Judaism, suggest that the architect of the Temple plan of the *Temple Scroll* had reached very similar conclusions. For him, the Temple and its courtyards were a source of holiness for all Israel. They had to be approached with awe and reverence and in the required level of ritual purity. The Temple symbolized the nation of Israel in its pristine perfection in the years of wandering in the desert. There God's blessings flowed out from the center, the Tabernacle, to the tribes encamped around. In his ideal, the tribes were to enter the sanctuary, approaching the sacred as closely as possible, to receive that blessing. With the adoption of these plans for the Temple, designed years before, the author/redactor of the entire *Temple Scroll* dreamt of a day when Israel would dwell, as it were, in the tent of the Lord. He looked forward to the reestablishment of Israelite society, within the courtyards of the House of the Lord.

---

[79]Meir Poppers, *Peri ʿEṣ Ḥayyim* (Koretz, 1779), pp. 2b-3a.

Index

Abraham 40, 69, 71-75, 98, 101, 151, 157, 158, 167

academy 25, 30, 41, 42, 50, 51, 54-56, 59, 194, 242, 277

accusation 84, 86, 88, 89, 94, 164, 173, 177, 179

accuse 174

administration 78, 102, 264

adversus Judaeos 172, 181, 190-194, 196, 198, 199, 201, 202

Ahad Ha'am 12

Akiba, Aqiba 195, 196, 244, 247, 249, 251, 253, 259, 261

Alexandria, Egypt 193-195

Alexandrian canon 62, 63

'allon bakhut 71

Amalek 5, 112

Amidah 238, 243, 245

androcentrism 35, 36

Answer to the Jews 191, 199, 200

anti-Christian 189

Anti-Judaism 8, 150, 151, 171, 191, 193, 201, 202

Anti-Semitism 149, 150, 169, 171-173, 182-186, 188

Asherah 73

Asian Brethren 17

autonomy 7-9, 20, 102, 243

Babylon 93

Bar Kokhba 37, 178, 234, 244, 254

Barnabas 191, 193-195, 202

Barnabas' Epistle 191, 194

Baron, Salo W. 13, 20, 181, 188

Barth, M. 149, 187

bear witness 78, 82, 84, 85, 152, 157, 164, 174

Beer-sheba 69, 70, 74

Berakhot 181, 233-236, 239-244, 247, 249, 250, 254, 262, 265

biblical interpretation 59, 190

Birkat haMinim 181

Blessings 33, 208, 233-236, 238-243, 249, 251-256, 258-265, 284

Boerne, Ludwig 14

Boethusians 205-207, 210, 211

bondman, bondmen 221-224, 226, 227, 228-230

Book of Jubilees 206, 210

"bread of life" discourse 169

Buber, Martin 20, 74, 123, 174, 175, 184

Camp, of the desert period 270, 271, 280-284

Canaanites 180

canon, canonical, canonicity 17, 18, 44, 48, 49, 59-68, 133-135, 141, 142, 145-148, 205, 255, 262, 265

capitalism 10

careerism 26, 28

Carthage 199, 200

Christ 151, 153, 156, 158-161

Christian Bible 61, 62, 64, 146

Christian canon 62

Christianization 144, 148

Chronicles 9, 73, 100, 104, 111, 112, 114, 116-123, 126

Chrysostom 33, 177, 181, 182

City as text 192

Clement of Alexandria 174

community 5, 7, 12, 13, 26, 29, 33, 35, 38, 40, 51, 55, 61, 62, 65, 93, 98, 141, 143, 145, 166, 169, 174, 179, 181, 190, 193, 198, 199, 212, 234, 243, 245, 255

Conservative Judaism 12

Constitution 98, 104, 106, 107, 114, 116, 117, 119, 121, 123, 125, 126, 133, 146

continuity 18, 37, 42, 43, 80, 81, 126

Counselor, The 162, 163

courts, courtyards 221, 222, 224, 226-268, 271, 273, 276, 278-282, 284

Covenant 5, 7, 14, 33-38, 71, 98, 99, 101, 102, 105-107, 110-112, 116-129, 186, 208, 209, 259

Crucifixion of Jesus 179

Culture, Jewish 5, 11, 13, 15, 138, 139, 148, 198

curriculum, curricula 25-31, 39, 40, 43, 46

daughter 108, 112, 224-226, 229

David 17, 31, 70, 97, 98, 101-104, 106-122, 124-129, 156, 183

Deicide 179

Destruction of Jerusalem 146, 176, 184

Dialogue with Trypho a Jew 196

Diaspora 6, 13, 20, 140, 143, 144, 184, 195, 198, 201, 202

Dinur, Ben-Zion 20

Division, Prayer of 240, 251

divorcee 225, 226

Domains, see also *ketarim* 97, 106, 114, 125

Driver, G. R. 78, 80, 86

Driver-Miles 79, 80, 84, 86, 92, 93

Dura Europus 283

Edah 99, 103-106, 125

Edict of Milan 179

education 23, 25-29, 31, 36, 39, 40, 50, 53, 55, 213

Egypt 5, 70, 74, 98, 112, 191, 194, 250

Eighteen Blessings, Prayer of 235, 236, 238, 239, 242, 243, 249, 252, 255

Eleazar ben Azariah 242, 243, 251

Elijah 123, 151, 174, 175

'el 'elyon 73

'el 'olam 72

'elah 71, 73

emancipation 12, 98

England 11, 53

Enlightenment 7, 10, 12, 52

Ephesus 196, 197

Epistle 140, 174, 176, 191, 193-195

eschatological 7, 136, 138, 139, 145

Eschaton 135, 136, 143, 146

'eshel 73-75

ethnicity 37-39

Evangelization 141

Exaltation of Jesus 173

Farewell Discourse 163

false testimony 81, 82, 85-87

Father and the Son, The 154, 162

festival 205-207, 211, 214, 239, 240, 268

Finkelstein, Louis 77, 78, 85, 91, 95, 180, 210-212

Former Prophets 99

fragmentation 26, 28, 30

France 11, 45

Frankfort, H.A. 209

Gamaliel 95, 96, 181, 242-245, 249, 253, 256, 258, 263

Gentiles 6, 7, 11, 33, 37, 135, 138-140, 143, 149, 159, 176

Germany 9, 10, 13, 183, 184, 187

Graetz, Heinrich 14, 63

Greece, Greek 12, 42, 45, 51, 75, 101, 165, 175, 177, 185, 190, 194, 196, 277

Hadari, H.Y. 213

halakhah 5, 265, 279, 281

halakic 33, 38

Haman 5

Hebrew Bible 4, 32, 33, 59-64, 66, 67, 73, 168, 177, 188

Hegel, Georg W.F. 15

Heine, Heinrich 14

Hess, Moses 12

hierarchy 36, 219-221, 223, 238, 255, 256, 263

High Priests 177, 178

Hillel 212, 235, 237-239, 242, 252, 262

Hippolytus 174

historical criticism 60

Holocaust 16, 20, 98

householder 222-224, 226-231

humanism 9

Ideengeschichte 13, 14, 16, 17, 21

ideology 6, 112, 121

inspiration 59-62, 64-67, 127, 136, 147

inspired 5, 10, 60, 63-66, 212

institution(s) 27-29, 41, 44, 45, 48, 49, 51, 54, 55, 61, 62, 70, 100, 102, 103, 105, 106, 114, 119, 121, 122, 124, 136, 138, 139, 144, 221, 226, 234, 236, 238, 242, 243, 248, 251, 253, 254, 258-261, 263, 265 interpretation 59, 73, 75, 80-82, 91, 92, 96, 100, 105, 106, 134, 141, 146, 176, 177, 185, 186, 190, 205

Italy 43, 44, 181

Jacob 71, 74, 98, 233, 236, 239

Jacob, sons of 273, 275, 276, 282

Jerusalem 70, 74, 75, 97, 98, 102, 104, 106, 109, 111, 112, 115, 116, 120-122, 124, 125, 129, 143-146, 152, 153, 156, 159, 161, 168, 169, 176, 177, 184, 194, 195, 208, 211, 213, 234-238, 242, 245, 246, 260, 267, 270, 277-280, 282-284

Jesus 134-140, 144-169, 171, 173-180, 183-187, 189, 192, 195, 238, 246

Jesus movement 136, 148

Jewish canon 62

Jewish Scripture 60, 61, 66

Jewish Studies 25, 28-32, 34, 39, 40, 61, 149

Johannine Comma 174

John the Baptist 145, 151-153, 159

Josephus 60, 175, 177, 206, 211, 278-280

Joshua 71, 97, 99, 102, 106, 117, 244, 245, 248, 249

Jubilee, year of 213, 214

Jubilees, Book of 206, 210

Judeo-Arabic 12

jurist('s) 87, 88-91, 96

Justin Martyr 174, 181, 188, 195

Kerygma 134, 138, 141, 142, 145

ketarim 100, 106, 116, 117

Kings 71, 72, 99, 100, 116-123, 125, 126, 175

knowledge 3, 26, 27, 31, 33, 36, 45, 46, 48, 49, 51, 53, 54, 90, 105, 107, 137, 147, 170, 219, 220, 246, 255

Kohelet 209, 216

Koran 180

Kraabel, A.T. 192, 198, 202

Last Supper 162, 186

Law of Moses 168

law(s) 12, 32, 36, 38, 43, 44, 46, 77, 78, 79, 81, 82, 84, 85, 86, 89, 91, 93, 94, 100, 102, 104, 124, 127, 128, 129, 133, 138, 140, 143, 151, 152, 153, 155-157, 161, 164, 165, 168, 176, 194, 211, 214, 219, 220, 233, 235, 237, 239, 241, 247, 253, 255, 257, 261, 265, 267, 273, 275

lawsuit 85

learning 23, 25-28, 30, 31, 39-56, 61, 101, 234, 254

legal 5, 7, 13, 33, 64, 70, 77, 78, 82-87, 89, 90, 92, 94, 95, 140, 194, 221, 227, 228, 231, 233, 244, 268

legal cases 77, 78, 83-85, 87

Leidensgeschichte 13, 14

Levites 100, 111, 114, 126, 221, 261, 271, 276, 281, 282

liable, liability 78, 81, 85, 87-89, 91-95

literary analysis 60

logos 151, 167

Luther, Martin 14, 62, 172

Maimonides 33, 37, 207, 213

Marcion 184, 200, 201

Marxism 16

Mary and Martha 159

Meeks, W. 175, 182, 190, 192, 193, 202

Melito of Sardis 175, 179, 191

Messiah 151-153, 168, 176-178, 184, 189, 192, 201, 250

messianic King 175

messianic Judaism 195

Miles, J. C. 78, 86

Mishnah 32-35, 37, 42, 44, 45, 96, 98, 146, 187, 189, 198, 205, 206, 212, 219, 220, 224, 233, 234, 236, 237, 239, 249, 254, 255, 262, 265, 279

mission 7, 26, 109, 155, 166

mlk 'lm 72

Mommsen, Theodor 14, 183

Mormon, Book of 180

Mosaism 12

Moses 97, 102, 106, 116, 117, 127, 151, 152, 154, 155, 158, 167, 168, 175, 176, 206, 234, 276, 283

Nation-state 7-9, 11, 14, 15, 17, 18

Neapolis, Samaria 193, 196, 197

Neusner, J. 40, 41, 59, 61, 96, 134, 140, 180, 182, 189, 192, 193, 202, 212, 236, 237, 239, 261

New Testament 35, 59, 62, 65-67, 133-135, 139, 141, 142, 144-150, 171, 173-179, 181-186, 190-192, 199, 200

oath 85, 88

Old consensus 198

Omer 205-208, 210, 212-214

oral 34, 98, 141, 142, 145

Oral Torah 34, 234

Origen 174, 188

Palestinian canon 62, 63

Paschal Homily, Melito's 191

Passover 152, 154, 160, 161, 164, 165, 169, 205, 207, 208

pattern of the two phases 134, 141

Paul 134, 137, 138, 140-145, 149, 169-181

penalty 6, 77-79, 81, 82, 85-92, 94, 95

Pharaoh 5, 175

Pharisaism 12

Pharisees 12, 150-152, 156, 160, 161, 163, 166, 167, 173, 177, 179, 180, 187, 189, 198, 205, 206, 210-212, 239, 261

Philo 15, 175

philosophy, philosophical 12, 15, 16, 26, 40, 42-46, 49, 77, 149, 188, 196, 209, 216, 220, 233, 234

Pilate 164-166, 169, 177

pneumatic 136, 145, 147

Polity, Jewish, see also *Edah* 97, 99, 101, 104, 106, 121-124, 128

prayer 32, 63, 112, 120, 121, 233-240, 242, 243, 246-252, 254-259, 262, 264, 265, 284

Presbyterian Church 187, 191

priests 100, 109, 111, 113, 114, 117, 126, 150, 151, 156, 160, 161, 163-165, 177, 178, 211,

221, 228, 236, 237, 243, 245, 260, 261, 271, 275, 278-280, 282

property 78, 90, 93, 95, 111, 182, 189, 214, 219-228, 230, 231, 260

prophetism 138

proselytes 37, 282

Psalms 34, 112, 126-129, 258, 260

Qumran 35, 62, 64, 210, 238, 267, 270, 273, 276, 279, 282

rabbinic Judaism 33-37, 198, 208, 236, 243, 263, 264

rabbis 13, 35-37, 42, 65-67, 75, 166, 189, 196, 198, 210, 213, 216, 233, 234, 236, 239-250, 252, 254, 256-265

reason 3, 35, 47, 52, 53, 55, 90, 109, 167, 175, 179, 180, 183, 188, 193, 199, 223, 227, 228, 230, 231, 235, 239, 243, 252

referent 93, 94

Reform Judaism 17

Reformation 9, 267

Regime, Mosaic 99

reign of God 135, 136, 139, 140, 143, 144, 148

relationship 5, 20, 66, 77, 84, 85, 108, 110, 117-119, 122, 126, 134, 140-142, 145, 153, 154, 162, 176, 186, 188-190, 192, 193, 201, 202, 219, 220, 222, 228, 229, 257, 275

religious system 124, 135, 136, 140, 142-148, 236, 255

Renaissance 9, 172, 190

responsible, responsibility 25-27, 30, 35, 53, 54, 80, 81, 88, 92, 94, 95, 98, 99, 105, 106, 117, 122, 164, 169, 179, 229, 244

Robinson Crusoe 216

Roman Empire 164, 172, 188, 201, 242

Rome 45, 72, 79, 81, 84, 134, 177-179, 188, 196, 197, 267

Rotenstreich, N. 8, 216

Sabbath 153-155, 158, 165, 205-207, 209, 210, 213, 216, 239-241, 251, 260, 264

Sabbath controversy 153

sabbatical year 213

sacred trees 71, 72

Sadducees 166, 205, 206, 210-212

Salvador, Joseph 12

Samaritan(s) 36, 63, 64, 69, 74, 150, 153, 157, 196, 206

Samuel 73, 99-115, 117-121, 123, 124, 126, 127, 215

Sanctification, Prayer of 240, 251

Sardis 175, 179, 191, 193, 196, 198, 199

Saul 73, 103, 104, 106-110, 115-119, 125, 215, 258

scholar 41, 55, 56, 95, 109, 171, 183, 219

scholarship 13, 16, 20, 29, 30, 51, 52, 54-56, 60-64, 67, 78, 106, 126, 173, 183, 185

Scholem, Gershom 16, 17

Scribes 34, 150, 166, 174, 236-238, 244, 245, 264

Sectarians 32, 36, 198, 276

Seder 244, 279

Sefer Ha-Bahir 283, 284

seven-day cycle 209

sexism 35, 36

Shammai 212, 235, 237, 238, 242, 252, 262

slave 83, 157, 163, 220, 228, 229, 231

Son of Man, The 152, 154, 155, 157, 158, 161, 162

Spain 45, 98

specialization 26, 29, 31, 39

Spinoza, Baruch-Benedict 15, 104

Spirit 7, 10, 53, 66, 103, 112, 135-138, 145-148, 152, 156, 160, 162, 163, 165, 174, 246

Stonehenge 45, 47

students 26-30, 32, 40, 43, 49, 51, 53-56, 61, 92, 129, 187, 190

study in depth 27, 28, 39

sukkot 212, 275, 276, 282

synagogue 143, 146, 158, 161, 169, 172, 181, 182, 188, 190, 193, 198, 199, 201, 206, 238, 251, 256, 257, 259, 265, 283

Tabernacle 70, 106, 277, 278, 280, 283, 284

Talmud 12, 13, 33, 35, 48, 49, 61, 75, 98, 185, 187, 189, 190, 200, 206, 242, 249

tamarisk 69, 70, 73

taxonomy, taxonomic 220-222, 224-226, 231, 262

teach, teaching 25, 27, 29, 30, 31, 37-40, 48, 50-56, 105, 106, 116, 137, 139, 142, 149, 152, 155, 156, 158, 162, 164, 169, 171, 179, 180, 184, 187, 195, 205, 214, 235, 249

teachers 26, 31, 32, 39, 43, 53, 54, 189, 196, 212, 242, 255, 263

temenos 270, 280-282

Temple 29, 32, 37, 47, 74, 97, 98, 112, 117, 118, 120, 121, 123-125, 140, 143, 144, 146, 152, 153, 155-159, 164, 168, 169, 177, 179, 191, 193, 195, 201, 208, 212, 221, 222, 224, 226, 234-239, 241, 242, 244-247, 249, 257, 261

Temple in Jerusalem 124, 169, 195, 234, 236, 237, 246, 260

Temple Mount 278-281

Temple Scroll 267-270, 272, 275-284

Temple, Ezekiel's 278

Temple, First 123, 270, 278

Temple, Herodian 279

Temple, Second 234, 277, 279, 282

Temple, Solomonic 277, 278

terebinth 71, 72

Tertullian 191, 193, 199-202

testify 71, 85, 86, 140, 155, 222

testimony 72, 78, 81-90, 92-94, 152, 156, 157, 182

"The Jews" 150, 151, 155, 158, 160, 162, 165-169, 181, 195, 197

"The King of the Jews" 164, 165

The true Shepherd 158

Titus 5

Tosefta 189, 233, 234, 236, 240, 248, 254, 255, 262, 283

Toynbee, Arnold 10, 15

transformation 26, 50, 69, 133-140, 142-144, 148, 255, 284

Treitschke, Heinrich von 14

Tribal Federation 97, 100-102, 105, 106, 117, 121, 123, 124, 127

Triumphalism 20

understanding 1, 27, 47, 49, 50, 61-64, 67, 68, 70, 79, 87, 91, 92, 94, 95, 99, 109, 129, 134-137, 145, 147, 148, 187, 190, 192, 199, 207, 212, 216, 217, 239, 241, 248, 255

United States 11

University of Bologna 42-45, 49, 133

university, universities 25, 26, 29-32, 39-56, 61

Usha 241, 252, 254, 255, 257, 259, 261, 262, 264, 265

Wegner, Judith R. 220, 224

widow 225, 226, 229, 230

wife 112, 115, 120, 225, 226, 229-231

Wissenschaft ('s) 30, 31, 183

witness(es) 36, 50, 78, 81, 82, 84-89, 91-96, 116, 120, 139, 152, 156, 157, 164, 174, 180, 213, 222

Wolfson, Harry A. 15, 16, 188, 267

woman, women 10, 18, 35, 36, 43, 50, 54, 138, 153, 156, 165, 189, 219-231, 256, 280, 282

Women's Studies 29, 30

Yavneh 63, 65, 144, 193, 198, 241, 242, 246, 249, 251, 252, 254, 256

Zerubavel 209, 210

Zion 7, 10, 71, 153

Zionism, Zionist 12, 15, 20, 104

Zohar 283, 284

Brown Judaic Studies

140001	*Approaches to Ancient Judaism I*	William S. Green
140002	*The Traditions of Eleazar Ben Azariah*	Tzvee Zahavy
140003	*Persons and Institutions in Early Rabbinic Judaism*	William S. Green
140004	*Claude Goldsmid Montefiore on the Ancient Rabbis*	Joshua B. Stein
140005	*The Ecumenical Perspective and the Modernization of Jewish Religion*	S. Daniel Breslauer
140006	*The Sabbath-Law of Rabbi Meir*	Robert Goldenberg
140007	*Rabbi Tarfon*	Joel Gereboff
140008	*Rabban Gamaliel II*	Shamai Kanter
140009	*Approaches to Ancient Judaism II*	William S. Green
140010	*Method and Meaning in Ancient Judaism*	Jacob Neusner
140011	*Approaches to Ancient Judaism III*	William S. Green
140012	*Turning Point: Zionism and Reform Judaism*	Howard R. Greenstein
140013	*Buber on God and the Perfect Man*	Pamela Vermes
140014	*Scholastic Rabbinism*	Anthony J. Saldarini
140015	*Method and Meaning in Ancient Judaism II*	Jacob Neusner
140016	*Method and Meaning in Ancient Judaism III*	Jacob Neusner
140017	*Post Mishnaic Judaism in Transition*	Baruch M. Bokser
140018	*A History of the Mishnaic Law of Agriculture: Tractate Maaser Sheni*	Peter J. Haas
140019	*Mishnah's Theology of Tithing*	Martin S. Jaffee
140020	*The Priestly Gift in Mishnah: A Study of Tractate Terumot*	Alan. J. Peck
140021	*History of Judaism: The Next Ten Years*	Baruch M. Bokser
140022	*Ancient Synagogues*	Joseph Gutmann
140023	*Warrant for Genocide*	Norman Cohn
140024	*The Creation of the World According to Gersonides*	Jacob J. Staub
140025	*Two Treatises of Philo of Alexandria: A Commentary on De Gigantibus and Quod Deus Sit Immutabilis*	David Winston/John Dillon
140026	*A History of the Mishnaic Law of Agriculture: Kilayim*	Irving Mandelbaum
140027	*Approaches to Ancient Judaism IV*	William S. Green
140028	*Judaism in the American Humanities*	Jacob Neusner
140029	*Handbook of Synagogue Architecture*	Marilyn Chiat
140030	*The Book of Mirrors*	Daniel C. Matt
140031	*Ideas in Fiction: The Works of Hayim Hazaz*	Warren Bargad
140032	*Approaches to Ancient Judaism V*	William S. Green
140033	*Sectarian Law in the Dead Sea Scrolls: Courts, Testimony and the Penal Code*	Lawrence H. Schiffman
140034	*A History of the United Jewish Appeal: 1939-1982*	Marc L. Raphael
140035	*The Academic Study of Judaism*	Jacob Neusner
140036	*Woman Leaders in the Ancient Synagogue*	Bernadette Brooten
140037	*Formative Judaism: Religious, Historical, and Literary Studies*	Jacob Neusner
140038	*Ben Sira's View of Women: A Literary Analysis*	Warren C. Trenchard
140039	*Barukh Kurzweil and Modern Hebrew Literature*	James S. Diamond

140040	*Israeli Childhood Stories of the Sixties: Yizhar, Aloni,Shahar, Kahana-Carmon*	
		Gideon Telpaz
140041	*Formative Judaism II: Religious, Historical, and Literary Studies*	Jacob Neusner
140042	*Judaism in the American Humanities II: Jewish Learning and the New Humanities*	Jacob Neusner
140043	*Support for the Poor in the Mishnaic Law of Agriculture: Tractate Peah*	Roger Brooks
140044	*The Sanctity of the Seventh Year: A Study of Mishnah Tractate Shebiit*	Louis E. Newman
140045	*Character and Context: Studies in the Fiction of Abramovitsh, Brenner, and Agnon*	Jeffrey Fleck
140046	*Formative Judaism III: Religious, Historical, and Literary Studies*	Jacob Neusner
140047	*Pharaoh's Counsellors: Job, Jethro, and Balaam in Rabbinic and Patristic Tradition*	Judith Baskin
140048	*The Scrolls and Christian Origins: Studies in the Jewish Background of the New Testament*	Matthew Black
140049	*Approaches to Modern Judaism I*	Marc Lee Raphael
140050	*Mysterious Encounters at Mamre and Jabbok*	William T. Miller
140051	*The Mishnah Before 70*	Jacob Neusner
140052	*Sparda by the Bitter Sea: Imperial Interaction in Western Anatolia*	Jack Martin Balcer
140053	*Hermann Cohen: The Challenge of a Religion of Reason*	William Kluback
140054	*Approaches to Judaism in Medieval Times I*	David R. Blumenthal
140055	*In the Margins of the Yerushalmi: Glosses on the English Translation*	Jacob Neusner
140056	*Approaches to Modern Judaism II*	Marc Lee Raphael
140057	*Approaches to Judaism in Medieval Times II*	David R. Blumenthal
140058	*Midrash as Literature: The Primacy of Documentary Discourse*	JacobNeusner
140059	*The Commerce of the Sacred: Mediation of the Divine Among Jews in the Graeco-Roman Diaspora*	Jack N. Lightstone
140060	*Major Trends in Formative Judaism I: Society and Symbol in Political Crisis*	Jacob Neusner
140061	*Major Trends in Formative Judaism II: Texts, Contents, and Contexts*	Jacob Neusner
140062	*A History of the Jews in Babylonia I: The Parthian Period*	Jacob Neusner
140063	*The Talmud of Babylonia: An American Translation. XXXII: Tractate Arakhin*	Jacob Neusner
140064	*Ancient Judaism: Debates and Disputes*	Jacob Neusner
140065	*Prayers Alleged to Be Jewish: An Examination of the Constitutiones Apostolorum*	David Fiensy
140066	*The Legal Methodology of Hai Gaon*	Tsvi Groner
140067	*From Mishnah to Scripture: The Problem of the Unattributed Saying*	Jacob Neusner
140068	*Halakhah in a Theological Dimension*	David Novak

140069	*From Philo to Origen: Middle Platonism in Transition*	Robert M. Berchman
140070	*In Search of Talmudic Biography: The Problem of the Attributed Saying*	Jacob Neusner
140071	*The Death of the Old and the Birth of the New: The Framework of the Book of Numbers and the Pentateuch*	Dennis T. Olson
140072	*The Talmud of Babylonia: An American Translation. XVII: Tractate Sotah*	Jacob Neusner
140073	*Understanding Seeking Faith: Essays on the Case of Judaism. Volume Two: Literature, Religion and the Social Study of Judiasm*	JacobNeusner
140074	*The Talmud of Babylonia: An American Translation. VI: Tractate Sukkah*	Jacob Neusner
140075	*Fear Not Warrior: A Study of 'al tira' Pericopes in the Hebrew Scriptures*	Edgar W. Conrad
140076	*Formative Judaism IV: Religious, Historical, and Literary Studies*	Jacob Neusner
140077	*Biblical Patterns in Modern Literature*	David H. Hirsch/ Nehama Aschkenasy
140078	*The Talmud of Babylonia: An American Translation I: Tractate Berakhot*	Jacob Neusner
140079	*Mishnah's Division of Agriculture: A History and Theology of Seder Zeraim*	Alan J. Avery-Peck
140080	*From Tradition to Imitation: The Plan and Program of Pesiqta Rabbati and Pesiqta deRab Kahana*	Jacob Neusner
140081	*The Talmud of Babylonia: An American Translation. XXIIIA: Tractate Sanhedrin, Chapters 1-3*	Jacob Neusner
140082	*Jewish Presence in T. S. Eliot and Franz Kafka*	Melvin Wilk
140083	*School, Court, Public Administration: Judaism and its Institutions in Talmudic Babylonia*	Jacob Neusner
140084	*The Talmud of Babylonia: An American Translation. XXIIIB: Tractate Sanhedrin, Chapters 4-8*	Jacob Neusner
140085	*The Bavli and Its Sources: The Question of Tradition in the Case of Tractate Sukkah*	Jacob Neusner
140086	*From Description to Conviction: Essays on the History and Theology of Judaism*	Jacob Neusner
140087	*The Talmud of Babylonia: An American Translation. XXIIIC: Tractate Sanhedrin, Chapters 9-11*	Jacob Neusner
140088	*Mishnaic Law of Blessings and Prayers: Tractate Berakhot*	Tzvee Zahavy
140089	*The Peripatetic Saying: The Problem of the Thrice-Told Tale in Talmudic Literature*	Jacob Neusner
140090	*The Talmud of Babylonia: An American Translation. XXVI: Tractate Horayot*	Martin S. Jaffee
140091	*Formative Judaism V: Religious, Historical, and Literary Studies*	Jacob Neusner
140092	*Essays on Biblical Method and Translation*	Edward Greenstein
140093	*The Integrity of Leviticus Rabbah*	Jacob Neusner
140094	*Behind the Essenes: History and Ideology of the Dead Sea Scrolls*	Philip R. Davies

140095	*Approaches to Judaism in Medieval Times,* *Volume III*	David R. Blumenthal
140096	*The Memorized Torah: The Mnemonic System of the Mishnah*	Jacob Neusner
140098	*Sifre to Deuteronomy: An Analytical Translation.* *Volume One: Pisqaot One through One Hundred Forty-Three.* *Debarim, Waethanan, Eqeb*	Jacob Neusner
140099	*Major Trends in Formative Judaism III: The Three Stages in the Formation of Judaism*	Jacob Neusner
140101	*Sifre to Deuteronomy: An Analytical Translation.* *Volume Two: Pisqaot One Hundred Forty-Four through Three Hundred Fifty-Seven. Shofetim, Ki Tese, Ki Tabo, Nesabim, Ha'azinu, Zot Habberakhah*	Jacob Neusner
140102	*Sifra: The Rabbinic Commentary on Leviticus*	Jacob Neusner/ Roger Brooks
140103	*The Human Will in Judaism*	Howard Eilberg-Schwartz
140104	*Genesis Rabbah: Volume 1. Genesis 1:1 to 8:14*	Jacob Neusner
140105	*Genesis Rabbah: Volume 2. Genesis 8:15 to 28:9*	Jacob Neusner
140106	*Genesis Rabbah: Volume 3. Genesis 28:10 to 50:26*	Jacob Neusner
140107	*First Principles of Systemic Analysis*	Jacob Neusner
140108	*Genesis and Judaism*	Jacob Neusner
140109	*The Talmud of Babylonia: An American Translation.* *XXXV: Tractates Meilah and Tamid*	Peter J. Haas
140110	*Studies in Islamic and Judaic Traditions*	William Brinner/Stephen Ricks
140111	*Comparative Midrash: The Plan and Program of Genesis Rabbah and Leviticus Rabbah*	Jacob Neusner
140112	*The Tosefta: Its Structure and its Sources*	Jacob Neusner
140113	*Reading and Believing*	Jacob Neusner
140114	*The Fathers According to Rabbi Nathan*	Jacob Neusner
140115	*Etymology in Early Jewish Interpretation:* *The Hebrew Names in Philo*	Lester L. Grabbe
140116	*Understanding Seeking Faith: Essays on the Case of Judaism.* *Volume One: Debates on Method, Reports of Results*	Jacob Neusner
140117	*The Talmud of Babylonia. An American Translation.* *VII: Tractate Besah*	Alan J. Avery-Peck
140118	*Sifre to Numbers: An American Translation and Explanation,* *Volume One: Sifre to Numbers 1-58*	Jacob Neusner
140119	*Sifre to Numbers: An American Translation and Explanation,* *Volume Two: Sifre to Numbers 59-115*	Jacob Neusner
140120	*Cohen and Troeltsch: Ethical Monotheistic Religion and Theory of Culture*	Wendell S. Dietrich
140121	*Goodenough on the History of Religion and on Judaism*	Jacob Neusner/ Ernest Frerichs
140122	*Pesiqta deRab Kahana I: Pisqaot One through Fourteen*	Jacob Neusner
140123	*Pesiqta deRab Kahana II: Pisqaot Fifteen through Twenty-Eight and Introduction to Pesiqta deRab Kahana*	Jacob Neusner
140124	*Sifre to Deuteronomy: Introduction*	Jacob Neusner

140126	A Conceptual Commentary on Midrash Leviticus Rabbah: Value Concepts in Jewish Thought	Max Kadushin
140127	The Other Judaisms of Late Antiquity	Alan F. Segal
140128	Josephus as a Historical Source in Patristic Literature through Eusebius	Michael Hardwick
140129	Judaism: The Evidence of the Mishnah	Jacob Neusner
140131	Philo, John and Paul: New Perspectives on Judaism and Early Christianity	Peder Borgen
140132	Babylonian Witchcraft Literature	Tzvi Abusch
140133	The Making of the Mind of Judaism: The Formative Age	Jacob Neusner
140135	Why No Gospels in Talmudic Judaism?	Jacob Neusner
140136	Torah: From Scroll to Symbol Part III: Doctrine	Jacob Neusner
140137	The Systemic Analysis of Judaism	Jacob Neusner
140138	Sifra: An Analytical Translation Vol. 1	Jacob Neusner
140139	Sifra: An Analytical Translation Vol. 2	Jacob Neusner
140140	Sifra: An Analytical Translation Vol. 3	Jacob Neusner
140141	Midrash in Context: Exegesis in Formative Judaism	Jacob Neusner
140143	Oxen, Women or Citizens? Slaves in the System of Mishnah	Paul V. Flesher
140144	The Book of the Pomegranate	Elliot R. Wolfson
140145	Wrong Ways and Right Ways in the Study of Formative Judaism	Jacob Neusner
140146	Sifra in Perspective: The Documentary Comparison of the Midrashim of Ancient Judaism	Jacob Neusner
140148	Mekhilta According to Rabbi Ishmael: An Analytical Translation Volume I	Jacob Neusner
140149	The Doctrine of the Divine Name: An Introduction to Classical Kabbalistic Theology	Stephen G. Wald
140150	Water into Wine and the Beheading of John the Baptist	Roger Aus
140151	The Formation of the Jewish Intellect	Jacob Neusner
140152	Mekhilta According to Rabbi Ishmael: An Introduction to Judaism's First Scriptural Encyclopaedia	Jacob Neusner
140153	Understanding Seeking Faith. Volume Three	Jacob Neusner
140154	Mekhilta According to Rabbi Ishmael: An Analytical Translation Volume Two	Jacob Neusner
140155	Goyim: Gentiles and Israelites in Mishnah-Tosefta	Gary P. Porton
140156	A Religion of Pots and Pans?	Jacob Neusner
140157	Claude Montefiore and Christianity	Maurice Gerald Bowler
140158	The Philospical Mishnah Volume III	Jacob Neusner
140159	From Ancient Israel to Modern Judaism Volume 1: Intellect in Quest of Understanding	Neusner/Frerichs/Sarna
140160	The Social Study of Judaism Volume I	Jacob Neusner
140161	Philo's Jewish Identity	Alan Mendelson
140162	The Social Study of Judaism Volume II	Jacob Neusner
140163	The Philosophical Mishnah Volume I : The Initial Probe	Jacob Neusner
140164	The Philosophical Mishnah Volume II : The Tractates Agenda: From Abodah Zarah Through Moed Qatan	Jacob Neusner
140166	Women's Earliest Records	Barbara S. Lesko

140167	*The Legacy of Hermann Cohen*	William Kluback
140168	*Method and Meaning in Ancient Judaism*	Jacob Neusner
140169	*The Role of the Messenger and Message in the Ancient Near East*	
		John T. Greene
140171	*Abraham Heschel's Idea of Revelation*	Lawerence Perlman
140172	*The Philosophical Mishnah Volume IV: The Repertoire*	Jacob Neusner
140173	*From Ancient Israel to Modern Judaism Volume 2: Intellect in Quest of Understanding*	Neusner/Frerichs/Sarna
140174	*From Ancient Israel to Modern Judaism Volume 3: Intellect in Quest of Understanding*	Neusner/Frerichs/Sarna
140175	*From Ancient Israel to Modern Judaism Volume 4: Intellect in Quest of Understanding*	Neusner/Frerichs/Sarna
140176	*Translating the Classics of Judaism: In Theory and In Practice*	Jacob Neusner
140177	*Profiles of a Rabbi: Synoptic Opportunities in Reading About Jesus*	
		Bruce Chilton
140178	*Studies in Islamic and Judaic Traditions II*	William Brinner/Stephen Ricks
140179	*Medium and Message in Judaism: First Series*	Jacob Neusner
140180	*Making the Classics of Judaism: The Three Stages of Literary Formation*	Jacob Neusner
140181	*The Law of Jealousy: Anthropology of Sotah*	Adriana Destro
140182	*Esther Rabbah I: An Analytical Translation*	Jacob Neusner

Brown Studies on Jews and Their Societies

145001	*American Jewish Fertility*	Calvin Goldscheider
145003	*The American Jewish Community*	Calvin Goldscheider
145004	*The Naturalized Jews of the Grand Duchy of Posen in 1834 and 1835*	Edward David Luft
145005	*Suburban Communities: The Jewishness of American Reform Jews*	Gerald L. Showstack
145007	*Ethnic Survival in America*	David Schoem

Brown Studies in Religion

147001	*Religious Writings and Religious Systems Volume 1*	Jacob Neusner, et al
147002	*Religious Writings and Religious Systems Volume 2*	Jacob Neusner, et al
147003	*Religion and the Social Sciences*	Robert Segal